Masochism

THE MYSTERY OF JEAN-JACQUES ROUSSEAU

Masochism

THE MYSTERY OF JEAN-JACQUES ROUSSEAU

Dr. Jaromír Janata

Rutledge Books, Inc. Danbury, CT

Interior design by Carlene Liscinsky

Cover design by Jason A. Cirillo

Copyright © 2001 by Jaromír Janata

ALL RIGHTS RESERVED
Rutledge Books, Inc.
107 Mill Plain Road, Danbury, CT 06811
1-800-278-8533
www.rutledgebooks.com

Manufactured in the United States of America

Cataloging in Publication Data
Janata, Jaromír

Masochism: The Mystery of Jean-Jacques Rousseau

ISBN: 1-58244-157-X

1. Jean-Jacques Rousseau. 2. Biography -- sexual masochist --
moral masochist. 3. French Enlightenment. 4. Contributions to
Humanity.

Library of Congress Control Number: 2001088143

For Julie

* * * * *

There are important associations between
morality and psychopathology
to which little attention has
been paid so far.

Table of Contents

Introduction

More than ten years ago, while attending courses on political science at the University of Eichstätt in Germany, I was given an assignment by Professor Graf Ballestrem to write a paper on Jean-Jacques Rousseau's book *Du Contract Social*. At this time my interest in Rousseau and the idea for this book were born. As part of my work on the paper I had to study Rousseau's biography, which I found very interesting. As a doctor I soon realized that Rousseau was a sick man and his sickness affected him not only physically but also mentally. Graf Ballestrem was probably not very enthusiastic about my paper, mainly because of its length (he preferred short papers), but also because it "showed medical teeth." In his view, medicine did not belong in political science.

Later I worked on other projects, but I never forgot about Rousseau and kept returning to his writings, the history of his life, and to his illnesses. Rousseau himself described his masochistic experiences of early life and youth, but few of his biographers paid attention to them. Study of more recent literature helped me to form a clear picture of Rousseau. I saw that he was primarily a moral masochist, not only a sexual masochist! It was then that the isolated pieces of the mosaic began to form a whole picture, and an explanation of the many mysterious circumstances and paradoxes of his life and his work slowly emerged.

Even his mysterious illnesses could be explained in a way which differed from the explanations provided so far by his biographers. Both Rousseau's novels and his literary works, the so-called philosophical works, reflect his personal problems; namely, the problems of a man with disturbed socialization placing him outside of a society which he could neither understand nor become a member of. Several physicians were concerned with Rousseau's life and illnesses, but their works were quite dated. They were mostly written in a relatively distant past and pay tribute to the time of their origin.

The book is divided into two parts. The first part, which can be read as the biography of Jean-Jacques Rousseau, could be likened to medical history with numerous medical notes. The second part is concerned with a medical analysis of data collected as part of the history and provides the summary diagnoses. The first part could be of interest for the general literary public. Rousseau's biography can be read as an exciting novel. The fact that its hero lived in the eighteenth century does not detract from it—it seems that masochism in the so-called civilized world is rather on the increase and, looking at ourselves with a little criticism, we all can detect some masochistic features in ourselves.

Even readers who are not professionals might be seduced and wish to learn more about this problem, one of the characteristics of which is that it is difficult to classify. We do not know whether it should be called a disease, a deviation, or in the United States, "paraphilia." As the masochistic deviation develops in early childhood at about two years of age during a period called socialization, and because for a child the central figure in this period is his mother, this part should be read by those concerned with child and developmental psychology. It should also be read by the parents of young children.

The development of Rousseau's personality in early childhood was the decisive factor, which determined and shaped not only his philosophical thought but also his whole life. Rousseau had many biographers. To my knowledge, however, none of them has attempted to interpret his life and work from this point of view. The renowned authority on Rousseau, Jean Starobinsky, who is a psychiatrist, is the only one who employs this approach, based mainly on the teachings of Freud. But only the most recent findings of modern medical science and psychology show us how far-reaching the influence of a disturbed personality development can be on the thinking and behavior of an individual. Here I have to refer the reader to the lifelong work of Professor Z. Matějček.

I have no intention, however, of limiting this book to the field of medical psychology, or of medicine exclusively, which deals only with Rousseau's illnesses. The description of the development of Rousseau's personality cannot be separated from the background of his time, which was to end in the French revolution, i.e. the eighteenth century, a century that has been dubbed the "women's century." The biography of Jean-Jacques Rousseau becomes the biography of the eighteenth century. It is a fascinating environment and Rousseau becomes a hero in it, not a fictitious hero but a real one. This picturesque, versatile man and adventurer suddenly takes on the shape of a great philosopher and moralist, and was regarded as such in his time. Rousseau's writings are full of paradoxes—the author often contradicts himself and admits it openly.

The present view of Rousseau varies between that of a great philosopher, genius of evil, prophet of fascism and communism, and even an enemy to science and progress. I myself was carried away by this view during my studies. Rousseau's biographers can be generally divided into those who admired him and those who refused him; all interpret him according to their positive or negative attitudes. I attempt to describe Rousseau as a patient, in other words, to provide as objective an account of his life as possible. Emotions distort, whereas objectivity enables one to keep a distance. Of course, as a doctor, I was also interested in Rousseau's diseases. Here, too, many discourses can be found. Most of them were written some time ago and as such are out of touch with recent findings of medical science.

A combination of such views should give rise to something which cannot be given an exact literary label at the present time. This is not a work of popular science; neither is it a book concerned purely with medical psychology, or mere biography or historical excursion. It is rather a literary experiment, the synthesis and formulation of a new picture, the various components of which have so far been described by medicine, psychology, political science and history in more or less separate ways.

This literary experiment was not born from a desire and passion for literary exotics, but rather it expresses the view that new knowledge can only be obtained by a new approach and a comparison of scientific disciplines which have not yet been interrelated. This interdisciplinary approach can be used to write an ambitious literary work which—in spite of its demanding character—can be of interest not only to historians, psychologists, physicians and philosophers, but also to educated readers who can be shown that "specialist" literature does not have to be boring. Demanding literature *is* popular, even though this view is not the view usually held by publishers, and, of course, it makes the life of literary critics and reviewers more difficult.

Part One—Personality and Time
Chapter One

The Birthplace of Rousseau—Geneva

Geneva (French *Genève*, Italian *Ginevra*, German *Genf*) is a beautiful town spread out on both banks of the Rhône, at the outlet of Lake Geneva (*Lac Leman, Genfer See*). At the time of Caesar's Roman conquest this place had already been settled by the Allobrogian Celts. Around A.D. 350, a bishopric was established here. The old part of the city was situated on the hills on the left bank of the Rhône and after the fourth century the town was often the residence of the Burgundian kings. In A.D. 534 it became part of the Roman Empire and passed to the German Reich in 1032.

The city was originally governed by the Genevese counts until 1124, when King Henry V entrusted the bishop of Geneva with the city's administration. The bourgeoisie of the city were gaining an ever-increasing independence and the differences between burghers and the bishopric formed a fertile ground for the future Reformation, brought about by Farel and Viret in 1532 and completed after heavy clashes in 1555 with John Calvin (originally Jean Chauvin or Caulvin, 1509–1564).

As a graduate of the faculty of law, Calvin had a high opinion of the law, which he called "written reason." He formed his own system of morals and a realistic theory of the administration of society and state. The Church and the state cooperated closely and governed their subjects by means of strict discipline. Calvin visited Geneva on his travels for the first time in August 1536 and Farel implored him to stay in Geneva as a teacher.

Both preachers, however, were forced to leave the city in 1538. Calvin went to Strasbourg, and later, in 1540, married Idelette de Bure, the widow of one of his converts and a member of a sect of "Baptists." In 1541, he was asked to return to Geneva, where the "Genevan catechism" was adopted in 1542. The in-fighting between various Protestant sects dragged on for a long time. S. Castello was expelled in 1545, followed by L. Bolsec in 1551 and M. Servet was burned to death at the stake in 1553. In 1555, Calvin at last asserted himself in

Geneva and, according to his ideals, formed a special branch of Protestantism characterized by discipline and strict religiousness. The influence of Protestantism in Geneva was so strong that Geneva was called "the Protestant Rome."

Neighboring Savoy remained Catholic and the Catholic bishop of Geneva transferred his residence to the Savoyan city of Annecy. The threat posed by the Catholic Savoy led Genevans to conclude the "eternal alliance" with Bern and Zurich in 1584, which proved its worth in 1602, when Geneva was attacked by Savoy in retaliation for "Eskalade." Geneva was then given a Republican constitution, which of course could not prevent the rule of the city aristocracy.

Calvinism developed its own form of Protestant faith that differed from the Lutheran conception by its attitude toward the Church as an ecclesiastical organization. Unlike Luther, Calvin saw the Church as a "nation of the chosen ones" and because of this, he imposed strict moral criteria on church members. His theology begins and ends with the profound experience of the immense power of God. The will of man is torn between man's own will and his obedience to God, who must be obeyed under all circumstances. Based on this assumption, Calvin introduced the idea of double predestination: God had decided in the beginning whether an individual would be damned or saved. The man himself does not know whether the one or the other will occur and he can only partly foresee it, based on successes or failures in his life. Wealth is a reward for outstanding diligence and at the same time a "sign of God's grace." Poverty is a sign of moral fault.

This psychological–ideological–religious trick (as atheists would interpret his idea) enabled Calvin to make people regard passivity with contempt (everything has been decided in advance) and to make them try to achieve success in life by a hectic attention to their work, which would result in a sign that they belonged to the group that was chosen by God, and not to the damned. In any case, by his dogmatic theology, Calvin put an end to the passivity of medieval Catholicism with its conception that this world is merely a preparation for life after death. Many years later, the sociologist, Max Weber, would deliver his thesis that Calvinism gave rise to modern capitalism; it appears, however, that Marx was right with his idea that changed economic relationships brought about a change of ideology.

Unlike Luther, Calvin did not disdain profit from commercial activities

and interests, and he thereby influenced later political and economic development in Western Europe and the United States. His teaching was partly the
result of external circumstances: the city of Geneva had to accept Huguenot
refugees (who came mainly from the south of France) and find work for them.
This necessity later on proved to have been worth the trouble—numerous
trades, industries and banking developed and Geneva became a prosperous
city-state. Politically, even before Calvin Geneva was a city-state similar to
Venice, Genoa or Florence. People with imagination, such as Isaac, Rousseau's
father, compared Geneva to ancient Rome.

The clever citizens of Geneva took advantage of the controversies between
the duke of Savoy and the bishop of Geneva. They took the bishop's part and
obtained numerous privileges and power in return. When the situation
changed and the duke was driven away, the Genevans turned against the bishop and gained their independence. Their "democracy," however, was not to
last for long and ended when the city elite, the Genevan aristocracy, came to
power. The advantage of this rule of oligarchy was that it did not spend its
strength in mutual in-fighting as was the case in Florence. Political power was
shared peacefully between several families and the city was governed successfully for two hundred years, keeping alive the myth of being "ruled by people." Geneva wanted to become part of the Swiss federation, but this was
blocked by the protest of Catholic cantons of eastern Switzerland.

The Genevan *conseil général* was turned into an independent Republic. At
the time, Geneva had about 20,000 inhabitants. Of those, only 1,500 or so were
citizens and burghers. The rest belonged to the category of foreigners born in
Geneva, new immigrants and "subjects," mainly farmers, who lived outside
the city walls. This class had no political rights and was not allowed to carry
on trades or commerce, particularly the remunerative watchmaking.

Social aristocracy was at the same time political aristocracy. From the
heights of Old Geneva they ruled the fates of the Republic, concentrating the
executive power in the *petit conseil*, composed of only twenty-five members
and four syndics. It is true that parallel to this decisive political power there
also existed a two hundred-member council and a *conseil général*, formed by all
voting citizens and burghers. The only task of these assemblies, however, was
to confirm the decisions of the council of twenty-five.

By the end of the seventeenth century certain opposition began to form,
led by wealthier citizens demanding more rights, but their efforts remained

largely unsuccessful. In 1707, five years before Rousseau's birth, these reforms were suppressed by force: the aristocrat Pierre Fatio was shot dead, Piaget was killed when he attempted to escape and Lemetre was tortured and killed. Stendhall called the fortified Geneva "a prison," even as late as 1811. Aside from the political elite, there also existed a Church and an academic elite in the Geneva of Rousseau's time. The latter two, however, had lost their political power in the early eighteenth century. Rousseau's mother came from this class.

Rousseaus in Geneva

Some of the Huguenots who found refuge in Geneva were the family of Rousseaus. They were part of the French Protestants flooding Geneva, hoping to find "the city of God."

In spite of initial misgivings, the Huguenots turned out to be beneficial to Geneva. They were not running away from poverty, but fled religious persecution. They brought with them money, industrial knowledge and culture. They came from all walks of life; they were middle-class as well as aristocrats and resumed their social hierarchy in the new environment, despite the formal equality of all Genevan citizens. The teaching of Calvinism led its supporters not only to live frugally but also to display an entrepreneurial spirit in financial affairs, which of course remained reserved for the wealthier among them. The effect of the Protestant ethics of Calvinism was therefore an increase in the inequality between rich and poor.

The first record of the Rousseaus' presence in Geneva dates from October 15, 1549, when a certain Didier Rousseau was mentioned as a foreign resident, earning his living as alehouse keeper, vine dealer and bookseller. Obviously his business activities must have been successful, because he became a free citizen of Geneva after a mere six years. In the Calvin epoch, the French Huguenots usually attained this promotion rather easily. In general they were more receptive to Calvin's dogmatic theology and accepted it more readily than did the original citizens of Geneva, who tended to come from rural backgrounds. The political support provided by the new Huguenot burghers must have been useful for Calvin.

Didier Rousseau died in 1581 and left a widow from his second marriage, Mie Miège (originally from Savoy), and a son, Jean Rousseau (senior). Jean Rousseau, as a son of a native-born burgher of Geneva, became a citizen and, at an early age, married Elisabeth Bluet, daughter of a Huguenot watchmaker. He himself was a tanner. He apprenticed his son, Jean Rousseau (junior), to his father-in-law.

At that time in Geneva, watchmaking was the most important industry and remained a family tradition for the Rousseaus for three generations. Jean Rousseau, junior, could be proud of his life success. He gained one house in town and a second house in the country; he owned jewelry; and at his death there remained 31,000 florins, which were distributed among his numerous descendants. From nineteen delivered children, ten had survived. One of them was David Rousseau, Jean-Jacques Rousseau's grandfather.

David Rousseau, also a watchmaker, was certainly an impressive personality. On a well-preserved portrait, painted by Rousseau Gardelle, we see an expressive face with aquiline nose, contemptuously lowered corners of the mouth and a slightly foxy expression. The face is framed by a long wig. We see an aristocrat rather than a watchmaker, quite possibly because watchmakers in Geneva at that time were highly regarded and cultivated.

David Rousseau loved music, dance and society. The Genevan consistory, the body which was designated to watch moral behavior, received a report that David Rousseau organized a dancing ball only a few weeks after his wife's death. He must have felt as if he were a nobleman because, though he had no license to it, he used a coat-of-arms.

It is therefore not surprising that he took part in political life as one of the Genevan "liberals," who sympathized with English and Dutch Protestantism, as opposed to the Genevan "conservatives," who tended to support Catholic France even though they were Protestants. The reasons were mainly social and political, and perhaps financial as well. Geneva's investments flowed predominantly to France.

In 1690, after the victory of William III (Prince of Orange) in the Battle of the Boyne over Irish Catholics (whose main ally was the king of France), David Rousseau and other "liberals" were celebrating this victory in such a noisy and, for the French residents of Geneva, dangerous manner that he earned punishment from the *petit conseil*.

Such a way of life must have been the reason that David Rousseau did not accumulate any wealth. Of his fourteen children only six survived. The three sons, who all became watchmakers, were Isaac Rousseau, father of Jean-Jacques Rousseau, David Rousseau (junior) and André Rousseau. The three daughters were Susanne ("Suzon"), Théodora and Clermonde.

Rousseau wrote in his *Confessions* that the sisters were "good and virtuous," which they might well have been, but not in the eyes of the Genevan morality consistory—they were reproached for having played cards on a holiday (holy day). Théodora was denied Holy Communion due to the fact that she gave birth to a child only a few days after her wedding, thereby committing the offence "scandalous anticipation of marriage."

Jean-Jacques Rousseau's father, Isaac Rousseau, and Isaac's sister, Théodora, found their counterparts for marriage in one family, the Bernards. The Bernards had come to Geneva from their native Savoy after the Rousseaus had arrived. In Geneva they became rich as merchandisers, and the first man of their family became a Genevan citizen in 1596. His son, Samuel, born in 1597, the great-grandfather of Jean Jacque Rousseau, became a wealthy and refined man. A circle of educated people would often meet in the big library of his home. One of his friends was also Jean de Clerc, a close friend of the English philosopher John Locke, and the first publisher of the abridged version of Locke's *Human Understanding*.

Rousseau wrote about the link between the two families: "Gabriel Bernard, one of my mother's brothers, fell in love with one of my father's sisters, and she refused to marry him unless her brother could marry my mother at the same time. Love overcame all obstacles, and the two pairs were wedded on the same day" (*Confessions*, 18). This account is a romantic one, but, as we will see later, totally untrue. The wedding between Gabriel Bernard and Théodora Rousseau had to be speeded up and took place in the fall of 1699 to make sure that the baby, due to be born soon thereafter, was legitimate. The wedding of Isaac Rousseau and Susanne Bernard, Jean Jacque Rousseau's parents, took place on June 2, 1704.

Samuel Bernard was a well-educated and wealthy man and as such he could have made his way in the highest walks of society, if only his children had chosen the right marriage partners. This was not to be. His son, Jacques Bernard, was known as a debauchee, and had to pay support for at least one child born out of wedlock. He was held in prison for immorality and got rid of two mistresses only after great difficulty—and he had managed all this by the age of twenty-three.

He married Anne-Marie Marchard, a lawyer's daughter, in 1672. His wife gave birth to three daughters. The oldest of them, Susanne, born on February

2, 1673 (six months after the wedding), was to become the mother of our patient. Here, too, similar to other parts of his life, Jean-Jacques Rousseau took liberties and embellished the situation: he proclaimed that the father of his mother was a pastor (Samuel Bernard, his uncle). To do justice to him, however, it is possible that Rousseau did not know of the existence of his debauched grandfather. He wrote his *Confessions* at an advanced age and that is probably why his descriptions are sometimes incorrect in terms of time as well as facts.

Jacques Bernard died at the young age of thirty-three, not surprising for a debauchee. His brother, the pastor and mathematician Samuel Bernard, (1631–1701), looked after Susanne from the age of nine years old and took care that she received an excellent upbringing. Rousseau was right when he wrote, "she had both intelligence and beauty." The beautiful and well-educated Susanne, however, was a true daughter of her father and was also fond of life. She had to give an account of her acts to the Genevan consistory several times, which reproached her for receiving visits from a married man, Vincent Sarasin. When he abandoned her, she became a close friend of M. de La Closure, a French resident of Geneva.

Sharp tongues maintained that he was the real father of Rousseau, a slanderous charge because this gentleman was definitely away from Geneva between 1709 and 1713. Similar to other wealthy Genevans, Susanne was also a Francophile and liked French literature and the theatre. Buying French books was no problem for her, but the theatre was prohibited in Geneva at that time. Good Calvinists regarded the theatre as immoral and her son, Jean Jacque Rousseau, later advocated this view as well, even though he himself wrote several plays for the theatre. His mother obviously did not share the Calvinist view. She is known to have disguised herself as a boy and visited the open-air theatre by the lake in secret at least once. Despite her disguise, she was caught and again reproached by the morality consistory.

It was not easy for Isaac Rousseau to marry Susanne, who could have married into the higher circles of Genevan aristocracy. Formally there was no difference between them. They were both citizens of the city and they were the same age. Susanne, however, was *plus riche*; her dowry amounted to 16,000 florins, and she inherited her uncle's library in addition to a house in Grand'rue, which was valued at 31,000 florins. More than that—she came from the hills of the "upper city" and her family belonged to Genevan elite. Isaac came from a family of traders who lived in the plain part of Geneva, Saint

Gervais. (The Saint-Gervais area was situated in the "lower city.") Isaac obviously credited his success with Susanne to his humorous and jovial nature, which must certainly have been a rare thing in Calvinist Geneva, and to the *légereté* of his character, which was even more apparent in his later life. He regarded himself as a sort of nobleman and preferred dancing and hunting to watchmaking. He went so far as to leave watchmaking at the age of twenty-one and, with some friends, open a school of dancing. Unfortunately, it could not sustain him and he returned to watchmaking.

Here the reader might wonder at the fact that a Calvinist Geneva should tolerate dancing schools. It is important to realize that the Calvinist ideology was in a sense quite pragmatic. Today it is nearly forgotten that the Reformation led to a profound reform in the organization of systems of education. Philosophy as part of theology was not rejected. The knowledge of classical languages (even a watchmaker in the Geneva of that time had to study Latin!) enabled the study of the Bible in the original, and supported logical thinking. Other important subjects were physics and astronomy. Faith and knowledge were closely related and one did not rule out the other. Melanchthon, preceptor of Germania, coined the saying "There is no greater threat for a state than uneducated serfs."

Calvin opened academies and seminaries in Geneva, which attracted pupils from aristocratic Protestant families in England and Germany. Geneva had the advantage that pupils could learn French without having to go to Catholic France. Some of the pupils criticized the situation in Geneva at the time of Calvin; these, however, were categorically punished: Michael Servet was denounced as a "Socinian" and burned to death and Jacques Gruet was killed after having been accused of atheism.

Fortunately, Geneva became richer in the course of time and religious fanaticism calmed down. Calvin's original dogmatic theology of predestination, selection by God and original sin receded and was followed by the spread of theological liberalism in Geneva. In the early eighteenth century, prominent Genevan theologians such as Jean-Alphonse Turrettini held views resembling Servet's "Socinianism." It is therefore not surprising that dancing schools were tolerated during the time of Isaac Rousseau. Noble foreign students found amusement there, and Geneva profited financially, gaining the reputation of a cultural and sociable city.

At that time, elegant clothing was already tolerated and those who could afford it were wearing fancy silk and jewels. Isaac Rousseau wore a sword and liked the noble society to which he actually did not belong (his son inherited this liking for aristocracy as well, though he always condemned it in his books). His flammable temperament involved him in several scuffles and the municipal chronicles of Geneva attest to at least four cases when Isaac used his sword: October 27, 1699 against four or five Englishmen; January 9, 1702 against another Englishman; and twice against the Genevan Pierre Gautier in 1722. Isaac was punished for these brawls and even jailed unjustly, according to some, as he acted in self-defense when causing injury to the English officer.

We can believe Rousseau when he says it was not easy for his father to marry Susanne. He wrote that his mother was "brilliant with respect to her descent." She was a good artist and singer, played musical instruments and even wrote passable poetry.

The wedding of Rousseau's parents took place on June 2, 1704. It was not long, however, before Isaac Rousseau felt restricted as a newly married man— perhaps partly because he lived with Susanne in the house in Grand'rue together with his mother-in-law. François, Rousseau's older brother, was born in this house on March 15, 1705. His life was not happy. He was born at the time of an economic depression when watchmaking was in decline.

The economic situation was probably the reason why Isaac Rousseau accepted an offer to work as a watchmaker at the court of sultan Seraglio in Constantinople, where he lived for the next six years, leaving his newborn son in the care of his wife and his mother-in-law, with whom he obviously did not get along well and which made the decision easy for him. According to a different view, he left Geneva and his family willfully and without reason. The fact remains that François grew up without the influence of a father, and was a semi-deprived child (partially deprived child) with disturbed upbringing and development, as was the case later with Rousseau as well. We cannot, therefore, be surprised that François left home when he was ten years old. No one heard of him again.

After his mother-in-law died, Isaac returned to Geneva, in September 1711, and as Rousseau lets us know, he himself became the "unhappy fruit of his return . . . For ten months later I was born, a poor and sickly child, and cost my mother her life. So my birth was the first of my misfortunes" (*Confessions*, 19) Rousseau was born on June 28, 1712 in the home at Number 40, Grand'rue. He was baptized in the Calvinist denomination on July 4, 1712, in the

Cathedral of Saint Pierre, and was given the Christian name of his grandfather, Jean-Jacques Valençon, a rich merchant-draper. Two days later Rousseau's mother, already in her fortieth year, died, perhaps of a puerperal fever. Rousseau wrote in *Confessions* that he "cost the life of the best mother," but he corrected himself in later editions and wrote that his delivery robbed his father of "the best woman." After Susanne's death, good fortune turned away from the widowed Isaac.

From a physician's point of view, the delivery of Jean-Jacques Rousseau was neither premature nor post-term. The remark that he was born as a "sickly" child does not refer to any abnormality. According to him all human beings are born "weak." He wrote in *Émile*, (Book One), "We are born weak and need strength: we are born poor and need the help of others . . ."

Literary tradition has it that Rousseau's mother died of puerperal fever a week after delivery. This claim is unsubstantiated and Susanne might have died of a disorder called postpartum gestosis (with symptoms of edema, hypertension, increased weight gain and renal damage, the latter leading to the occurrence of proteins in urine). Postpartum gestosis is a disorder which can be without symptoms in pregnancy itself and full-blown symptoms manifest only after the delivery (cramps, unconsciousness, renal failure, hypertension, or even cerebral hemorrhage). This would be in keeping with the reference to the weakness of the newborn baby. Though this assumption might be—with respect to the reference to the weakness of the newborn—more probable, we might never be able to learn the true reason of Rousseau's mother's death.

Our information about Rousseau's birth can be found in *Confessions*, a book he began to write when he was fifty. His claim that he was born as a "sickly and weak" child and that he "brought with me into this world the germ of a defect that got stronger with the years and grants me some peace only from time to time to torment me with still more cruelty in other ways," must be subjected to critical analysis. His first claim, that he was "sickly and weak" at his birth might but need not be true. If it were true, we would have to assume that he heard about his birth from one of his aunts, who took care of his upbringing after his birth.

The other possibility that must be taken into account is that Rousseau made it up to evoke the reader's sympathy and forbearance for his future. In addition, his reference to "weakness" fits stylistically into the whole sentence, which reads: "For ten months later I was born, a poor and sickly child, and cost my mother her life. So my birth was the first of my misfortunes."

His second claim, that he was born with a congenital defect (this defect is interpreted by his biographers as the cause of a nearly permanent retention of urine—see Dr. Susanne Elosu 1929) is obviously totally made-up. If he had suffered from a real congenital developmental defect (such as a valve in the urethra), accompanied by urinary retention, he would not have been able to survive, despite all available care. That this claim is a fabrication is also evidenced by the fact that Rousseau does not mention any urinary problems during later childhood and adolescence and that none of his contemporaries have ever mentioned his having such problems.

The first symptoms of urinary problems in Rousseau's life occurred only after he came to Venice and their character was clearly *inflammatory*. In adulthood, Rousseau's urinary tract infections, accompanied by intense pain, were an open secret and Rousseau himself mentioned them quite often, writing about them and nearly indulging himself in them (Starobinsky).

Another fact speaking against the existence of congenital urinary system defects is that he had not experienced any problems until 1748, at the age of thirty-six. At this time, August 26, 1748, he first mentioned his problems in a letter to his friends Alcuna and Mme de Warens. Most of his contemporaries who had such symptoms had sexually transmitted diseases. Rousseau tried to refute the suspicion that he might be infected by such disease and referred to his problems as due to congenital defect. This strategy was successful and most of his contemporaries were convinced that he suffered from a congenital defect. This conviction has been accepted by medically uneducated biographers up to the present time. A picture intrudes itself here—the archetype of a suffering savior of humanity. Rousseau regarded himself to be such a savior and this image undoubtedly required that this illness be inborn and not acquired by immoral conduct.

D. Bensoussan (1974) holds that Rousseau suffered from hereditary intermittent porphyria, but this thesis has not been proved.

Regarding deformities of the urinary tract at birth, it would have been possible to find only external penis deformities, which most often occur in the form of the urinary meatus being found on the underside of the penis (hypospadias), or on the dorsum of the penis (epispadias). Rousseau himself would have certainly mentioned them, as complaints connected with these deformities would have caused him to suffer in his childhood. It was *not possible,* at that time, to detect internal deformities of the urinary tract. In her work, Dr. Susanne Elosu argues that Rousseau suffered from congenital malformation of the prostatic part of the urethra, but this assertion is not provable. The postmortem after his death did not reveal any anomalies.

The picture of his parents as painted earlier in the chapter makes it sufficiently obvious that Rousseau must have inherited from them an emotionally unstable character. Mother and father evidently had musical talent, which could explain Rousseau's love of music (he kept repeating all his life that his profession was that of "note copyist") and would also explain his achievements in this field, which were made without any deeper musical education. He physically resembled his father and also inherited his father's unstable, difficult, irresponsible and obstinate character, though the arguments of his life were fought by pen and not by sword.

Childhood Development: Missing Mother—Deprivation and Semi-deprivation—First Masochistic Experiences

Let us now return to Rousseau's childhood years, according to his account in *Confessions.* His postpartum weakness slowly got better and though it is true that he was a child of shorter stature, he was lively and strong.

After his mother's death, Rousseau was put in the care of his father's sisters. He particularly loved his Aunt Suzon, who was thirty at that time, single, and basically his "surrogate mother" (she was born in 1682 and married Isaac-Henri Concerut to Nyon in 1730). Rousseau recalls that he was with her all the time, observed her at embroidery, listened to her singing (Suzon was the first to enkindle his love for music), was generally happy in her presence and remembered her later quite often. He went for walks with the maid, Jacqueline Faramond, daughter of a Genevan shoemaker, born January 20, 1695.

In 1717, when Rousseau was five, his father sold the house in Grand'rue though it actually was not his property. According to the last will of Rousseau's mother, half of the house belonged to both sons. The Rousseaus settled in the Saint Gervais quarter, which meant social decline from the heights of the "upper city" or Old Town.

Rousseau's education was remarkable and would generally be considered unsuitable and one-sided for a child of his age. The age at which he was able to read cannot be determined with certainty. In *Confessions* (Book One) he remarks that he does not know what he did before the age of five or six and that he does not remember how he acquired the ability to read. He remembers, however, what he read and his self-consciousness dates back to this time. He first read light literature (novels and comedies), but later his interest in literature became so strong that he and his father read out loud together, sometimes till early morning hours. By this dangerous method he had soon acquired facility in reading and an understanding for what is called passion. He had not the slightest idea about the meaning of the things they read but he knew all the emotions connected with them. He wrote, "I had no idea of the facts, but I was already familiar with every feeling. I had grasped nothing: I had sensed everything. These confused emotions which I experienced one after another, did not warp my reasoning powers in any way, for I had none."

Rousseau therefore remained, according to his *own* words, a captive of the fantastic ideas about life that he had formed in childhood and he was never able to free himself of them. Between his seventh and ninth year (1719–1723) he read serious literature: Le Sueur's *History of the Church and the Empire*, Bossuet's *Discourse on Universal History*, Plutarch's *Lives*— which was his favorite book and described the biographies of famous men in ancient Rome and Greece—Nani's *History of Venice*, Ovid's *Metamorphoses* and other books from the library of his late mother's uncle. These books and discussions with his father filled him with republican principles. He felt himself to be a Greek or Roman and identified with the characters he read about.

Isaac, Rousseau's father, about whom Rousseau always wrote only the best despite his numerous character defects, was not sufficiently educated to offer his son a systematic education. He was emotionally unstable and it is an established fact that he beat both sons, especially François, whom he did not like. Rousseau recalls how he once sprang between his father and François in order to protect his brother from the blows of their father, who was "correcting him severely and angrily." We can see that François, who was seven years older, suffered an even greater neglect than Jean-Jacques, a fact admitted even by Rousseau—this is one of the rare criticisms directed at his father. Given François's disposition, which was certainly shaped by the upbringing he received, the older brother was apprenticed at an early age to a watchmaker and later followed a "wrong path" (further details were not revealed) and ran away from Geneva. Perhaps he died in Germany. Things that were not granted to his brother were bestowed upon Jean-Jacques Rousseau.

Rousseau wrote that he was brought up with love, but that he was never pampered. He said he never attended school, though he was always loud in his praise of the Genevan schools and system of education (for example, in his *Lettre à Monsieur d'Alembert*). In fact, he had no direct experience with any of the Genevan schools. He never made clear whether he regretted this or not. In a letter to Dr. Tronchin, he more or less prided himself on the fact that he got no such education normally provided by formal institutions, but was instead influenced by traditions, transmitted from generation to generation, which provided true understanding and feeling. In the same letter Rousseau also wrote, "when I was twelve I was a Roman." Usually, by the age of twelve, boys who have been brought up normally have their own ideas about the world around them, based on direct experience. His letter reveals that he himself lived in a dreamed-up world of idealized ancient Rome unrelated to reality.

As it is clear that Rousseau's education played an important role in his life, it is interesting to quote his own recollections of his childhood: "No royal child could be more scrupulously cared for than I was in my early years. I was idolized by everyone around me, what is rarer, always treated as beloved son, never as spoilt child. *Never once, until I left my father's house, was I allowed to run out alone into a road with other children.* They never had to repress or to indulge in me any of those wayward humors that are usually attributed to nature" (italics added).

As we can see, the childhood moods of Rousseau were not repressed. He confesses to typical children's transgressions: fondness of sweet things, petty thefts, lying, and he was a chatterbox. As a small boy he had once urinated into one of the kitchen pots of their neighbor, Mrs. Clot and laughed over this remembrance even at the time when he wrote his *Confessions*. But he had never done any harm to anybody and was never cruel to animals. He tells us, "How could I have turned out wicked when I had nothing but examples of kindliness before my eyes, none but the best people in the world around me? . . . My desires were so rarely excited and so rarely thwarted, that it never came to my mind to have any."

Rousseau was content when he could spend all day sitting beside his aunt "watching her embroider, hearing her sing, always sitting or standing beside her: and I was happy."

The result of this upbringing was a "heart that was at once proud and affectionate, and a character at once effeminate and inflexible, which by always wavering between weakness and courage, between self-indulgence and virtue, has throughout my life set me in conflict with myself . . ."

This is his own idealized description, which nevertheless bears witness to the fact that Rousseau's personality was split since his youth, a fact of which he was well aware when he wrote *Confessions*.

It can be deduced from these quotations that Rousseau was a pampered child with an unstable and moody nature, whose every wish was fulfilled. He was brought up in an environment formed exclusively by women, deprived of the possibility of meeting other children and becoming familiar with their real world and thereby that of human society. Brought up in a "women's isolation," his character had gained feminine features. This kind of education is often encountered in children who have lost their mothers. The compassion of those surrounding such a poor child leads to pampering and forgiveness of bad behavior. The child is overprotected and eventually becomes semi-isolated, a situation that can be, as was the case with Rousseau, further worsened by reading unsuitable books. From his childhood, therefore, Rousseau lived in a world of dreams, which he regarded as good and fair, and condemned the reality of daily life. His situation was typical for that of a social reformer.

Once, in a fit of ill temper, Isaac said to his son reproachfully and in tears that he was the cause of the death of his wife. Such statements must have had a lasting influence on Rousseau's mental life. He remembered them for many years and, sensitive as he was, he must have been traumatized by them (see Part 2).

His father inculcated in Rousseau that Geneva had a political system which was nearly ideal, a republican city-state, and Rousseau held these views stubbornly up to his forties.

It is interesting to compare the "fragmentary" education of Rousseau with that of Thomas Hobbes: the latter could write, count and read at the age of four, studied classic languages at private school when he was eight and was therefore able to translate poetry from Latin at the age of fourteen; later he studied at Magdalena College in Oxford, where he took a Baccalareus Artium degree, which entitled him to lecture on logic. This comparison makes Rousseau appear to be an uneducated, self-taught person. The difference in the basic education is reflected in the life work of each philosopher. Hobbes produced logical philosophical work, without contradictions and with respect for the reality of daily life, which was certainly a reflection of his strong and fundamental education, whereas Rousseau's chaotic and paradoxical philosophical opinions reflect his limited, chaotic education.

Rousseau's unrealistic ideas about the society around him were further strengthened because he was not allowed, as a child, to join other children on the street. His isolation might not have been absolute, for in *Rêveries*, written toward the end of his life, he records the following episode: while playing with his friend Pleince, they had a fight and Rousseau was struck by a bludgeon with a force that almost knocked the brain out of his head. Even taking this episode into account, it is very probable that Rousseau's contacts with his peers were rather limited (peer semi-deprivation).

This fact is very important, as we know that the basic knowledge of human society is formed in children's communities. In contacts with peers, be it on the street or at school, every child automatically acquires the codes of social behavior of a given group. All children's communities have their own realistic morality, their own principles of behavior that develop with age and are continually transformed into a knowledge of the rules followed by people in their social contacts.

Rousseau was stupefied by literature that idealized the real social conditions in ancient Rome (which were in fact unbelievably cruel) and was at the same time totally unfamiliar with the society in Geneva of that time. His father aroused in him pathetic patriotism, which was not unusual, as the Genevans thought of themselves as "better" people, especially with regard to their "papal" neighbors. They took pride in their morals, simple way of life, conversation about serious matters and their contempt of worldly pleasures.

This moral superiority was adopted also by Rousseau. He remained an obstinate and not particularly polite citizen of Geneva for his whole life; this clumsiness was only partially softened by his personal charm. As he declares in *Confessions*, the model of ancient Rome inspired his dreams about self-sacrificing heroism and "helped to create in me a free and republican spirit of a proud and firm character, unable to tolerate any kind of serfdom or slavery, and causing me to suffer in situations in which it was most uncalled-for."

He stressed, in a totally unrealistic way, that his "education" was better than the education provided in school and suggested, with the same lack of realism, that he was born in a family whose ways differed from the lifestyle of others, though there were occasions when he admitted that he came from an artisan's family.

In June 1722 Isaac was hunting on lands lying outside the city walls which were the property of the patrician Pierre Gautier. They had a quarrel, which came to a head four months later, when the two men met in Geneva. Isaac challenged Gautier, a French army captain, to a duel. Gautier, being a soldier, had to refuse it, but remarked that he did not fight with people such as Isaac with a sword, but used a cane instead. Isaac hit him in the face with the sword. Gautier drew as well, but the people around them prevented them from fighting and both parties were summoned to appear for court.

Isaac Rousseau did not wait till the trial and fled the Genevan territory on October 11, 1722. The court decided in his absence, and sentenced him to three months in prison and imposed a fine on him. Isaac took refuge in the nearby Nyon Bernese territory. He later got married there for the second time with Jeanne François (March 5, 1726) and subsequently led a quiet life, living on the income he had inherited from his first wife. He remained in this exile till the end of his life. He certainly could have taken Rousseau to Nyon, but did not do it.

Rousseau, who was later to give his five children to a foundling home, does not reproach his father in *Confessions* for anything and restricts himself to the remark that he was given in the care of his maternal uncle, Gabriel Bernard, whose son, Abraham, was of the same age as he. Colonel Bernard belonged to Genevan nobility. He looked down on Rousseau who was a child of a mere artisan, but made the right decision in the sense that Rousseau needed to receive a proper education.

Both boys were sent to live outside Geneva with a Calvinist minister, Jean-Jacques Lambercier, in Bossey, an idyllic small town at the foot of Mont Saleve, now a part of France. In the eighteenth century, Bossey was part of the dukedom of Savoy, but due to a strange treaty it was entrusted into the care of a Calvinist pastor. It was not until the Treaty of Turin in 1754 that this rarity was abolished and Bossey became Catholic according to *cuius regio, euis religio*.

The two years spent in Bossey were happy and Rousseau, who was a semi-deprived child, felt good there. The disturbed development of the previous ten years was partially halted and even slightly rectified. Rousseau himself observes that the stay in Bossey "modified my harsh Roman manners and brought me back to the state of childhood." His development at this stage, however, was already beyond any rectification, because the first decisive years of life were past.

The strength of Rousseau's feelings of happiness can be judged from his *Confessions*. He described in detail how the house was arranged inside and wrote about small adventurous episodes and trips in the surroundings of Bossey. The sheer amount of detailed memories bears witness to his strong emotions, which are necessary for a child's memory to record these kinds of details. In this setting, Rousseau discovered his love of nature, which he retained for his whole life and which, described in his writings, has had a profound effect on the understanding and discovery of nature in the whole of the Western world up to the present day. Solitude in nature relieved him of the demands and pressures of a society whose rules he was never able to understand.

This is also the place where he expresses his strongest desire, typical of all masochists: "My strongest desire was to be loved . . ." Under normal circumstances, all children are happy when they are praised. Rousseau, however, shows a deviation: "I was not very susceptible to praise, I was always extremely sensitive to disgrace." Punishment—also in a sense disgrace—was for him a stronger stimulus than the happy feeling of praise.

He had here a friend, Abraham, who was of the same age, and a relationship developed such as he had not known before. As Rousseau wrote later, this relationship "opened his heart to the joys of friendship." Here, allegedly, his lifelong desire to live a simple life in the country also was born, where he would later find refuge again and again when not succeeding in finding "a place" in the society which he found incomprehensible.

He was stronger than Abraham and took up the lead position in their play. He was also his superior in learning. In Bossey his education became more systematic and he learned the basics of Latin and mathematics, as well as other subjects.

Pastor Lambercier was a very educated man, as were all Calvinist clergymen at that time. Calvin relentlessly required that all pastors acquire a thorough education and all his ministers had to be able to compete in education with the best of Catholic clergymen. Rousseau speaks with contempt of the "general education" that he got there in addition to Latin. Pastor Lambercier did not overburden the boys with learning and Rousseau praises him for that in *Confessions*, for he had already developed a strong "dislike for compulsion," which he retained all his life.

This rhetoric formulation indicates that Rousseau was an undisciplined and disobedient child. Pastor Lambercier was apparently aware of it and that was why he did not put any greater demands on his education. Rousseau gave here the first detailed account of his masochistic experiences, which is important for understanding Rousseau's character and work. He described them with certain bewilderment ("It embarrassed me to be more explicit"), nevertheless in great detail, so that they take up several pages in *Confessions*. He justified this extensiveness by saying that parents should take an example "from so common and unfortunate a case as my own." He assumes mistakenly that his masochistic deviation was the result of the thrashing he got from Mlle Lambercier. (According to today's knowledge, however, masochism becomes encoded in early childhood, at the age of two years or so.) Masochism permeated all of Rousseau's life, thinking, behavior and work, a fact that will be discussed in the concluding part. Here, it is necessary to say that Rousseau described the strength and duration of his "raging passion" very explicitly.

The two boys were indeed no angels and Mlle Lambercier, who assumed the role of their mother, threatened to apply corporal punishment for their transgressions. For Rousseau this was something entirely new and terrible. But to his great surprise he found out that the thrashing itself was not so painful as he had feared: "[The] very strange thing was that this punishment increased my affection for the inflictor . . . I had discovered in the shame and pain of the punishment an admixture of sensuality." Sexuality was already playing a part: "No doubt, there being some degree of precocious sexuality in all this, the same punishment at the hands of her brother would not have seemed pleasant at all . . . Who could have supposed that this childish punishment, received at the age of eight at the hands of a woman of thirty, would *determine my tastes and desires, my passions, my very self for the rest of my life and that in a sense diametrically opposed to the one in which they should normally have developed*" (italics added). This question will be dealt with in the second part of the book. The above quotation shows that Rousseau was aware that his development was not normal and that his deviation affected his subsequent life.

Rousseau treated facts freely, to say the least, in a way that suited his needs and this diminishes the trustworthiness of his *Confessions*, a fact we will be able to see later. At that time Rousseau was eleven and not eight and Mlle Lambercier was not thirty but forty. He experienced the urge to behave deliberately badly in order to obtain punishment, but at the same time he did not want to irritate Mlle Lambercier.

The second punishment came about without his fault, without any intention on his side, as Rousseau tries to make us believe, and so Rousseau could enjoy the thrashing "with an easy conscience." Delivering this "undeserved" thrashing, Mlle Lambercier "no doubt detected signs that this punishment was not having the desired effect" and declared that she had no intention to use corporal punishment in Rousseau's case "since she found it too exhausting." It can be assumed that Mlle Lambercier noticed that corporal punishment sexually aroused the young Rousseau. This is confirmed by the recorded fact that after this punishment took place the beds of the boys were moved to another room—before that they had slept in the same room as Mlle Lambercier (and in winter in the same bed with her).

Rousseau remarked that after the second thrashing he had been regarded as a grown-up boy, an honor which he would have preferred not to have. Rousseau confessed that ever since these thrashings he had been sexually aroused by fantasies of being physically punished by beautiful women. These openly masochistic confessions, as important as they are for our understanding of Rousseau, most often have been omitted by his biographers. Rousseau wrote that his three aunts, who took care of his upbringing, had never spoken about sexual matters so that he had no idea until his adolescence of what sexual intercourse was, and that these rather confused ideas always evoked feelings of disgust and aversion in him. He felt the same about prostitutes, which certainly was contributed to by the puritan spirit of Geneva. This type of deviation usually can be prevented when a child's upbringing takes place in the presence of other children. The pages of *Confessions* are filled with extensive descriptions of Rousseau's deviation and will be dealt with separately.

To summarize the rather extensive masochistic confession, Rousseau passionately desired torture, physical as well as mental, at the hands of a woman. His masochistic pleasure—to be punished physically by a woman, was later joined by another sensual pleasure, to which he never referred directly (see below).

Besides his semi-deprivation, his masochistic experiences are of major importance in an analysis of Rousseau's personality.

Rousseau could not have known that people in Bossey suspected Pastor Lambercier of having incestuous relationships with his sister, and of neglecting his pastoral duties. It might be interesting, from the point of view of our time, to mention the "transgressions" committed by the Lambercieres. The pastor was once seen through the window helping his sister set her hair, and the next "scandalous" case was when brother and sister rode on the back of one horse, as they could not afford two horses.

Rousseau's happy period in Bossey ended in the fall of 1724. On August 21, 1724 he must still have lived in Bossey, because he recalls an episode that occurred on the same day: the King of Sardinia, the ruling member of the House of Savoy, passed through Bossey on his way from Thonon to Annecy, which was a never-to-be-forgotten experience for Bossey. Mlle Lambercier was so excited that she fell down a slope on which she had been standing, turned a somersault, and showed the king her backside. Rousseau remarked about how this painful incident hurt his feelings, because, as he says, "I loved her as a mother, or perhaps even more dearly."

The end of their stay in Bossey was not happy for the boys, who, as already said, were no angels. Rousseau was accused of having broken a comb, and Abraham committed a transgression as well. Pastor Lambercier asked Colonel Bernard to punish both boys by a proper thrashing. This was done with a ceremonial pomp and Rousseau, who felt innocent, lets us know theatrically that this undeserved punishment, unlike what he knew from his father or from Mlle Lambercier, put a definite end to his happy childhood. The shock of this experience became a lasting trauma for him, as it was a sign of inhumanity. He later said that after that time he never again experienced "the feeling of pure happiness."

Both boys returned to Geneva to live in the house of Colonel Bernard which was situated on the hills of the Old Town. According to Rousseau his uncle Bernard was a worldly man, similar to his father, without much interest in the boys. They enjoyed freedom, but did not socialize with other boys on the street and preferred instead to stay at home and play together: "So little we were in need of companions indeed, that we even neglected opportunities to finding them . . . we watched the children's game without envy, from a distance, and did not so much as think of joining in." They were never accepted as members of other boys' groups (nor did they attempt to become such members). "I have never come into contact with young people, who could have spoilt me." The "contacts" with other boys were restricted to fights in which Rousseau was the more active and regarded himself as protector of his weaker cousin. Rousseau was the stronger, and when children made fun of Abraham, he was ready to fight for his friend, as Abraham refused to fight. "I fought and I was beaten," Rousseau lets us know. As they were afraid of the other boys, they ventured to the streets only when others were at school and they could be sure they would not be attacked.

Abraham was preparing for a career as a military engineer, in the steps of his father, whereas Rousseau was meant to become a watchmaker or a lawyer, or was to be sent to studies to become a priest. Rousseau's financial resources were modest and insufficient for the career of a priest, though Rousseau would have liked the profession of a priest as he enjoyed preaching. His father, Isaac, retained a disproportionate part of the income left by his late wife, although Colonel Bernard wanted him to pay five hundred twenty florins for Rousseau annually. Abraham studied drawing and mathematics and Rousseau stood by, preferring drawing to arithmetic. Both friends tried to produce watches and even puppets and then used their puppets to arrange a performance. During his friendship with Abraham, Rousseau's social isolation was replaced by the isolated friendship of two boys.

Rousseau's statement in *Confessions*, that he lived at his uncle's for two or three years, is also incorrect. In the spring of 1725, he was sent to work as a clerk for City Registrar Jean-Louis Masseron (1686–1753), who worked at city hall not far from their house. This was the first independent step made by Rousseau into the world of adults, which he—considering his disturbed childhood development—did not understand. It is not surprising that he was soon sacked as a "donkey" who was suited to trade only. His uncle suggested that he take a position as an apprentice with an engraver and Rousseau agreed.

He was apprenticed to Abel Ducommun, an engraver (born in 1705). This man had a violent nature, not even modified by marriage. Unlike Rousseau's grandfather, David Rousseau, who had been a learned watchmaker, Ducommun was a simple man. For Rousseau this position as an apprentice meant social decline from a refined environment. According to the work contract from April 26, 1725, Rousseau was obliged to spend five years in apprenticeship and live in the house of his master. He was unable to put up with the new, plebeian way of life and, as was usual for him, he tried to find the reasons for his faults and failures elsewhere and not in his own behavior. His character got worse in this under-civilized environment and "never did a precocious Caesar so promptly become a Laridon" (degenerated dog).

He forgot Latin and history, which he had learned in Bossey, and learned instead lying, stealing and cheating. He stole food, allegedly because he was hungry. At that time the apprentices usually left the table before the pudding was served. He mentions euphemistically that he did not steal the engraving instruments, but only concealed them and stresses that he had never stolen money. His transgressions were discovered and, as was customary at that time, he was punished by beating. At this time of early adolescence he fell in love for the first time, with two girls he met in Nyon, where he was visiting his father Isaac, who was known to be in great favor with women.

Mlle Charlotte de Vulson was his "spiritual love" and Mlle Goton his "sensual love." As he remarked later, he was capable of falling in love in both ways even later in his life. Mlle de Vulson was ten years older and got married shortly to a lawyer, Jean-Pierre Cristin, whom she followed to Orbe, a small town in canton Vaud. She was engaged to this man all the time she was flirting with Rousseau.

Psychologically more interesting was his "sensual love" for Mlle Goton, a girl of the same age, although we have no further details about her as a person. Mlle Goton invited Rousseau to play "school," where she would be a strict teacher and he an obedient schoolboy. She revived his masochistic desires that had unknowingly been awakened in him by Mlle Lambercier (see Part 2). Rousseau wrote about her—in different versions of *Confessions*—with a certain contempt, but the large number of his memories and observations gives evidence of a much greater influence on him than that of Mlle de Vulson's. Mlle Goton may have spilled the secret of their play, because the children on the street shouted at Rousseau that Mlle Goton was beating him. After his return from Nyon, Rousseau never met Mlle Goton again.

The years of his apprenticeship were not happy. He actually liked drawing and had a flair for calligraphy, but thought of himself, (as had his father thought of himself), as a "natural aristocrat" and, though he took over some of the habits of other apprentices, he never became fully immersed into their vulgar world. Having had a childhood with disturbed development he did not know how to fit into society and lacked the emotional flexibility that would allow him to adapt to his environment. Semi-isolated from his youth, nurtured on literature which glorified famous personalities and their deeds, which he partially identified with, he felt degraded in the environment in which he found himself, which punished him physically and for which he felt only contempt.

He described in detail all the thefts which he committed during his apprenticeship and which were not restricted to food only, but included everything he felt attracted to: instruments of his master, stamps, the best drawings. It was typical of him that he assured himself automatically that these thefts were in fact "innocent." Later on, still as a youth, he admits to another theft in Turin, thefts of small amounts of money at Mme de Warens's and during his stay in Lyon, where he appropriated several bottles of wine, which probably led to his dismissal as educator. Rousseau "stole" seven livres and ten sous in Paris; the whole story can be found in *Confessions*.

Portraying his excitable and passion-ridden character, he does not forget to emphasize that money has never been important to him and that his "almost sordid avarice" contrasted with "the greatest contempt for money." He admits, however, that money one owns serves as a means of freedom, whereas money which a person tries to win leads to enslavement. This is why he needs so little. His character is unstable and wavering. He described his fearfulness, irresoluteness, and feelings of shame with great exactness: "Everything alarms me, everything discourages me. I am frightened by a buzzing fly . . . So much am I a slave to fears and shame. If action is necessary I do not know what to do. If I must speak I do not know what to say . . ."

Unable to adapt to reality he tried to escape it as he in fact did all his later life. During the years of apprenticeship he read indiscriminately—like one possessed—everything he could find. He paid Mme La Tribu, who owned a lending library, even selling his clothes, to get the only drug which allowed him to flee from the reality of life and which transferred him to a different world. Books were his substitute for reality. "my restless imagination took a hand which saved me from myself and calmed my growing sensuality . . . I became one of the characters I imagined, and I saw myself always in the pleasantest situations of my own choosing . . . the fictions I succeeded in building up made me forget my real conditions, which so dissatisfied me." His "love of fantasies" left him indifferent toward his surroundings and contributed to "a tendency to solitariness," which became his permanent trait and created the impression of misanthropy. The only books he refused were books on sex because sex had never attracted him. This was abnormal in his age, but characteristic of a person with masochistic disposition.

Occasionally the claim can be encountered that even the idea of freedom, which plays such an important role in his writings, was the result of his adolescent experiences. Here one should be rather cautious. Rousseau's concept and understanding of freedom undoubtedly has its roots in his youth. His "freedom" is always related to ideas of the exceptionality of his own personality, which is seen as above the usual societal restrictions. He was "different" from others and claimed a different freedom for himself. "My mind is impatient of any sort of restraint, and cannot subject itself to the rules of the moment." Rousseau's freedom is unbalanced and egoistic: he claimed individual freedom for himself, without any social obligations. It is not surprising. Rousseau had never learned the mechanisms of social interaction and could not therefore be aware of the fact that society cannot tolerate absolute individual freedom. This would disturb the needs of society as a whole. Society is always more likely to restrict the personal freedom of individuals. This is another reason for his later contempt of society and for his view that it is bad. His contemporaries considered him a misanthrope.

Part One—Personality and Time
Chapter Two

Flight from Geneva

The apprenticeship contract with Master Ducommun was supposed to last five years, but was ended on March 14, 1728 after only three years, just three months before Rousseau's sixteenth birthday. He had returned late from his Sunday walk outside the city walls and found the city gates already closed (a certain Captain Minutoli had closed the gates half an hour earlier, before the ordered time). This had happened once before and Rousseau had spent the night outside the gates and the following morning was beaten by his master for being late. By March 14, Rousseau had become fed up with "the tyranny of the master" and was probably also unhappy with being forced to work daily, which he was not used to. He made up his mind and decided, after the night spent outside the city, not to return to his master but to run away from Geneva.

He sent his friends to let his cousin Abraham Bernard know that he intended to leave Geneva. He tried to persuade his cousin to run away with him, but Abraham refused, although it seems certain that he later left Geneva. (Rousseau remarks in *Confessions* that Abraham died in the employ of the Prussian king in 1736; on March 20, 1750 Théodora Bernard testified to the fact that her son did not live in Geneva and said that she did not know whether he was alive or not.)

Rousseau turned south and found his way to the Catholic Savoy, at that time still an independent dukedom, before it became part of France in 1860. In 1712, the year of Jean-Jacques Rousseau's birth, the governing member of the House of Savoy, Victor Amadeus II, a strict Catholic, succeeded in gaining the crown of Sicily through his diplomacy, as part of the Peace of Utrecht, trading for that of Sardinia in 1720. This was the same king Rousseau had seen in Bossey, when the embarrassing episode had occurred to Mlle Lambercier.

It might appear that Rousseau's flight to Savoy, without any means, was an ill-considered adventure. That was not the case—refugees from Geneva were welcome in Savoy because they were willingly accepted as converts to

Roman Catholicism. Geneva did the same, willingly accepting refugees from Savoy and converting them to Protestantism. The capital of the dukedom was Turin, which was better protected by its position in the Alps than was the original capital, the city of Chambéry. This change in the location of the capital had taken place in 1563, under Emmanuel-Phillibert.

Rousseau found the romantic feudalism of Savoy very convenient. The old aristocratic culture was still alive here—noblemen frequently lived at their country residences. The city aristocracy in Geneva was formed by the newly rich burghers, whom Rousseau had never loved, whereas the absolutist monarchy of the House of Bourbon in France forced its aristocracy to live in Versailles as courtiers, as graceful but politically powerless puppets.

He spent the first night in the house of a peasant-friend. Rousseau was not afraid of the foreign country: "I marched confidently out into the world's wide spaces." He got rid of the necessity to work on a daily basis. "The only thought in my mind was the independence I believed I had won." His modesty was remarkable. "A single castle was the limit of my ambition. To be a favorite of its lord and lady, the lover of their daughter, the friend of their son, and a protector of their neighbors: that would be enough." At the age of sixteen, Rousseau dreamed of a future in which he would be protected and loved. He is silent on work or responsibility. Such was the goal of his life, to which would return again and again in his later life, in various forms. He was always magically attracted by aristocratic society.

Rousseau decided to ask a Catholic priest for help, but not just any priest: he chose the aristocrat Benoit de Pontverre, who held the office *curé* of Confignon (a two-hour's walk from Geneva). In 1728, the priest was already a seventy-two-year-old man and had spent his life writing lampoons and sermons directed against Calvinism. The priest, a good host, entertained Rousseau and explained to him the sins of Genevan Calvinism. Out of politeness, Rousseau did not want to oppose him. "I had certainly more learning . . . and I felt my own superiority," he remarks with modesty in recalling the incident. He compared his behavior to that of coquettes, who raise more hope than they intend to meet in order to obtain what they want. In his politeness he was supported by the Frangi wine he was offered by the *curé*. No, he was no "dissembler," he was just "grateful," he eagerly assures the reader. His host provided him with a letter of recommendation to a Swiss baroness in Annecy, herself a convert and well known for her helpful attitude to Protestant refugees.

The journey to Annecy became longer because he stopped to visit several feudal seats, singing there below the windows and trying to attract the attention of the lady of the manor, or her daughter. He was surprised that no one appeared.

Annecy of that time was the Catholic counterpart of Calvinist Geneva. Enclosed by city walls, in the shadow of the Palais de l'Isle, it was the seat of the counts of Geneva from the tenth century. When the Catholic bishop was forced out of Geneva in 1535, Annecy became the ideological seat of the Counter-Reformation. Unlike Geneva, under Counter-Reformation *joie de vivre* was not prohibited; Catholic piousness did not exclude worldly pleasures. It is a characteristic feature of religions with longer historical traditions that after an initial stage of asceticism there comes the recognition that it is necessary to tolerate the worldly pleasures of their believers. Emotions become an acceptable part of religious life. Strict asceticism is socially unacceptable.

In Annecy, on Palm Sunday 1728, a week after he left Geneva, Rousseau met Mme de Warens for the first time in a church consecrated to Saint Francis of Assisi. This woman was to play an important role in his life. Rousseau was overwhelmed by her beauty and had nothing but words of praise for her. She insisted that he return to his father, but the young, spellbound Rousseau had already made the decision to stay with her. In his *Rêveries du Promeneur Solitaire*, a work written in the last years of his life, Rousseau says it was owing solely to her that he was able to develop his mental capabilities, which made him what he was and helped him to achieve the goals of his life.

In view of the important role Mme de Warens played in Rousseau's life, involving both his mental and sexual development, it is necessary to offer a short biography of this remarkable woman, which will also provide a charming background picture of the era.

Mme de Warens

Françoise-Louise de la Tour was born in Vevey on March 31, 1699. Her mother, Jean-Louise Warnéry died a year later, after giving birth to another child. The father, Jean-Baptiste de la Tour de Chailly remarried, but died in 1709. At the age of ten, the future Mme de Warens was an orphan. She was brought up by a stepmother and her aunts. Her main educator was a well known pietist, Father François Magny.

Pietism came to the canton of Vaud from the German-speaking Bern. Its teaching was rather heterogeneous and represented a reaction to the declining religiosity of Lutheran Protestantism. Mme de Wares lived in Father Magny's house and received instruction in religious philosophy, and a literary and musical education. Of the churches of that time, hardly any were well disposed toward pietism. A consequence of working out matters to their conclusion has the effect of bringing about the end of every religious doctrine. To think matters to their conclusion means to reduce them to absurdity. Pietist mysticism had no strengthening effect on moral laws but, on the other hand, did not infringe upon everyone's freedom to follow their own "inner light" and inner feelings. Feelings were valued more than reason. These and similar views were later presented to Rousseau, whose first reaction to the moral principles of Mme de Warens was deep horror and shock.

Mme de Warens had married in Lausanne on September 22, 1713 at the age of fourteen. Her husband was Sébastien-Isaac de Loys de Villardin, who later became Baron de Warens. There was no romantic love between them; it was a normal middle-class wedding. The bridegroom was twenty-five and had already served in several armies. On the occasion of his wedding his father bought him the estate of Vuarens, located above Lausanne in the direction of Neuchâtel. The estate carried with it the right to use the title of a baron. The formalities of the purchase took some time so the newly married man could not use the title until 1723. In 1728 debts forced Baron de Warens to sell the estate and he ceased to use the title of a baron; however, his wife decided to keep the title and in fact used it, as Mme de Warens, till the end of her life.

Their marriage remained childless, which probably sped up the development of a financial crisis. The young wife was energetic, enterprising, and full of emotions. She compensated for her childlessness by business activities. She tried to introduce the industrial revolution into the canton of Vaud: she set up companies, built factories, and produced socks and soap. Unfortunately she was unable to keep the founded factories going and to make even a small profit. We will see later that her unsuccessful entrepreneurial spirit was to remain with her till the end of her life.

She had several lovers. Her first lover, a friend of her husband, Colonel Étienne-Sigismonde de Tavel, was an English lord who had entered the French army. Allegedly, he taught her more than her own family and educator. He also taught her to make light of unfaithfulness and to prevent the development of scandals, which was then a modern sexual attitude held mainly by the highest echelon of French society. For an ambitious and enterprising young Swiss woman such a philosophy must certainly have been exciting. Her lover gained the rank of a colonel at the age of thirty and must have been more successful than her husband. Tavel remained her faithful friend, even at times when she was doing badly.

Mme de Warens was also interested in botany and the preparation of drugs from medicinal plants. Her stay in Aix-les-Bains, where she took the waters at the age of twenty-six, became the dramatic turning point of her life. She realized that it was possible to flee Vevey. Vevey was governed by German-speaking, Protestant Bern and was of the same stringent and cheerless nature as Geneva. The young, active baroness was fond of social life and was enchanted by the Catholic Savoy, which impressed her as a place that was much more lively, cultured and tolerant than Switzerland. It was full of French culture. Pietism, in which she was raised, had the effect of reducing the differences between religions. She declared on her return to Geneva in the summer of 1725—in front of her husband's friends, to his great consternation—how charming Savoy was compared to Switzerland. She declared that she was fed up with Switzerland, and she soon decided to leave. As an enterprising woman, she found a doctor, Dr. Viridet of Morges, and persuaded him to prescribe a new stay for her at the health resort of Amphion near Évian. She crossed Lake Geneva to its southern shore in July and left Vevey for good.

At that time the king of Sardinia, Victor Amadeus II, was visiting Évian and, according to Rousseau, Mme de Warens fell to the king's feet and declared that she wanted to convert to Catholicism. The king, who liked the idea of being seen as a fervent Catholic, promised to protect her and provided her with an annual pension of 1,500 Piedmont livres. To forestall the suspicion that he had fallen in love with her, he sent her under the protection of his personal guard to Annecy, where she was to renounce the Protestant faith under the supervision of Monsignor Michael Gabriel de Bernex, the titular bishop of Geneva.

There are several versions of this spectacular flight; in one account, a friend of Mme de Warens—François-Joseph de Conzié—wrote in a letter several years later that Mme de Warens fell to Bishop de Bernex's feet with the words: *In manus tuas domine commendo spiritum meum.* Another version springs from the pen of Bishop de Bernex's biographer, Claude Boudet, who wrote that the educated and rich Swiss baroness realized her mistaken belief through her studies of holy scriptures and got carried away by the sermons of Mgr de Bernex to such extent that she asked him for an audience, in which she implored him to help her with conversion to the Catholic Church.

All these descriptions agree in one point: Mme de Warens was a politically important convert and was brought to Annecy promptly. Another factor may have been the concern that the Swiss present in Évian might abduct and bring her back to Geneva; the Swiss claimed that everything was just a pompous performance and a put-up repentance. The baroness simply wanted to escape from her financially ruined husband. This same view was also given in a letter from 1732, six years after the event, by the deserted husband himself, who described his wife as a calculating person. According to him, his wife took the best bedclothes and silver and a large amount of money from the factory in the winter of 1725–1726, before she went to Évian. As she planned to spend the whole summer in Évian, she took with her also the best part of their kitchen equipment and goods from the factory. She decided to travel overnight, because it was too hot for her by day. She left him very early in the morning (at two o'clock), was unusually sweet and implored him to stay in bed, obviously because she did not want him to see the many pieces of luggage she took with her. Loys visited her in Évian later (she asked him to bring her walking stick and Bayle's dictionary) and she ordered still other goods from their factory to be sent to her behind his back.

The messenger, who was sent to bring her the stick and the book, informed Loys that Mme de Warens had left Évian. The following search of the house revealed that the valuable things, which were allegedly locked up, were in fact gone. The husband did catch some pieces of luggage in Geneva, but these were already sealed in the name of the King of Sardinia and lost to the owner. The flight of his wife put the unhappy husband into serious difficulties with the authorities. According to Bernese laws, possessions of those who turned away from the Protestant faith could be confiscated.

When she arrived in Annecy, Mme de Warens was received with enthusiasm. The story of a young, beautiful and rich Swiss baroness, who left her home and family to convert to the true religion, was as if made up just for the purposes of the Counter-Reformation. Bishop de Bernex was proud that the conversion turned out well with his help and felt responsible for her well-being. He ordered a pension to be paid to her from his resources and tried to obtain other resources for her as well. He had a portrait of her painted which is said to be one of the pictures in the Museé Cluny in Paris. It was generally expected that the prominent convert would enter a convent where she would complete her conversion. Mme de Warens, however, was not enthusiastic about the idea of a life spent in the solitude of a convent and succeeded in persuading the bishop that she would be more useful for the Catholic Church if she lived in a house as a noblewoman, accepting Protestant refugees there and helping with the work of their rectification.

That was why she sent a letter to her former teacher, Father Magny, who had returned to Vevey in 1722, after his Genevan exile. She asked him to obtain a brief pedigree for her that was to show her peerage in as advantageous a light as possible. She wrote that it is not a question of vanity but a question of daily bread. Her baptism in the Roman Catholic faith took place on the day of the Blessed Virgin Mary. She lived in a flat not far from the bishop's residence and received the pension provided by the king; the king even bought her some furniture. Her income amounted to fifteen hundred livres from the king, one hundred fifty livres from Bishop de Bernex who had converted her, and two hundred livres from Bishop Valpergue de Maurienne.

These material advantages and gifts were not granted for unselfish reasons, for she was expected to succeed in converting her husband to Catholicism. We have a report on that directly from her husband, who visited her in Annecy on September 24, 1726. He tried to persuade her that her conversion to Catholicism was a mistake. He wrote that she was crying, because she knew that tears had always mollified him. She told him about the financial support that she was receiving from Turin and suggested that he could receive similar support. But her husband withstood the persuasions and they agreed, in order to prevent their property in Switzerland from being confiscated, that his wife would donate her property to him. The donation was authenticated by a notary public.

When he returned to Switzerland, however, he received a letter from his wife asking him to regard her as dead and to forget about her. He applied for divorce to the Bernese authorities and as a Protestant had no difficulties with it. Mme de Warens, however, remained married for her whole life, according to her Catholic faith, and kept using the title Baronne de Warens. The debts, which the baroness left to Loys, led to his ruin. He had to leave Switzerland and eked out a miserable existence in London.

Mme de Warens was followed to Annecy by a youth, the gardener from Vevey, Claude Anet, who was her servant and at some point became her lover.

This was the woman Rousseau addressed in church and to whom he was bringing, in addition to the letter of recommendation from M. de Pontverre, his own letter, which was written in an oratorical style in most eloquent phrases borrowed from the books he had read. When this meeting took place Mme de Warens was twenty-nine and Rousseau was not quite sixteen. Two kindred souls met on that day—motherless child and childless mother, romantic youth and sentimental woman, adventurer and adventuress. Mme de Warens was fond of young men and it is very difficult to distinguish between her religious feelings and her erotic emotions. The philosopher Bataille shares the same view of the connection between both emotional states.

There exist several portraits claimed to be of Mme de Warens, but it is not clear which of them may be genuine and which are only mistakenly ascribed to her. Rousseau described her looks with enthusiasm but perhaps a more realistic picture originates with M. de Conzié, who met with her somewhat later. According to him, Mme de Warens was of medium stature with a tendency toward plumpness already showing on her shoulders and bosom, the latter being measured as too big by the French ideal of beauty of that time. Her nature was jovial and capricious, her laugh charming and her manner attractive and intelligent. This assessment of her character was different from the view of the bishop, who saw in her "a devout Swiss noblewoman," and the view of her husband and several others who regarded her as "a perfect actress."

Mme de Warens listened to the story of the young Rousseau's life and had no idea what to do with him. She fed him and gave him a bed in her flat, which he had not the slightest desire to leave. But he realized that he had already reached the age when it is not possible to live together with a young woman. There was also Claude Anet, who officially was her steward—it took quite a long time before Rousseau discovered that Anet was also her lover. No one had any idea what to do with Jean-Jacques, who quickly settled in at Mme de Warens's. His father did not want him and Rousseau had no intention of returning to Geneva to continue his apprenticeship.

One of Mme de Warens's guests suggested a solution: Rousseau should go to Turin, enter a hospice, where the stay was cost-free, and formally realize his conversion there. Mme de Warens and Bishop de Bernex would jointly finance the journey. Rousseau had no heart for this suggestion but had to accept it. The journey was in fact a plot by a married couple, Mr. and Mrs. Sabran, who wanted to go to Turin. They accompanied Rousseau and lived on his money. The day after Rousseau's departure from Annecy his father Isaac arrived there on horseback from Nyon, but when he heard from Mme de Warens that his son had already left for Chambéry, he did not try to catch him. He would certainly have succeeded in it, because Rousseau was traveling on foot whereas Isaac had a horse.

His behavior was similar to that of young Rousseau's uncle, Colonel Bernard, who followed his nephew on the latter's journey to Annecy, but only up to Confignon, where he turned back to Geneva. Rousseau's father probably was not very unhappy about the fact that both his sons had left home, because he could use the whole income from the real estate he had inherited from his first wife and would not have to share any of it with his sons, even though he had to pay his son's former employer, the engraver Ducommun, a financial penalty to compensate for Rousseau's running away.

Rousseau was always happy when he could travel on foot and was in good spirits on his way to Turin. He was healthy and the future was wide open, everything he could see seemed to guarantee his future happiness. To his view he was the young Hannibal crossing the Alps. He often thought about Mme de Warens: "I looked on myself as the creature, the pupil, the friend and almost the lover of Mme de Warens . . . By sending me to Turin they had, as I saw it, assumed responsibility for my existence there . . . I need have no further care for myself: others have undertaken to look after me." But sex still remained a secret for him. He slept in one room with the married couple (the Sabrans) and complained that his sleep was disturbed by their noisy sleeplessness, which certainly would have disturbed him more if he understood its meaning.

The Sabrans traveled with him but at his expense, which was the reason that a week after his arrival in Turin he had nothing left from his traveling money. They even stole his linen and the small sword donated to him by his cousin Abraham, beautified by Mme de Warens with a silver-pink ribbon. When he knocked on the hospice gate in Turin, he had only the clothes he wore, a letter of recommendation and his conviction that he would soon become a person worthy of himself. Already he began to feel more important than a mere apprentice.

His journey to Turin shows in many respects how defective his upbringing and socialization in fact were. At the age of sixteen he had no concrete plans for his life—other children of this age already have such plans, even though they may later change them several times. He is convinced he will become an extraordinary personality, but he desires at the same time to be protected, preferably by Mme de Warens, who assumes the role of his surrogate mother. His behavior reveals a complete lack of knowledge of the human community. He knows nothing about sex, he is not able to take care of his own things, and knows nothing about the reality of life.

Turin—Conversion to Roman Catholicism

Turin of the early eighteenth century was the capital of the duchy of Savoy and contained many expensive buildings. The building to which Rousseau was sent can still be found today. It is Number 9 via Porta Palatina, next to Santo Spirito Church. We can still find a record there that "Rosso, Gio Giacomo, di Ginevra, Calvinista" was accepted on April 12, 1728. According to these records, he abjured the sinful Protestant teaching on April 21, and was baptized two days later. Though Rousseau wrote in his *Confessions* that he spent two months there, because he contested the theologians and did not want to disclaim Calvinism without resistance, his statements are not very reliable, as is often the case.

We can hardly conceal a smile reading his accounts of the theological disputations with monks and how he made one after another doubt their own positions by his arguments. According to him, religion can be best attained by education. He himself came from a virtuous, religious family and "if ever a child received a sound and reasonable education that child was I." This is an impassioned, uncritical and unrealistic claim, which is at the same time typical of Rousseau's way of thinking. The reader might ask why then had Rousseau converted at all? Actually, he had realistic reasons: he did not want to return to Geneva, and he was terrified by the prospect of remaining alone in a foreign environment, or of having to re-cross the Alps again.

The people in the hospice were probably no good. There were vagrants among them, who let themselves be baptized as many times as needed. Besides the men, women also lived in the hospice. He even liked one of the girls, a Jewish girl from Amsterdam named Judith Komes. Both sexes were strictly separated, not for reasons of sexual prudery, but because of homosexuality, which Rousseau encountered here for the first time. He described in detail his experiences with a "Moor," who tried to seduce him into mutual masturbation.

This episode is remarkable for medical reasons, as it is known of Rousseau that he later masturbated for much of his life, though he pilloried this kind of sexual gratification in *Émile*, and one form of masturbation (masturbation of the urethra) was obviously the cause of his later urinary tract disorders. He told the monks of his sexual experiences. They were by no means surprised and one of them regarded it as his duty to enlighten him about life.

Rousseau tried to speed up his conversion in order to leave an environment he did not like as quickly as possible. It was typical of Rousseau that he embellished his conversion to Catholicism in his *Confessions* in a way which showed him in the best light. We are told that during the ceremony, where he had to give an account of his life to the inquisitor, he thought of the prince of Navarre, Henry IV of France, who converted to Catholicism to save the unity of France. He thought of himself as being in the same situation. We must of course realize that the description of the situation of the young Rousseau springs from a much older and more knowledgeable Rousseau in his *Confessions*. It is rather improbable that Rousseau, at the age of sixteen, would think of, or even know anything about, the conversion of Henry IV.

We know Rousseau successfully abjured Protestantism because he was baptized two days later. He was given the name Francesco after his godmother Francesca Christina Rocca, a name that by coincidence was also the name of his lost brother. The money collected at his baptism amounted to as little as twenty francs. We know that later Rousseau was fond of solitude and repeatedly fled bigger cities, but as a youth in Turin he had no such tendencies and felt quite well there. After two months of this monastery imprisonment he enjoyed his regained freedom and the twenty francs made him feel rich.

His talents and advantages would certainly help him to find a way to important people. He fell for Piedmont cuisine and Italian music and singing, which he was fond of and promulgated for his whole life. King Victor Amadeus had "the best orchestra in Europe" and the everyday mass in royal chapel, which Rousseau attended regularly, was something like a concert of that time, where symphonies and sonatas were performed. The papal restrictions regarding church music were not yet in force and admission to church was free. Rousseau preferred the solitude of the church environment and did not attempt any active enterprise, which was rather unusual for a boy of his age. Further, he felt congeniality with the king when he was in his presence in the chapel. He indulged in music and expected that a young princess would appear whom he could court.

He passed the nights at a lodging house in Po street, where he paid one sou for a night. The owner of the house was a soldier's wife. She slept with her children in the same room as the lodgers. Rousseau was soon short of money and he had no other choice than to start visiting different shops and offering his services as an engraver. He spent some time working for the beautiful Signora Basile, a businesswoman of twenty-two, whose husband was serving in the army. A romance developed between them, which Rousseau described as the most sweet and most pure joys of love. "No passions were ever at once so pure and so strong as mine."

Once Rousseau knelt down behind her and raised his arms in her direction. She saw him in a mirror and ordered him to lie down on a small carpet at her feet without saying a word. But the romance was brought to an end because the returning husband ordered Rousseau out of the house.

With the help of the lodging house's owner he then got a job as servant to Comtesse de Vercelli, a widow of fifty-eight who suffered from breast cancer. She dictated letters to him, which she was unable to write due to the illness. Rousseau admired her style, comparing it with the style of Madame de Sévigné. He showed her the letters he sent to Mme de Warens. In his position as a servant, the proud citizen of Geneva, the born aristocrat, the "Roman at the age of twelve," who crossed the Alps "as Hannibal" and converted "as Henry IV," took comfort from being a secretary and even cherished hopes of inheriting something from the countess.

She died in December 1728 and Rousseau got from her nephew and heir, Count della Rocca, only thirty livres and was allowed to keep the clothes he wore. The end of his employment was speeded by an embarrassing affair which, according to him, gave rise to his later *Confessions*: in his disappointment he stole a pink and silver ribbon and, when the theft was discovered, he blamed the maid, Marion, saying it was she who gave it to him. They were both sacked and Rousseau suffered from pangs of conscience for the rest of his life—the attempt to clear his conscience was allegedly one of the motives that motivated him to write *Confessions*.

It should be mentioned that Rousseau made the acquaintance of abbé Jean-Claude Gaime, who was employed as tutor of the children of Count Mallarède at the time of his employment with M. de Vercelli in Palazzo Cavour. This young, poor and unconventional priest served as the model for a character in Rousseau's *Vicaire savoyard*. Gaime instructed Rousseau in moral virtues, in the importance of getting to know oneself, and tried to dampen his admiration of noble personalities. He further taught Rousseau the principles of good and evil, that people who have climbed up high can fall easily, that every-day good deeds are as deserving as heroic deeds, and that it is better to be respected by people all the time than to obtain a short-lived admiration. In doing so, he laid the foundations of Rousseau's moral code, which made him a moralist to the Europeans even though Rousseau did not follow these principles.

So Rousseau found himself in the old lodging house again. On the first pages of his *Confessions* he described in detail how he showed his naked backside to women (see Part 2), a behavior that was misinterpreted as exhibitionism. The nephew of the late Mme de Vercelli, Count della Rocca, helped him find the next employer. He was admitted as a servant in Palazzo Solaro, the residence of Count de Gouvon, head of the Solaro family, who was then a man of eighty. The count had worked earlier as ambassador to various European courts, and as a minister and highly positioned courtier (main marshal of the royal household). Rousseau was personally introduced to other members of the family as well, who were all employed at the court.

He was dazzled and satisfied to hear that he did not have to wear servant's livery. At table, however, he had to be in attendance and meet the duties of a lackey, but "in greater freedom." His further development was deeply influenced by the learned abbé Gouvon (Carlo Vittorio, a second son from Count de Gouvon's second marriage), who had studied at the University of Siena. Rousseau became something like his secretary and his pupil. The abbé recognized Rousseau's talent and, as he was a literary and educated man, taught him Latin and Italian and loaned him books of contemporary and classic authors. Rousseau had never been able to use Latin correctly, but his knowledge of Italian was a great help for his later life.

Our hero and patient fell in love platonically with Pauline-Gabrielle de Breil, abbé Gouvon's niece, who it must be said did not take much cognizance of him. Rousseau saw in her a demigoddess who belonged to an aristocratic family and he was always trying to make the acquaintance of such people. His disturbed childhood development left him no other choice than to look for his loves in a dreamed-up and, for him, inaccessible world.

Never in his life was he able to find sexual partners who would be appropriate to his age and status. His sexuality developed in an abnormal direction.

Abbé Gouvon's teaching activities obviously were well-directed and met with some success. Count de Gouvon allegedly went so far as to speak about Rousseau with the king and suggested that the youth could be sent to him for studies to obtain education for royal diplomatic service. One might think that Rousseau stood at the start of a promising career, a position attained by a combination of chance, talent and apparently good manners, (helped along by considerable self-confidence), a career which would mentally suit him more than that of an engraver.

But as we observe very often in his later life, there appeared a sudden interruption of Rousseau's positive and advantageous position, driven by motives of which biographers, who are not acquainted with recent knowledge on moral masochism, cannot make much sense. Moral masochists do not like situations where they are successful, where activity and diligence are required. Rather they try to find a subordinate position, where they do not have to overexert themselves and where others will take care of them. On the other hand, they do not perceive the subordinate position to a person who takes care of them and whom they "love" as a restriction of freedom. This should help us understand Rousseau's words that such a career would mean "a long period of time where I would be subject to other people," an explanation which sounds rather sublime and keeps returning later on, because he wants to retain his personal "freedom," the particular character of which has been described. The meaning of his freedom is characterized by passivity: he is free when he does not have to do what he does not want, and not when he is allowed to do what is not forbidden.

At this time, a friend from his apprenticeship days, the savage Pierre Bacle (born 1714) turned up in Turin—he also had run away. Though younger, he succeeded in persuading Rousseau that he should not endure his present "enslavement" any longer and that he should leave his job as servant. Rousseau began neglecting his duties in Palazzo Solaro and sought various diversions in the city. He was rebuked, reprimanded and then sacked. He also insolently ignored all attempts at reconciliation. One reason may have been his longing for the maternal care of Mme de Warens, to whom he was still sending letters and who adjured him in her letters to hold onto his job at Count de Gouvon's and not to destroy his situation by behaving foolishly. Both boys fought their way back to Annecy. According to Rousseau their separation in Annecy was an easy one. Pierre Bacle said, "Your are at home here, so good luck!" and disappeared. Their renewed friendship lasted six weeks but influenced the whole of Rousseau's life. The friends never met again, as Pierre returned to Geneva and died there at the age of seventeen.

Life at Mme de Warens's in Annecy—Rambles

Rousseau returned with trembling heart to Mme de Warens in summer 1729, threw himself to her feet and kissed her hands. Apparently she was not surprised to see her poor small boy return. She asked him to tell her his story, which Rousseau did, concealing only a few details. Mme de Warens offered him accommodation in her house once again and decided that Rousseau would stay indefinitely this time. Rousseau was finally at home after a long time. He felt very happy there, although it could not be compared with Turin's palaces, and he was assigned a small room that formerly had served as a chamber for cleaning utensils. He was very pleased about the fact that his room afforded a view of the garden.

Mme de Warens was a good-natured woman who invited everyone to dinner (Rousseau was jealous of her guests), she had too many servants for her income and thrift was not her strongest point. She had debts despite her income of 2,000 livres a year. According to Rousseau, "a sweet intimate relationship" formed between them from the first day of his return. She called him *"Petit"* and he called her *"Maman,"* which corresponded with their relationship. The intimacies they exchanged had the same character as those between mother and child. Rousseau felt "a gladdening peace" and pleasure in her presence without having any idea why.

Their conversations can be best described as an endless gossip. Rousseau did not need any encouragement to talk; on the contrary, it was often necessary to use a certain pressure to make him keep quiet. He was extremely happy in her presence and cried when she left. Rousseau described their relationship with exaggerated enthusiasm, gratitude and infatuation, which, as he assures us, was totally asexual despite the round surfaces of her body, sometimes only partly concealed. He renounced even the masturbation he had practiced before (and also later): "I was chaste because I loved her." He started masturbating in Italy and says, "I had preserved my physical not my moral virginity." He records an episode that happened at that time, which will be analyzed in the medical section, Part 2: Once at table with Mme de Warens, he cried out that she should not swallow a morsel, as he saw a hair on it. *When she spat out the morsel on the plate, he ate it.*

In the first weeks after his return to Annecy, Rousseau helped Anet (Rousseau did not know that Anet was not only Mme Warens's servant but also her lover) to collect medicinal plants and prepare drugs from them, a permanent activity of Mme de Warens. Rousseau hated medicines, but despite his aversion *licked Mme Warens's fingers smeared by "the most disgusting remedies."* (This, too, is typical of masochists—see Part 2.)

Mme de Warens tried to improve his education. She loaned him various serious books: works of Hobbes, Voltaire, Pufendorf, Addison and Saint-Évremond; authors who fell within the category of "moralists" in France of that period. At this time Rousseau was rather critical of the writings by Bayle, or La Bruyére, and regarded Mme Warens's literary taste as "somewhat Protestant."

These books nevertheless had an influence on Rousseau's later literary activities. Rousseau's disinclination to appear in public and salons was already becoming apparent, even though he was to become more at ease there later. He was well aware that men of society knew that in social settings certain subjects were not mentioned and that they were more self-confident with their conversation. It has always been dangerous for an unsociable man such as Rousseau to express something spontaneously in front of other people. He was unable to dispel the uneasy feeling that he could make a fool of himself, or that he could be misunderstood. He wrote, "I cannot understand how a man can have the confidence to speak in company." He adds that his memory for words had always been very poor and that he was unable to learn even a few verses by heart. "I . . . have never been able to memorize half a dozen verses in my life." According to his own words, his feeling was much faster than his thinking, which he described as slow.

His letters, which he had enough time to write and to reflect upon, contained formulations that were much better then his conversations. ("I have a passionate temperament, and lively and headstrong emotions. Yet my thoughts arise slowly and confusedly, and are never ready till too late . . . I do not suffer from this combination of quick emotion and slow thought only in company . . . Ideas take shape in my head with the most incredible difficulty.") His thoughts straightened out slowly and he could achieve best results during walks or at night.

The best feelings he experienced were those when he was alone with Mme de Warens in her boudoir.

Mme de Warens had to ask herself with increasing urgency what to do with Rousseau. One of her relatives suggested the career of a priest, and as this also found the full support of Bishop de Bernex, Rousseau entered the Lazarists' seminary in Annecy to study theology, His studies were financially supported by the bishop. His teacher was Father Gros, a small clergyman.

Rousseau was by no means enthusiastic about this decision and his stay in the seminary. He went there "as if to a torture chamber." He missed his room at Mme de Warens's. He had to study regularly, especially Latin (which he had never properly mastered), and all of it was causing him real suffering. Before and after this period of his life, he had never been able to study in a systematic way, once again the result of missing an education at school where the pupils learn to work regularly. This explains the fact that he always made an impression of an irresponsible pupil.

Father Gros soon realized the abilities of his pupil and asked the gentle and intelligent abbey, Father Jan-Baptiste Gâtier, to take care of Rousseau's education. Rousseau used many of the features of this second teacher for the main character of *Vicaire savoyard*. His first model for this literary character was the young priest Gaime whom he met in Turin, "as I wrote *Émile,* combining M. Gâtier with M. Gaime, I made these two excellent priests the models for my Savoyard vicar."

In spite of his gentle disposition and patience, Jean-Baptiste Gâtier was unable to teach Rousseau Latin, and when he left Rousseau had to be discharged from the seminary, where he had spent less than three months, with the unflattering remark that he was "unfit even to be a priest." The only book Rousseau had studied in the seminary was the *Cantatas* by Clérambault, loaned to him by Mme de Warens.

Even though he lacked any formal musical education, Rousseau had easily learned the cantatas by heart, and as Mme de Warens was fond of music as well, she agreed after his return from the seminary that her *petit* should study music. She found him a position in the chorus school of the local cathedral, which was led by Jacques-Louis-Nikolas Le Maistre (sometimes written as M. le Maître). Rousseau spent six happy winter months here, and he could visit Maman daily as she lived not far off. He acquired some rudiments of music; however, he turned out to be unable to concentrate and motivate himself to work systematically. As a child he had not been a pupil and these two habits were never demanded from him. He admitted to being a dreamer, unable to concentrate, "But what can I do about it?"

At this time an adventurer and musician, Venture de Villeneuve, came to Annecy. Just as in Turin, where Rousseau had become enthusiastic about the young villain Pierre Bacle, Rousseau was bewitched by Venture de Villeneuve, who acted the polished, popular, ingenious globetrotter with aristocratic manner, even though his clothes were worn through and he spoke with a Provençal dialect. All these were features that the eighteen-year-old Rousseau wanted to have. Rousseau introduced him to Mme de Warens, who quickly saw through him, did not recommend that Rousseau see him and banned the adventurer from her house.

Mme de Warens's friend, M. Le Maistre, had a dispute with local church authorities and decided to leave Annecy. Mme de Warens asked Rousseau to accompany M. Le Maistre and stay with him as long as he needed him. She wanted Rousseau to be removed from the influence of de Villeneuve. Anet, her servant, helped carry their luggage out of town. This was Rousseau's second departure from Annecy, this time with an epileptic music teacher who was fond of drinking.

The musician's last days turned out to be most unhappy. In Lyon, having been accused by Annecy church authorities of the theft of musical materials that were the property of the cathedral, his luggage was confiscated. Rousseau left his master when the latter suffered an epileptic attack and was badly in need of a friend's help in a foreign town. In *Confessions* Rousseau admits he was ashamed of this behavior, but realized it only after his return to Annecy.

We will see similar behavior on many occasions in his later life. People who do not grow up in the company of peers lack any knowledge of the necessity of mutual altruism. They behave egoistically and expect good deeds from others, but are unable to behave in such a way themselves. Masochists are collectors of their own transgressions, because these serve the purpose of confirming the feelings of guilt hidden at the back of a masochist's consciousness.

Rousseau was back in Annecy again but did not find Mme de Warens there. Most probably she had been persuaded to take part in a rather unsuccessful secret diplomacy. Her relative, Colonel d'Aubonne had set his heart on trying to achieve the secession of the canton of Vaud from German-speaking Bern and wanted it to become part of the Francophile kingdom of Sardinia. They were both trying to find support for their undertaking at the French court. But the royal courts were not enthusiastic about this undertaking and their mission was doomed to failure.

When in Annecy, Rousseau contacted the adventurer Venture de Villeneuve. He declared in his *Confessions* that he is a good judge of human character ("I have studied people and regard myself to be a good observer"), but the entire course of his life shows that his judgment of people was often wrong.

This was certainly true of his relationship with Venture de Villeneuve, who gained the reputation of the local Casanova and whom Rousseau admired as such. Like his friend, he amused himself with local girls and says of some that they fell in love with him. One of them was the maidservant of Mme de Warens, Anne-Marie Merceret, a good Swiss girl from Fribourg, whose father was musician. Anne-Marie must have inherited musical talent from her father, since we hear from Rousseau that they sang duets together. Even though this girl fed Rousseau in Mme de Warens's house, he did not appreciate her much. She attracted his stomach, not his heart.

Another girl who was in love with Rousseau was Ester Giraud, the daughter of an upholsterer and a converted Calvinist. She was ten years older than Rousseau, who found her disgusting. He admits quite openly that he had never been attracted to girls of lower origin. For him, the ideal girl would be of aristocratic origin though not necessarily the most beautiful one. Here again, his unfamiliarity with society becomes obvious. He does not know his place in society and dreams of something unattainable. Eventually he would have to face the reality of his social life. Years later he spent a long period with an illiterate laundress, marrying her toward the close of his life.

Rousseau vividly recalls in his *Confessions* a romantic episode, described as "the idyll of a cherry orchard," that he had during the summer of 1730. In Mme de Warens's absence, while making a trip to the city's surrounding area, he had met two girls traveling on horses who were having difficulty crossing a river. One of them was Mlle de Graffenried, a descendent of a noble Bernese family who had escaped from Bern to convert to Catholicism. Rousseau had previously met Mlle de Graffenried in Mme de Warens's house. Mlle de Graffenried's companion, Mlle Galley, came from Savoy. Rousseau forded the river on one horse and followed with the second horse.

Both girls were on their way to the Château de la Tour near Thôn and, when Rousseau was about to go on about his way, they told him laughingly that he must come with them as their prisoner of war to have his clothes dried out. They should be alone in the château and intended to return to Annecy the same evening. The amazed and enchanted Rousseau was asked to mount Mlle de Graffenried's horse and hold on to her waist to keep from falling off the horse. His heart was thumping and, according to Rousseau, he suspected that Mlle de Graffenried had the same feelings, although he did not have the courage to ask her.

When they arrived at the château, the girls prepared a dinner for him, about which Rousseau wrote only in superlatives. The only thing that he missed was wine, which Rousseau was fond of. He made up for it by the courteous compliment that they could charm him even without wine. After the meal they all went to a cherry orchard, where Rousseau climbed the trees and threw cherries at the girls, some of which fell into Mlle Galley's neckline, which provoked an outburst of laughter.

The trip ended innocently, probably to the disappointment of both girls. Rousseau must have felt he behaved contrary to their expectations and in the *Confessions* finds an excuse for himself: the experience was as beautiful as it was because he was innocent. The only thing he took the liberty of doing was to kiss Mlle Galley's hand. On the return journey he rode behind Mlle Graffenried again, though he would have preferred to ride together with the more beautiful Mlle Galley, who cast seductive looks at him, but he did not work up the courage to suggest a change. When they parted, they promised each other to meet again.

The whole episode demonstrates Rousseau's lack of sexual experience although, according to him, innocence has its own sensuality, which lasts forever. This statement shows the inadequate inability he had, for his age, to obtain sexual gratification. He contends himself with flirtation. He was unable to make up his mind and did not know what he wanted from the girls. He found Mlle Galley the prettier of the two and assigned Mlle de Graffenried the role of a confidante. Rousseau tried to see them again but failed, as the participants of this episode do not meet again. He wrote a letter to Mlle de Graffenried and received a reply but we are left without further details. Mlle de Graffenried entered a convent in Bonlieu, where she died in 1748 at the age of thirty-eight and Mlle Galley married a much older Savoyard senator and died childless in 1781.

Mme de Warens was still on her travels and Rousseau decided to accompany her maidservant, Anne-Marie Merceret (at her expense), to her parents who lived in Fribourg. They traveled through Geneva and Rousseau described his emotion at the sight of the city, which was always to stand for freedom, equality, concord and moral purity in his eyes, all things he had lost.

He believed in these qualities of his native town, because as he says, "I carried it in my own heart." While on the journey to Fribourg he also visited his father in Nyon, whereupon they embraced each other and both shed tears. Isaac Rousseau did not try to force his son to stay with him, and Rousseau added with some criticism aimed at his father that "he felt not the least temptation to hold me back by force, and in that I think he was right." Their mutual relationship, which he always described as good, was probably idealized, because—as can be judged by a letter sent to his father—it is obvious that that there was dissention between them and we know that Isaac had renounced him under the pretext of his conversion to Catholicism.

Anne-Marie did her best to seduce him on the way—they even slept in one room—but nothing happened, despite the fact that Rousseau was twenty and Anne-Marie twenty-five. The reason for this abstinence was undoubtedly due to Rousseau's complete lack of experience with sex. It must be said that he was unable, even at this age, to imagine how sexual intercourse was initiated, and had the idea that extensive preparations were necessary. No wonder that Anne-Marie's interest in him cooled off rapidly after their arrival in Fribourg. Later on, from the perspective of middle age, he regretted that he had missed the occasion, which was offering him the opportunity of marriage with this girl. He could have lived peacefully in Fribourg and take over the position of an organist from her father. But at that time he was young and his adventurous tendencies led him to Lausanne.

He had no money but, in Lausanne, inspired by the adventurer Venture, he posed as a music teacher from Paris and even changed his name to Vaussore de Villeneuve. His "school of music" ended up as a failure when he was asked to compose a piece of chamber music for a local attorney. No one had ever had such a "caterwauling" and the musicians split their sides laughing. During his stay he made several trips to the former house of Mme de Warens in Vevey. Lausanne was later used as background for his most successful novel *La Nouvelle Héloïse.*. In the first manuscript of his *Confessions*, which was written in Neuchâtel, the length of his stay in Lausanne is not mentioned. In the Parisian and Genevan manuscripts, he lets us know that he left Lausanne and spent the winter in Neuchâtel.

Neuchâtel was part of the kingdom of Prussia, reigned over by the "enlightened" Frederick II, who had inherited it from the Orléans-Longueville family in 1707. Frederick II had very progressive views, loved culture and so even as bad a music teacher as Rousseau found pupils here. "I have gradually learned music by teaching it," he noted. He did better than in Lausanne, his situation improved, and he was able to pay his debts made in Lausanne.

But here again, as was typical of him, Rousseau unfortunately made another bad choice of friends, this time a Greek adventurer who posed as the Archimandrite of Jerusalem (a Greek priest commissioned to take up a collection in Europe for the restoration of the Holy Sepulchre). As a Greek he did not speak French and asked Rousseau to work for him as an interpreter. Rousseau agreed with enthusiasm. They traveled together to Fribourg, then to Bern, where Rousseau held his only public speech in the local senate. Rousseau liked the wanderings so much that "he could not imagine anything more beautiful than to go on traveling all his life." Their adventure ended in Soleure (Solothurn), the diplomatic center of the Swiss Confederation.

The French envoy Marquis de Bonac, who was familiar with circumstances in Jerusalem from his diplomatic activities there, had no difficulty in finding out about the true nature of the fraudulent Greek. Rousseau escaped punishment only because he succeeded in persuading the envoy that he was only the impostor's instrument.

He was even allowed to stay at the French embassy in Soleure and obtained from them a letter of recommendation for work in Paris. According to other sources he returned to Neuchâtel and tried unsuccessfully to reopen his musical school. The lost pupils refused to return to school.

Rousseau was without means of support, foundering in debt, and wrote his father Isaac a letter asking for financial help. He received a message from Annecy that he had fallen into disgrace with Mme de Warens as well. It appears that his friends from the French embassy helped him out of his debts.

He was recommended to a Swiss colonel in Paris, where he should work as an educator. His journey to Paris was a pleasant experience. The French embassy gave him one hundred francs and he traveled alone, accompanied only by his sweet dreams.

This time, for a change, he imagined he was a soldier. His near-sightedness would not matter—he would make up for it by his courage and dauntlessness. Graf von Schomberg, the marshal of France, was also near-sighted, so why could there not also be the near-sighted Marshal Rousseau? Reality set in when he discovered that both Paris and the colonel's family disappointed him—they were not ready to pay for his work as educator.

Because he could not find out any news about what his protector, Mme de Warens, was doing, he decided to locate her on his own. He went to Lyon, and visited Mlle du Châtelet, a friend of Maman. He was received with kindness, but his hostess did not know the whereabouts of Mme de Warens. Rousseau mentions his conversation with Mlle du Châtelet with appreciation, describing her as "neither beautiful nor young, but capable to converse with charm and intelligence. She lent him several novels by Le Sage, especially *Gil Blas*, which Rousseau did not find appealing.

At this age he preferred sentimental novels. According to him, conversation with an intelligent woman of culture is a much better education for a young man than all the pedantic philosophies. This idea of his does not surprise us when we realize Rousseau's lifelong dislike of systematic work of any kind, and his masochistic weakness for older women. Being without any means of support, he slept in the open, and it was probably at that time when he met a laborer who invited him to masturbation, which Rousseau already practiced. This episode scared him so much that he was "cured of this sin for some time." He had a similar experience with a monk who offered him shelter in one-half of his bed. After that time he regarded Lyon as the most rotten city in Europe.

One morning Rousseau was in a good mood. He set about singing and Rolichon, a monk who heard him, employed him as a note copyist. He was assigned a room and provided good food, which was important, as Rousseau was gaunt and starved. Rousseau made note copying his livelihood from time to time in his later life. It must be said, however, that his first steps in this profession were infamous. He made a lot of mistakes, lacked carefulness and felt bored by the work for which attention to detail was essential.

In this connection he made a psychologically interesting remark: he admits that he felt at his best at those times when he did badly in real life, and when he suffered. As soon as he was getting on better, the feeling of happiness was lost. "It is a very odd thing that my imagination never attains pleasanter heights than when my condition is most unpleasant and that, on the contrary, it is less cheerful when all is cheerful around me . . . I have said a hundred times that if I were put in the Bastille, I should paint a picture of freedom" (see Part 2). The life of a tramp, with its hardships and uncertain future, must have been to his liking. This admission shows that the masochistic features have already influenced a non-sexual sphere of his life. His contemporaries were well aware of Rousseau's "delight in suffering."

He received a letter from Mme de Warens at this time. She wrote him that she had moved from Annecy to Chambéry, and invited Rousseau to come to her. Knowing him well, she sent him also the money for the journey, but Rousseau traveled on foot, since he had the time. He knew he would be safe in her house and that he would be taken care of, but he also knew that the tormenting uncertainty of his vagabondage will disappear.

Chambéry, Les Charmettes, Lyon

The reasons that led Mme de Warens to move from Annecy and settle in Chambéry were purely rational. Annecy was too provincial for her taste; everything revolved around the Church. Chambéry had ceased to be the capital of Savoy for some time, but it still remained the administrative center for the province of Savoy. It was possible to meet more influential people there who were more interested in culture, business and industry, an environment which Mme de Warens found more congenial. She lived in a rented house belonging to a governmental official, Count de Saint-Laurent. The house was so ugly that the count had difficulty renting it. Mme de Warens knew this and in spite of that she reached an agreement on the lease with the count and made sure that her royal pension, which was sent to her from Turin, would be forthcoming, because Count de Saint-Laurent expected the payments to be sent regularly.

Rousseau, who was then nineteen, arrived in Chambéry in the fall of 1731, walking on foot from Lyon, and took immediate dislike to the house as well as to the room he was to live in. Everything was dark and decrepit. The reunion with Mme de Warens, after such a long separation, passed without the usual embraces and tears. Mme de Warens was not alone. There was a governmental official in the room, the general director Don Antoine Petitti. Mme de Warens allegedly held Rousseau's hand and introduced him with the words, "Here he is, sir, the poor young man. If you will only protect him for as long as he deserves it, I shall have no further anxiety about him for the rest of my life." She then turned to Rousseau. "My child, you are in the king's service. Be thankful to M. Intendant, who is offering you a living."

Rousseau took up the position of an official in the administrative office of King Victor Emanuel, which employed three hundred clerks. He was to map and file the distribution of property in Savoy to prepare for the collection of taxes, even from nobility. Rousseau found the job interesting at first, as it was something he had never done before. He was not familiar with mathematics and was forced to study elemental arithmetic from books as a self-taught person. He spent the time drawing plants and landscapes, which he found a great help later in his life, when he was preoccupied with botany as a hobby. After the many years of crazy adventures, for some time Rousseau was proud to earn his living in an honest way. He lived with Maman and even made friends with Anet, whose character he described with appreciation.

Because of its enforced regularity, even this work became unendurable for Rousseau. As soon as this profession became routine work, he began to feel contempt for the clerical simpletons and left the position of safety. He wrote in *Confessions* that he worked in the office for two years, but, according to the dossier of the office, his employment was terminated after eight months, on June 7, 1732. He tried to convince Maman that he would support himself as music teacher. She tried to convince him about the foolishness of giving up a reliable position and becoming a music teacher, particularly when he had no musical education, but it was all in vain. Rousseau forced a consent out of her by unceasing entreaties combined with caresses.

He was in Besançon once or twice, where he took music lessons by abbé Blanchard. This episode was to end soon, because his teacher was unexpectedly forced to leave Besançon and Rousseau had to return to Chambéry. Mme de Warens supported him in organizing musical evenings visited by the notabilities of the town. It is obvious that Rousseau loved teaching music. He cherished the memory of sweet hours at the harpsichord when he taught the local aristocratic girls and young women who were attending his classes. He mentioned here his own chronic unpunctuality and inaccuracy and justified it as usual by "noble" motives: all limitations and restrictions are unbearable for him.

Claude Anet recommended to Mme de Warens that she should buy a garden in the suburbs of Chambéry, where they could grow medicinal plants. There was a furnished house in the garden, which offered the possibility of staying overnight, which Rousseau loved. He was ill at this time and Maman treated him and took care of him, which led to the development of stronger emotional links between them. Rousseau does not describe the character of his illness, the only thing we hear from him is that it was an infection. During the course of his illness he read Rameau's book on harmony.

At this age he was also attractive to the mothers of his pupils and some of them tried to seduce him, though they were unsuccessful. He told his experiences to Mme de Warens, who as a woman of the world did not make light of them and decided to take the initiative and instruct Rousseau in sexual intercourse. It was 1733 and Rousseau was twenty-one.

Maman proposed this step of his education openly to him and gave him eight days for reflection. Rousseau assured her hypocritically that this time for reflection was not necessary, but was in fact grateful for the delay of such a delicate lesson (see Part 2). He wrote that he was torn by contradictory feelings during the next few days. Mme de Warens did not experience any such mental complications. She had already had many love affairs and neither "virtue" or "abstinence" had any value for her, as opposed to Rousseau, the romantic and unrealistic dreamer. For her, sexual relationships were purely matters of reason. She knew that a man could be bound strongly to a woman only when he can possess her. Rousseau said that she had "a sensitive soul, and cold temperament." She was not a "passion-ridden" woman and regarded the fact that she would instruct Rousseau in sexual intercourse simply as a part of education, in the same way as she would, for example, see the necessity to send him to receive instruction in dancing and fencing.

Rousseau admitted that she used the wrong philosophy for altruistic purposes. She was not the kind of woman who would let her lovers support her. She preferred younger and rather simple lovers, perhaps acting in accordance with the motto that people with simple taste experience more pleasure in life. Now she had two lovers. It remains unclear whether Claude Anet, who came with her from Savoy and converted to Catholicism as well, was aware that Rousseau's relationship to Maman had changed. It is very likely that he was.

He was reticent and taciturn, but practical-minded and Mme de Warens accorded him certain authority. He was able to hold the purse strings of Mme de Warens at least in a state where her debts did not increase too much. Rousseau allegedly got along well with him, if we want to believe what he says in *Confessions*. Anet, who succeeded in protecting him from many foolish acts, should have been his tutor, but it is possible that he was jealous of Rousseau. He had attempted suicide once, by drinking laudanum, but had been rescued when Maman and Rousseau succeeded in making him vomit the ingested fluid. In her excitement over Anet's resuscitation, Mme de Warens mentioned for the first time that Claude Anet was her lover, a relationship which her *petit* had not suspected in the least. Rousseau assures us that this attempted suicide had nothing to do with jealousy, *that all three of them loved each other as one family*, but this stilted and exaggerated assurance make the suspicion of Anet's jealousy even stronger.

Anet must have known of the seduction in the garden house, but he did not let anything show. Mme de Warens told Rousseau about her strong affection for Anet, but added that she needed both Anet as well as Rousseau in order to be happy. "In this way a relationship between the three of us came into being, which might have occurred on this earth for the first time," declares Rousseau. It is doubtful that Anet shared his satisfaction with the triangle.

Anet was supposed to become a paid teacher in the royal garden Mme de Warens wanted to establish, but died unexpectedly and under mysterious circumstances. According to Rousseau's version, Anet had gone to the Alps to collect rare medicinal plants. While there, he developed a fever, followed by pleurisy, and died on the fifth day of his illness despite all efforts to save his life. But the parish registers state that Anet died on March 13, 1734, at a time when there are no plants growing in the mountainous areas of the Alps.

Rousseau did not show himself in the best light after Anet's death. He asked Mme de Warens if he could have the clothes left by the deceased, by which the good Maman was moved to tears. He inherited from Anet the duties of caretaker of her household as well. Unlike the correct and methodical Anet, Rousseau turned out to be entirely incapable of managing the finances, which were soon moving in a bad direction. Maman had never taken Rousseau seriously and so he began concealing small amounts of money to make sure that at least something would be left. To put it more simply he was stealing and, as usual, rationalized his behavior as a result of higher motives: he was acting in a way deserving contempt, but was driven by "noble motives." He justified his miserliness, which became one of his character traits, by this experience.

Mme de Warens knew of his incompetence in financial matters and tried to at least make him into a man who would be able to live in society. She found fencing and dancing courses for him, both of which lead to nothing. Rousseau said that he could not dance because he had learned to walk "on heels" and suffered from corns, and he could not fence because he had a "weak arm" and would be unable to kill anyway.

In *Confessions* he speaks of going to Besançon in 1735. By his account he convinced Maman he had to go to Besançon in order to study music at abbé Blanchard's—in reality, this may have been his way of trying to turn away the menacing financial disaster. Maman agreed and contributed eight hundred francs to his equipment, by which she only precipitated her own financial ruin. When trying to cross the French border, Rousseau's luggage was confiscated, the music lessons in Besançon came to nothing, and Rousseau had to return.

There is an air of mystery about the whole thing, remarks Cranston. Rousseau's own letters tell us that he went to Besançon in 1732, but by 1735 the abbé Blanchard was far from Besançon, and Rousseau knew it. The real purpose of the trip is dark. It may have had something to do with one of Mme de Warens's abortive secret projects. He had by this time fully committed himself to her service: "weighing everything up, and seeing that bad luck dogged all my own enterprises, I decided to attach myself entirely to Maman, to share her fortune, and not to trouble myself fruitlessly about a future I could not control."

Maman had gradually renewed his clothing and both of them (as Rousseau assures us) had soon forgotten about this incident. It became clear that Rousseau could assert himself in company only by his music and that was why there were many musical evenings in Mme de Warens's house for people from the upper classes. Rousseau felt happy during these *soirées*. It was here that he met the rich Gaffecourt, who later became his long-term sponsor. Gaffecourt came from Geneva as well.

Mme de Warens's hospitality did not improve her finances, which explains the fact that she became increasingly involved in business activities, although she had already lost money several times. In his twenty-third year, Rousseau was still dreaming about making a career as a musician and tried to acquire at least the basics of music theory. The rather busy social life in Mme de Warens's house forced him to undertake journeys from time to time (to

Nyon, Geneva, and Lyon), which certainly mollified his worries, but at the same time these journeys further increased his cost of living.

An interesting episode at this time started with the fact that he had inherited from his Uncle Bernard, a military engineer who died in the United States of America, plans of Genevan fortifications, actually their critical assessment by Micheli du Crest, and these fell into the hands of the king of Sardinia. Rousseau wrote in a poem dedicated to Mme de Warens, *"Genève jadi sage ô ma chère Patrie,"* but the fact remains that he betrayed his dear native town. It also cannot be ruled out that the instigation of this espionage came from Mme de Warens, who delighted in secret diplomacy.

Writing about this period Rousseau also mentions his frequent nervous illnesses, melancholy, sadness and feelings of nervous exhaustion. He was sighing and crying for no reason. Though he might have in fact suffered these mental states, it is more likely that it was all autosuggestion, or dissimulation. In connection with this, his *Confessions* contain the sentence: "My passions have aroused me to life and they have also meant my ruin." What he needed was a real mistress and could not find such in Mme de Warens. The image of Maman killed all erotic feelings. Sometimes he would leave his bed and go to her room to talk over with her the anxieties that disturbed him. Only after she had succeeded in soothing his fears would he go back to his own room and sleep contentedly. Sickness had become a road to happiness with Maman: "Our mutual attachment . . . became somehow more intimate and more moving in its great simplicity. I became entirely her creature, more of her child than if she had been my real mother. We began, without thinking about it, to become inseparable, to share our whole existence."

A Genevan called Bagueret taught him the game of chess and Rousseau "threw himself into the deepest chess frenzy." He shut himself off in his room and studied chess theory, but never excelled in the game.

He succeeded in convincing himself several times that he was to die soon—Mme de Warens responded always with nursing and "saved" his life—strengthening by her behavior the emotional links between them. He described his illness also in several letters sent to his father; it is clear from them that he believed he was developing tuberculosis. We know from the draft of the letter that he recovered from his illness in June 1735 "as a result of the good care of Mme de Warens," and that he had also been on a journey.

In his replies his father asked him to try to find a proper job, but in the fall of 1735 Rousseau sent him a long letter full of excuses: he has not the means that would enable him to study theology or law; business and trade had never appealed to him and so he can only be a musician, private educator or secretary to some important personality.

The only thing he aimed at was to improve his education in a rather unsystematic way; he ordered and bought books, despite the difficult situation of Mme de Warens's finances and his declared efforts to behave in a thrifty way. These books were sold to him by the Genevan bookseller and publisher Jacques Barrillot, who had also published the works of Montesquieu and Burlamaqui.

As Rousseau was discontented with life in the dark house in Chambéry, he tried to persuade Maman to rent a holiday house not far from the town, in the valley of Les Charmettes, which was situated on the estates of M. de Conzié. They probably lived in several houses before finally renting the most beautiful one (Maison Noeray, which now serves as a Rousseau museum).

Rousseau described their stay in the valley and their common life there in *Confessions* with exaggerated enthusiasm (Book Six). It is not certain whether this "idyll" of country life really existed. There is no reason to doubt that Rousseau spent the summer and autumn of 1736 with Mme de Warens at Les Charmettes—he may well have stayed with her there as early as the summer of 1735—but their happy life *à deux* ended in 1737. Even here he was to suffer attacks of "mental illness," palpitations, headaches, sleeplessness and shortness of breath caused by the slightest exertion.

All this corroborated his worst fears that he would not live much longer. He was constantly contemplating his approaching death and, surprisingly, felt no sadness by these grim thoughts but rather a certain sweet tiredness, which had its own charms. In spite of this he had a feeling in his bones that he would *"have to live to endure still more suffering."* Until that time he had always slept long hours and even enjoyed sleep, but he says that he suffered from "total sleeplessness" from that time onwards (an untenable claim). Once a doctor even had to be called in. He could not tolerate the milk diets prescribed to him and the water treatments had only upset his stomach. The suspicion arises again that his illnesses of that time were pretended, or exaggerated, to attract Maman's attention. His good appetite, which had never failed him, could not be spoiled by any illness.

It became evident that he was entirely unsuitable to work as an agricultural laborer—he shrank from manual work for his whole life. He was capable, on the other hand, of taking long hikes in the mountains where he had no shortness of breath at all. This provides further evidence supporting the suspicion that many of his illness were simulated.

At that time he showed a greater interest in religion, especially in Jansenist authors. The description of his usual day shows us a man who could be best described as an irresponsible idler, whose only activities included reading books after breakfast for a while, going for walks and observing pigeons, whom he tried to tame. It is barely conceivable that such a life would be to Mme de Warens's taste. She was a woman of the world and society, and was fond of young and strong lovers.

Their neighbor in the valley, M. de Conzié (François-Joseph de Conzié, 1707–89, Comte de Charmettes, Baron de Rumilly), who had previously attended Rousseau's school of music as a pupil, was a literary, educated man. He described Mme de Warens as a well-read woman of culture and an intelligent conversation partner. According to de Conzié she tried to educate Rousseau, who appeared to be docile and even *submissive in the relationship toward his Maman.* In consideration of Rousseau's penchant for reading, Mme de Warens suggested he should study medicine, which he refused with disgust.

It was then that Rousseau first attempted to write. He wrote prose and poems and his first work printed was a poem, *"Un Papillon Badin,"* published in *Mercure de France.* Rousseau had allegedly decided to become a writer. He admitted—in a rare moment of realism—that his illnesses were partly caused by his own fantasies and gloomy thoughts, which are often the illness of happy people: he cried for no reason, was scared by a falling leaf or a flying bird, and his feelings were tossed about in an environment of uniform happiness. He suffered attacks of "boredom from happiness." *In his view man was not created to feel happy on earth. The soul or body must necessarily suffer.* Rousseau luxuriated in the feeling of suffering and hardship and looks for them.

Once he was almost blinded by an explosion during his lay experiments and the fear that he would die led him to write his own last will and testament. The reader might ask what it was he wanted distributed after his death, when he had nothing? He was to come of age on July 28, 1737 and, according to Genevan law, he had the right to receive his part of the inheritance from his late mother, which he eventually did get. Unlike Bern, the Genevan Republic did not confiscate the property of apostates who converted to Catholicism; these had only lost the right to have permanent residence in Geneva. He was not entitled to his brother's portion because there was no document confirming his death—this portion was used by his father till his death.

Rousseau's share of 6,000 florins was only a small part of the whole inheritance, but it was huge when measured by his situation at that time. He spent part of it for the books he bought in Geneva, and laid the rest "to the feet" of Maman, where it did not remain for long, as we will see. When he was in Geneva, he was offered the position of secretary to Count de Lautrec, who was one of the visitors to Mme de Warens's salon in Chambéry, but Rousseau turned this rare opportunity down.

In the idyllic environment of a mountain valley in Les Charmettes, where he had everything, did not have to work and was well-provided for, there was actually only one thing missing: his health. He felt ill there all the time. He was reading numerous medical books and felt himself to be a doctor to the extent that he even diagnosed the cause of his own medical problem: he suffered from a "heart polyp." Mme de Warens told him of a well-known professor in Montpellier, Dr. Fizes, who had successfully cured a case similar to his.

This was enough for Rousseau to decide to travel to Montpellier. Part of the inheritance covered his traveling expenses and treatment. Maman supported his decision—for her own good reason—as presently a new man turned up in the house, Jean-Samuel-Rodolphe Wintzenried, who sometimes (by right) called himself M. de Courtilles. He was six years older than Rousseau and was quite different by nature: virile, dominant and active. He was a hairdresser by occupation and came, as did Mme de Warens, from the Swiss canton Vaud. He carried out all her wishes and as a lover certainly surpassed the weak and bashful Rousseau He looked down on women and had an affair with both Mme de Warens and her servant soon after he arrived in the house.

It seems that Mme de Warens, in spite of all her affection for Rousseau, had had enough of his incessant illnesses, his spoiled childishness, egoism, excessive sentimentality, laziness, and his incapacity for any practical occupation, not to mention his insufficiency as a lover. She needed a man with a strong personality that she could lean on. But Wintzenried was not Anet and her choice was a bad one.

Rousseau wrote his first letter from Grenoble, where he was well-received he says, and where he was happy. His only complaints were again heart palpitations. These occurred after a theatre visit, where Voltaire's *Alzire* was played. On his journey Rousseau got into the society of people from better circles. He did not want to admit he was a convert to Catholicism and pretended to be an Englishman, a Jacobite, even though he did not speak a single word of English. He gave himself the name "Dudding." His youth aroused the interest of Mme de Larnage, who was described by Rousseau as a very attractive woman, although not young or beautiful. She was actually forty-four and the mother of ten children.

This experienced woman had no difficulty seducing the young Rousseau, who was very proud of it and regarded the seduction as his success (see the medical analysis in Part 2). He was now a man and this feeling increased his self-confidence. These feelings of happiness after sexual intercourse contrast with feelings he had after intercourse with Mme de Warens—melancholy and a feeling of guilt and the degradation of his partner (see Part 2). The unequal lovers spent three days in Montélimar and parted on the bridge of Pont Saint-Esprit, where they were crossing the Rhône, each of them continuing their respective journeys. They promised to see each other again; Rousseau was to visit Mme de Larnage at her residence in Bourg-Saint Andéol on his way back from Montpellier and spend the winter with her, continuing his "treatment" in her house.

The affair with Mme de Larnage had made him forget Maman and, strangely enough, even cured all symptoms of his "heart polyp." When parting with Mme de Larnage, Rousseau was physically exhausted and therefore not too unhappy about the separation. His illness had been totally forgotten on the way to Montpellier and he recalled it only after arriving in the university town. He visited Dr. Fizes, but found the visit disappointing. Dr. Fizes declared that Rousseau was a hypochondriac (which was probably correct). Rousseau, however, passed his own judgment on this pronouncement: because the doctors did not know anything about his illness, they decided he was not ill.

There are two versions of his stay in Montpellier. The description in *Confessions* is filled with enthusiasm (time makes us forget unpleasant things) about the good time he had there in the presence of Irish students. He lived with an Irish doctor named Fitzmorris, from whom he picked up some English words. The student life of that time was pleasant; they played games, took walks and lunched in taverns. This was to Rousseau's liking because, as he wrote, he was able to enjoy a life which did not make any demands on him.

In his letters (written in November 1737) to Jean-Antoine Charbonel from

Chambéry, who had once loaned him some money, Rousseau described Montpellier as an overcrowded town with tortuous narrow streets and ostentatious palaces as well as miserable shanties, where one half of the inhabitants are rich and the other half are extremely poor. The women of Montpellier are depicted as morally corrupt, foreigners are robbed in all possible ways and dealt with worse than Jews in Spain, or Protestants in Italy. He asked his benefactor for a new loan, because he is once again on the rocks. He wrote reproachful letters to Mme de Warens because she had not answered his previous letters and he complained that he had no means because she had made an error in a letter that should have given him a credit of two hundred livres. Their relationship had cooled down and by the end of 1737 it had become clear to Rousseau that his privileged standing with Mme de Warens was lost.

According to the account in *Confessions*, he left Montpellier with the intention of visiting Mme de Larnage and staying with her. While on his way he devised all sorts of conjectures, which spoke against the visit: "How would the family of his sweetheart accept him? . . . What if he falls in love with Mme de Larnage's daughter?" and similar thoughts which prove that unconsciously he was not enthusiastic about the visit as it promised to be an uncertain enterprise with stressful sex—and uncertainty and stress were emotions he was always trying to avoid.

Ultimately, he decided to solve the dilemma in a much safer way: he decided not to visit Mme de Larnage and to go directly to Les Charmettes instead, returning to Maman. Mme de Warens did receive him kindly, but without the usual enthusiasm. His place was occupied. There was a new favorite and Rousseau saw nothing good in him. She suggested that all three live together, but Rousseau refused the life à trois and in addition refused to have sexual relations with Mme de Warens, which must certainly have insulted her.

Women will never excuse such a rejection, as Rousseau correctly judges in *Confessions*, because they always see in it a sign of indifference to their personality: "The most unpardonable crime a man . . . can commit is that of not possessing her when he has the chance of doing so. This rule admits no exception . . ." The idyll of Les Charmettes (if there was any) ended. When Mme de Warens and Wintzenried were at Chambéry, Rousseau lived alone in Les Charmettes as a hermit and sought solace in religion. M. de Conzié bears witness to Rousseau's *desire for solitude, combined with contempt of other people*, in whom he saw their weaknesses and imperfections (it is true that Conzié wrote these lines later—at a time when Rousseau was already notoriously known to be a hermit). All of this contributed to Rousseau's contempt and mistrust of human nature.

Such was his frame of mind when he wrote his second poem, "*Le Verger de Madame la Baronne de Warens,*" in 1738. It was published in 1739 with a limited number of copies being printed. The poem contains ostentatious praise of Mme de Warens for her help—she makes it possible for the poet to live a life in peace and solitude, a life disturbed only by the poet's bad health, which places him on the brink of the grave. The poet would work for the good of human society, if only he were healthy—but in his condition he can only work to his own satisfaction.

The question intrudes itself into the reader's mind of what it is that the poet could do for the good of human society, when he lacks systematic education, when he does not know very much about this society and has never been able to force himself to work. His exaggerated hypochondriac "illnesses" are seemingly just a pretext used to justify his own laziness.

The fact was that the house in Les Charmettes had become a source of anxiety and fear for him. He had no one who would take care of him and he felt isolated. In all his later periods of hermitage there was always someone around, usually a woman who looked after him and some neighbors (again mostly women), whom he could be with; therefore, one cannot take his "hermitage" literally. But in Les Charmettes he really was alone and lonely.

In 1738 his grandfather died, the former liberal and lover of arts, David Rousseau. It is characteristic of the emotional coldness of this family, so proud of the name Rousseau, that he died in a poorhouse because no one in the family would care for him.

It was at the beginning of 1739 when Mme de Warens probably told him that she could not provide financial sustenance for him anymore. This induced Rousseau to try again to get the portion of inheritance belonging to his lost brother François, who was said to have died in Breisach. He also applied for a pension from the king of Sardinia, because "he, as convert to Catholicism, had studied hard but was wrecked by illness, and is now a dying man." Mme de Warens, Wintzenried and Rousseau lived in Les Charmettes in the summer of 1739 till the end of fall, when Rousseau made the decision at the age of twenty-seven to leave Les Charmettes for good and to work for his living. Mme de

Warens agreed with his decision and probably embraced it with relief. She found him the job of an educator; he was to tutor the youngest son of the chief of gendarmerie (Prèvôt-Général) in Lyon, Seigneur de Mably.

Rousseau left Les Charmettes in spring of 1740, on April 20, and took up the tutor post on May 1 with a salary of 350 livres and fifty livres premium. The Mably family was an intellectual family of high standing. Already two generations of lawyers had sprung from this family. Jean Bonnot, born in 1696, known as Seigneur de Mably was his employer. He was the oldest son of Gabriel Bonnot, born in 1675, who was one of the secretaries of the king of France. His younger sons were Gabriel (born in 1709), known as the abbé de Mably, who wrote several theoretical works on socialism, and Étienne (born in 1714), known as the abbé de Condillac, a well-known philosopher and prominent expert on John Locke. The mathematician and scientist d'Alembert, though formally a foundling, was the cousin of these brothers.

Without knowing it, Rousseau was coming from provincial Savoy Catholicism into a family of the French Enlightenment, governed by a strong belief in Reason. Rousseau's employer had twelve children and Rousseau was entrusted with the education of two sons: six-year-old François-Paul Marie, known later as M. de Sainte-Marie, and five-year-old Jean-Antoine, known as M. de Condillac. The wife of his employer (with whom Rousseau immediately fell in love) was to work on the improvement of Rousseau's behavior. Rousseau assumed that he had all the necessary knowledge and talent to be an educator. He was to be cured of this mistaken idea soon.

Life in Lyon filled Rousseau with enthusiasm. He had been introduced into a highly cultivated, intellectual society. He could attend the meetings of the Lyon Academy of Sciences, where various scientific discourses were lectured and discussed and concerts were performed at the Academy of Arts, and where humanistic subjects were taught as well. He made the acquaintance of many educated people. Among these was Charles Bordes, "the Voltaire of Lyon," who returned from Paris and astounded Rousseau, a provincial Swiss to whom the courteous French society was foreign, by the sophistic and doubting conversation of a city-dweller.

Rousseau dedicated to him the poem "Épître à Monsieur Bordes," in which several interesting verses can be found that praise the manufacturing industry and economic prosperity of Lyon—things which he will later vehemently deny in his *Discours sur les arts et les sciences*. It is not uninteresting that this was the same Charles Bordes who was to come out publicly with a critical assessment of his friend's discourse when it was later published.

Another important acquaintance for Rousseau was the composer Jacques David, a most prominent municipal musician. He learned many useful things from him about musical technique. Earlier, in Chambéry, Rousseau had been trying to write a tragic opera, *Iphis et Anaxarcte*, but burned it. In Lyon he wrote an opera with the aid of Jacques David *"La Découverte du noveau monde"*—a strongly Francophile work glorifying Europe's influence on America, wherein Rousseau evoked the idea of the "noble savage" for the first time, though a similar character had appeared in literature before Rousseau. Rousseau wrote another letter in verses similar to that dedicated to Jacques David, this time it concerned a Lyon physician, the surgeon and gallstone specialist, Gabriel Parisot. Even here evidence can be found that young Rousseau was by no means a prophet of egalitarianism, in contradiction to the views of many authors. According to his verses, too much equality is not beneficial to society:

> *"Il ne serait pas bon dans la société*
>
> *Qui'il fût entre les rangs moins d'inégalité."*

Rousseau also made friends with Camille Perrichon, another prominent member of Lyon society, despite the fact that he was a foreigner in Lyon and had a rather minor position as a tutor. Perrichon was a senior civil servant, a mayor and member of the Academy of Sciences. He collected books and even knew Mme de Warens, to whom he had once loaned money to finance her numerous business projects. The money was lost.

All these encounters make it obvious that the spirit of the French Enlightenment, a movement based on the conviction of Francis Bacon that humanity can be saved by science, which can at least help to solve some of its problems, left its mark on Rousseau.

The only problem Rousseau had in Lyon was his own activity as educator. He admits quite openly that he was too "short" for both of his wards. There was no educational success. To be a successful tutor, he would have to be more patient and would need more self-control (as he admits); without these two attributes, he was simply lost. The only educational measures he knew were beseeching requests, logical arguments and displays of irritation. The children regarded it as their greatest triumph to drive him to a flash of anger, so that they would appear to be the philosophers whereas he would be the child.

All of his actions were precisely the opposite of what he should have done. As a semi-deprived child, brought up in semi-isolation, Rousseau was unable to understand the emotions of a child. He did not understand himself and consequently he could not understand the emotions of other people, particularly those of children. He was also incapable of forming lasting emotional bonds, which are vital not only to educational activity, but also to social life in general. In Lyon he was soon regarded as a misogynist who shunned the company of other people.

It is therefore remarkable that, despite his practical failure as educator—inevitable on the strength of his personal development—he should begin to regard himself to be an expert on the theory of education and that we should regard him as such expert even today! He wrote another treatise for M. de Mably, "Project for the education of M. de Sainte-Marie," which some authors regard as the beginning and initial step to Émile. Here also his requirement (a doubtful one from a contemporary point of view), that a child's education be entrusted to an educator, is presented for the first time.

His educational "Project" contains more rationalistic elements than Émile. He recommends that in the education of children rational argumentation be used and that a child should be taught to understand Latin, but does not have to be able to write in Latin. He further recommends that instead of extensive historical data on Greece and Rome, the child should be taught the history of France, and instead of complicated theological concepts, moral principles and humanities should be taught. He stresses the necessity of a knowledge of the natural sciences and particularly mathematics, ethics and natural laws, and treats Grotius and Pufendorf as authorities on these subjects. Logic, rhetoric and scholastic philosophy are not treated as important. Another important subject is physical education—equitation (horseback riding) and fencing—of which, as we know, Rousseau had no command.

This project (submitted in 1740) could not have filled the rationalistic M. de Mably with enthusiasm. In France a translation of Locke's De l'Éducation des enfants had been available since 1695, and Locke's pupil Charles Rolin had published the book Traité des études. It is interesting that these works have fallen into oblivion, whereas Rousseau's Émile has survived as an educational work in spite of its confused character.

Rousseau dedicated the essay "Mémoire" to his employer M. de Mably.

This is a valuable source of his psychology at that time, because he reveals his soul and character in it. He says *that he has a mournful and misanthropist character,* that people considered him an uncultivated pedant, who is unable to conform to polite society and who therefore cannot educate his pupils in this spirit. He admits that there are some shortcomings: *mistrust,* silly shyness, and dry, dull conversation. These are all shortcomings which are very difficult to overcome. He has a melancholic nature which he cannot change, *he has spent most of his life in isolation, was often ill and the proximity of death has deepened his inner sadness.* He suffers further from an insuperable bashfulness and has a deep aversion to everything "that is called brilliant." He then expresses a remarkable and correct observation: *a man endowed with such character finds it very difficult to achieve any real success in his personal life as well as in society.*

Rousseau sees himself correctly: he had never been able to maintain enduring interpersonal relationships. His unusually frequent, short-term friendships have invariably ended in incomprehensible separation, or rift. After his departure from Lyon for example, Rousseau lost nearly all his friends, which he explains is due to his own inability to write letters on a regular basis. This is, of course, a rationalization, for he wrote letters practically every day. His success as a writer cannot be described in terms of a successful career. He had become the idol of his time because he wrote *Héloïse,* a book that corresponded to the ladies' taste in every respect.

Because he did not know any other society and did not want to be in a bad one, he preferred to be alone. However, it would not be Rousseau as we know him, who never doubted his true origins, if he did not add that there was nothing in his character that would prevent him from living in a society of cultivated people, by which he means the nobility. On the one hand there is a personal insecurity, on the other an impassioned certainty of his character and abilities.

It is not certain whether this memorandum got into M. de Mably's hands. If he did read it, he must have come to the conclusion that Rousseau could never be a good tutor. There was also the fact that Rousseau committed certain misdemeanors. He was entrusted with the keys to the wine cellar and, being unable to withstand the temptation, stole a few bottles of wine and drank them in his bedroom. Food, drinking and reading compensated him for the company of other people: "it has always been a fancy of mine to read as I eat when I am on my own: it makes up for the lack of society. I devour a page and a mouthful alternatively, and it is as if my book were dining with me." M. de Mably was a reasonable man and did not blow up the whole thing. But Rousseau did not get the keys again. Let us remember that Rousseau repeatedly stole minor things throughout his life. This bears witness to a low level of self-control and self-discipline.

Rousseau wrote in *Confessions* that the decision to leave was made by him, because he saw that he could not be a successful tutor for the children. It cannot be ruled out, however, that his year's contract was over and he was not asked to return. Rousseau was once again overcome by the desire for Maman and her tenderness. He succeeded in convincing himself that if he would love her more and be more patient their old intimacy could return again. The fact was that Mme de Warens was facing dire financial difficulties and had no other choice but to sell her silver. So she sent a silver pot to Rousseau in Lyon and asked him to try to sell it for five louis. Rousseau succeeded in selling the silver to Mme de Mably for four-and-a-half louis, which he sent to Maman together with a small amount as a gift, "which is made possible by my present poverty."

Rousseau's career as a tutor in Lyon was definitely over in May 1741 and he hurried back to Les Charmettes. The reception by Mme de Warens was friendly again, but their "old happiness" was dead "for good." Wintzenried had a dominant position in the house and Rousseau tended more and more to seclusion, where he read and wrote. Having no income, he was forced to sell his books.

He made several trips to Lyon, where a young girl, Susanne Serre attracted him. Susanne's ancestors came from Spain, and, according to many researchers, she was Rousseau's only true love and the model for Julie in *La Nouvelle Héloïse*. The two in love were too poor to think of a normal life and Rousseau had, according to his own words, other plans and ambitions and would not think of a wedding. When Susanne told him she would marry a young merchant who wanted to marry her, Rousseau agreed and left Lyon. He did not want to disturb their innocent lives.

December 1741 was particularly cold and Rousseau fell ill and returned immediately to Mme de Warens, as usual, who was now living in Les Charmettes for the whole year. He recovered with her help in spring of 1742 and, as he wrote later in a letter to M. de Conzié, Mme de Warens "brought him back from the gate of death." He wrote a new poem about her, dedicated to

"Fannie," which is an abbreviation of Françoise, her Christen name. He helped Mme de Warens by writing letters in connection with the arguments she had with her neighbors in the valley caused by some of her new activities, this time in agriculture. But again, she had no financial success in it, similar to her previous trade and business activities.

Rousseau was retiring to his study more and more often. He developed a new approach to writing notes, namely with the help of numbers, and expected that his invention would bring him acknowledgement in Paris. In summer 1742 Rousseau became fully aware of the fact that he could not expect any more hospitality and decided to go to Paris and gain fame, happiness and money there.

Once again he had to sell some of his books, in order to pay for the journey. Of the several letters of recommendation he had, one proved helpful: abbé de Mably recommended him to the doyen of French authors, Fontenelle. According to Rousseau's plans, fame and happiness would be gained by his new method of writing notes and by his play *Narcisse*. In August 1742, at the age of thirty, he arrived in Paris with every intention of conquering it.

Part One—Personality and Time
Chapter Three

Departure for Paris—Search for Fame

Rousseau described his stay in Paris in the second part of *Confessions*, Book Seven, which contains the years 1741–1749. Here he points out that he wrote the memoirs according to his memories, so certain errors and inaccuracies are therefore unavoidable in the first and particularly in the second part. It is necessary to bring these words to the attention of the reader, because some regard Rousseau's *Confessions* as an exact and objective account of his life. He wrote the second part two years after the first and his memory certainly did not improve during this time. Any correct description of this period of his life, more than that contained in the first part, must of necessity depend on the accounts of his contemporaries and other correspondence of that time.

On his way to Paris, Rousseau made a stop in Lyon, where he tried to get some letters of recommendation. He was successful and these letters turned out to be helpful later. Even so, he soon forgot his friends in Lyon and did not write to them.

Paris of the mid-eighteenth century was made for smart and talented people with go-getter natures. The aristocracy, modeled in Versailles, was committed to a rigid protocol, but Paris was bourgeois, prosperous, progressive, skeptical, open to new ideas and personalities, pursuing worldly pleasures, and looking for more political power and changes. The city was bustling with people possessing new and opposing views, and these people were willingly received. One of them was Rousseau, who had come to Paris to achieve success and happiness. He also would not turn down the prospect of making money, if only to help Mme de Warens in her penury. Compared to other people coming to conquer Paris, Rousseau had the advantage of letters of recommendation, which acquainted him with all sorts of useful as well as less useful personalities. He had fifteen louisidors in cash, the rough draft of the comedy *Narcisse* in his possession, and his new system of musical notation to tout.

He found accommodation in Hôtel Saint-Quentin near the Sorbonne, "in an ugly room, ugly house and ugly street." One of the guests of this house particularly recommended Rousseau to Daniel Rougin, a Swiss who came from canton Vaud, who remained his faithful friend. His other acquaintances were Count d'Almézin (1707–1794), lover of the wife of Prince Charles de Rohan-Soubise, Anne-Thérèse de Savoie-Carigan; the Jesuit secular clergyman Louis-Bertrand Castel, who was a known philosopher, inventor, and mathematician; and Newton's adversary, the numismatist M. de Bose, secretary of the Academy of Archeology, who was interested in the new system of musical notation which Rousseau had brought to Paris.

Rousseau was also introduced to the renowned scientist Réamur, who made it possible for Rousseau to present his proposal in front of the Academy of Sciences. His presentation was received with kindness, but rejected with the same kindness after a preliminary assessment by a special commission. His proposal was said not to be quite new (a monk named Souhaitti had had a similar idea before), and besides it was more suitable for singers than for musicians. Rousseau received the criticism with indignation and was willing to accept only the critical comment of the most famous musician of the time—Rameau—as legitimate, who said that the traditional way of notation required a greater mental effort by singers. To defend his proposal he wrote and published a long letter in *Mercure* (printed in February 1743) and went so far as to write a book with the title *Dissertation sur la musique moderne*. As he expected, the book was not successful but its publication attracted some attention to his name.

He also had contacts with the writer Marivaux, a successful playwright, which proved to be useful. Marivaux read his play *Narcisse* and suggested that he make some changes in dialogues and reassured Rousseau, saying that he could become a writer and gain success in literature after his lack of success in the world of music. Marivaux's witty plays were performed in Téâtre des Italiens, which competed with the classic and recognized la Comédie-Française.

Another important man that Rousseau met in Paris was Fontenelle, who was then already eighty-five years of age (he lived longer than Hobbes and died as a centenarian). He appeared as a dinosaur from the distant age of Racine and Corneille (Cranston 1981). Fontenelle had never accepted the rationalistic view of the Enlightenment, that reason played a decisive role in human behavior. He believed that man was guided more by his imagination. As a true man of the seventeenth century, Fontenelle abhorred human passions so much that Mme de Tencin (who laid her own child, the future scientist d'Alembert, on the steps of the Church of Saint Jean de la Ronde) allegedly said to him that he had a brain in his chest instead of a heart. The human soul cannot, according to Fontenelle, rule people, but can be at best helpful in gaining equanimity by curbing human passions, and enabling people to act reasonably. David Hume later elaborated on this theory, which from today's perspective was very progressive; we would call this a theory of emotional management. It was from Fontenelle that Rousseau heard the idea that science will increase mankind's knowledge but not its happiness.

His financial means were diminishing and so Rousseau invented all sorts of dubious ways to earn money. He wanted to recite poems by heart, but was unable to memorize anything. He thought he could earn money by playing chess and spent his afternoons in the Café Maugis, or so he reported in *Confessions,* (actually, from Diderot we know that the chess players met in Café Régence), where he met the best chess players of that time: de Légal, Husson (wrongly named de Bussy by Rousseau), Mayot and Philidor. One of the visitors was also Voltaire. Diderot described the atmosphere of Parisian chess players in the play *Le neveu de Rameau (Rameau's Nephew)* and the *Encyclopédie* dedicated an extensive chapter to the history and rules of the game of chess. Even though Rousseau says that he invented his own game strategy, he could not assert himself against the leading players. In his encounters with Philidor he always had to be given the advantage of having one extra castle to keep the game even. This notion was dropped as Rousseau was unsuited to earn a living at it.

The Jesuit clergyman, Castel (according to Rousseau, "a madman, but otherwise a good fellow"), gave him a practical tip: "Since musicians and theorists will not sing in unison with you, change the string and try the women." Castel's advice was to try to win over the women of Paris to his side, because "nothing is achieved in Paris except by help of the ladies." He was right. Paris of that time was managed from great salons, governed by women who were playing the role of "communicators." Here careers, connections and relations were steered and decided. Those who did not succeed in penetrating this environment and gaining the support of the women governing the salons did not achieve anything. These women, who had their hands in high politics, influenced even the king of France. Rousseau himself became a "cult person" after he wrote a typical ladies' novel, *Héloïse.*

The advice of the clever clergyman was certainly to Rousseau's taste. For his whole life he had been trying to be under the protection of a "mistress," who would take care of him, help him and support him. Suffice it to remember his masochistic tendencies. The clergyman Castel added to his advice several letters of recommendation and Rousseau used them in spite of his bashfulness. He visited Mme de Besenval (Baroness Catherine Bielinska by birth), who had connections with the court, and her daughter Mme de Broglie.

His visit has been recorded and is worth mentioning here as it is characteristic of both the time and the manners of the young Rousseau. Both ladies had already read his book on new musical notation, were enthusiastic about it and were trying it on the clavichord, together with Rousseau. Around one o'clock Rousseau was invited to stay for dinner, but when he discovered he would have to dine with the servants, he excused himself, saying he had another appointment. Young Mme de Broglie saved the situation by whispering to her mother to allow Rousseau to stay in the drawing room, and soon Rousseau was having dinner in the company of the ladies and Gouillame Lamoignon de Malesherbes, president of the parlement of Paris (his son Chrétien-Guillaume Lamoignon de Malesherbes, 1721–1794, known as M. de Malesherbes, was later a popular liberal politician).

Rousseau was so overwhelmed by the president's eloquence that after the dinner, to keep the ladies' attention, he started to recite his poem "*Épître à M. Parisot.*" He was reciting with such a zest that his listeners were sobbing at the end of the poem, which was an emotional expression regarded at that time as appropriate even for men. Mme de Broglie flatteringly assured Rousseau that he was going to arouse attention in Paris and become the favorite of all the women. As a reward, she gave him the novel by Charles Duclos, *Les Confessions du comte de* ——, which in fact was a textbook on seduction. Rousseau did not understand her message. He had never been a courteous lover and was only seeking fame in the field of literature.

Charles Duclos was a historian and writer and his literary fame was coming to the end at the same time as Rousseau's literary career was starting. Rousseau remembered him even at the end of his life as his only friend and the most honest man he had met among the men of letters, which can only mean that Rousseau had never quarreled with him. Duclos contributed significantly to the sociology of this epoch by his description of the atmosphere of Parisian salons, which is interesting even from the present point of view.

Besides the previously mentioned book, Duclos also wrote one unsuccessful ballet and the books *Considérations sur les moeurs* and *Mémoires pour servir à l'histoire des moeurs du XVIII siècle* and several contributions to Diderot's *Encyclopédie*. He was a protégé of Mme de Pompadour, a royal historian (after Voltaire left for Prussia in 1750) and a permanent secretary of Académie française (after Mirabeau's abdication). He spoke with a deep voice and everything he said was interesting. This experienced man provides insight regarding Rousseau's success in the salons and why he was not hampered by his shyness. The essential thing was that Rousseau was different. He was a Swiss whose provincial manners were largely condoned. He had written a book, had held discussions at the Academy and was regarded a man of letters. He had fresh ideas and was not boring; in fact, while in company, Rousseau was either silent or saying shocking things. Either was permissible. The deadly sin would have been to conduct a boring and arid conversation.

Rousseau's closest friend, however, was Denis Diderot. Both were roughly the same age (Diderot was one year younger), and both had come from the province and later achieved glory and literary fame. Diderot was born in Langres as son of a cutler and had received a much better academic education than Rousseau. He had attended an excellent Jesuit college. He did not, however, acquire Catholic faith there. He believed in science instead, in which he had not received any further education—here his fate was identical with the fate of Rousseau. Both friends were amateur scientists. It is not uninteresting that Rousseau was a better chess player than Diderot and got the upper hand on him in most of their encounters. Diderot was not a very successful author although he wrote several plays for the theatre.

Both young men shared the same desire for cultural innovation in France. They did not see each other as rivals, but planned their literary attempts together. Both were paying tribute to the moderate empiricism of John Locke, whose teaching had been introduced to France by Voltaire and Montesquieu, and with which Rousseau had made his first acquaintance in the house of M. de Mably, in Lyon. In the first years of their friendship, they had similar views. In 1740 both were influenced by the beginning of the Age of Enlightenment. Later on, each of them followed his individual path. Diderot, originally a deist and not an atheist, did not yet have the materialistic views which he developed later under the influence of Baron d'Holbach, and Rousseau had not yet become the radical adversary of all progress—this attitude was to develop later in the *Discours sur les sciences et les arts*. In the years to come, Rousseau was to renounce the Enlightenment while Diderot developed it in the extreme.

Rousseau lived on the income he gained through teaching the few pupils who attended his music lessons. According to his own words, he was indulging his laziness, and committed himself into the hands of divine providence. He made the decision to visit the café only once every other day and the theatre twice a week.

One could ask how it was possible that Rousseau survived at all? We must not forget there were the Parisian salons and the advice of Castel, the clergyman, that to achieve anything in Paris one must rely on *les femmes du monde*. After Mme de Broglie, Rousseau got into the salon of Mme de Dupin, who was not as noble, but was unbelievably rich. She was one of three daughters of the financier Samuel Bernard and his mistress, the former actress Mme Fontaine. The much older husband of Mme de Dupin, Claude Dupin, owned the palace Hôtel Lambert in Paris and the most beautiful of the châteaus in the Loire Valley, Chenonceau.

At the time when Rousseau handed Mme de Dupin, on his first visit to her salon, his *Dissertation sur la musique moderne*, this lady was thirty-six, and she was as beautiful as she was rich. For reasons nobody in Paris could understand, she remained faithful to her much older husband. Mme de Dupin's salon was the most renowned in Paris. Representatives of aristocracy, politics, literature and science gathered there: abbé de Saint-Pierre, abbé Salier, M. de Fourmont, de Bernis, Voltaire, Fontenelle, Marivaux and Buffon.

Rousseau was received in her dressing room—and Mme Dupin was only half-dressed. Later, at dinner, he was seated next to her. No wonder the young Rousseau immediately fell in love with the beautiful lady. He visited her daily and made the mistake of writing love letters to her. Mme Dupin left the letters unnoticed at first, but rebuked him for his behavior several days later. For reasons which remain unknown to us (again, most likely his unsuitable behavior), he stopped visiting Mme Dupin's salon, as he was not welcome.

This unpleasant message was brought to him by Mme Dupin's stepson Charles Louis Dupin de Fracueil (born in 1716 from Dupin's first marriage with Marie-Jeanne Bouilhat). The two were on friendly terms and together they had attended chemistry courses given by Professor Guillame-François Rouelle. His friend was said to prefer in public the company of his beautiful stepmother to that of his plain wife, Sousanne Bollioud de Saint-Julien. Rousseau bore his rejection with silence for some time, but asked for forgiveness on April 9, 1743 and even applied for the job of tutor for Mme Dupin's twelve-year-old son. On this occasion he sent her the treatise on education he had written in Lyon and originally had dedicated to M. de Mably. Rousseau was apparently forgiven and he even got the tutor position, but admits that he instantly regretted having asked for the job. He did not know what to do with young Chenonceaux (who probably had some illness) and resigned from his position one week later.

In *Confessions* he described this episode differently: Mme Dupin herself asked him to look after her son for eight to ten days. Rousseau added to this a sentence which is very interesting from the point of view of his masochistic tendencies: "I spent the week in an agony that would have been unbearable but for my *pleasure in obliging* Mme Dupin" (italics added). The man who would later be celebrated as a theorist of education lamentably failed in practice once more and conceded defeat after a mere eight days. He remarks he would not have stayed another eight days even if Mme Dupin offered herself as a reward.

While taking the chemistry courses, he fell ill with pneumonia which nearly killed him. While he was convalescing, he returned to music, for which he obviously had talent. The result of his hard work during this time was the composition of three acts of an opera, *Les Muses galantes*.

Secretary in Venice—First Signs of Illness

The beautiful marquise, Mme de Broglie, who knew of Rousseau's financial difficulties, quite unexpectedly found him a very good position as a private secretary to the newly appointed French ambassador in Venice, Count de Montaigu. Rousseau rejected the offer at first, because the salary appeared too low to him. But he got the position in the end due to a fortunate coincidence—the secretary employed instead of Rousseau got involved in a smuggling scandal and was sacked. Rousseau was to be paid 1,000 livres plus expenses—although he was originally demanding 1,200 livres plus expenses. Before he left for Venice, Rousseau had purchased some smart clothing, expecting he would have to represent the embassy and the king of France in Venice.

Rousseau decided to accept the offered job at the end of June 1743 and set out on his journey for Venice shortly thereafter.

The journey itself was rather strange and took an unexpectedly long time, which made his employer very angry. The grand diplomat (which Rousseau felt himself to be) did not travel to Venice via Switzerland, but made a short trip to Chambéry, where he wanted to pay Mme de Warens a brief visit, but she was not there. He does not mention this short trip in *Confessions*, but the cost did appear in the statement of expenses which was submitted to his new employer. He continued his journey from Toulon aboard a ship, but arriving in Genoa he was immediately put in quarantine. He spent this time in an unfurnished house, where he felt quite like Robinson Crusoe.

He was later the guest of the diplomat François de Jonville, the man who originally was to get the ambassadorial post in Venice, but which was instead given to Montaigu. The latter had known the right people at the court though his diplomatic education was not as good as that of Jonville. The diplomat in Genoa got a favorable impression of Rousseau in the course of his visit and congratulated his more successful colleague in a letter on obtaining such an intelligent and talented secretary, who, in addition, had an excellent command of conversational skills.

This positive opinion as well as previous events make it obvious that Rousseau was no simpleton, as he was often purported to be, and that he had adapted to life in Paris quite well. Let us remember the fact that it did not take him long to make his way into the Parisian salons and to become a relatively well-known person; he was able to push through his financial requirements and had even improved his conversation, which is supported by the letter of the diplomat Jonville. Rousseau's letters are written with eloquence and skill, and it is on record that he had a talent for calligraphy. It would thus appear that his character defects, no doubt partly caused by the semi-deprivation of his childhood, could have been corrected by the influence of a different environment. As we will see later, however, a disturbed childhood development leaves traces that are much deeper and must manifest themselves sooner or later, even in individuals as intelligent and gifted as Rousseau.

On his way to Venice, Rousseau was probably very fashionable and incurred various expenses which he put on the bill and asked to be reimbursed for. On the way from Genoa he was not behaving niggardly and was generously getting acquainted with Milan, Padua and Verona, according to his ideas of the manner suiting a French "diplomat." He arrived in Venice at the end of September 1743—at the age of thirty-one. The architectural beauty of the city did not enchant him so much as the Venetian way of life, which he liked for its charming style, thinking it had some similarity to his own character. (His hermit-like lifestyle was still to come.)

In Venice, Rousseau bore himself as a young man of the world who wanted to excel, to astound by eccentric behavior, to meet new people and do important things. He felt the view, expressed by abbé de Gouvon in Turin, who first suggested that he be employed in diplomatic service, to be confirmed. Now he was working as a diplomat for the king of France! He wanted to enjoy himself in Venice, too. This should not have been very difficult, because indulging in life's pleasures was in a sense one of the Venetian "industries," as we learn from Casanova's *Memoirs*. Venice itself became an important center of diplomacy.

Let us remember that 1743 was the year when war between Spain and the kingdom of Sardinia began; a war in which France sided with Spain. This was one of the many wars which broke out after the death of emperor Charles VI (1685-1740) of Austria, in 1740. The death of his only son had prompted Charles VI to promulgate the so-called Pragmatic Sanction (on April 19, 1713), by which he made his oldest daughter, the archduchess Maria Theresia, his successor. The emperor's relatives claimed the throne, or at least part of the Habsburg Empire. France supported Charles Albert of Bavaria (who was elected Holy Roman emperor with the help of France in Frankfurt on the Main in February 1742). Other interested monarchs were August II, king of Poland, the king of Spain and the king of Sardinia. The king of France, too, claimed part of the Austrian Succession, but was intelligent enough to realize that this could not be achieved. He restricted himself to supporting the claims of others. Italy was an important scene during these wars. Two Bourbon royal families—of Spain and of Naples—tried to weaken Austrian positions in Italy and the third Bourbon royal family of France became their ally in the fall of 1743.

Maria Theresia had numerous supporters in Italy. Her Husband, Francis Stephen of Lorraine, was the grand duke of Tuscany and some Italian territories preferred good relationships with Austria to the largely unknown influence of the House of Bourbon. The king of Sardinia, who was known as a traditional enemy of Austria, which stood in the way of the Savoy expansion in northern Italy, was bribed by English money and the offer of Austrian territory.

Consequently, he entered the war as an Austrian ally. In this conflict, diplomatic moves were as important as military moves. One of the major tasks for French diplomacy was to achieve a split between Sardinia and Austria. The Venetian Republic declared neutrality and French diplomats were given the task of assuring Venice that its neutrality would be respected.

In September 1743, when Rousseau arrived in Venice, Austrian-Sardinian troops were facing Spanish troops between Pesaro and Rimini, after the battle of Campo Santo (in February 1743); this rather quiet period of the war continued till spring of the next year. Efforts in the field of diplomacy were quite active, and this applied even to such a small representation as the French embassy in Venice.

Comte de Montaigu, who was new to diplomacy after his previous military career, did not understand the coded dispatches and did not know how to reply to them. He spoke no Italian and even his French was rather simple, in keeping with his military past. Neither was he a rich man, although French envoys were expected to have a private fortune. Payments were made by the French court and were forthcoming only with great delays. The conflict between the militarily rigorous and discipline-demanding de Montaigu, who saw in Rousseau only an employee whose main task was to obey his orders, and Rousseau, who was well aware of the professional, language and social shortcomings of his employer and who regarded himself (unrealistically) to be a diplomat in service to the king of France, was preprogrammed. Rousseau had learned Italian during his stay in Turin and had quickly mastered the Venetian dialect. He was on friendly terms with the French consul in Venice, Jean Le Blond, who had been born in Venice. Le Blond was the son of a French consul who had inherited his father's office. No wonder he understood the Venetian circumstances much better than those in France. Unfortunately, Montaigu made this influential man into his enemy by ordering that he could not import wine duty-free.

In view of the numerous diplomatic tasks Comte de Montaigu had to deal with at the embassy he had to work closely with his new secretary. Rousseau easily mastered the system of encoding used by the French army, which was rather primitive. His employer (who also had to pay him) had a favorable opinion of his secretary at first, despite the latter's demand to be assigned his own gondola, which was very likely requested in his haughty style. The gondola was painted in gay colors, which was a privilege of ambassadorial gondolas. Rousseau had one more demand—he wanted to visit clavichord concerts.

Initially, Rousseau liked the work at the embassy and he was obviously able to handle it. Between September 14, 1743 and June 25, 1744, the period Rousseau spent at the embassy in Venice, the weekly work schedule included two dispatches to the king of France to inform him about matters concerning the state, and one dispatch to the foreign secretary Amelot, or to the undersecretary in Versailles. The dispatches sent to Montaigu from Versailles had to be answered. On top of that, the Venetian embassy had to write weekly reports and send them to the other French embassies in Italy. There was thus a lot of work to be done and even when the embassy in Venice had a second secretary, abbé de Binis, Rousseau had to bear the main brunt of the work.

Rousseau had no reason to feel satisfied with his employer. He soon became aware of the ambassador's weaknesses, saw that the latter was dependent on him, and his own behavior grew increasingly arrogant. He criticized the ambassador for his thrift bordering on miserliness, the bad quality of the food at the embassy, where the ambassador did not employ any women, and the fact that Montaigu had a second residence on the mainland.

The Venetian protocol to be followed by foreign diplomats was not a simple one. The presentation of credentials was preceded by a complicated procedure. The new ambassador had to make an appearance on the island Santo Spirito, where he would be visited by a delegation of sixty Venetian senators, who would greet him and escort him to his embassy in Venice. This would be followed by an overnight masked ball, and only thereafter, as a reward, could the ambassador be received in the doge's palace, present his credentials to the doge and be introduced to members of government. The immense cost of such an inauguration deterred many ambassadors from holding this ceremony, as it had no practical meaning at all. Even when inaugurated, the new ambassador could not meet the doge or members of his government. This led many diplomats to postpone the inauguration ceremony as long as possible. Montaigu postponed it so long it never took place.

Communication with the government was possible either via letters or by *viva voce*, a Venetian representative, called a *conférent*. During Rousseau's time, no such *conférent* had been appointed and all communication with Venetian authorities was done in writing. Rousseau got acquainted with the secretary at the Spanish embassy, François-Xavier de Carrio, and the French consul Le Blond, who initiated him into the mysteries of Venetian administration.

Behind the republican facade of Venetian government a secret and despotic patrician rule was hidden. Executive power lay with a board, mainly with six of its members, the so-called *Savii-Grandi*, who were selected for a period of six months. This government depended on an extensive network of informers and made its decision behind closed doors. This despotic system was based on the old truth that people prefer *panis et circenses* to freedom, and was undoubtedly popular.

Rousseau compared the republican system of Venice with that of his native Geneva and started writing a book on political institutions. The unfinished and sizeable fragment of this attempt is his *Du Contract social*. At his age Rousseau was uncomfortable with the Puritan spirit of Geneva but was attracted by the Venetian *joie de vivre*. He loved carnivals and masked balls, he enjoyed the ambience in the more than two hundred Venetian cafés, and visited the many theatres. He did not enjoy gambling and the only game he valued and enjoyed was chess because it did not involve the possibility of betting. He complained (in a letter from February 1744) that his health suffered from the cold winter weather in Venice, *when he probably experienced symptoms of urinary problems for the first time*. We cannot find any mention of the "deadly illnesses" from which he suffered earlier. The thing, however, he loved most in Venice, was the music, which could be heard at every step. This folk music could be heard every day: Italian barcaroles, operas, or church music. The latter was sung by orphaned girls sitting behind curtains and singing with angel voices. Rousseau imagined them as beautiful angels and was unpleasantly surprised when he was once taken behind the scenes by consul Le Blond, and discovered that some of the girls were ill with smallpox or were disfigured in other ways.

In spite of the fact that he later condemned the theatre as an institution, he helped two Venetian actresses, Coralina and Camille, and their father, Carlo-Antonio Veronese, to get to Paris where they were to attain great success. This intervention (probably somewhat exaggerated in *Confessions*) paid off later. Coralina was to be the mistress of Prince de Conti for several years and finished her career marrying Marquise de Silly. Prince de Conti later became Rousseau's protector at a time when he needed help badly.

The French embassy in Venice had to deal not only with politics, but also with actresses. A feverish activity surrounded the best dancer of the time, Barbara Campanini—La Barbarina—who, after her successes in Paris, signed a contract with the court of Frederick II in Berlin. Because she fell in love with a Scotsman named Mackenzie, however, she changed her mind and disappeared in Venice. French political circles did not want Frederick II to become angry so La Barbarina was located, arrested and escorted to Berlin. Her lover followed her but was expelled from Berlin. The misfortune of the famous dancer was relieved by a pension she got from the king, and possibly disappeared completely when she married an enormously rich Prussian aristocrat.

Another beautiful Venetian actress, Zanetta Farussi, departed for the court theatre of the Saxon electoral prince. She left a small boy in Venice, Giacomo Girolamo Casanova (1725–1798), whose father was a wandering actor, Caetano Casanova. Casanova, who bestowed a peerage on himself and posed as Chevalier de Seingalt, was another semi-deprived child whose fate was somewhat similar to Rousseau's. He had been brought up by his grandmother, Marzia. Like Rousseau he also had a sexual variation, but of a different kind.

The spring of 1744 brought new military and diplomatic activities. The Austrian army, led by Fürst von Lobkowitz, took the offensive and the Spanish-Neapolitan army, led by Count de Gages, marched back strategically to Velletri. Rousseau wrote in *Confessions* that he discovered a pro-Austrian insurgency in Naples and thereby saved the Bourbon ruling structure in Naples, but it appears that everything was rather a mistake. His *Confessions* were written many years after his Venetian stay and contain, despite his good memory, a lot of inaccuracies.

Rousseau had only two amorous adventures in Venice. He admitted that he had not lost his unfortunate habit of cheating his passions (masturbation) and he lived in Venice with the "same chastity as in Paris." Only after he was mocked because of his scornful attitude toward seductive Venetian courtesans did he give in to their persuasion and visit a courtesan, *(padoana)*, who had a nice face. Rousseau, however, did not find her beauty appealing. He wanted to leave without sexual intercourse and he put one ducat on the table. The padoana, however, refused to accept it, saying she had not earned it and Rousseau was "strangely stupid as to try to dissolve her objections." Immediately after he came home he sent for a doctor and was prescribed drugs because he was afraid he had caught a sexually transmitted disease. "The surgeon himself had the greatest imaginable trouble in reassuring me. He only succeeded in the end by persuading me that I was so peculiarly made that I could not easily catch an infection."

The second episode started when a Captain Olivet, whose ship had collided with another ship, was released from prison and Rousseau wrote that he was released "as a result of my efforts and without the help of others." In any event, the released captain organized a party and invited Rousseau and his friend, Carrio, from the Spanish embassy. As a present, the captain gave to the two secretaries the courtesan Ziulietta (Giulietta), a beautiful brunette with dark, Oriental eyes. She pretended to mistake Rousseau for her former lover and embraced him immediately. When he protested, saying he was a foreigner, she told him he was so similar to her former lover he had to be her lover, too. After dinner, the beauty took both secretaries to the island of Murano where they bought a lot of little glass trinkets and returned to her home.

Rousseau made a date with her for the next day. His description of their meeting cannot be left out as it is remembered in most of his biographies. Rousseau wrote in *Confessions*: "I found her *in vestitio di confidenza*, in a more than seductive undress, which is unknown except in southern lands . . . her ruffles and bodice were edged with silk thread and ornamented with rose-colored tufts, and this seemed to me to enhance the beauty of her skin." In spite of this Rousseau did not feel any necessity to succumb to the sensual pleasures offered to him. He admitted that: "Never was such sweet pleasure offered to mortal heart and senses. Alas, had I only known how to enjoy it fully . . . No, Nature has not made me for sensual delight. She has put the hunger for it in my heart, but what might be ineffable pleasure turns to poison in my wretched head." And so his passions began to cool down during their embrace. *His feet were trembling; he felt a weakness and started to sob as if he were a child.* He says that he was overwhelmed by the contradictory awareness that this beautiful and good woman, this miracle of nature who would be the pride of every king, was an ordinary prostitute.

To justify his aversion toward her he had to find some fault with her. The beautiful Giulietta tried to conform him, to dispel his fears and relieve his sense of shame. "Then," he continued, "just as I was about to rest my head on a breast that seemed to be receiving for the first time the touch of a man's lip and hands, I noticed that she had a malformed nipple . . ." He compared both nipples attentively and came to the conclusion that what he saw was a serious natural disturbance and that *"instead of the most charming creature, I held in my arms some kind of monster, rejected by Nature, men and love"* (italics added).

Naïve as he was, he began talking about her defect. Giulietta considered this to be a joke at first. When she saw, however, that he was serious, she took umbrage, arranged her dress and said derisively, "Jacko, give up the ladies and study mathematics." (*Zanetto, lascia le donne, e studia la matematica.*) Rousseau wanted to visit her a day or two later, but was told she had left for Florence. Rousseau regretted that he had lost her, but it was too late. He was able to put up with the fact that he lost her, but could never tolerate the thought that Giulietta would remember him with contempt.

The story with Giulietta is interesting for several reasons. It confirms the observation of disturbed sexual behavior made in semi-deprived individuals, who have difficulties in establishing normal emotional relationships and fear emotional bonds, which might be due to fear that expectations invested in them will be frustrated (see the attachment theory of J. Bowlby).

The episode is also a good example of the problematic thinking of our patient. He uses unrealistic arguments to convince himself of something which he then believes, and then he reacts and behaves according to this firm conviction. In addition, he is prepared to persuade other people of his illogical conviction, with a cogency supported by brilliant eloquence. "How frightful are the illusions in human life!" wrote Rousseau in his *Confessions*. It is very remarkable that Rousseau felt no need to have normal sexual intercourse at the age of thirty-one and resorted to autoeroticism. Being a masochist Rousseau found normal sexual intercourse disgusting. Giulietta did not provide any masochistic foreplay. Only such activity could have aroused him and enabled the intercourse.

The last recorded "love" affair shows a deviation from sexual norms. His friend from the Spanish embassy, Carrio, suggested that they could keep a mistress together, which was a common practice in Venice at that time. He found a twelve-year-old girl, Anzoletta, "sweet as a lamb." They paid her mother and took care of the education of the "lamb." They taught her to sing and play the spinet. According to Rousseau they enjoyed being with her and playing with her. As far as Rousseau was concerned, it might well have been true—he says that what attracts a man to women is not sexual gratification, but the delight of being in their company (this view certainly corresponds to a feminine way of thinking, but by no means to the thinking of an average man). It is more than doubtful whether Carrio treated their "lamb" in the same way. Rousseau assures us that Carrio had similar views, but this is difficult to believe. The good work of educating Anzoletta could not be completed—Rousseau clashed openly with his employer and had to leave Venice.

The feuds between Rousseau and Montaigu occurred with increased frequency and grew increasingly bitter. Obviously both parties were to blame. In January 1744 a quarrel broke out between them over the question of whether Rousseau should attend a dinner to which the duke of Modena had been invited. Montaigu considered sacking Rousseau then, but the duke canceled his participation at the dinner and the crisis could be averted.

At the end of April 1744 Rousseau wrote a letter to Montaigu's brother, Chevalier de Montaigu, in which he described his difficulties and assured him he would do his best to catch up with his work and would make up for lack of talent by more diligence. Rousseau evidently was attending to most of the embassy's correspondence, but not always with sufficient concentration and not without mistakes. As early as November 1743, dispatches from Venice, which were Rousseau's responsibility, contained more mistakes than did those from other French embassies. Rousseau admits to only one or two errors in encoding and rejects any accusation of neglecting his duties, which is remarkable in a person, "who is as absent-minded as I."

Another incident broke out when the ambassador found out that Rousseau collected the charges for a visa and put them in his own pocket; it has to be said, however, that this was probably his only income, because his employer did not pay him any salary.

At the same time, the letters written by the ambassador make it obvious that Rousseau was an arrogant and foppish employee with whom it was difficult to get along. He appropriated the right to sit in the ambassador's chair. And worse—when the ambassador was dictating a letter to him and paused, trying to think of the right word or the right formulation, Rousseau took a book and started to read! (Every chess player knows how unpleasant it is when his opponent reads a book during the game, making clear how impatient and surprised he is by the slow thinking of his opponent.)

Rousseau was also refusing to obey when he was ordered to bring papers from the embassy to the ambassador's house on the mainland, because it was something for servants to do, "but not for a man in my position." The controversy came to a head in early August 1744 when—in an open quarrel—the ambassador accused Rousseau of selling the code the embassy used for dispatches. Rousseau laughed in his face and said that no one in Venice would pay anything to him for such a code. The ambassador threatened to throw him out of the window, but Rousseau says it was his decision to leave forever.

It is likely that his departure was not so dramatic and took some time. He announces on August 4, in a letter directed to his friends at the French embassy in Switzerland, that he stopped being a secretary at the embassy in Venice. In fact he left the embassy a day or two later. After another two days, he wrote a long letter to the undersecretary of the foreign office in Versailles, M. du Theil (Louis XV had dismissed the office principal, Amelot, and intended to head the office himself). In this letter, he describes his version of his departure from the embassy and continues to describe his present situation with typical eloquence: he has been sacked, he has no money and is without help, has nowhere to go, is a thousand and two hundred miles away from his friends, and he has incurred debts because the ambassador has cancelled his contract. The letter remained unanswered, and was later stolen and passed to Voltaire, who distorted its contents and portrayed Rousseau as a mere servant at the embassy.

Rousseau's situation was in fact far from being that desperate. His friend, the French consul Le Blond took him to his house and gave a dinner in his honor, which was attended by the entire French colony. Rousseau was offered financial loans and overwhelmed by invitations. Montaigu learned about it and asked the Venetian senate to expel Rousseau. The senate did not reply to Montaigu's request and, when Rousseau heard about the request, he enjoyed the Venetian life for another fourteen days, at least in part to irritate the ambassador.

A week before Rousseau left, he wrote a second letter to M. du Theil in Versailles, which was as exalted as the first: he complained bitterly about the behavior of his former employer, who sent people to persecute him "night and day, day and night." It was not until September 1744 that the Venetian senate finally sent a memorandum to the ambassador, via consul Le Blond, stating that the man "who was to be expelled" had left Venice on August 22. Consul Le Blond accompanied Rousseau to his boat and loaned him money for his return to France, where Rousseau wanted to seek the protection of the foreign office and justice from the king. His fate was to receive neither.

Back in Paris—Acquaintance with Thérèse

Rousseau's journey back to Paris was neither precipitous nor direct. It took nearly seven weeks and resembled a long excursion. He traveled via the Simplon Pass to the Valais canton and halted in Sion, where he was warmly received by a French resident, M. de Chaignon, despite the fact that the latter had been warned by Montaigu that Rousseau was a "an adventurer." He continued his journey to Geneva via Nyon without visiting his father. He says he did not want to meet his stepmother, especially after he had been so humbled in Venice. In Geneva, however, an old friend of his father, the bookseller Duvillard, persuaded him that he should see his father and both of them returned to Nyon and had lunch with Isaac Rousseau in an inn, where Rousseau also spent the night.

On the next day he hurried back to Geneva where he had many friends. An old admirer of his mother's, M. de la Closure, received him with great kindness, and his secretary, M. de Gauffecourt, who held a monopoly for the collection of tax on salt in Geneva and Valais, provided him with money. He later became Rousseau's faithful friend. Originally, Rousseau wanted to stay in Geneva until "a happier fate should, by removing the obstacles, enable me to rejoin my poor Maman."

The continuing argument with his former employer, Montaigu, with whom he haggled about the customs charges for his luggage, led him to Lyon and then to Paris, where he wanted to "clear his name." In Paris, he wrote a third emotional letter to M. du Theil in Versailles, but again in vain. Rousseau described his arrival in Paris as a near triumph: everyone in Paris was allegedly surprised by the behavior of the Venetian ambassador. The truth was that his arrival left practically no traces in Parisian society. He did not mention that he was not invited to visit the salons of aristocracy again. It could be hardly expected that aristocratic circles would ever believe that a simple Swiss could be right in a dispute with a member of their stratum. Rousseau fared the same as Voltaire when the latter was whipped by Duke Rohan's servants for a joke he ventured.

It was then that Rousseau turned his mind to the injustice of the social system. For the first time, contempt for oppressive institutions stirred in his breast; he began to identify the systems in which real public interest and real justice were sacrificed to a semblance of order, though they destroy the real order, and where public institutions oppress the weak while permitting the injustice of the strong,. These thoughts later became part of the *Discours sur l'origine de l'inégalité*.

Rousseau, however, never evaded contacts with these same privileged classes, nor did he refuse their support. On the contrary, he had actively sought them since his youth, and was dependent on their charity for most of his life.

But his views started to change. Let us remember that in Lyon, in the house of M. de Mably, he was still writing poems in which he claimed that more equality would harm society.

After his arrival in Paris, he immediately took advantage of help offered to him by the aristocracy. When he was still in Venice, he was introduced to a young Spanish nobleman, Don Manuel Ignacio Altuna y Porta. Rousseau recommended that he go to Paris and study science. In Paris they met again. The young Spaniard suggested that Rousseau could live in his flat free of charge, an offer which Rousseau gratefully accepted. Rousseau spent the winter of 1744 in his company, till spring of 1745 when Altuna returned to Spain. Rousseau has only words of praise for him, which means he had no quarrels with him, probably because of Altuna's smooth politeness. He wrote, "He was the only truly tolerant man I have met in my life, with the exception of my person." Both friends were frequent guests of the pub operated by Mme La Selle, near the Palais Royal.

The alehouse was notorious for bad food, jovial company and *risqué* conversation. Beautiful girls worked nearby in Mme Duchapt's tailor shop. Rousseau admits he would have liked to enjoy himself in the same way as others, if only he were more daring.

We know from a letter dated February 25, 1745, which Rousseau wrote to Mme de Warens, that before he returned to Spain, Altuna invited Rousseau to come and live on his estates where they could philosophize for the rest of their lives. We do not know why Rousseau did not accept this attractive offer. In the letter he says the reason was his love for Mme de Warens. He would have wished "to be the lucky one who could spend the rest of my life with you." But beforehand he must show the whole world he was not only better than Montaigu, but also more respected (masochists are collectors of insults).

We can believe these words, or we need not. Perhaps he knew in his subconscious that if he lived longer with his "tolerant" friend they would get to know each other so well they would become enemies. Even a philanthropist is a person who loves all people with the exception of those he knows well—and we know Rousseau was considered to be a misanthrope.

Altuna returned to Spain in the spring of 1745 and Rousseau entered a difficult period of his life, in which he found himself without protectors and support. The dispute with Montaigu and his dismissal, or rather the marching orders from Venice, did him more harm socially than he was ready to admit.

There are no reports of him being invited to salons again, where he would at least have gotten something to eat and had a chance to establish new contacts. He moved back to the Hôtel Saint-Quentin near the Sorbonne. This time he did not write that the hotel was bad, but that he had chosen it because of its "quietness."

It is unclear on how he managed financially. He did not receive the money ambassador Montaigu allegedly owed him and was therefore unable to pay his debts. Necessity is the mother of invention, and so out of necessity Rousseau set about finishing *Les Muses galantes*, the opera which he had begun in Venice. Probably for the first time Rousseau was working steadily and with concentration—he had no alternative—and the opera was finished within three months.

At a time when he was forced to work hard and reside at the ugly Hôtel Saint-Quentin, Rousseau met a person who was to become not only his mistress, but also his nurse, companion and, in the end, even his wife until his death. The character of Thérèse Levasseur appears at the stage of his life.

From previous pages the reader knows of Rousseau's enthusiasm for aristocratic mistresses who did not have to be beautiful or young. Rousseau fell in love with them just for their origin and despised girls from lower classes who he regarded as unworthy of him. That makes his relationship with Thérèse all the more surprising. Thérèse was a twenty-two-year-old chambermaid in the hotel where Rousseau was staying. The landlady, her guests and all employees ate at the same table. Rousseau lets us know he was carried along by the young woman's modesty and lively, sweet expression at first sight. He recalls that the party at the table often made fun of her and he was her only defender.

He did not find her attractive, rather he felt pity for her because she was lonely in the same way he was lonely. In addition, she suffered from the same bashfulness as he did. It did not take long before a kinship of hearts developed. According to Rousseau, Thérèse saw in him an honest man and he saw in her a sensitive and simple girl without coquetry. He was not disappointed. Thérèse came from a very simple family. Her father had been employed at a mint in Orleans which had been closed, and Thérèse had to support not only her father, but also her mother, who had gone bankrupt in a business venture.

Rousseau, of course, portrays her family in a better light than they deserved, which is not surprising. If he had described her parentage correctly, the question would have arisen as to how it was possible that a man of his stature could have chosen a woman from such a low social stratum. According to those who knew her, Thérèse was an imbecile and Rousseau himself admits he was only wasting his time when he tried to "improve her soul." She could write, but hardly read. She could not count or tell time. She did not understand many words and Rousseau, as her protector, once put together a list of her errors to entertain Mme de Luxembourg. On the other hand, she allegedly had well-developed common sense and was able to advise Rousseau in his difficulties—protecting him successfully against the many dangers of his impulsive nature. This would explain his remarks, "I attained more happiness though I thought only of my pleasures."

We must take everything Rousseau wrote about Thérèse with a grain of salt, because his description of her varied over time. His statements regarding Thérèse are often contradictory (as are his philosophical views) and evolved from their developing and changing relationship. At the time he wrote *Confessions* he held different moral views than he did in 1745. At first he wanted Thérèse as a mistress and told her (in the style of an *honnete homme*) that he would never marry her but would never leave her either. This was the posture of a young roué who saw in Thérèse a girl of low origin. His views did not change until the time when he experienced what he called his "reform."

Thérèse refused his first amorous proposal which led Rousseau to the conclusion that she suffered from a venereal disease. Thérèse guessed his misgivings, burst into tears and told him she had been seduced at young age and had lost her virginity. Rousseau banished her fears saying that no one in Paris would expect a twenty-year-old to be a virgin. He said he was happy to have a good and healthy girl.

According to Rousseau, Thérèse was slowly replacing Maman's position in his life. She had not the culture and background of Mme de Warens, but appeared to attract Rousseau sexually. Starobinsky's view that Rousseau saw in Thérèse someone he was able to identify with is rather improbable. Rousseau regarded himself from his youth as someone who was different from, and better than, other people. Later on he even felt himself to be the "prophet" of humanity and identified more with Christ. He was proud of his fragmentary and unsystematic education, of his subjective views, which he was always prepared to defend as objective truths, and of his origin and birthplace. In addition, he had never valued women of low origin.

It appears that Cranston gets nearer to the truth. He points out that

Rousseau and Thérèse must have had more or less regular sexual intercourse, especially in the first period of their "cohabitation." This is supported by the fact that Thérèse gave birth to five children. It cannot be said with certainty, however, that Rousseau was the father of all of them. Some of them might have been foisted on him, because Thérèse was often alone and without any means of support, and in Paris of that time prostitution and promiscuity were quite common. Her deliveries would also support the assumption that she was not infected by a sexually transmitted disease. Venereal diseases are accompanied by pelvic inflammations which cause lower fertility.

The reader knows from previous sections that Rousseau never regarded sexual intercourse as his primary object. He was attracted by abnormal sexual experiences.

What made Thérèse so indispensable to Rousseau? According to my view Rousseau did not masturbate in the usual way but did so by introducing various objects into his urethra and obtained sexual gratification in this way. Urethral masturbation is very painful and his sexual experiences were much more intense and pleasurable when these painful practices were performed by a woman. The masochist wants to suffer from the hands of a woman. (Remember Mlle Goton?) That was why Rousseau taught Thérèse to render sexual gratification to him in a way he desired but was unable to ask from other women. When the masochistic component was missing he was unable to have intercourse even with the beautiful Giulietta. The painful and humiliating masturbation, with Thérèse was inserting objects into his urethra, satisfied his masochistic demands and intensified his sexual arousal. He was capable of sexual intercourse only after such masochistic foreplay. At a later time Rousseau says in his *Confessions*, "from the first moment I saw her till this day I have never felt the least glimmering of love for her: that I no more desired to possess her than I had desired Mme de Warens and that the sensual needs I satisfied with her were for me purely sexual and nothing to do with her as an individual." This statement makes it obvious that Thérèse was not a substitute for Mme de Warens because he had never gratified any sensual needs with his Maman.

This proposed thesis is supported by Rousseau's mysterious urinary tract diseases, from which he suffered for many years and over which so many of his contemporaries and later researchers puzzled. It also explains why he fell ill in the first place.

Now we can understand the reason for his changing attitude toward Thérèse. As we understand how important these masochistic sexual experiences were for him, it becomes obvious why he could never break away from Thérèse. Comparing Thérèse to Anne-Toinette (Nanette) Champion, whom Diderot married in 1743 and whom Rousseau never liked, Rousseau wrote that Thérèse was "sweet and docile." We know that Thérèse was by no means docile, or teachable, in the intellectual sphere. It must have been her docility in the sexual sphere that was making her so sweet.

His dependence on Thérèse was gradually increasing. Later, during his hermitic way of life, he would need someone who would care for him, especially with respect to his deteriorating health, and who would at the same time comply with his sexual tastes. As soon as he arrived at a new place one of his first concerns was to make sure always that Thérèse be near him.

One could ask why Rousseau did not write about his sexual practices in *Confessions* and the answer is that the confessions Rousseau left behind are far from comprehensive. It would be more appropriate to say they were written to *create the impression of confession*. This work is in fact a defense and justification, invented by Rousseau and skillfully put into effect. The reader learns about numerous ticklish details from his life, about his errors and misdemeanors. Almost invariably, noble motives are added as explanations of those misdemeanors. *Confessions* creates the impression that Rousseau really confesses something, but it is in fact a retouched self-portrait. It papers over most of the cracks of his life with the goal of saving his reputation for future generations by explaining his abnormal behavior. Rousseau was extremely intelligent and saw clearly that his personality was full of contradictions and so he found it necessary to present his life in the favorable light of apparent openness. And he succeeded in it. Without *Confessions* Rousseau would be more or less forgotten today—his *Confessions* amounts to a readable monument of the personality and its time. One can hardly expect to find objective truths in a subjective account of the writer's personality.

Thérèse and Rousseau did not live together. Thérèse had to support both her mother and father and Rousseau had to work on his opera. When the work was ready, his next step was to try to get it performed. He knew that he could not achieve anything in Paris living in seclusion. Gaffecourt, a rich secretary of an old admirer of his mother, came to Paris from Geneva and recommended him to the house of M. de La Poplinière, a rich tax collector who was affluent enough to be a patron of music. But Rousseau had bad luck because another well-known musician, Jean-Phillipe Rameau, who was thirty years older, was already established in this house. Rameau was not interested in a rival.

Les Muses galantes was performed by orchestra in the house of M. de La Poplinière, to the great dissatisfaction of Rameau, who declared the work could not have been written by Rousseau because one part of the opera must have been written by a genius and another part by an ignoramus, who did not understand music at all. Mme de La Poplinière, a *grande horizontale* of her time, and a relative of Mme Dupin, did not show any enthusiasm for Rousseau; however, her lover at the time, Duke Richelieu, whom Rousseau had met in Lyon, treated Rousseau with greater friendliness. He organized the performance of the whole work in the house of M. de Bonneval, the Atendant des *Des Menus Plaisirs,* and was so pleased with the ballet that he promised to perform it in Versailles; however, this was never realized.

As a next step, Rousseau offered the composition to the Paris opera, but did not receive any reply—according to Rameau, the opera was rejected as a product of Italian taste combined with the worst of French music. Duke Richelieu found him some work as musician. The victory of French armies in the battle of Fontenoy, after which Marshal de Saxe invaded and occupied most of the Netherlands, was marked with numerous theatre performances in France. Voltaire's *Princess de Navarre* was rewritten as *Les Fêtes de Ramire* and Rousseau participated in the adaptation, working on the scores. The first written contact between Rousseau and Voltaire occurred in connection with it. Voltaire's letter was very friendly, probably because he thought that Rousseau was Duke Richelieu's protégé. Rousseau did not get paid for the adaptations he performed—and he was allegedly so ill in the autumn of 1745 that he was unable to ask for payment for the adapted work. No further details are known about the illness he suffered. It is possible he experienced the first symptoms of urinary tract infection, which would correspond to the time when he taught Thérèse the specific sexual practices mentioned earlier.

His friend Gaffecourt told Rousseau he should stop visiting Mme de La Poplinière's salon, because La Poplinière's wife could not tolerate Rousseau's presence, and it was not until early 1746 when Rousseau returned as a guest to Mme Dupin's salon. The two women were relatives, but did not know each other socially.

Rousseau studied chemistry with Mme Dupin's stepson, Francueil (they had attended chemistry courses before Rousseau's stay in Venice). Rousseau was offered the job of a paid secretary in Mme Dupin's house, which he accepted.

His goals were to become a musician and literary author, but so far he had had no financial income from these activities. He needed the income, particularly then, because he and Thérèse had moved closer to Mme Dupin's house—at the Hôtel Lambert. Thérèse's relatives lived in the country and visited her regularly, expecting Rousseau would support them. Rousseau's life was thus divided in two lines: on the one hand he was taking part in a glittering life where he had good meals, wine and conversation, and had access to an excellent library he could never have afforded as poor man. On the other hand, he lived in the simple environment of Thérèse's family.

The secretarial job turned out to be quite difficult and demanding. The young Francueil wanted to become a member of the Academy at all costs and therefore had to write at least one book. Literary ambition was by no means restricted to Francueil. His father, Claude Dupin, set out to write a book on economics in his old age. Mme de Dupin regarded herself a born writer, because her mother was an actress and her grandfather was the dramatist Dancourt.

It is interesting that Mme Dupin was a feminist and tried to prove that all women were men's equals in every respect, including physical characteristics, and that many distinguished deeds in human history were the work of women and so made them men's equals. Rousseau held no such feminist views and, according to him, women should be subordinate to men. Rousseau did background research for the whole family, and also wrote from their dictation. His work was very exhausting (he was paid eight hundred to nine hundred francs a year), but it held the advantage that Rousseau was forced to read numerous authors, which contributed to his general education. The Dupin family employed him without interruption from 1746 to 1751.

The whole family, including Rousseau, often lived outside of Paris, especially in summer when they resided at their summer residence, Château de Chenonceaux, the most beautiful of the châteaus in the Loire Valley. This château was once the residence of royal mistresses and widows. It was founded by Thomas Bohier, financial minister in Normandy, and was later confiscated by Francis I. King Henry II presented it to his favorite Diane de Poitiers, who was forced by queen Catherine de Médicis, to leave the château when the king died. The queen bequeathed Chenonceau to Louise de Lorraine.

Francueil and Rousseau continued their chemical experiments in a laboratory established on the château. Rousseau had all he needed and got "thick as a monk." He wrote several trifles of no account to entertain Mme Dupin: *L'Engagement téméraire*, a comedy in three acts; the poem *"L'Allée de Sylvie"*; and several arias for three voices. In the poem he dreams of love—but nothing more specific is known about this love.

His dreams were definitely not concerned with Thérèse, though the latter had enough reason to think of him. She was pregnant, and Rousseau frivolously remarked on his return to Paris in December 1747 that, whereas he had put on weight in Chenonceau, Thérèse had put on weight, too, but for other reasons. He admits that Thérèse's pregnancy interrupted his life and that he had found a practical solution: his companions in the pub of Mme La Selle, which he started visiting again, probably initiated the suggestion that the unwanted child be sent to a foundling home. "Since it is the custom of the country I told myself if one lives there one must adopt it . . . I cheerfully resolved to take it without the least scruple." He was pleased by this solution and his mind was not fraught with remorse. The only obstacle was Thérèse. He persuaded her with only "the greatest difficulty in the world" to accept his plan.

He was convinced it would save her honor (a typical example of Rousseau's way of thinking: a wrong act is rationalized as noble intention). Thérèse's mother supported this plan too because she feared another hungry life in the household, and Thérèse gave way in the end. Rousseau wrote succinctly that the same situation recurred a year later, whereupon the same solution was found. "No greater hesitation on my part, no greater agreement on the mother's part: she obeyed sobbingly."

His decision shocked the whole world, but that came later. At the time it was made, Rousseau was poor and not yet known as aspiring to fame. There were hundreds of similar men in Paris and his act was nothing exceptional. The foundling home in Paris admitted 3,274 children in 1746 and 950 of these children had been found on the streets. All five of his children were sent to a foundling home—here Rousseau's egoism can be seen, together with his irresponsibility and lack of interest in his children, which is typical of deprived and semi-deprived individuals; we know this behavior from experiments with primates.

Another honest excuse for his behavior was his love for his Maman. He said he wanted to become rich to be able to pay back all the good she did for him and live with her till the end of life. It is difficult to judge whether his words were true. Mme de Warens was indeed facing immense financial difficulties at that time. One of the results of the War of the Austrian Succession was the occupation of Savoy by Spain. Don Felipe became the ruling prince in Chambéry and Mme de Warens lost her pension, which had been coming from Turin. In 1745, after her stepmother died, she undertook several incognito journeys to Switzerland and tried to save at least part of the family property, but her efforts came to nothing. In debt and without any experience she rushed into new business activities. She gave up soap production and turned to mining in Savoy. She succeeded in persuading her friends about future prosperity and they invested in undertakings that were a lost cause.

In 1747 Rousseau's father, Isaac, died at the age of seventy-five (in *Confessions* Rousseau states he was "about sixty years old"). With the help of Gaffecourt, who had become his close friend, Rousseau received 6,000 florins as an inheritance from his mother, the revenue from which was used by Isaac so far. Rousseau sent a small part of this amount to Mme de Warens with the note, "I regret, in my eyes the tears of happy days, when I would lay everything at your feet." He did not tell Mme de Warens anything of the inheritance despite the fact that he wrote to her quite often.

In a letter to Mme de Warens from August 1748 he does not mention money but wrote about his health. It is one of the first written proofs of the character of his illness because he described his symptoms. He wrote he developed "renal colic, fever, burning pain and urinary retention." According to him the illness was caused by a urinary stone, which had descended into his bladder and "can be removed only by an operation," which is out of the question because of his health and financial situation. All he could do was to be patient and resigned, the two means that are always on hand but do not have any healing power. In addition to all the previous problems, he had developed a severe stomachache with incessant vomiting and severe diarrhea, which had exhausted him despite the "thousand worthless cures" he had tried in vain.

Looked at from the medical point of view it has to be said that the self-diagnosis of a urinary stone (similar to the diagnosis of a heart polyp) that was accepted by his biographers without raising any doubts is totally uncertain and unproven. To objectively prove a urinary stone at that time was impossible. It would also have to pass and leave the urinary pathways and bladder after previous fragmentation, a thing that Rousseau has never mentioned, or it would have been discovered during the postmortem after his death, which was not the case. It appears to be far more probable that Rousseau suffered a urinary tract infection as a result of the masturbation practices that were already mentioned. Rousseau must have developed not only an infection of the urethra and prostate (burning, painful urination and urinary retention), but also of the bladder (cystitis), with ascending renal infection (ascending pyelonephritis). The latter causes flank pain similar to that seen in urinary stone disease.

Let us recall the fact that he met Thérèse in the spring of 1745, after his friend Alcuna returned to Spain. The first report of Rousseau's illness appears in the fall of 1745, even if we do not know exactly what kind of illness it was. When he lived outside Paris at Chenonceau, he was healthy and put on weight. As soon as he returned to Paris and lived with Thérèse, he suffered from serious urinary tract infections. His self-diagnosis of "urinary stone" could have been a camouflage as he was intelligent enough to recognize the connection between urethral masturbation and his problems, which must have worsened immediately after these practices.

It is true that he wrote in *Confessions* that he was born with a congenital malformation, which, according to him, had caused a nearly permanent urinary retention in his childhood and that it was only due to the care of his Aunt Suzon that he reached the age of thirty without having felt any consequences of the alleged malformation.

But the first symptoms did not appear until his stay in Venice. He explained the painful urination and flank pain as the result of a tiring journey and the hot weather in Venice. These problems lasted till winter.

What we learn from *Confessions* is medically doubtful. It is difficult to imagine a penis deformity that would lead to urinary retention and could be cured by the "good care" of Aunt Suzon so it would not become manifest until the age of thirty. And how would Rousseau learn of his deformity and of Aunt Suzon's care at all? A congenital deformity is something permanent and any problems that it caused would have had to last for his whole life.

Explanations that his urinary tract infection in Venice was caused by a tiring journey and hot weather are unprofessional. Recurrent urethritis and cystitis improve with warmth as opposed to cold, which leads to their worsening. Painful urination is a symptom that is almost exclusively linked to urethritis and cystitis, and the reference to flank pain in Venice shows that the infection had already ascended to his kidneys.

The fact that Rousseau had no enduring girlfriend in Venice and that the symptoms occurred immediately after his arrival suggest that Rousseau must have performed urethral masturbation on himself (on his way to Paris and when he arrived there) and that these repeated urethral manipulations led to his complaints.

The data in *Confessions* regarding Rousseau's illnesses are also chronologically unreliable. He wrote that he suffered the renal attack on his way to Vincennes where he wanted to visit Diderot in prison. Diderot, however, was imprisoned as late as July 1749, whereas Rousseau described his first renal "colic" in the letter to Mme de Warens that was written in August 1748. Still earlier, on June 30, 1748, he wrote a letter to his friend Altuna in Spain; in this letter he mentioned his illness and urinary retention: *"une colique néphritique, la plus effrayable qu'on jamais sentie."*

This is just one of many contradictions that come to light when *Confessions* is compared with his letters. One can only agree with Cranston who says that the diagnosis of Rousseau's illnesses can be only surmised, but it is very difficult to accept his assumption that, "It seems probable that he had a malformation of the penis which impeded sex life and made him subject to chronic urinary pain, inflammation and infection." Cranston was not a physician and depended on the assertions handed down by Rousseau's biographers and on outdated medical essays (Elosu 1929).

Thérèse did not live with him during his illness. He was staying in the Hôtel du Saint-Esprit in rue Plâtrière, but they were able to meet all the time, which is evidenced by the fact that Thérèse was pregnant again.

The literary work he had to cope with in the Dupin family increased significantly when Montesquieu, Baron de La Brède, who was already a half-blind old man, published his book *De l'Esprit des Lois* in Geneva in October 1748—a book on which he had been working for more than twenty years. Rousseau does not mention this book in his *Confessions*. Mme Dupin and her husband did not agree with Montesquieu and tried to refute his book by publications and counter-arguments, the first version of which appeared promptly and was revised a year later.

The Dupins' criticism actually represented a clash between the bourgeoisie and the aristocratic Montesquieu. He had criticized tax collectors and the financial system, which was defended by Dupin. Montesquieu claimed that all rights were the result of agreement and conventions; he advocated polygamy and did not concede any rights to women. His opponents held the view that there exist objective "natural laws" which give women the same rights as men.

Mme Dupin took part in the ensuing literary polemic, mainly to defend women's rights though she has never been remembered as an author. Rousseau may have agreed with some of the views held by his employers, but on the whole preferred Montesquieu's views. Montesquieu's famous book has survived up to the present (it reached twenty-two editions in a short time) whereas the Dupins' criticisms has sunk into oblivion.

The central theme of the whole book is the author's endeavor to prevent state despotism and to restrict its role. Similarly to Hobbes, Montesquieu defended a pessimistic anthropology and was convinced that those in power would always be tempted to misuse it. They would continue to increase the abuse of power till they reach the limits. Who would think of it: "Even virtue must have a limit." Political freedom is actually a question of legal safeguards. According to his ideas, the nobility should play the role of protector of freedom. One of the postulates of the so-called "English chapter" involved independence; the well-known postulate of division of political authority into legislative, executive, and judicial powers. Another was that everything is connected with everything: the type of state with its size (which was later emphasized by Rousseau), the climatic conditions with morality, the institutions with political freedom.

All of this must have had an enormous influence on Rousseau's political views. At the time when he was employed at the Dupins, and when he found himself "between the front-lines," Rousseau started writing *Discours sur les arts et les sciences*. He wrote in it that "the statesmen of antiquity spoke incessantly of morality and virtue: our statesmen speak of business and finances." From this sentence one can tell that he tacitly agreed with Montesquieu, but of course he still could not afford to show his views openly.

It is interesting that Montesquieu knew the Dupins and they could have invited him to dinner when he was in Paris: Dinners were given once a week by Mme Dupin to honor various prominent personalities. Montesquieu was a valued companion: being a universal personality and excellent speaker he was familiar with all sorts of subjects. He was interested in physics, botany and geology; he studied human behavior, geography and meteorology; he was a winegrower and a pharmacist; and he proposed the study of the sociology of law and history of art.

According to Grimm, the dinners were deliberately given on days when Rousseau was on furlough to make sure that nobody would ask uncalled-for questions about his occupation in the Dupins' house. There is no direct evidence that Rousseau met Montesquieu. It is obvious, however, that he admired his work and that he drew on it as well.

Rousseau must have been important to the Dupins at the time of these literary disputes—so much so that Mme Dupin raised his salary to fifty francs a month and offered him, in the spring 1749, the post of a "companion" to her son, Chenonceaux, who was then nineteen. Rousseau had been employed as his tutor many years previously, but had given up the position because of Chenonceaux's nature. The character of this youth had not improved at all, which explains why Rousseau hesitated to accept the offer. He accepted it in the end mainly because he had no other choice.

The young Chenonceaux married the only daughter of Viscount de Rochechouart-Pointville. It was a bond between aristocracy and rich bourgeoisie. Rousseau was supposed to work as a moral adviser to the newly-married couple, a task which failed completely in the case of Chenonceaux. The latter lost 700,000 livres in one night in a game and the family had to sell Hôtel Lambert to pay his debts. Rousseau's relationship with the young wife was much better, he admired her not only for her beauty but also for her aristocratic origin, and he felt sympathy for her isolation in the Dupins' house, which was caused mainly by her refusal to take part in their social life. In *Confessions* Rousseau recalls with delight how he taught the young lady arithmetic three to four hours daily. But he described his situation as strange in a letter to Mme de Warens. He was doing nothing but had no time for himself, because he had to be the companion of people who were doing nothing.

Rousseau could not complain about lack of work at that time. In addition to his work for the Dupins and the life with Thérèse, he spent many hours with Diderot, Condillac and others who were to become leading philosophers of the Enlightenment. The label "philosopher" has been attached to the name Rousseau, though he was not a philosopher in today's sense of the word. In the eighteenth century philosophers were intellectuals, essayists in the style of Francis Bacon, and not systematic philosophers as were Descartes and Hobbes. Philosophers were men who were looking for a new lifestyle, new values and ideology—who were trying not only to change the world but also to understand it.

A prototype of a philosopher of the eighteenth century was Diderot, who stood ideologically somewhere between Voltaire's deism and Hollbach's atheism. His political views fluctuated between the constitutional liberalism of Montesquieu and the doctrine of Enlightenment despotism propagated by Francis Bacon. A certain turn occurred in his middle age, changing him from a frank and friendly man who was easy to get along with (as opposed to Rousseau), to a person who did not publish and was hiding his best works, such as *Jacques le fatalist, Le Rêve de l'Alembert* and others, which were unknown to his contemporaries. His ambition was to become the Molière of the eighteenth century, in which he did not succeed. Like Voltaire he was proud of his bourgeois origin and was convinced that the theatre must proclaim values of modern bourgeoisie and denounce outdated aristocratic ideas.

Diderot and Rousseau worked together in 1740 and planned to publish a periodical, *Le Persifleur.* Rousseau introduced Diderot to Condillac, through whom Diderot found the publisher for his book *L'Essai sur l'origine des connaissances humaines.* Condillac and Diderot, who were brought up in Jesuit colleges, philosophized together and Rousseau usually did not take part in their disputes. Condillac was the pupil of J. Locke, or the Irish Christian philosopher Berkeley, whereas French Encyclopédistes were looking up to Bacon. But abbé Condillac, who was said to have never officiated at a mass, had never fully identified (similar to Rousseau) with the anticlericalism of the Enlightenment.

The periodical *Le Persifleur,* the first and last copy of which was written in manuscript by Rousseau alone, is interesting in that it provides Rousseau's self-portrait as he saw himself at the age of thirty-five. He sees quite correctly that he had a divided personality, which is typical of masochists, a personality indulging in paradoxes. He described himself in the following way: "Sometimes I am a hard and fierce misanthropist: at other moments I am enraptured by the charm of society and the delights of love. Sometimes I am austere and pious, but soon become a downright libertine . . . In a word, a Proteus, *a chameleon and a woman are less variable creatures than I am . . . It is this very irregularity which forms the basis of my character* . . . I am liable to two main moods which change fairly constantly from week to week and which I call my weekly souls: through the one I am wisely mad, and through the other madly wise" (italics added).

Like Rousseau, Diderot had constant financial difficulties. He married Nanette Champion in 1743, but had a mistress after only two years of marriage—Madeleine de Puisieux. He wrote *Les Bijoux indiscrets* for her, an obscene novelette sold only under the counter. His novel *Pensées philosophique* was published in 1746, but was publicly burned and Diderot was declared a dangerous man in his parish a year later. He was planning to write the greatest monument of the Age of Enlightenment—*Encyclopédie*. The purpose of this work was to realize Bacon's dream of a compendium that would unite all sciences and would show the world in a new form and do away ideologically with traditional philosophy and religion.

The beginnings of the work were modest. The publisher André Le Breton wanted to adapt and bring out a French translation of the book *Cyclopaedia* that was written by Ephraim Chambers in Scotland. Diderot became editor and undertook to change the work into something different from the *Cyclopaedia*, which was an alphabetically arranged collection of information.

Diderot believed in the power of science, that it was able to save mankind. Because his scientific education was not sufficient for such a task, he was looking for an assistant, whom he found in the scientist d'Alembert, a small man with enormous self-discipline.

D'Alembert was four years younger than Diderot and five years younger than Rousseau, but had already gained a distinguished position in the world of science. The history of his life was quite remarkable. He was the illegitimate child of a famous hostess, Mme de Tencin, and her lover Chevalier Destouches. His mother abandoned him in a basket on the steps of the Church of Saint Jean Le Ronde, from which he derived his Christian names—Jean Le Rond. His father sought out the child and gave him the name Daremberg—which he later changed to d'Alembert—found him a foster-mother and provided for his education at a prestigious Jansenist school. D'Alembert was given an annuity of 1,200 livres which made it possible for him to study science and he excelled in mathematics and physics. In 1741, at the age of twenty-four, he became a member of the Academy of Sciences where he wrote *Traité de dynamique*.

D'Alembert became coeditor of *Encyclopédie*—a decisive step ensuring the future success of the work. He had to calm down the impulsive Diderot (but did not always succeed), who used every opportunity to attack the regime. D'Alembert edited all contributions, not only the scientific ones, but also the entries on history, music, literature, law, society and philosophy. Rousseau contributed to *Encyclopédie* all articles pertaining to music, as we learn from his letter sent to Mme de Warens in January 1749. His contributions were corrected by d'Alembert, who was familiar with music, especially its physical aspects (he wrote *Les Élements de musique* in 1752).

Rousseau's life during that time was active and versatile. Besides his work in Dupin's house he worked for *Encyclopédie*, continued his contacts with Thérèse, and, following the advice of Father Castel, started to seek the company of society ladies again—he became *salonard*.

At the age of thirty-five he met a woman who was to play an important role in his later life, Mme d'Épinay. Similar to Mme Dupin, she was the wife of a financier. She was not as rich, virtuous and beautiful as Mme Dupin, but she was young and had an aristocratic pedigree, which Rousseau valued. Her maiden name was Louise-Florence-Pétronille de Tardieu d'Esclavelles and she married the tax collector Denis-Joseph Lalive d'Épinay at the age of nineteen. It was a bond between impoverished nobility and rich bourgeoisie.

Rousseau characterized Mme d'Épinay as "shallow and simple." It is not uninteresting that her first infidelity was an affair with Rousseau's employer and friend Dupin de Francueil, the stepson of Mme Dupin. With the latter she had her second daughter Pauline, who later became Mme de Belzunce. (Her first daughter, whom she had with her husband, died.) Her husband kept his own mistress—the dancer, Mlle Rose—and visited brothels where he contracted syphilis. He infected his wife who passed the infection on to de Francueil.

Mme d'Épinay's salon attracted writers and artists and she herself had literary ambitions. She wrote *Histoire de Mme de Montbrillant*, an autobiographical work in which she gave her friends various pseudonyms. Francueil was given the nickname "Formeuse" and Rousseau was called "René." We learn from her what she thought about Rousseau and his character because Mme d'Épinay was, unlike Mme Dupin, a prolific writer. She described René as a man with dark complexion and lively eyes that brightened up his face. "When you are in his company and listen to him, he looks nice, but when you recall him later you see an awful man . . . he is not polite, or rather he *does not appear* to be polite. He is a man *who acts the role of an unworldly man, but is in fact very cunning*" (italics added).

One could agree with her observation that Rousseau was a cunning and artful actor. Rousseau's description originated at the Château La Chevrette, during the winter of 1747–1748, after her first (legitimate) daughter had died.

At this unhappy time she saw in Rousseau a beloved "bear," who kept her company. The château, situated twenty-five kilometers from Paris at the edge of the Montmorency forest, did not belong to d'Épinay's family. Its owner was her husband's brother, M. Lalive de Bellegarde, whose adolescent and plain daughter Elisabeth—at the age of seventeen she was plagued by acne—was later to blossom out into the magnificent Comtesse d'Houdetot with whom Rousseau fell passionately in love.

Mme d'Épinay and the people around her staged an amateur play in the château's orangery in the summer of 1748; the play, *L'Engagement téméraire*, was written by Rousseau for the Dupin family during his stay at Chenonceau. Rousseau was playing the role of the servant Carlin and though he had been studying it incessantly for six months in a row he had to have a prompter during the whole performance.

At the Château Fontenay-sur-Pois, Rousseau met two royal suite members, Christophe Klüpfel (the founder of the "Gotha Almanac") and an impoverished German baron, Melchior Grimm, who was looking for a permanent occupation in France and soon became Count von Friesen's companion. In several ways Grimm and Rousseau were similar to each other. Both were foreigners living in Paris and both were seeking fame. They both loved music and often played and sang together.

The company of his German friends enabled Rousseau to get into the bed (for the last time in his life) of a *fille de joie*, Klüpfel's mistress. Klüpfel offered the latter to both companions when they joshed him. Whereas Rousseau obviously made use of the invitation, Grimm swore he had never touched the girl. Rousseau insists he felt deeply ashamed and he made use of these feelings later when he wrote *La Nouvelle Héloïse*—in it, St-Preux is ashamed of having got drunk. Rousseau told Thérèse of his experience before Grimm could do the same. Rousseau says that Thérèse reproached him only "slightly and sweetly," but without any signs of anger or umbrage. Obviously she was confident about her position in her relationship with Rousseau: how could there be another woman who would be so "sweet and docile" as she and who else would know what type of love Rousseau needed?

Many people around Thérèse were convinced that she was not faithful. Rousseau says nothing about the it. He might well have known, but we cannot be sure. Should this have been the case, it is very likely that Rousseau was not the father of all five children Thérèse gave birth to.

Provocation of the *First Discourse*—Fame, Reform and Illness

The political situation in Paris got worse in 1749. The wars of Austrian Succession ended in a peace that was not advantageous for Louis XV. France had lost its Flemish provinces and taxes were increased. The political situation radicalized and the government tightened censorship. Even the scientist Buffon was forced to declare he had never said anything against the Catholic orthodoxy.

On July 23, 1749 Diderot was imprisoned and his household was searched. He must have been informed about his imprisonment because the police sent in to secure everything that was against "religion, state, or morality" found nothing. He had to swear that he had not written some of his books and was imprisoned in the tower of Château Vincennes located ten kilometers outside of Paris. Rousseau says he wrote a letter to Mme de Pompadour in which he demanded that Diderot be set free, otherwise he wished to be imprisoned with his friend. He remarks in *Confessions*, however, that he did not receive any reply to his letter, since it was "injudicious" and could not achieve any result.

Diderot's imprisonment was relaxed after a month. He was transferred from a prison cell to a room in the château and was allowed to walk in the château gardens; it was even allowed that his wife could live with him. This change may have been the result of a letter written to the warden of Château Vincennes, Marquis Chatelet, by his cousin, Mme de Chatelet, Voltaire's mistress. Count d'Argerson, who had signed the arrest warrant and also had anticlerical and liberal views, did not want to be looked upon as a persecutor of philosophers. The well-known prisoner was also given the privilege of receiving visitors.

On August 25, 1749, on a hot summer day, Rousseau set off on foot to visit his friend for the first time. He described one of these journeys in *Confessions* in detail and everyone who has written about Rousseau has felt obliged to repeat his description and attach comments to it. According to Rousseau he had a "revelation" on one of these journeys to Vincennes (although not on the first) that induced a change in his life and led to what he described as his "reform," or "conversion."

It is necessary to point out that Rousseau's "reform" and "revelation" were described and depicted several years after the fact, in his letters to Malesherb, at a time when—contrary to all expectations—his *First Discourse* had become a great success. Rousseau decided to change his way of life, and to enhance it, based on this success. The circumstances themselves, under which the first discourse was written, were obviously quite simple and its success a mere coincidence.

Rousseau wrote that he set out from Paris on foot and marched fast. The trees on the side of the road were pruned and did not provide any shade. Owing to the heat and fatigue Rousseau was so exhausted that he had to rest along the way.

He found Diderot in the company of d'Alembert and a priest. They embraced each other, moved to tears, and Rousseau saw the "terrible" changes left behind by the imprisonment in the prison cell, which had now been exchanged for a more convenient accommodation in the château. (According to Diderot's daughter he was even asked to the table of the château's warden.) As Rousseau was Diderot's closest friend and could offer him the best comfort of all, he visited him at least every other day, either alone or with his wife, and spent the afternoons with him.

During one of these journeys to Vincennes (in October) Rousseau had, according to his own words, a vision which could be compared to the revelation Saint Paul had on the way to Damascus. On the way he read *Mercure de France* from which he learned that the Academy in Dijon was advertising a prize for an essay entitled "Has the progress of the sciences and arts done more to corrupt morals or improve them?" The moment he read these lines Rousseau became "another man and beheld another universe." He saw in a flash of inspiration that the progress had not in the least improved the morals, but on the contrary had worsened them disastrously.

He described his revelation in greater detail, and much more eloquently, in a letter written to Malesherb in 1762 (at a time when he was already famous and could properly embellish the revelation on which his popularity was based). The newspaper advertisement had led to a sudden inspiration, "a thousand lights illumined his mind, and a multitude of beautiful thoughts that appeared to him dazzled him and put him in indescribable confusion." He felt dizzy as if he had been poisoned and his heart was pounding. He could not breathe or walk—he sank in "the throes of death" under a tree where he stayed on the ground for half an hour. His clothes were wet with tears he had shed, though he was not aware he had been weeping. If he had been able to write down everything he felt and saw he would have been able to pinpoint the contradictions of the social system, he would have been able to show the abuse of institutions and the fact that *man was good by nature but has been corrupted by these very institutions.*

It is necessary to say here that the view of the innate goodness of man was the predominant view of the eighteenth century and by no means the original thought of Rousseau. These thoughts appear in all three of his fundamental works, which are inseparable and form a unity: discourses on arts and sciences, upon the origin of inequality, and on education (*Émile*). It is remarkable that in this letter, written in 1762, Rousseau does not mention his other works, *Du Contract social* and *La Nouvelle Héloïse* since by this time (1762) these books had already been written. The letter to Malesherb was written at a time when Rousseau was already well known as a moralist. In other words when his decision in favor of this view had already been made, and Rousseau lived up to it with an obstinacy of his own.

It is known that Rousseau delighted in exaggerations and dramatic descriptions in his letters and they did not necessarily always correspond to the truth. It was in his interest to depict his revelation-conversion, or "reform," in the most dramatic style, because in doing so he enhanced its mysterious nature and credibility as heavenly revelation. Let us recall that Rousseau regarded himself as a sort of a "prophet." Rousseau as chess player and author of theatre plays as well as writer of impassioned phrases knew all this very well. Returning to Rousseau's own words in *Confessions* we read that when he arrived in Vincennes he was very upset, almost in a delirium. "The moment I read this I beheld another universe and became another man. Though I can vividly remember the effects of these lines, I have lost the details in the moment I have described them in one of my four letters to Malersherb."

Diderot listened to him and encouraged him to write down his views and take part in the contest. In his memoirs Diderot wrote that Rousseau came to him and simply sought his advice on what view he should take. Diderot advised him to approach the essay in a way different from others, and Rousseau agreed. According to other sources Diderot gave Rousseau the advice to express a pessimistic view because most contenders would defend the optimistic opinion of the day and his original opinion would receive the highest assessment.

Diderot was well aware that this view was contradictory to the entire ethos of the Enlightenment, which was also his own, but perhaps he assumed that everything was just a temporary chapter in his friend's life, and would disappear after the literary contest was over. He was a tolerant man and regarded the whole affair as an amusing paradox that could help Rousseau to achieve popularity. It is therefore very likely that Rousseau's "revelation" and "conversion" were not as unexpected and dramatic as Rousseau wants us to believe in his description, a version that was written more than ten years later.

Everything was rather a gradual process. It could have been estimated from the entire course of his life and the experiences of his childhood and adolescence that Rousseau would arrive at this view, even though he did not anticipate at first that his life would be influenced by it to such an extent. He *had* to become a social critic because he had never been able to understand social events, had never been initiated in them, and above all, had never had any material benefit from social progress. In spite of his Calvinist origins he was lacking the Calvinist-Protestant work ethic that forced its supporters to work in order to achieve material success in society. He also lacked any systematic scientific education and self-discipline. It is only human that something that people do not understand, or are unable to cope with, becomes the object of their criticism. But as Rousseau yearned for success and recognition he was able to discern that he would become famous when he took views that were extremely different from those held by the French society of that time, which saw salvation and future religion in science.

Rousseau's masochism may have played a role as well because it was not limited to physical masochism. He was able to imagine that when he wrote something that would shock all of society he would be punished and persecuted—he would become the martyr of his prophetic visions.

According to his own account, Rousseau had formed the thoughts in his mind overnight and dictated them in the morning, still in bed, to Thérèse's mother, Mme Levasseur, using her as a secretary. He showed the completed work to Diderot who was satisfied and recommended only minor changes. Rousseau himself did not think much of the essay that was to establish his fame. He said "it lacked logic and inner order." He considered his first essay to be the weakest of all his works as far as the logical skeleton was concerned, and the poorest stylistically. His *First Discourse*, similar to his other works, was not based on logical or scientific analysis. Rousseau had never been able to work systematically and this type of work went against his grain. He reveals the way in which he created most of his works in the seventh promenade in *Rêveries*:

Sometimes I thought deeply, but seldom with pleasure and almost entirely with reluctance and under pressure. I enjoyed dreaming and dreaming was always setting me free. Thinking made me tired and sad. I have always considered thinking a tiring and unattractive occupation. My dreams have sometimes resulted in reasoning. More often, however, my thinking resulted in dreaming. And in this losing of my self my soul wanders and flies on the wings of fantasy in space and this enchanting pleasure surpasses all other.

Dreams and fantasies made up for rational thinking. Thought caused pain.

Rousseau decided to take part in the contest in Dijon in summer 1749. The jury of the Dijon Academy announced in July 1750 that the winner was the essay with the quotation of Horace: "*Decipimur specie recti,*" which was Rousseau's work. The jury consisted of two clerics, two officials and three lawyers. The Dijon Academy was a newly founded provincial bourgeois institution.

Rousseau did not receive the prize personally in Dijon. The gold medal, worth three hundred livres, was received in Rousseau's place by Jacques Tardy in a ceremony at which Rousseau's essay was read aloud in public. Rousseau contented himself with a letter, which he sent to the jury members, and in which he congratulated them on their courage to award an author whose views were opposite to the academy's interests.

Rousseau knew well that his eccentric views were untenable and to moderate his nonsensical argumentation he added an appendage, which actually ran counter to his own arguments: science, in spite of all dangers, can be an excellent thing for a man of excellent spirit and kings should not despise the advice given to them by philosophers. Such advice has no meaning for simple people who should be satisfied with their ignorance. This is an obvious contradiction that allows all interpretations and is impenetrable to any criticism.

Diderot helped Rousseau prepare the discourse for the press and did not pay much attention to its contents since it was the opposite of all postulates of the Enlightenment. Diderot replied to Helvétius's opinion that Rousseau had become a writer by chance saying, "Rousseau did what he did because he was

Rousseau." He himself would have never spent several months supporting a weak paradox by sophistic arguments dressed up in rhetorical elegance as did Rousseau, who had in the end spun a whole philosophical system out of an intellectual game. In this essay, Rousseau laid the foundation stone of his "philosophy," i.e. the thought that man is good by nature (a common view of the eighteenth century) but has been corrupted by society. People who form society are bad.

His thought has a subjective background originating in his personality: Rousseau as a person, who has grown up in considerable isolation from society, is essentially good and becomes gradually corrupted by life in society. The logical conclusion is his later flight from society and his inclination toward life in seclusion.

It is most likely that the essay would have fallen into oblivion if it had not been for his friend, Guillaume Raynal, who became the new editor of *Mercure de France*, the most popular literary newspaper in the kingdom. Guillaume Raynal was a former Jesuit clergyman who had resigned from his duties as a priest in 1747 and pursued a career in literary newspapers. He probably realized that Rousseau's views were controversial to such a degree that they would evoke wide criticism and thereby support the circulation of the paper. The abbé asked Rousseau to write a contribution for his paper in July 1750. Rousseau replied, with artful timidity, that he hurried to return back to being an unknown person, which was more suitable for his "talent and character," and he did not want to attain the fame of an average author. Raynal published the letter together with several of his verses in September. A short summary of the discourse appeared in November, written probably by Raynal himself, and parts of the discourse were published in January 1751.

At that time Rousseau was ill and had to remain in bed, and it was Diderot who informed him of the immense success caused by his work. The whole text was then published as a pamphlet, thanks to Diderot, by the Parisian bookseller, Jacques Pissot, without official permission. Diderot and Rousseau were counting on their friendship with Malesherb, who was appointed a censor by his father, Lamoignon, the new chancellor of France. The whole edition was sold out quickly and in the meantime the articles in *Mercure* continued to remind its readers of Rousseau's work: some critical comments were published in June 1751, most likely written by Raynal, together with Rousseau's reaction.

A more extensive review of the work was published in September, partly written by the Polish king Stanislaw I and the Duke of Lorraine (father-in-law of the king of France). Charles Bordes from Lyon published further criticisms, as did abbé Gautier and Claude-Nikolas Lecat, a member of the Dijon Academy who voted against the prize being awarded to Rousseau. Rousseau's discourse occupied the front pages in *Mercure* all year long and each article increased Rousseau's popularity and the general interest in the pamphlet.

The criticism revived Rousseau in a positive sense. He abandoned some of his untenable formulations but remained faithful to the main thesis. It was held against him that he wanted to destroy cultural institutions, burn libraries and introduce rustic barbarism (Gautier). He was even asked whether music was also one of the arts to be forbidden, when he had written many contributions about music to *Encyclopédie* (Lecat).

Rousseau's opinions were very changeable. At first he considered as rightful only those wars that were fought for freedom whereas later he was to condemn all wars, including civil wars, which he feared similar to Hobbes, provided that the existing social order was peaceful on the outside and had moral values which contributed to peace inside society. Without freedom no real peace can exist. Science itself is not bad but is unsuitable for human nature, because man is subject to very powerful passions that lead him to abuse science. According to Rousseau *science and art are the consequences of wealth and not its causes*. This argumentation prepared the ground for his assertion that all wealth meant moral corruption. The primary source of evil, however, is inequality. Inequality has made possible the accumulation of wealth. Wherever men are equal, there will be neither rich nor poor. Wealth inevitably leads to luxury and idleness. Wealth enabled the development of the arts. Idleness enabled the development of science.

It is not necessary to prove here that these thoughts are untrue. Rousseau has developed a speculative anthropology, which runs counter to all empirical knowledge. His philosophy is deeply pessimistic. Sinners cannot be reformed and it is not possible to return to original innocence and equality once these have been abandoned. This is why he does not intend to abolish sciences and arts and why these are to be preserved. "Do not assume that we should burn libraries and abolish universities and academies. We would throw Europe into barbarism and would not gain any moral profit," he warns King Stanislaw.

Asked if it is not a paradox to assume that the sciences, which had corrupted humanity, are now to help alleviate the evil they had caused, Rousseau answered that he preferred to be a man of paradoxes than a man with prejudices. His views, modified by various interpretations, have become the ideology of the French Revolution, National Socialism and Communism. Rousseau's pessimism was, however, always replaced by the optimism of the future saviors of humanity. When he was unable to defend himself against his critics he simply declared that they did not understand him. It was not from the original discourse itself but from the ensuing criticism and his answers to it that Rousseau's "philosophical" system developed.

In 1751 Rousseau became a literary celebrity. To enhance his popularity and to persuade others that he himself was convinced of his views he started playing the role of a simple, unconventional person. To literary provocation he added provocative behavior unusual for his time, which had the effect of enhancing the general interest in him. He gave up his well-paying job as a cashier at his friend Francueil's, and officially became a mere note copyist working for a minimum wage of a few sous. He gave up all luxury. The most difficult task, to give up his luxury clothes, was made for him—his thirty-two shirts were stolen. His wigs were simple and poorly combed, he did not shave and his behavior in society was more impertinent than before.

> My first publication led me on unsuspected paths to a new spiritual world . . . I was really transformed. All my friends and people around me did not recognize me anymore. I stopped being that shy, embarrassed and humble person . . . Daring, proud, undaunted, I showed my firm certainty everywhere . . . What a transformation! All of Paris echoed my bitter and biting sarcastic remarks—in a sense I stopped being myself.

> Precipitated against my will into the world without possessing its manners, and in no state to learn them or to conform to them, I decided to adopt manners of my own which would excuse me from necessity. Since my foolish and tiresome silence, which I could not overcome, arose from my fear of making social blunders I elected, in order to give myself courage, to trample all courtesies underfoot. I became cynical and sarcastic out of awkwardness, and

affected to despise the manners I did not know how to practice. It is true that, to harmonize this rudeness with my new principles, I embodied it in my mind until it assumed the shape of dauntless virtue." (*Confessions*, 343–344)

This entire behavior was met with enthusiastic tolerance. Though he wrote that women were vying with each other to lure him into their salons, which he was tired of, the truth is that he did not live in seclusion and was in fact indulging in his successes in society. His paradoxical views took him into paradoxical situations. He spoke out against the arts but wrote a successful opera. He experienced the urge to live up to the ideals expressed in the first essay immediately after he received the award and saw the glory it brought to him. He decided to earn his living as a note copyist and left a well-paying job. He excused the fact that his work was not of the best quality by his ill health, by his busy literary activity (polemics about the discourse) and the social life that, as he says, was forced on him.

The success of his *First Discourse* resulted in the disappearance of his shyness and timidity. His self-esteem increased and he spoke with great self-confidence in public. He acted misanthropic and cynical only in the salons. To play this role in the circle of his friends who knew him well was more difficult, and as he says in *Confessions*, he was not very good at it.

Though the winter of 1749–1750 was not tough, Rousseau was ill again, as was usual at this time of the year. He complains in a letter to Mme de Warens that he had fever and urinary attacks and said of his improvements that they "were mere pauses between bouts of illness." His description is correct: it is known that urethritis, cystitis, and prostatitis become worse at lower temperatures and their course is characterized by frequent remissions.

He wrote that he lives alone and his thoughts are all the time with his dearest Maman. That was simply not true for he had rented a flat on the fourth floor in the Hôtel de Languedoc (in rue Grenelle-Saint Honoré) and he and Thérèse lived in it "peace-lovingly and comfortably" for seven years. This idyll was spoiled only by Thérèse's family, especially by her mother, Mme Levasseur, who was a prototype of a bad mother-in-law, sticking her nose into everything and spreading malicious gossip about Rousseau's life with Thérèse. She even begged people for gifts for them. Rousseau found her unbearable though she was sometimes quite useful. She had a better education than

Thérèse and was able to write Rousseau's thoughts from dictation.

No wonder Thérèse became pregnant for the third time in these favorable circumstances, putting Rousseau in a difficult dilemma. He had proposed certain principles in his essay and was now in a situation where he would betray them. In his heart he felt love for the child to be born, but reason advised him to act otherwise. As before, he also sent this child to a foundling home and, as usual, found a noble justification for it: he saw himself as a citizen in Plato's Republic where all children were handed over to the state and did not know their fathers.

But his situation had changed. Formerly, as an unknown man, he could send his children to the foundling home but now he was becoming well known as a person and the public watched his private life and compared it with his writings. Now he was in a position where it was not enough to justify his controversial acts to himself—he had to find a justification for others as well. The private life of a celebrity is in the focus of attention of the general public and there is no way around it. Suddenly it was interesting to know that a known moralist had abandoned his children and sent them to a foundling home.

Mme de Francueil touched on this delicate issue and the letter she wrote was soon known all over Paris because at that time the letters were read aloud in salons. Rousseau replied to her accusations by a lengthy letter in April 1751, and certain parts of it are worth quoting:

> Yes, Madame, I have sent my children to the foundling home. I have entrusted them into the care of a charity established for this purpose. With respect to my poverty and bad health, which have robbed me of the pleasure to realize my duty, I should be commiserated with for my misfortune, and not accused of crime. I owe my children care for their life and I have arranged for a life that is better for them, or at least more secure, than the life I could offer them myself. This is my first reason. There was also the duty to avert shame from their mother. You know my situation: I earn my living with great difficulty, from one day to the next. How could I earn for a whole family? And since I have become a writer, how could I attain peace of mind, so necessary for

profitable work, in an attic room disturbed by household chores and noisy children? Excuse me, Madame, but Nature wants us to have children because Nature provides enough for everybody: it is the way of life of the rich, it is your way of life that robs my children of bread. Nature, too, demands that we provide security for our children: and that is precisely what I did. If there had not been a foundling home I would have fulfilled my duty and would prefer to suffer from hunger till my death than to leave them without food."

We do not know whether Rousseau ever posted this letter. Its existence is evidenced only by a coded (!) copy that was found in his documents.

The letter illustrates Rousseau's eloquence and cruelty. He completely overlooks the fact that foundling homes of that time were by no means ideal organizations in which to raise or educate children. In 1741, 68 percent of children received into these homes died in their childhood.

Mme de Francueil's granddaughter, George Sand, remembered that her grandmother was asking herself whether Rousseau was able to have children at all. Mme d'Houdetot said that Rousseau did not believe himself to be the father of all his children. Determination of paternity was not practicable. It is probable that only Thérèse's first children were his and that later, when he was ill and unable to have sexual intercourse with her, other children were born who were not his.

Rousseau never stopped being haunted by remorse. Ten years later, on June 12, 1761, he wrote a letter to the Duchess of Luxembourg and tried to trace the fate of his first child, born sometime in the winter of 1746–1747. According to *Confessions*, the duchess wanted to adopt his child and asked him to describe the sign with which the child was then marked. Rousseau did so but the duchess informed him the search was extremely difficult and that her steward, La Roche, had been unable to find out anything about the fate of the firstborn daughter. Here we are able to learn the gender of Rousseau's first child for the first time because *Confessions* contains no information in this respect. After the search had ended unsuccessfully Rousseau wrote another letter and asked the duchess to stop the search and not to undertake any further steps. At the time he was very ill and assumed he would soon die.

He wrote in Book Twelve of *Confessions* (1762–1765) that even though the decision regarding his children seemed correct to him, it "had not always left me easy in my mind. While thinking about my Treatise upon Education, I felt that I had neglected some duties from which nothing could excuse me. So strong did my remorse finally grow that it almost drew from me a public confession of my fault at the beginning of *Émile*."

This is the paragraph to which Rousseau referred:

> When a man fathers and brings up his child he fulfills thereby only a third of his duties . . . the man who cannot fulfill the duties of a father has no right to be a father. Poverty, work or human considerations cannot set him free from the duty to earn a living and bring up his children. Reader, you can believe me indeed: Who has a heart and neglects these holy duties, for him I prophesy that he will shed bitter tears for his guilt and will not find solace in all eternity.

This paragraph was part of the original manuscript of *Émile* (the so-called Favre manuscript) but was added only in the final version, demonstrating that it was inserted later during Rousseau's work on *Émile*. It thus appears that it was not the regret over the abandoning of his children that led Rousseau to write *Émile*. On the contrary, it must have been during his work on *Émile* that he came to realize his fault. As late as 1768 he wrote in his letter to Thérèse: "We both have to bewail and repent our misdemeanors." It is not clear that this sentence can be associated with the abandonment of their children to a foundling home. Thérèse had always opposed this step, she was forced to it, and it is hardly acceptable to refer to her as a wrongdoer. It is also possible that this inconspicuous sentence is a tactful allusion to their sexual practices that cost Rousseau his health.

The first volume of *Encyclopédie* was published at the end of June 1751. This work was based on the idea of an interdisciplinary approach to science with special attention to applied sciences in the spirit of Bacon's empiricism. At the same time, the work was meant to remove the "rubbish" which meant traditional religious, moral and philosophical views. Diderot's *Encyclopédie* had the ambition to become the new materialistic bible of progress. Originally planned as a work of eight volumes, it later spread to seventeen volumes of text, eleven volumes of illustration and seven volumes of supplementary material.

The work has thus become the monument of the French Enlightenment. Rousseau contributed to the *Encyclopédie* mainly articles on music and spoke of Diderot as of a virtuous philosopher whose friendship "creates the glory and happiness of my life." Rousseau obviously had no problems cooperating with the Encyclopédistes, despite the fact that their ideals did not correspond to his "philosophy."

He was assigned articles on other topics as well. He wrote the contribution *"Économie politique,"* in which the signs of his cooperation with Diderot cannot be overlooked. Rousseau knew very little about political economy, mostly from books. Accordingly, he soon got into contradictions and inconsistencies. On the one hand, he follows Locke and his views on property rights: "We must bear in mind that the social contract is based on property and the first premise is the assurance that everyone can derive pleasure from what belongs to him."

In fact Rousseau could not have agreed with Locke because, according to him, the natural right to own property and the property itself were sources of evil. Rousseau saw Locke's concept of a social contract as a mutually beneficial arrangement to be basically a fraudulent arrangement, in which the rich perpetuate their rights and property. His contribution is totally inconsistent, because he combines liberal economics with his subjective view that the so-called "natural right" to property is an injustice that has been made into law.

Encyclopédie was tremendously successful and all contributors to it became more or less known in Paris. Rousseau was known as a person who was contributing to the progressive *Encyclopédie* and writing about science and arts, but had also published an essay in which he condemned the same sciences and arts.

His paradoxical views evoked interest and everybody wanted to get to know the eccentric person who defended them. His controversial views were entertaining and what was entertaining was also permissible and acceptable in Parisian salons. Conversation in these salons had to observe the rules of politeness and permissiveness, but otherwise one could discuss anything, provided the discussion was witty. At that time it was still possible to contest the traditional religious and moral ideas. Voltaire demonstrated this style and declared that it was obligatory. Following the publication of *Encyclopédie* the intellectuals or *philosophes,* as they called themselves, became sought after in Parisian salons.

Formerly one could become a member of any of the salons only by virtue of his aristocratic origin, or when he had attained a high status in society. Now, as Voltaire wrote in his contribution to *Encyclopédie,* "writers have become a necessary part of refined society." Philosophes came from all strata of society: Diderot, Raynal, Marmontel, Morellet and Duclos were of middle-class origin, Saint-Lambert, LeRoy, Helvétius and Chastellux belonged to old aristocracy, Holbach to new aristocracy and Grimm to German aristocracy. Condillac and Buffon belonged to *nobles de robe.* In their political views the philosophers concurred in condemning the *ancient régime* and demanding freedom, but their opinions regarding the form of "liberty" varied. Gradually two movements crystallized. The first was based on the teachings of Locke and Montesquie and tried to reform France in accordance with the English example. Its advocates wished for a parliamentary monarchy with guaranteed individual and property rights. The second movement espoused the views of Bacon and Voltaire. The concept of freedom was combined with the idea of Enlightenment despotism, in which the absolutist institution of the Bourbon monarchy would have to accept a planned society governed by scholarly experts.

One of the most extreme proponents of this movement was Holbach. Paul-Henri Dietrich Baron d'Holbach (1723–1789) was the most influential philosopher of the Enlightenment. He was a German who had studied in Holland. In 1749, at the age of twenty-six, he moved from Holland to Paris. Because of his studies he was even more important for Diderot than d'Alembert. He was an expert on the applied sciences, which corresponded to Bacon's notion of mastering nature by technology.

Holbach contributed more than four hundred articles to *Encyclopédie.* He did not deny his German origin. He had the German propensity to take things to an extreme. He developed Diderot and Voltaire's deism to uncompromising atheism. He regarded all knowledge that was not based on positive scientific evidence to be nonsense. In politics, he went beyond the limits of liberalism and arrived at political radicalism, which claimed that the sciences could save society solely on the assumption that they had the necessary power. His views, partly shared by Diderot, were the most influential politico-philosophical movement of the French Enlightenment. Rousseau did not espouse any of these movements but tried instead to create his own philosophical system.

It would seem that these extreme political views could become dangerous and speed up the advent of a revolution, but the Bourbon government did not perceive such danger. Bacon's ideas in particular were not entirely unwelcome—the monarchy considered itself to be enlightened already. The king saw in Montesquieu just a member of the old aristocracy who was trying to recover old privileges. Though the attacks of the philosophes on the Church were formally rejected, the establishment did not make many efforts to disguise their half-heartedness.

In the seventeenth century the Bourbons had needed the Church because it helped them to undermine the influence of aristocracy. Now the Church and its influence could be disposed of as it had already fulfilled its historical mission. As a result the philosophes were persecuted only rarely and when imprisoned, as happened to Voltaire, Diderot and Marmotel, it was never for long and their imprisonment was never severe. Also, Rousseau was later forced to leave Paris and he went into exile, but the decision was not made in Versailles but by the parlement of Paris. Most authors contributing to *Encyclopédie* were soon assimilated by the state and appointed to various positions in the Academy and state institutions. From those positions they determined the cultural life in France between 1750 and the French Revolution.

Meanwhile Rousseau's popularity was steadily rising and he was invited to most of the salons. Women employed various tricks to get him to accept their invitations. His household was overwhelmed by visits. Rousseau took it into his head that he would never accept gifts. These views, however, were not shared by his mother-in-law and Thérèse, who accepted the gifts willingly and secretly.

Rousseau was again in a situation that caused him inner conflict: according to his teaching, he should desert society and live in seclusion. But instead he was accepting invitations in real life and continued, through his letters, to maintain contacts with influential friends.

The society around him did not mind the fact that Rousseau was not behaving in compliance with the etiquette of the time. It only further enhanced his desirability and his reputation as a misanthrope.

In spite of all of his fame Rousseau's financial situation remained bad. From time to time he received some money from the editor of *Mercure de France*. But he was paid nothing for the publication of his discourse in book form. It has already been mentioned he had the offer of a well-paying job of cashier made by his friend Francueil. He could have had a secure position without financial worries.

We know that Rousseau was pursuing only fame in Paris. He wanted to donate any wealth that he might possibly gain to Mme de Warens. When Mme de Créqui congratulated him on his position and happiness, Rousseau's answer was characteristic: *"I have never felt as bad as now, when I became rich"* (italics added). He soon abandoned the well-paying job. When he was in the office with his friend Francueil he was able to work, but as soon as he was alone and the burden of responsibility weighed on him, the work had became unbearable. (Masochists are unable to bear the burden of responsibility and feel better in subordinate positions.)

His animosity toward wealthy people grew. It is interesting that he tolerated the wealth of hereditary aristocracy and his strongest criticism was aimed at the newly rich bourgeoisie, such as the Dupin family or Voltaire. While he was employed, he visited only the salon of Mme d'Épinay, who was Francueil's mistress, and the salon of young Baron d'Holbach. Rousseau did not like him (he referred to him as the son of a parvenu) and ignored his invitations for a long time—he even went so far as to let Holbach know his reason: "You are too rich."

In the summer of 1751 he fell ill again and had to stay in bed. Mme Dupin sent for the surgeon Morand, who caused him "unimaginable pain" but could not help him and referred him to another surgeon, Jacques Daran. This doctor introduced flexible wax catheters into his urethra and told Mme Dupin that Rousseau would not survive six months. Rousseau learned about this prognosis and decided "to spend the little time I had still to live in independence and poverty." He took to the flexible urethral wax probes of doctor Daran (as an aid to urethral catheterization and perhaps as a means of masturbation), so much so that he ordered a large amount of the catheters though he knew of the doctor's prognosis. He paid fifty louisidors for them and used them often in the next eight to ten years (*Confessions*, Book Eight, 1749–1756).

Relating to this time, Rousseau offers his own description of the illness, which is very interesting from a medical point of view—he explains that his illness was caused by a congenital defect of his urinary bladder:

> I have mentioned in my first part that I was almost born
> dead. A defect in the formation of my bladder caused me,
> during my early years, an almost continuous retention of
> urine, and my Aunt Suzon, who looked after me, had

incredible difficulty in keeping me alive . . . My health grew so much stronger during my youth that except for the attacks of languor, which I have described, and the frequent necessity of making water, which the slightest heating of the blood always rendered an uncomfortable duty, I reached the age of thirty almost without feeling my early infirmity at all. *The first touch of it I had was on my arrival in Venice.* The fatigue of the journey and the terrible heat I had endured raised the temperature of my urine and gave me pain in the kidneys, which did not leave me till winter set in (*Conf.*, 336–337, italics added).

What Rousseau wrote here is untenable from a medical point of view and apparently is completely made-up. It is surprising that this has been taken at its face value for so long. A congenital urinary bladder defect would have caused manifestly *permanent* symptoms and Aunt Suzon would not be able to save him. There must have been other reasons for Rousseau to employ this argumentation and it is highly probable that he wanted to hide something.

In 1763, when writing his last will, Rousseau described his urinary complaints precisely. The description suggests that he suffered from recurrent cystitis, urethritis and prostatitis. According to Rousseau, his illness was chronic. He wrote that he had never been able to pass water through a fully opened urinary canal—it was always more or less blocked and caused him permanent pain. A complete urinary retention, however, had never occurred. The most plausible cause of these well-described symptoms of recurrent inflammations was the practice of urethral masturbation that was probably performed by Thérèse.

Another possibility that cannot be ruled out is that he was infected by venereal disease by Thérèse who became infected during her amorous escapades. Rousseau kept assuring the people around him—including his doctors—that the cause of his illness could not be a sexually transmitted disease. It is worth mentioning that Rousseau decided to live with Thérèse permanently only after he received the award for his *First Discourse.* Up to that time she was his *petite amie* and he visited her only from time to time. She could have had other lovers and Rousseau did not have to know about them. The doctors did not believe his assurances (that he did not get infected by venereal disease) and so Rousseau stopped visiting them.

Duclos introduced Rousseau to the salon of Mme de Graffigny, who had literary ambitions as well, and this is where Rousseau met Voltaire. We have no details about the encounter of those two men. Voltaire probably assured Rousseau of his friendship, which did not prevent him from speaking of him with derision. For Voltaire, Rousseau's views were unacceptable and absurd. In this sunny period of his life Rousseau was also visited by his friends from Geneva who lived in Paris: François Mussard, Isaac-Ami Marcet and Toussaint-Pierre Lenieps. Memories of his native Geneva filled Rousseau with nostalgia even at this time of fame and glory.

It was probably at this time that he wrote the relatively unknown and never completed essay *Discours sur les richesses*, that was published in 1853 (the manuscript is part of the depository of the library in Neuchâtel). Rousseau does not recommend getting rich to anyone, not even to the poor man, Chrysophile, (who obviously is Rousseau himself), even if he wanted the wealth to do good for other people. A nouveau riche views things in a new light. In getting rich one has to abandon ethical ideals to make a profit and thus cannot remain honest.

He succeeded in persuading himself that even virtuous intentions about what will happen with wealth are too weak to withstand the sinister power of money. This is why he made a virtue out of poverty. Psychologically it is again a noble rationalization justifying the fact that he remains poor despite his having had several jobs where he could have at least achieved a good income. But this would have required submitting to the rules that govern society, which Rousseau was never able to do.

Economists maintain that economic relationships between people result in mutual dependencies, which are beneficial for them. Rousseau says this is a fallacy. Economic interests of society did quite the opposite—dividing people rather than uniting them. A modern society is divided into two classes: a rich, educated and corrupted *minority* of wealthy people and an uneducated *majority* condemned to poverty and scruffiness.

Rousseau essentially was always antisocial, which is a typical trait of all social reformers. B. Shaw remarks wittily, "A reasonable man adapts to the world around him. Unreasonable people try to adapt the world to their ideas. This is why the progress of mankind depends on unreasonable people." There are important associations between morality and psychopathology to which little attention has been paid so far.

Rousseau wrote, "The success of my *First Discourse* made the realization of my decision easier"; this "decision" was to live in poverty as an eccentric despising the corrupted society (but visiting it diligently). He was not attracting attention solely because he wrote an original essay. Such attention is always temporary. But when he started living in conformity with his views he became still more interesting as an eccentric original: "Judging that in order to gain a hearing I must reconcile my actions to my principles, I adopted that singular course" (*Conf.*, 387) This is the reason why he contemplated a life in "seclusion," but, of course, not complete seclusion—Thérèse had inevitably to be around and he needed also a noble protector with whom to meet.

Simultaneously with his moral "reform," his religious views started to change and the love of nature that substituted for society in his life became stronger. In nature he felt closer to God, his Father. He saw nature as his mother and he regarded himself to be her son. In this way he was living in a divine family where he felt secure.

His escape from society and the fact that he took refuge in nature was, in fact, a withdrawal into an ideal society because he was unable to live in normal human society. This inability is evidenced by the fact that, at the age of forty, he was famous but as poor as before. He lacked any entrepreneurial spirit. He lived so simply that even his clothes attracted the attention of visitors. Isaac Iselin from Basle recorded that the worn-out clothing and the shabby exterior of the renowned "philosopher" shocked him.

He lived on the very small amount of forty sous a day and when paid more by his noble friends, for whom he did the copying of notes, he returned the money. In his eyes poverty represented freedom and he wished to die in freedom (his doctors told him that he was going to die soon). A good act makes one obliged: Rousseau did not want to be indebted to anybody. Social life is based on reciprocal obligations and Rousseau rejected what he did not know.

Rousseau was always glad when he could escape from Paris. His favorite refuge was Mussard's house in Passy (Mussard came from Geneva). Mussard loved Italian music—*opera buffa,* and particularly Pergolesi's opera *La Serva padrona.* This opera had served as a pattern for Rousseau's opera *Le Devin du village* (The Village Soothsayer) which he had composed in a very short time. This opera glorifies the simple life, reunion with nature and the plainness of an "uncorrupt man."

It was an irony of fate that his work was admired by the most sublime audience. It was under consideration that Rousseau's opera would be first performed at the Parisian *opéra* but it turned out that the first performance was in front of the royal court at Fontainebleau.

Rousseau attended the premiere (with a rough beard, in an ordinary suit and an ill-combed wig) and considered his "unkempt state an act of courage." Opposite to him sat the king and Mme de Pompadour. Rousseau asked himself, in view of the fancy dress of the noble audience, whether or not he was suitably attired but was able to convince himself that he did the right thing.

The ladies attending the performance were moved to tears. The success of his opera meant for Rousseau a personal satisfaction because Rameau had previously rejected his *Les Muses galantes* and ridiculed his articles on music in *Encyclopédie*. Of course he also cried pathetically with the other spectators but felt like a slave: "This recollection made me feel like the *slave* who held the crown over the head of the Roman general in triumph" (italics added). Rousseau did not savor his success only as a celebrated composer but also sexually, in agreement with the sexual tendencies (see the analysis of Rousseau's feelings in the medical analysis in Part 2) that are a typical example of what is technically called pikacism, which is common in masochists. The word denotes the eating of women's excrements, or of food masticated and spat out by a woman—see Rousseau's pikacism in the case of Mme de Warens.

The king was so enthusiastic about the opera that he commissioned the director of *Des Menus Plaisirs,* M. de Cury, to introduce Rousseau to him on the next day. M. de Cury suggested that Rousseau could be given a pension from the king. Rousseau, however, was paralyzed by shyness. His urinary tract problem forced him to pass urine very often (pollakiuria), as did any nervous excitement, and he felt unable to appear in front of the king. His uneasiness would certainly increase the urge to urinate. He knew he would not be able to go to the bathroom and he would risk the dishonor of having wet trousers. He asked himself whether his timidity would make it impossible for him to utter a word in the king's presence: "Would my confounded shyness, which afflicts me when in company . . . have left me in the presence of the king of France, or would it have allowed me to choose the proper answers on the spur of the moment?" These were the real reasons that led him to turn down the invitation.

And again, as was typical of him, he concocted other and more noble justifications for his behavior the night before the audience: it was his moral conviction that did not allow him to visit the king. This way of thinking was typical of Rousseau and exposes him as a mere rhetorical moralist who always has to moralize: "It was necessary to clothe some great and useful truth in the form of a choice and well-deserved eulogy," he wrote openly. If he accepted the pension from the king he would have to accept the ensuing obligations. Could he accept the pension and preserve his independence, integrity and uncorrupted soul? The answer was No:

> "This danger alarmed me, terrified me, and made me trem-
> ble so violently that I decided, come what might, not to
> expose myself to it. I was losing, it is true, the pension . . .
> but at the same time I was freeing myself from the depend-
> ence it would have imposed upon me. How should I be
> able ever to speak again of independence and disinterest-
> edness? I concluded, therefore, that by refusing it I was tak-
> ing an action highly consonant with my principles and was
> sacrificing the illusion for the reality."

In fact he was sacrificing reality to illusions. After these deliberations he decided to leave Fontainebleau the next morning and not to obey the king. Grimm was the only person Rousseau informed about his true reasons, officially he announced that he was ill and had to return to Paris. Jelyotte, who presented the play, wrote him a letter and reproached him for having ran away from the court at the height of his triumph. The king, otherwise no music lover, is singing his arias in the worst voice in the kingdom, day after day, and demands that the opera be performed again within a week. His refusal of the royal pension led also to the first serious quarrel between Rousseau and Diderot, who reproached him for his lack of responsibility for Thérèse and her family. But Rousseau remained convinced that he was right and enjoyed his Spartan independence.

But still, Rousseau continued to seek fame. He offered his play *Narcisse*, which he brought to Paris in his pack and allegedly wrote when he was eighteen (but worked on it for some time), to Comédie-Française. It was indeed performed, but only twice: on December 18 and December 20, 1752. The reaction of the audience was polite to enthusiastic, which came as a surprise to Rousseau, because he considered it weak and left the performance prematurely.

In spite of it he endeavored to have the play printed. The bookseller, Pissot, gave him a first retainer 240 livres for the rights to *Le Devin du village*. Rousseau sent the whole sum to Mme de Warens in Chambéry together with a letter notifying her that his illness had gotten worse, so much so that he assumed that he would not live till next winter and would go to his grave with the only sorrow that he leaves her unhappy.

The opera *Le Devin du village* was performed at the Paris opera on March 1 with great success. The royal court performed it at the Château Bellevue for the second time. On the stage appeared members of the royal court. Mme de Pompadour sang one of the leading roles and Rousseau, who did not want to attend the performance at the château because he knew it was going to be sung with bad voices, sent Mme de Pompadour a copy of the opera, which he signed as "her humble servant." He got a present of fifty livres for it.

This time coincides also with a remarkable "Cultural Revolution," in which Rousseau took an active part, and which entered history as *querelle des bouffons*. The controversy started in the summer of 1752 when an Italian theatre company, led by Eustachio Bambini, visited Paris and staged here *opera buffa*, a genre of comic opera written by the composers Pergolesi, Scarlati, Vinci, Jomelli and others.

The argument concerned the question of whether the French or the Italian opera was better. The whole cultural community was engulfed by a controversy that can be understood only with difficulty from our point of view. The background of this controversy was not so much art as ideology (the Chinese Cultural Revolution was also based on ideology).

The Encyclopédistes and Rousseau vociferously advocated the merits of Italian music and opera. According to them, French opera was not only nationalist but also traditional, authoritative and academic. They said its composition was similar to Descartes's philosophy, being mathematical and regular. Its pomp represented the self-confidence of the kingdom of France. The sounds of drums and trumpets were meant to speak to the ears of its subjects in the same way as the architecture of Versailles was intended to influence their eyes. The librettos of French opera should glorify the glory of Bourbons.

Italian opera, on the other hand, wanted to entertain. It needed only a small orchestra, a small stage and several singers singing appealing arias related to folk music. The declamations of French opera were missing. *Opera seria* was a form of tragedy and *opera buffa* was comic opera, as can be seen on the following names: *La Donna superba, Il Medico ignorante, Il Maestro di musica, La Finta cameriera* and the most popular of them—*La Serva padrona*. Italian opera was more melodious, vivacious and not so intellectual, which made it more popular. The characters of Italian opera were taken from real life. There were not so many kings or gods on the stage but there were people. According to Lady Sydney Morgan, Paris was divided into two musical parties holding different political views.

It is not uninteresting that Rousseau wrote his *Le Devin du village* in the Italian musical style as he had learned it in Turin and Venice, whereas the story deviates radically from its model, *La Serva padrona*. In *La Serva padrona* the maid marries a rich man and becomes the lady of the house. The message of the opera is egalitarian. Rousseau's opera shows that people should not overstep the class barriers and can find the best love among their equals. It is therefore understandable that the performance before the royal court was so successful. Its musical composition was liberal, but its story was conservative and corresponded to the system of French society.

Rousseau lead the advocates of Italian music and wrote the sharp and polemic, but eloquent, *Lettre sur la musique française* where he contended openly that it was impossible to reform French music, with or without the help of Italian music. He said that every nation had its own music, and a national music is derived from national language. Italian language could give rise to good music, which was not the case of French. French did not have the qualities necessary for good music: it was coarse, monotonous, guttural, full of nasal consonants, lacking sonorous vowels. When asked how it was possible even for French music to arise Rousseau gave the answer that French composers had rejected melody and turned to harmony. He ends his essay saying the French have no music because they are unable to have any. (Here we see a typical example of manichaeistic thinking, characteristic of the mode of activity of the right hemisphere: good-bad, correct-wrong, compromises and relative truths do not exist.)

Such aggressive, rough and one-sided criticism must have aroused resistance, not only through its content but also by virtue of its form. One could discuss anything in Paris provided it was done in a witty, elegant and entertaining way. Rousseau criticism was written eloquently but with too much boldness, which was unforgivable, especially when the author was a Genevan citizen. Political issues were forgotten and France united against Rousseau.

The general political situation was very strained indeed. In November 1753 the king made an attempt to dissolve the great chamber of Parisian parlement with the intention to replace its function by a royal chamber, which provoked a resistance bordering on rebellion. French parlements were municipal legal corporations and cannot be compared with the English parliament; in France of that time the latter is most comparable to Estates-General, which had not been allowed to assemble since 1614. Most of the French municipal parlements were controlled by Jansenists, who were uncompromising in questions of religion and censorship, which was why they could not be regarded as advocates of freedom. It was, according to Rousseau, his controversial work that focused attention on this area, and it was thanks to him, as he humbly presumes, that no revolution broke out. It is certainly an irony that Rousseau, who is often dubbed the father of the French Revolution, considers himself to be a man who prevented a revolution. Of course, we know from other sources that Rousseau was always against revolutions and has never been a revolutionary.

Likewise, Grimm wrote in his *Correspondence littéraire* that people were more interested in the disputes which Rousseau caused by his *Lettre* than in the issues of the royal chamber. The outcry of Paris against Rousseau was great. Rousseau wrote in *Confessions* that there were plans made to murder him, which was most probably pure fantasy. Rousseau was to have been expelled from Paris but the order was revoked. During his theatre visits, excited advocates of French music attacked Rousseau and so he had to have his own bodyguard, the musketeer officer M. Ancelet. He was barred from free access to all operatic performances. No less numerous were literary rejoinders from many of his critics.

The gravest criticism came from the doyen of French music, Rameau, the author of theoretical works from which even Rousseau studied music. In the spring of 1754 Rameau published a booklet *Observations sur notre instinct pour la musique*, in which he attacked Rousseau. Rameau maintained, contrary to Rousseau, that harmony was primary and melody secondary. Harmony was not only the basic principle of music but also of all "fine arts." Their dispute was actually a controversy about the reality of the world. Rameau demanded unity and Cartesian order. Music had the same principles as mathematics. Rousseau claimed that music differed from mathematics, and musical styles changed in the same way as nature. Harmony was artificial, invented by the intellect, whereas the genius of music revealed what was natural.

The dispute between Rousseau and Rameau was "a dispute of the deaf": Rousseau did not want to understand where Rameau was right and vice versa, Rameau did not understand things emphasized by Rousseau. Encyclopédistes supported Rousseau, but the dispute had nevertheless resulted in a certain cooling of their relationship with Rousseau, because they feared that Rousseau's exaggerated criticism might turn damaging in the end. The disputes over the new opera also influenced Mozart. His opera *Bastien und Bastienne* is grounded on Rousseau's *Le Devin du village*. Gluck created a novel type of French opera after Rameau's death and did not conceal the influence Rousseau had on him.

This musical controversy is also a good example of Rousseau's way of thinking. He thought in absolute categories that were based on his subjective convictions. The logic is to be replaced by eloquence and so it is no wonder that his absolute views cannot have absolute validity. In his thinking everything is either positive or negative, compromises do not exist (i.e., French music cannot be reformed), and any detailed analytical discrimination is missing, as are any doubts about his own views. Rousseau becomes entangled in contradictions. He maintains that French music, because it is based on French language, cannot be reformed—but composes a successful French opera, *Le Devin du village*. This contradiction was mentioned as an example by Grimm in *Correspondence littéraire*. The whole dispute reveals also Rousseau's masochistic tendencies. Rousseau *must* have known his criticism was provocative and exaggerated, yet he used it in this absolute form: he desired "punishment" by society, he wanted to suffer in the name of truth.

After his musical dispute Rousseau decided to pursue only philosophy in the future and gave up composing. This was in keeping with his "system," because in his discourse he exposed the decline of science and in his controversy with Rameau the decline of music, which in turn led to his conviction that language, too, was in the process of decline (music depends on the nation's language); the decline of the latter was more or less identical with the decline of human society. His *Essai sur l'origine des langues* was published only after his death, and was probably written over a longer period, after 1750. The idea underlying this discourse and stated in it, was still that man is good by nature, but is corrupted by society. He differentiated northern languages (he ranks French among them) and southern languages, the latter preserving their poetic and musical character. But languages, like civilizations, develop only for the worse. Instead of being a means for the exchange of feelings only thoughts are exchanged. Languages become more accurate and distinct but at the same time become more humming, dull and cold. Even modern Italian has lost the original purity of emotional language. The reason for its ability to give rise to music is that it contains the remnants of its original melodiousness. He even went so far as to maintain that some languages are suitable for freedom. Such languages are poetical, harmonious and sonorous.

Chapter Four

Provocation of the *Second Discourse*

The Italian opera company left Paris in March 1754 and Rousseau, who did not feel comfortable in the hostile environment, intended to leave as well, or rather to escape the Parisian society. It is probable that his departure from Paris was also precipitated by what became known as his *Second Discourse*, which represents a further elaboration of the ideas of the first (*Discours sur les arts et les sciences*). The content and social consequences of the *Second Discourse*, however, were of much greater impact and rather explosive. It is also possible that Rousseau feared political persecution and left Paris to find a new refuge in case he would face serious persecution later.

His *First Discourse* is full of paradoxes but is not politically dangerous. In his *Second Discourse*, Rousseau denounces the existing social order as such. Let us now examine the history of the *Second Discourse*.

In the fall of 1753 the Dijon Academy announced another literary competition, this time raising questions concerning inequality among men. The subject of the essay was: "What is the origin of inequality among men and is it authorized by natural law?" This question came for Rousseau at just the right time—this issue had fascinated him for a long time. He notified the Academy promptly that since they had had the courage to raise such an issue, he would have the courage to write about it. He added that the Academy would have to "hold the baby" for any reactions to his interpretation of such an explosive issue. We read elsewhere that he felt it was his duty to tell people the truth, or what he thought of as truth, but he expected a more powerful voice ought to force the people to love this truth. He decided to write as a person who is not afraid of anything or anybody.

He left Paris accompanied only by Thérèse and two other women who cared for him. November of 1753 was unusually sunny and Rousseau walked in the forests of Saint-Germain, reflecting on his upcoming essay. Here, he looked for and found (in his imagination) the original man, whose history he "injudiciously" set about to write. The final version of this discourse was finished after his return to Paris. He was walking in Bois de Boulogne and then hurried home to put his thoughts on paper.

The *Discours sur les origines de l'inégalité* is probably his most influential work, in spite of the fact that it only consists of about one hundred pages; it is for this discourse that Rousseau is dubbed the father of the French Revolution (Hegel, Burke, Napoleon) and the founder of modern social science (e.g. Lévi-Strauss), which appears to be a rather controversial opinion. It is true that Rousseau addressed the changes people were undergoing in the course of their evolution before Darwin. The idea of such changes in the course of evolution was nothing new and to regard Rousseau as Darwin's precursor of this is doubtful. Rousseau admitted that humans could be distant relatives of orang-utans and could have developed from simple bipeds. He viewed the evolution of man as a process of adaptation and fight.

He starts his essay with two kinds of inequality among people. The *first* is the natural inequality given by nature. People are taller and smaller, stronger and weaker, more intelligent and less intelligent. The *second* inequality is what he calls the "artificial inequality derived from the conventions that govern human society. Some people are richer than others and occupy higher ranks—others have to obey. He deals in the *Second Discourse* with this "artificial inequality" and does not raise the question as to why nature endowed people so unevenly. It is strange that it did not occur to him that a man, endowed by nature by greater intellect, or by greater physical strength, simply must assert himself more forcefully in the fight with those who were endowed sub-normally or normally, and thereby achieve more in life.

To be able to find out when this change occurred and man was struck by this "artificial inequality" he had to determine first what this "original" man looked like. This was the reason for Rousseau's search for the "original" man, who existed before the civilization process set in. He was not studying any appropriate sources about the appearance and behavior of primitive cultures though such data was already available in the eighteenth century. He made up the picture of a primitive savage during his walks in nature, and he did it so that this picture suited his ideas and his philosophical "system." His original man is healthy, happy, good, and isolated.

None of these claims were correct, which he could have learned from experts on primitive tribes—but Paris did not want to believe these experts.

The picture of a savage, invented for them by Rousseau enchanted everyone. The gravest fallacy is Rousseau's claim that the "natural" man was an anti-social individual living in isolation. Even the most primitive humans were gregarious animals, living in groups of various sizes, with a hierarchical structure already in place—a stratification, which forestalls intra-social aggression. This had been correctly understood by Hobbes, who started with a detailed analysis of the psychology of human nature (from the perspective of his time) and arrived at the conclusion that people were aggressive, miserly, and thought only of their own good. This is why they needed rules of social behavior, established for them by their ruler, to bring peace into a war that would otherwise be fought as a war of all against all. The fact that man has a social instinct was already clear to Locke, and Voltaire shared this view as well.

Rousseau, however, arrives at quite the opposite conclusion: people have become bad *because* they became social; he overlooks that man *has never been anti-social*. Using doubtful premises he arrives at doubtful conclusions, which of course does not rule out that he can occasionally come up with a correct thought.

His view that in nature only the fit and healthy survive did certainly occur to others before him. Here his old admiration for ancient Sparta appears again, in which only healthy individuals were allowed to survive, an attitude in agreement with Rousseau's own. Of course, these laws would have resulted in his own death after delivery because he was born "a poor and sickly child."

Reading Rousseau's description of natural man one cannot get rid of the idea that Rousseau must have had his own childhood in mind. As a child he lived in isolation, or semi-isolation, and dreamt up his primitive man after the image of his childhood. He sees himself as a noble "savage" who is being corrupted by human society. His natural man is free. He has free will, as opposed to other animals that are driven by nature. According to Rousseau there exists in this archaic state also an archaic freedom, because there are no governments and no laws to restrict it. In the *Second Discourse* this pre-political freedom is described as positive, though Rousseau later condemns it, in *Du Contract social*, with the same enthusiasm as does Hobbes.

The third kind of freedom of a man in his natural state was his personal freedom, and Rousseau considered this freedom the most important. Primitive man has no employer—there is nobody who would stand above him. The life of the original man did not depend on anybody. He was economically independent, which was no doubt Rousseau's wish as well, because he was dependent on various people for his entire life and this was why he so vehemently emphasized personal freedom.

Besides these many types of freedom the natural man has another feature, called by Rousseau *perfectibilité*, the ability to improve or to become worse. According to Rousseau there occurred a deterioration at a certain stage of human development. The original man did not have a great capacity for thinking and he did not have language, he was subject to only a few passions, he was happy, free, and innocent. This original man did not know what evil was because he did not know what good was. At that time a view started to emerge, later elaborated on by Hume, that people are driven mainly by their passions (emotions) and these must be controlled. This was why Rousseau emphasized that primitive man had only a few passions. It is only in society that his passions multiply and corrupt human morals.

Rousseau's views concerning family as a basic unit of society are very controversial. At first he claimed that family did not emerge as a result of the natural state. In other essays, however, Rousseau says that family is a natural society. He says this not only in *Du Contract social*, which he wrote later, but also in his *Essay sur l'origine des langues*, written at about the same time as his *Second Discourse*.

The turning point in the evolution of man occurred when people became settled and built "cottages" where they lived together. It was here that natural man left his natural state, in which he had lived in isolation, and formed a society characterized by sexual promiscuity. The building of dwellings brought about a primitive society that led to the first revolution, which introduced property ownership. This stage underwent evolution as well. The idea of private property did not occur before agriculture was introduced. Rousseau considered the nascent society to be closest to an ideal state, but this is not described by him in detail.

In his natural state man had what Rousseau called *amour de soi-même*, a self-saving instinct, which kept him alive. Through the influence of society this instinct was transformed to *amour-propre*, a form of self-love, and the desire to surpass others and seek their admiration. According to Rousseau *amour-propre* is the main driving force of human society. It leads man to the greatest inventions in industry and advances of knowledge in science and art but, at the same time, to the greatest decline, which he described in his *First Discourse*.

Rousseau differs from Hobbes in his attitude toward war. Hobbes claims that wars result from an aggressiveness in people that is inborn. Rousseau considers wars to be the result of uneven distribution of wealth. Both concur in the view that anarchy can be prevented only by a social contract. Whereas Hobbes treats this social contract as beneficial for all, in Rousseau's writing this contract is described as a deception profiting only the rich. Economic inequality causes all evil. Rousseau knew that social development cannot be reversed and that a return to pre-political society was impossible. He differed in this from the theoreticians of socialism who would later declare that social changes are possible at any time.

All attempts to classify Rousseau as a social reformer must be therefore regarded with a grain of salt. Rousseau attacks all of human civilization in his essay but has never called for it to be changed. None of these views prevented Rousseau from savoring all the positive sides of civilization: he frequently visited the theatres and salons of Parisian society. It was only later that his views grew more radical and he attempted to act the natural man who, in his view, lived alone, was lazy and appreciated food and freedom. But this always was, and remained, just a façade meant to put him in a certain position in the eyes of society.

It is difficult to accept that he ever personally believed in what he wrote. He had never been completely alone. He not only had Thérèse to care for him, but there were also influential protectors with whom he remained in personal contact and to whom he wrote many letters. He was not lazy, as we can judge from his extensive literary legacy. What he produced must have been time-consuming and bears witness to activities that characterize a rather civilized man.

In his own words the "civilized man" is incessantly active, industrious, willing to do everything for honor, might and glory, of which he can never have enough. The "civilized man" generally appears to be something which in fact he is not. Here Rousseau hints of the discrepancy between reality and appearance, a discrepancy which is always present. In German this is called the contradiction of *sein* and *schein* (of being and appearance), the contradiction of the real SELF-being and the IMPRESSION the man wants to project for others to see. Rousseau rejected all pretension (semblance) as morally bad, but he himself was a pretender in front of the entire world—a pretender who lived up to his ideas of a "noble savage."

One could ask, in view of the fact that Rousseau considered a reversal of civilized society to its original state impossible, why it was that he tried to imitate this state by his own behavior? Considering his intelligence it must have been sufficiently clear to him that his attitude lacked trustworthiness and had to appear rather as a caricature of "primitive man." The answer is given by his psychology, which makes his behavior understandable. He withdrew from social life, for which he had not been prepared by upbringing and which he did not interpret realistically, but rather according to his illusory constructs. His withdrawal from society served to underscore his views about society. The society saw in him a scrupulous moralist. It was by his own *amour-propre* that he was driven to untiring literary activity, ergo a characteristic of the "civilized" man he so much despised. We have here the following picture of Rousseau: he was a civilized man who acted the role of noble savage.

The *Second Discourse* was therefore much more radical than the first. It could not appeal to anybody. Even the Church must have noticed there was no reference to God in it.

Rousseau completed the *Second Discourse* in the winter of 1753–1754. He did not expect to get the prize (the competition was won by abbé Talbert). Parts of the essay were read at the meeting of the Dijon Academy on June 21, 1754, but he wanted it published as soon as possible and left a copy of it with Diderot and asked him to have it published by Pissot.

The *Second Discourse* should have answered questions left unanswered by the *First Discourse* and add scientific arguments to the previous work, which was eloquent in a brilliant way. But the *Second Discourse* too was a victory of dazzling eloquence and a creation of catchy and emotionally explosive phrases over reasonable thinking. Rousseau was partly aware of the paradoxes exposing his work to criticism and implored the reader to read the text twice before passing judgment on it. It appears that Rousseau fell victim to his literary rhetoric and ability to construct unforgettable phrases. His views were probably less radical than his writings.

We can see by the way he attacked mainly the "rich" and less the "powerful" that he was disgusted by the rich bourgeoisie such as the Dupins and Poplinières, who gave him employment. He was dependent on them but despised them. His admiration for the French aristocracy of the eighteenth century was more or less romantic. According to his dreams, only the best people should occupy leading positions. Though the aristocracy of that time still had the titles it had no political authority. Bourbon absolutism and the rich bourgeoisie were the real rulers of the French kingdom.

Diderot sympathized with Rousseau's arguments and helped him to prepare the text. It appears that Diderot put his own radical views into the discourse because it matched his political orientation, and it is not clear whether Rousseau himself would have used such radical formulations.

Rousseau wrote many years later (when he broke with Diderot) that his former friend abused his faith in him and put a "coarse note and black tone" into the discourse, which he himself did not use later. It is nevertheless necessary to record that Diderot did not participate only in the work on the first, but also the *Second Discourse*.

At the age of forty Rousseau was a personality of renown but found it increasingly difficult to continue his way of life in Paris. He visited the salon of Baron Holbach, which could also be described as an Encyclopédistes' club. The rich Holbach gave dinners twice a week (on Tuesdays and Saturdays) with the guests meeting as early as two o'clock in the afternoon and staying till seven or eight o'clock. The topic for discussion was open. According to others (Marmontel), Rousseau's behavior was quite normal, he was not yet acting the part of a "savage," he was rather timid, or rather pretended his timidity. Others saw in him a sort of capricious and lofty woman and felt he did not trust any of them, living very much by the motto, "Live with your friends as if they should become your enemies one day."

Holbach recorded one of Rousseau's embarrassing tantrums. Rousseau became enraged when one of the visitors (abbé Petit) read the manuscript of his play, one that Rousseau regarded as worthless. Jean-Jacques sprang from his chair as a madman, ripped the manuscript from the abbé's hands, threw it on the floor and shouted that the play was worthless and the abbé should return to his parish. In the end both had to be separated to prevent the otherwise imminent fight. This incident is not mentioned in *Confessions*—Rousseau wrote only that his relationship with Holbach was becoming increasingly colder. Rousseau stopped visiting his salon. His interest shifted to the salon of Mlle Quinault, a former actress, where he met with more acknowledgement than at the Holbachs' (Mme d'Holbach died in 1754 and Rousseau wrote such a warm condolence that Baron Holbach made an attempt to renew their old friendship, but not for long).

In the salon of Mlle Quinault, Rousseau met Chevalier de Saint-Lambert, a decorated soldier, poet and women's favorite. Saint-Lambert was discovered by Voltaire who praised his poetical talent. He repaid Voltaire by seducing his mistress, Mme du Chatelet, who became pregnant from him and died at the delivery. Voltaire had lived with Marquise du Chatelet—the "divine Emilia"— in Cirey (Champagne) for fifteen years. Frederick II, the king of Prussia, called this lady "Venus-Newton," because she was at home in astronomy as well as in the art of love. Saint-Lambert served Rousseau as the model for the character of Wolmar in his *La Nouvelle Héloïse*, in which he creates a love triangle similar to that of his later relationship with Mme d'Houdetot.

At the beginning of 1754 Rousseau is thus still a *salonard* and man of society. He finds, however, that he cannot live permanently in a society where he attained glory but no wealth. His friendly relationships become cooler, his friends begrudge him, and are annoyed by his changed behavior. His supercilious critique of French music made many people in Paris into his enemies.

This was further compounded by fear and uncertainty over the unfavorable response of the French government and the Church, which he feared might follow the publication of his *Second Discourse*. He remembered the turmoil and criticism caused by his *First Discourse*, which was in fact politically innocent. His *Second Discourse*, however, was an open and provocative attack on contemporary civilization and therefore on the monarchy. Being a chess player he prepared his steps in advance: an unknown journalist wrote on August 1, 1753 that Rousseau intended to renounce the Catholic faith. Rousseau does not mention this event in *Confessions*, but informs the reader that life in Paris became ever more difficult for him and that he longed for a life in the country.

He must have been fully aware that after he had written all these things about religion, science, the arts, morals and politics, he could not go on living in the center of a morally bankrupt society and participate in its social life. He therefore started to prepare for the departure back to his hometown, which he saw as provincial, puritanically simple and less corrupted, and tried to find there a safe haven in case he was forced to leave Paris.

Rousseau realized that his *Second Discourse* condemned everything, that it was absolutely negativistic and pessimistic, but also that this attitude was not enough. In a work that was written later, *Du Contract social*, Rousseau tried to outline some possibilities on how people could enjoy freedom and laws and create a functioning society. In his personal life, he sought to resolve the consequences to which his discourse had led by leaving the place governed by the greatest inequality. Cranston asked the legitimate question of whether Rousseau himself was sufficiently honest when he started to lean to Calvinism and prepare for his departure to Geneva, which was certainly not the well-organized Republic Rousseau declared it to be. Geneva was ruled by patrician despotism and Rousseau must have known it. Yet still, he dedicated his *Second Discourse* to Geneva and in the preface he praised the city-state and its institutions as the best of that time. Even if he saw the flaws in the Genevan political system, which is probable, what else could he do? He would be expelled from Paris after the publication of his discourse and where would he go? It is therefore only natural that he tried to find a new refuge by flattering the Genevan government.

Geneva and Conversion to Calvinism

Rousseau set out for Geneva on June 1, 1754. He took advantage of an invitation by his old friend, the rich bon vivant Gauffecourt (who used to consume oysters and champagne seven days a week) and traveled with Thérèse in a carriage. She accompanied him because, as he said, he did not feel well enough to get along without her. One can ask how Thérèse could care for him? Only by catheterizing him! Rousseau was not in need of other care.

Rousseau described in *Confessions* how Gauffecourt tried to seduce Thérèse during the journey (who was not a paragon of faithfulness, and, according to Rousseau's own words, was neither beautiful nor young). In his correspondence from that time he keeps quiet about it, and this affair (which occupies enough space in *Confessions*) did not cause any disruption of his friendship with Gauffecourt (masochists find infidelity of their partner sexually arousing).

They parted in Lyon, Gauffecourt continuing directly to Geneva, while Rousseau and Thérèse decided to visit Mme de Warens in Chambéry where they arrived on June 12, 1754. Rousseau was horrified by the situation in which he found Mme de Warens. Her financial situation was so desperate that she had had to be entered on the official list of paupers. Her pension was discontinued on behalf of her creditors. Rousseau says that he gave her a small part of the money he had with him and suggested that she solve her situation in the way he had already proposed in his letters: to leave Savoy and live with him and Thérèse—a happy life *à trois*. Mme Warens refused this solution and Rousseau left Chambéry, ashamed and filled with guilt.

Still in Chambéry, he wrote a dedication for his *Second Discourse* (for

Geneva) the draft of which had been finished earlier in Paris. He did not want the dedication to be dated in Paris or Geneva. At the time of his journey to Geneva the *Second Discourse* was not yet printed and existed only as manuscript. His Genevan visit served not only the purpose of ensuring a safe haven, but he also wanted to find out what the reception of his paper in Geneva would be.

He told his friends in Paris that the sole purpose of his journey to Geneva was to obtain official permission by Genevan authorities to publish his enthusiastic foreword about Geneva in his *Second Discourse*, and that he would then return, at the latest, in early September. The text of the foreword itself, however, is so sententiously overblown that it does not testify so much to Rousseau's naiveté as to his intention to win the favor of Genevan authorities and gain back his lost citizenship.

He signed his *First Discourse* as Rousseau, *citoyen de Genève*, which of course was not correct. He had never been a Genevan citizen in the first place and had forfeited his civic rights after his conversion to Catholicism in Turin. He wrote in *Confessions* that it was only after the enthusiastic reception in his native city that he started to contemplate settling in Geneva for good. It is much more likely, however, that he made up his mind earlier, before he set out for Geneva, and that this was his primary intention and reason for his journey to Geneva.

After their arrival in Geneva at the end of June 1754, Rousseau and Thérèse settled near the Genevan lake in Eaux-Vives, at the city gates. His decision was influenced not only by the location of this residence outside the city, but also by the fact that it belonged to the parish of Jacques Maystre (1703–1755). With his help Rousseau's conversion to Calvinism passed off without any great difficulty.

Normally, he would have to go before the *petit conseil*, spend several days in prison, undergo public interrogations by the consistory and ask for forgiveness on his knees. Thanks to Maystre's help, who spent about a month instructing him in Calvinism, Rousseau was spared all these degradations. Genevan authorities were practical enough to decide that it would be in their interest to regain their famous countryman into their ranks. Even the inquiry, which should have been held in public, was carried out in private and the considerate theologians did not ask any contentious questions so that Rousseau did not have to disclose his unorthodox views.

The inquiry by the consistory was held on Thursday, August 1, 1754. As soon as he was formally granted Genevan citizenship, the first syndic of the Republic, Jean-Louis Du Pan, sent Rousseau a cordial letter notifying him that he would be taxed based on an annual income of only eighteen florins and that his arrears would be forgiven.

The religious atmosphere of Geneva of that time was not as dogmatically stringent as it had been. At the beginning of the eighteenth century the philosopher Robert Chouet at the Genevan Academy introduced the Cartesian method of systematic dispute that was later extended to Calvin's dogmatics by the theologian J. A. Turretini. Turretini's pupil, Jacob Vernet, developed the process of elimination of dogma still further. This process was also influenced by the liberal views of the Anglican Church.

Rousseau had no reason to be afraid of the questions of the dogmatics. He had his own private religion and his religious views were foreign to any church. He acknowledged at the same time that any working society needed some form of religious institution however controversial it might be. In this he resembled Hobbes and Voltaire. His conversion to Protestantism was not a conversion based on conviction but a matter of pure utilitarianism: he wanted to acquire Genevan civic rights and therefore had to embrace the official religion of Geneva.

But the Genevan Calvinists were intransigent in questions of morality. It is true that adultery was no longer punished by death, nor were prostitutes thrown into the lake, but cohabitation without marriage, as practiced by Rousseau with Thérèse, was still considered to be a major offence. In Paris no one would have bothered about it, but provincial Geneva was different; however, Rousseau succeeded in getting around even this. He was able to show to the authorities (which were obviously inclined to believe him) that he was ill—he said he had protuberances in his urethra—that Thérèse was not his mistress, but was nursing him and that he was certainly not able to do the things they thought he did.

We have testimony disproving this; Pastor Vernes once appeared unexpectedly in Rousseau's room, surprising the couple during intercourse, and Rousseau told him (without interrupting the intercourse), "She is helping me and I am helping her." The same pastor reveals that Thérèse accompanied Rousseau everywhere and was even invited with him to prominent Genevan houses, which would have been unthinkable if Thérèse had been a mere nurse.

In Geneva, now politically calm (the Treaty of Turin that guaranteed peace between Geneva and Savoy was signed on June 3, 1754), Rousseau spent several joyous months and wrote enthusiastically to Mme Dupin in a letter from July 12, 1754, "It seems to me that Geneva is certainly one of the most charming places in the world and its inhabitants are the wisest and happiest of all people I have ever met. Unrestricted freedom prevails, the government is peace loving, the Genevans are enlightened, decent and gentle; they know their rights and make use of them fearlessly, not forgetting to respect the rights of others . . ."

Though Geneva was not quite the paradise Rousseau described in this letter or in the foreword to his discourse, it had some positive features distinguishing it from other governments of that time. In 1754 Genevans contended with a government that consisted of twenty-five "ruling" families. There was a big difference between the ruling class formed by a 6 percent minority of Genevan patricians and the remaining population. The burghers pursued lucrative trade, banking, and foreign investments but did not exploit or restrict the freedom of the working class. A "cereal board" guaranteed that Genevan citizens could buy food at normal prices even at times of bad harvests. There was a public system of education. These benefits were certainly not available in all neighboring countries.

In spite of his complaints about bad health, Rousseau visited many people in Geneva and its neighborhoods—among others his former wet nurse Jacqueline Faramond, married to the dyer Jacques Daniel in rue de Countance, and also his beloved Aunt Suzon—Susanne Concerut—who had moved to Nyon and was more than seventy (she lived to be more than ninety, similar to her father, David Rousseau).

Rousseau also met many members of the Genevan ruling oligarchy who were glad to have regained Rousseau as a citizen of Geneva. Among others he became acquainted with the politician Jacques-François Deluc (who was a critic of Genevan government), Professor Jallabert, and Vernet, Lullin and Pedriau. Rousseau read parts of his *Second Discourse* to Jallabert (leaving out the foreword), who reportedly was enchanted by it. (It is not clear whether this was true.)

It can be assumed that Rousseau read his disruptive essay to other important people as well, to test their reaction. But we have no accounts that this actually happened. It was rumored by August that Rousseau was going to stay in Geneva for good. Professor Jean-François Pictet, for example, wrote in a letter from late August, "Rousseau gave us a hope" that he would settle in Geneva after he had sorted out his personal matters in Paris. Rousseau expressed himself similarly in *Confessions* but it is obvious that he was still hesitating to take the final step. He wrote that he could return in the spring of the next year and stay in Geneva, but that there was still time to talk about it during the winter.

In August 1754 Rousseau met Mme de Warens at the Genevan Grange-Canal when she was passing through Geneva on her way to Jussy. It was the last time he saw her. She had no means whatsoever and Rousseau who had no money with him sent her a small amount by way of Thérèse. He wrote in *Confessions* with remorse that he should have paid back to her all he owed her, that he should have stayed with her till death and shared her fate whatever it might be. "I did nothing of it . . . I was sighing: but I did not follow her."

The encounter at Grange-Canal caused him the greatest remorse he had ever experienced in his life. Yet he had built a new personal relationship and felt that his ties with Mme de Warens were waning. He was unable to help her financially and it was clear that his Maman was not interested in anything else. She knew about his situation and it is likely that she did not want Rousseau to follow her. Jussy, near Thonon, was a small "hermitage" provided for her by Marquis de Coundré where she spent the rest of her life in ever increasing poverty and died seven years later. She was a remarkable woman and we might not have known about her colorful life if it were not for her ungrateful *petit*.

In summer 1754 Rousseau rediscovered his love of nature and admired the beautiful lake with the silhouette of the Alps. He collected plants, fed fish in the lake and taught them to swim to the shore at a certain time. He took long walks and rowed on the lake with his friends. One of these rowing trips, in September 1754, lasted seven days and the company, including Thérèse, rowed across the lake as far as Valis and back. Rousseau remembers this trip vividly in *Confessions*. He used the description of the natural splendors later in the novel *La Nouvelle Héloïse*.

He did not admire only nature in Valis. He was interested in its inhabitants and intended to write a history of Valis but never completed it. According to his theory, the souls of people who live in places with such beautiful nature must be more noble than those of other people. Since the people of Valis earned their living as simple farmers, they were not yet spoiled by the sophistry of modern life and had to be morally better, according to his *First Discourse*. He repeated this view in 1758, in *Lettre à Monsieur d'Alembert sur les spectacles*, where he argues in favor of the rustic simplicity of the people living in the Alps and values it higher than the trivial distractions of advanced societies. Rousseau's other plans included a tragedy in prose and a book that was to deal with forms of social order and state. In this period he also translated the first book of Tacitus's *Histories*.

On October 10, 1754 Rousseau left Geneva together with Thérèse to "settle his matters in Paris" as he declared to his friends, with plans to return the following spring to stay for good. Before his departure he was asked by the Genevan library to secure the complete edition of Diderot's *Encyclopédie*.

It is likely that, in spite of all his admiration for Geneva and the surrounding natural beauties, Rousseau felt a certain nostalgia for the literary life in Paris. Though his status had changed in Geneva, his identity had not. Perhaps he simply attained what he wanted: he had built a safe haven and a new home where he could return should the situation in Paris become too dangerous for him. The possibility of his expulsion obviously occurred to others as well, as can be surmised from the letter he sent to Vernes in Geneva after reaching Paris. He wrote that his arrival in Paris surprised many people who thought he had been banished to Geneva and would not be allowed to return to France.

He spent part of the winter of 1754 proofreading the *Second Discourse* on inequality among mankind, which he commissioned to be printed at Reye's in the Netherlands. (He had met Rey in Geneva.) Concerning his return to Geneva, Rousseau wrote in *Confessions* that he wanted to wait until he knew how the dedication in his discourse was received in the Republic.

What is more probable, however, is that he wanted to determine the reaction of Geneva to the complete work. "As this work was dedicated to the Republic, and as this dedication might be displeasing to the Council, I decided to wait and see what the reception in Geneva would be before returning there. Its effect was unfavorable to me: and that dedication, which had been inspired by purest patriotism, brought nothing but enemies on the Council and the jealousy of some citizens." The response was not favorable; the rulers of Geneva were unlikely to approve of the book, in spite of the patriotic dedication. Rousseau complained that not a single citizen of Geneva rendered thanks to him for the inward fervor, "which spoke from his entire work."

There were many circumstances that spoke against his intention to settle permanently in Geneva (if he had such intention at all). The most important was the matter of employment. The work of a note copyist was possible only in Paris, certainly not in Geneva, where music and theatre were not yet publicly performed.

In Paris he could assume the role of a moralist preaching to the modern society, and lash out against the corruption and false values of the modern world, pointing to his immaculate soul. Paris teemed with hedonistic materialists, skeptics, atheists and libertines, and it was easy for him to demonstrate that he was a better Christian than others. To play this role in Geneva with its puritan spirit was practically impossible. On the contrary, he could be reprehended by anyone as he was breaching moral codices daily by his loose life with Thérèse.

He had not attained the professed purpose of his Genevan visit—to obtain official permission to dedicate his *Second Discourse* to the city. Soon after his arrival he was informed by Jean Pedriau that the dedication of his *Discours sur les origines de l'inégalité* to the Genevan Republic was not going to be welcome. The summer spent in Geneva opened his eyes and he had probably come to realize that Geneva was not the Promised Land he described with such enthusiasm. He regarded himself as the best censor of his works but Jean Pedriau reminded him that all publications in Geneva were subject to censorship. Rousseau must have come to the conclusion that his *Second Discourse* would not to be read with enthusiasm in Geneva.

The real achievement of his journey was his regained citizenship in the city-state. Being formally a foreign national in Paris, he could express his views more freely and was immune with respect to possible punishment as long as his books were not printed in France. (The only city in Europe without censorship was Amsterdam.) Such a freedom would be impossible in Geneva: "I will even admit that as a foreigner living in France I found my position most favorable for truth-telling . . . I should have been much less free even in Geneva, where the magistrates would have the right to censure the contents of my books . . ." The fact was that the Genevan government had the power to affect his books even if they were printed outside of Geneva.

These were all considerations that were critical to his decision not to return to Geneva and to accept the offer of Mme d'Épinay to settle in Hermitage. The decision was influenced by personal reasons as well. In spite of all this he described the situation as if he *had to submit* to Mme d'Épinay's coercion and accept the "yoke" of her friendship. It would have appeared that Rousseau's situation in Paris could be characterized by a verse by François Villon: "I dwell abroad, which is my home." Actually he could not feel at home in any society because he had not learned the rules of social life in his youth and had never become integrated in any society. For him, society was something alien, perverse and bad, and he could live in it only as its critic. He anticipated subconsciously that he would have to withdraw from society anyway, sooner or later.

Meanwhile, he returned to his old flat in Paris (in rue Grenelle-Saint Honoré) and lived there with Thérèse and her mother from the fall of 1754 until the spring of 1756. He was haunted by his own work: he had to live up to his writings. He had to live morally out of sheer necessity to preserve his status as a renowned moralist.

He loathed steady work, which was the only way to secure a regular income. Poverty had always seemed moral and pure to him, and that was why he cultivated it with such pleasure. As a note copyist he earned the necessary minimum to support his household, but this income was never such that it would satisfy Mme Levasseur. Rousseau was not bothered by his personal poverty because it was offset by public fame and recognition. He forgot about it in the salons he visited, where he found not only intellectual amusement, but he could also eat and drink his fill. The leading philosophers of the French Enlightenment were still his friends.

He was popular in the salons though he himself maintains he was always bashful and awkward. His contemporaries, however, prove he was a brilliant speaker and had a personal charm in spite of the peculiarity of his nature. He returned to Holbach with whom he had previously broken (but, after writing a warm condolence on Mme d'Holbach's death, he had been invited back). He also loved to visit the salon of Claude-Adrien Helvétius (1715–1771) who had resigned from a lucrative post at the revenue office and became notorious by his atheistic and materialist work *De l'Esprit*, which he was called on to recant several times.

Rousseau recalled the carnival ball given by Helvétius in February 1755 in *Confessions* as a great experience. The aged Fontenelle, together with a four-year-old girl (the future Comtesse De Mun) opened the ball. In such company it was easy for Rousseau to forget about his poverty and he mixed with these people contentedly even though he condemned such civilized society in his works.

He was not only the censor of his works but decided for himself as well as others which kind of morality was correct and which was not. He wrote in one letter to a friend in Geneva that one could find in Paris a certain purity of taste, a certitude of style which was rarely found in the provinces. In Rousseau's *La Nouvelle Héloïse,* St-Preux says to Julie: "There is not any other country in the world where women would be as enlightened as the women of Paris, or generally speaking more sensitive and prudent; you cannot receive better advice in the whole world."

Rousseau never forgot to praise women. He wrote of them even in the dedication of his *Second Discourse*: the women of Geneva "are remarkable and honorable daughters of the Republic whose sex will always rule men." He continued, saying that their pure strength, working only in marriage, pursued the future glory of the state and public good. As with the women of Sparta who ruled Sparta they, the women of Geneva, deserved to rule Geneva.

His links with the Encyclopédistes continued unabated and, along with them, he celebrated enthusiastically when d'Alembert was elected as a member of the French Academy in November 1754, after defeating three Catholic candidates.

He got along well with Voltaire, too. At that time Voltaire decided to settle in Geneva with his mistress, Mme Denis (who Rousseau knew from the salon of Mme Dupin and also from François Mussard's house in Passy). As soon as he learned about Voltaire's decision he sent a letter to Pastor Vernes in Geneva with the recommendation that he visit Voltaire. He praised Voltaire as the most brilliant writer of the century and added his hope that Voltaire would not disturb the peace between the Genevan writers.

Several weeks later he wrote to his Genevan friend, Pastor Pedriau, about Montesquieu's death whom he had admired like Diderot, though the concept of Montesquieu's liberalism differed from the conception of the Enlightenment's avant-garde. Montesquieu recommended that political freedom be secured by a division and balancing of governmental institutions (legislative, executive, and judicial powers). Voltaire and others did not share this view and tended more to Enlightenment absolutism. It is certainly an irony that Voltaire, who descended from the bourgeoisie, supported the king, whereas the aristocrat Montesquieu advocated municipal parlements—the *noblesse de robe*—in the fight against the absolutism of the king.

It has already been mentioned that Rousseau made the acquaintance of the bookseller and publisher Marc-Michel Rey (1720–1780). Rey was an auto-didact of humble descent who had made a fortune by publishing books in Amsterdam. Rey received the manuscript of *Discours sur l'inégalité* from the Parisian publisher Pissot and later became the publisher of all Rousseau's most important works. Rousseau demanded twenty-five louis which he got imme-diately. The publication of the discourse wore on slowly and the reasons were not just technical. Both Rousseau and Rey knew that it was a politically explo-sive work. Rousseau himself knew that the controversial views contained in his essay were going to increase his literary renown but he was afraid of the response of the general public (Rousseau was always very anxious).

Rey asked Rousseau to visit the chief royal censor, Malesherbes, personal-ly, and request that he intervene so the book could be sold in France. Chrétien-Guillaume de Lamoignon de Malesherbes, the son of chancellor M. de Lamoignon, was a censor at the age of thirty-four, but in practice advocated lit-erary freedom. He later defended the king at the court and was executed in 1794. Rousseau refused and replied in his letter that he regarded himself as one who would have nothing to do with the book if it were to be published in France. "Act as if I did not exist." These words betray the fear Rousseau had. He nevertheless asked Rey to advertise the book in England where, in his opin-ion, it had the greatest prospects for success, and to ask Malesherbes to prevent the publication of pirate copies in France. After he read the fascicles of the dis-course, Malesherbes granted his permission for the book to be sold in France on May 12.

Rousseau wished longingly for his work to be received favorably in Geneva. He wrote in *Confessions* that the reason for his not settling in Geneva was the failure of his work there. The correspondence from the time shows, however, that the response was more favorable than Rousseau admits. The for-mer syndic of Geneva, Jean-Louis Du Pan, praised Rousseau's efforts as the work of an honest man and avid patriot who depicted in his dedication the cit-izens of Geneva as they should be and not as they were.

In the summer of that year Rousseau sent one copy of the book to Voltaire in Geneva (At that time Voltaire lived in a villa that he himself called Les Délices and which is now a museum and Voltaire's institute.) Voltaire replied to Rousseau in a letter which later became well-known. It starts rather offensively and derisively: "I have received, Sir, your new book against the human race and I thank you for it . . . no one has ever used so much intelligence to make people into animals. After the perusal of your book one cannot but experience the desire to run on all fours but because I have forfeited this habit more than sixty years ago I am afraid that I will not be able to renew it." Other parts of the letter are friendlier. In conclusion, Voltaire even recommended that Rousseau move to Geneva, the Republic where Voltaire himself had chosen to live, where he was happy living as a peace-loving savage in isolation, and where Rousseau should live as well. Rousseau could enjoy the freedom there with Voltaire and drink together with him the milk of their cows and eat vegetables.

Rousseau's answer was very friendly and he wrote that he would come to Geneva in the spring provided his health would allow it but that he would prefer spring water to the milk. We can not know what the writers were actually thinking because both of these artificial letters were destined for publication and formulated accordingly. The writing of such letters and their immediate publication was an interesting practice of the time. Their purpose was to enhance personal reputation or arouse interest in a work that was yet to be published.

Voltaire's opinion of Rousseau was probably much worse than Rousseau's of Voltaire. His hostile attitude toward Rousseau can be gauged from Voltaire's annotations on a dedicated copy written by hand (it can now be found in St. Petersburg). Voltaire was of bourgeois descent and became rich during his career, of which he was proud. He hated aristocracy. One of his annotations reads, "a person who builds a fence around his plot, and plants and sows it, should have no right to reap the results of his work?"

According to some researchers, it was the very presence of Voltaire in Geneva which explains why Rousseau did not want to settle there. Both had (hitherto) hidden antipathies toward each other. It is more likely that Rousseau had never considered settling permanently in Geneva in earnest. He was simply preparing the ground for the possible necessity of using Geneva as a refuge if one was needed. He wrote in a letter to Jallabert in November 1755 that even if his health improved he would hardly be able to sustain himself as a note copyist in Geneva while this possibility to earn a scarce living was available in Paris where he "carries on frivolous activities that he himself condemns." According to his theory, music, being a refined art, would be harmful to the unspoiled Swiss, but was beneficial to the contrived Parisians. It should be mentioned that Rousseau also worked on a dictionary of music in early 1755, which was not published until several years later.

In the summer of 1755 Rousseau was ill again. He had problems with urination, which he ascribed to the bad air in Paris. His friends recommended he visit the well-known Genevan doctor, Théodore Tronchin, whose fame started when he vaccinated the children of the royal family against smallpox. Dr. Tronchin himself offered his services to Rousseau, but Rousseau refused with reference to his conviction that medical science was useless in his case, and added that he had stopped consulting doctors three years ago. His verdict that doctors were helpless in his illness was justified. Medical science of that time was unable to help him because it did not have antibiotics, which would have been necessary to treat his urethritis, prostatitis and cystitis—antibiotics were not discovered until two hundred years later.

The catheterization of the urethra, which was obviously performed by Thérèse and which—at her hands—produced at the same time the painful sexual gratification, could not cure his complaints. On the contrary, it led to relapses that occurred with increasing frequency, and produced progressive anatomical changes in the form of inflammatory strictures. Rousseau's relapse in the summer of 1755 receded in early fall.

The fifth volume of *Encyclopédie* was published in November and withstood, partly helped by Malesherbes, the attacks of the Church and others who tried to prevent its publication. The volume contained also a contribution on political economy written by Rousseau which can be regarded as a link between his *Second Discourse* and *Du Social contract*. He wrote in it that every human being has a "private will," but has also, and must have, a "general will," which is the source of laws that determine what is correct or incorrect.

The economic views espoused in this article correspond more to the views typical of Locke and Diderot than to those of Adam Smith. The task of the government is to regulate economy and to protect national interests and industry by intervening on their behalf and not to rely on the regulatory power of market forces. In this connection Rousseau presented the example of Genevan granaries storing the corn that was bought up by the Republic; this corn was sold at acceptable prices at bad times when there was a shortage of it so that the occurrence of famine was prevented.

Rousseau came out against high taxes which would finance the activities of state and advocated a simple, mainly agrarian economy which would prevent greater differences in the ownership of property. It is remarkable that he speaks of ownership here, which he identified in the *Second Discourse* as the source of conflict and injustice between people. Here he speaks of it as the "holiest right of citizens, in some respect even more important than freedom itself." These contradictory thoughts are typical of a split personality of a moral masochist. His contradictory statements have always made it difficult to arrive at a consistent interpretation of his views. Every political movement could choose from his political writings the views that were useful for it and simply omit those that were in opposition.

His *Second Discourse* appeared on the bookshelves in August 1755, which was less than a year after Rousseau commissioned its publication. There was no immediate controversy following the publication, unlike after his *First Discourse,* and the book confirmed his reputation as a philosopher and writer. Rousseau was not forced to leave Paris as he had obviously feared.

Noble Savage: Life and Illness in Hermitage and Montlouis

The published work pilloried wealth, which did not prevent Rousseau from making use of the hospitality of his wealthy aristocratic friends. He paid visits mainly to Mme d'Épinay whom he visited either in Paris or at her Château La Chevrette, north of Paris in the valley of Montmorency. They were bound by their mutual pains. Rousseau was ill and Mme d'Épinay had difficulties with her lovers. They comforted each other but were obviously not lovers, contrary to rumors circulated in Paris. Mme d'Épinay's lover, Dupin de Francueil, was unfaithful to her with the sister of the actress Mlle Rose who had an affair with Mme d'Épinay's husband. Francueil offered to give up Mlle Rose but Mme d'Épinay was offended and refused to see him, fixing instead her friendly affection upon Rousseau.

He had comforted her eight years previously upon the death of her first child, and proved to be useful once again in her new difficulties. Mme d'Épinay called him her "bear." She used this word for other friends as well but Rousseau was her first bear. She was no beauty and was well aware of it. She was no match for the brilliant Mme Dupin, yet she was intelligent, lively, loved culture, and was generous. Rousseau enjoyed her warmth and affection.

Mme d'Épinay's celibacy did not last long—immediately after her break with Francueil her old friend Baron Grimm started paying court to her. At one of the dinners given by Grimm's employer, Count de Friese, a certain baron mentioned the defamation circulating in Paris (Mme d'Épinay was alleged to have burned, after the death of her sister, some papers attesting to outstanding debts incurred by her husband, which should have been paid to her sister's heirs). Grimm declared he was a friend of Mme d'Épinay and challenged the baron to a duel, in which both of them were slightly injured. Mme d'Épinay promptly invited Grimm to become her beau and lover, to the discontent of Rousseau who thus forfeited his privileged standing. He never forgave this Grimm for this, and the episode started their subsequent enmity as Charles Duclos recorded it.

During one of their autumn trips to the Château La Chevrette, Mme d'Épinay showed Rousseau some reconstruction efforts made there. In an outlying spot of the estate, an old country house near the forest had been rebuilt to a new cottage. Rousseau had seen this dilapidated building previously, before he left for Geneva, and had exclaimed then, "Ah Madame, what a delightful place to live in! Here is a refuge absolutely made for me." Mme d'Épinay had said nothing at the time but Rousseau was surprised to see during his second visit, in the fall of 1755, that the cottage had been totally rebuilt and stood in the midst of a garden. Mme d'Épinay said, "Here is your refuge, Mr. Bear. You chose it yourself. It is offered to you out of friendship. I hope it will put an end to your cruel idea of parting from me." Rousseau's "answer" was characteristic of him: "I was deeply and pleasantly touched. I moistened the hand of my friend and benefactress with my tears." He added, however, that he did not accept.

This was not to be his last word and refusal, however. In his letters he told Mme d'Épinay that he wanted to spend his life in her proximity. In the end he could be easily persuaded to accept Hermitage: "I renounced the idea of living in my native country and promised to move into Hermitage." He wrote in an unpublished autobiographical fragment that Mme d'Épinay did what she could to persuade him to change his plans to leave France, and when she saw he could not live in Paris she rebuilt Hermitage and promised that he could live there. She even provided the furniture for the cottage.

This episode is psychologically interesting. Rousseau deprecated, as a matter of principle, all presents, even minor ones, brought to him occasionally by his visitors. He refused to be paid more than was his fee for note copying by his clients. But here he suddenly betrayed his principles and accepted a present, the value of which was incomparably higher. We can conclude, therefore, that his refusal of smaller presents was a mere posture by which he intended to make a mark for himself as an incorruptible, morally elevated person. He had to act in keeping with this posture to make his writings credible, at least in this way. By accepting Hermitage, however, he ran into dependencies that were of much greater consequence. This fact was perhaps the reason why he later referred to the friendship of Mme d'Épinay using characteristically masochistic expressions of total submission: "I realized that I *hung a chain round my neck* . . . this *tie* considerably diminished my pleasure . . . I had to submit to this *yoke* . . . I found that the liberty she had so lavishly promised me was only granted me on condition that I never make use of it" (italics added). The friendship fettered him, robbed him of freedom, and hung a chain round his neck!

His protectress and benefactress was shining in society and Rousseau liked to enjoy the entertainment with her, but their conversation in private was boring; they had nothing to say to each other, so they even played chess (Rousseau had a similar problem with Mlle de Vulson in his youth). Mme d'Épinay did not attract Rousseau sexually. They exchanged kisses but that was all. She was very thin and "her chest was as flat as my hand" as we can read in *Confessions*. This was enough to transform him into an ice cube. Rousseau loved luxuriant bosoms, which he had been accustomed to when he lived with Mme de Warens. He reproached the women of Paris for having small bosoms and fondly recalled the fuller shapes of Swiss women.

Thérèse and her mother were far from being enthusiastic about his intention to live in the country. Grimm rebuked Mme d'Épinay that she was not rendering good service to Rousseau. The solitude would poison his soul and he would become an unbearable neighbor. The company around Holbach was of the same view. Rousseau wrote to Mme d'Épinay on March 18, 1756 and informed her that he was making preparations to move to Hermitage and asks her to help him sell his books to pay his taxes and his rent for three months (but rebukes her for making several errors in his favor when he checked the bills for the sold books).

Mme d'Épinay found various ways to help Rousseau to settle into Hermitage. She did not believe Grimm who said that Rousseau would bite the hand which fed him. Rousseau left Paris on April 9 and decided not to return to the city again.

The relocation was carried out by Mme d'Épinay's servants. Rousseau described the journey enthusiastically but Mme d'Épinay recorded that the roads were full of snow and mud and that Mme Levasseur (who was around eighty) had to be carried by the servants. Rousseau claimed that he was awakened by a nightingale during the first nights at Hermitage. That was certainly not true because nightingales arrive in France at a later time. The letters, which he wrote on the first days of his stay, express only enthusiasm.

Rousseau claimed that his character improved for the better because he had left the corrupted metropolis. He was not looking down on others, and had become more tolerant, gentle, timid and good: "I have regained my true nature." Even his relationship with Thérèse allegedly got better, and even though she was not accompanying him on his walks, he spent many a pleasant hour with her under the trees, where she seemed to be happier than ever before and where "she opened her heart to me as never before." But he says in the same chapter, quite antagonistically, "the day that had united me with my Thérèse was the day which determined my moral being," and further, "I have never felt the least glimmering of love for her . . . the sensual needs I satisfied with her were for me purely sexual and had nothing to do with her as an individual."

These sentences support the thesis proposed in this book: he needed Thérèse as an obedient instrument rendering abnormal sexual practices (urethral masturbation), which he required to achieve sexual gratification, as he was ashamed to solicit it from more educated or more intelligent women. He declared later that they lived together as "brother and sister." But it is much more likely that he saw in Thérèse a mere maidservant who cleaned his catheters and brought them into his bedroom when he did not feel well.

In Hermitage Rousseau was soon missing the people who visited him in Paris. He missed Diderot in particular. He tried to invite Lenieps (1694–1774), a radical opponent of the patrician Genevan government who lived in Parisian exile as a rich banker. Mme d'Épinay could not come because she was ill herself and was being treated by Dr. Tronchin. Rousseau himself traveled to Paris only once to visit his old friend Gauffecourt whom he called "papa." He forgave him for once having tried to seduce Thérèse and for showing her pornographic pictures on their joint journey to Lyon in 1754.

Rousseau felt lonely in Hermitage but the loneliness and peacefulness of the place helped his literary work. He copied notes in the morning, walked in the forest in the afternoon, recording his thoughts in a notebook (like Hobbes), and wrote in the evening. He abbreviated and prepared for publication the voluminous literary inheritance of abbé Saint-Pierre (mainly to please Mme Dupin). The abbé had died twelve years earlier.

It is interesting from the point of view of our time to dedicate several lines to this rather unknown writer and compare his ideas with those of Rousseau. Saint-Pierre (Charles-Irénée Castel, abbé de Saint-Pierre, 1658–1753, originator of various economic theories) was the pupil of Thomas Hobbes who held that in the natural state (without any government) people were in a state of permanent war. Saint-Pierre widened this thesis and recognized that this state of incessant war characterized also the relationships between nations, in analogy to Hobbes's state of individuals at war. Like Hobbes, who claimed that society could not do without a firm government, Saint-Pierre proposed the establishment of an international organization, a confederation of individual states, representing the rulers of the states. Individual countries would then lose part of their sovereignty but would gain a guarantee of peace. International trade promotes peace (a universal view of the Enlightenment) and, vice versa, trade is possible only during peace. International trade is beneficial for all and lowers the probability of war.

This led him to predict the foundation of an international economic community, together with a political international confederation. The present existence of a developing and expanding European Union, NATO, and the establishment of the United Nations shows the clarity of his foresight.

His views made Rousseau an unsuitable editor of the literary heritage of the far-sighted abbé. Rousseau rejected Hobbes's view that a natural state was equal to a state of war between people. He claimed that this state was a consequence of the development of the modern state. According to Rousseau no international community could guarantee peace but would be rather a cause of permanent wars. He thus rejected Saint-Pierre's views because "to be wise in the world of fools is a form of lunacy." He included his ideas relating to an eternal peace (regarding which he was not at all optimistic) in his work *Jugement sur le project de paix perpetuelle* where he again rejected Saint-Pierre's views and postulated that peace could be attained only between smaller, economically independent and self-sufficient nations. Rousseau's work appeared after Saint-Pierre's death—the abbé's *Project* appeared in the fifth year of the Seven Years' War that broke out in the summer of 1756.

That same summer, Voltaire sent Rousseau a copy of his poem "*Le Désastre de Lisbonne,*" which had been written in 1756 after the November 1755 earthquake in Lisbon, in which many people died. The earthquake shattered Voltaire's deistic faith as well as the faith that the order of the world was right.

The issue of theodicy reemerged. His poem expressed doubts about the goodness and justice of God.

> *Élements, animaux, humains, tout est en guerre Il le faut avouer,*
> *le MAL est sur la terre.*

Rousseau replied with a carefully drafted letter intended for publication. He contended in it that God was not responsible for the disasters humanity was afflicted with on the earth. Most of the evil was of peoples' own making. If they did not build multi-story buildings and overcrowded cities there would not occur such tragedies or no tragedies at all. His faith in the goodness of God could not be shaken by anything. He agreed here with the papal motto "Whatever may be it is right."

Voltaire's reply was rather short and was not concerned with Rousseau's arguments; Voltaire referred to his illness and the illness of his niece as he stated, "I have with me one of my nieces, who is dangerously ill. I am a sick-nurse, and I am sick myself." Voltaire's real reply was the novel *Candide*. Rousseau later complained about it to Prince von Württenberg, saying that in it Voltaire was making fun of him. In *Confessions* he writes something else: "Voltaire has published the reply that he promised me. It is nothing else than his novel *Candide*, of which I cannot speak because I have not read it (*Confessions*, 400).

At Hermitage Rousseau experienced the first signs of indignation. His "freedom" was questionable. On the one hand he did not know when Mme d'Épinay would call him to the château, on the other he could never be sure when unexpected visitors would come and disturb him. Hermitage could not be compared to his refuge in Les Charmettes. His common life with Thérèse had lasted for some time and they had nothing to say to each other. They understood each other without saying a word and Thérèse was incapable of intelligent conversation. She also did not like going for walks, which Rousseau loved, and he did not force her to accompany him. Rousseau's dislike of his mother-in-law continued to increase, especially when he learned she was running up debts behind his back and which Thérèse had not mentioned to him.

On his solitary walks, Rousseau took more and more refuge in sexual fantasies and recalled all the women he had met in his life, "I saw myself surrounded by a seraglio of houris . . ." Among these were Mlle Galley, Mlle Grafenried, Mme Basile, his pretty music students, Mme de Larnage. He believed he no longer had a chance with women, being an older man. He did not want to disturb the peaceful home atmosphere with Thérèse, whom he really loved (at least at this time, according to *Confessions*), by falling in love with other women.

Amid these sexual fantasies, governed by "Love" and "Friendship" as two goddesses of his heart, Rousseau began his work on the story of *La Nouvelle Héloïse*, an imaginative projection of Rousseau's idealized longings transformed through the deliberate creation of a seemingly independent world (Grimsley 1969, 118). He described the creative process in detail: he created two friends in his fantasy, two young women with different characters, both of them agreeable to him; one blonde, the other with brown hair; one lively and the other gentle. "I gave one of them a lover to whom the other was a tender friend and even something more" (another love triangle). This is how Rousseau described the genesis of his famous novel in the summer of 1756, the work which he started in addition to his work on *Du Contract social*.

La Nouvelle Héloïse is a romantic novel par excellence. It was written in June, at the season of summer as well as the summertime of Rousseau's life, when he realized he himself lacked real love. In this autobiographic novel he transformed himself into a good-looking young man (with accompanying strengths and weaknesses) and summoned up in his fantasy all the erotic experiences of his youth. He placed the story in the environment of the lake of Geneva with the natural panorama of the Alps, an area which he knew intimately and which was frequently the Promised Land of his fantasies. The emotion, nature and passionate love of *La Nouvelle Héloïse* was not just Rousseau's own creation, but rather the culmination of a great movement of emotionality that was characteristic of the eighteenth century, as was faith in reason. This movement is sometimes called "Rousseauism before Rousseau."

In comparison with previous sentimental novels, Rousseau made his work great by skillfully manipulating a combination of the cults of feeling and love. To this powerful combination, he added virtue. His sentimentalism is made morally legitimate.

Considering the immense success of the novel, primarily among women, it is necessary to offer the reader an outline of its contents, which engulfed all layers of the readership of that time, though today most of us are only familiar with its name. The novel was written as a series of letters and Rousseau did not pose as the writer but as an editor of the letters: "There have to be theatres and novels for the corrupted people of the big cities. I watched the morals of my time and published these letters," wrote Rousseau in one of two forewords to his novel. While he was working on the novel, Rousseau met Mme d'Houdetot and his affair with her changed the character of the novel. The original erotic fantasies were subordinated to more moral considerations. He appended religious themes at the end of the work and let the dying Julie confess to a religion which reappears later in *La Profession de foi du vicaire savoyard*.

It is interesting from a psychological point of view that Rousseau's masochism and his masochistic demands become projected into all of the main characters of the novel. The parallel between St-Preux and Rousseau is striking. Their "weakness" leads them into grievous errors. St-Preux is tormented by anxiety and insecurity and he is "easy to subjugate." He has a weak, unstable personality with another essential trait of Rousseau's own character: his persistent tendency to see himself through other people's eyes (emotional experiences of his early life). He is able to feel that he has become in some way transparent to the gaze of others. Similar to Rousseau, St-Preux needs another's esteem: "I must be esteemed by Julie . . . all my worth lies in your esteem." It is a matter of concern to him to gain not only the acknowledgement of Julie but also that of other people who "stand higher," as for example Wolmar.

The masochistic perspective of St-Preux (and Rousseau) is clearly described: "I no longer belong to myself, my alienated soul is completely in you . . . Yes, my Julie, it is indeed you who form my life and being . . . Your will is enough for me . . . I shall be nothing but a part of you."

At the beginning of the novel Julie appears to be convinced of her love but, similar to Rousseau, sees in love a platonic relationship, "which speaks to the heart without stirring the senses," and which is even defiled by the senses. "My too affectionate heart needs love, but my senses do not need a lover." She constantly treats their passion as a source of shame and guilt. Their relationship was a "criminal intercourse." She has an "ungrateful" and "unnatural" heart that has been "degraded" by this shameful relationship with St-Preux.

Her sense of guilt is exacerbated by her belief that this illicit love hastened her mother's death. Here Rousseau's own sense of guilt resurfaces, which had been deeply rooted in his unconscious: the sexual intercourse that resulted in his own birth caused the death of his mother. This is also why Julie feels she is "an impure victim who defiles the sacrifice at which she is to be offered up." She is "weak" and "guilty," but not "depraved" and "sinful." Rousseau often used these expressions when he referred to his own person. Julie then shows an attitude toward love which is curiously reminiscent of Rousseau's own views (Grimsley 1969, 135). Sex is identical with guilt.

Rousseau identified with Julie also in religious matters and put his own convictions in her mouth. The author projected into the character of Wolmar his moral conscience. Wolmar symbolizes his moral self or superego. He is the discerning, omnipotent and all-wise father figure, and "has some supernatural gift for reading into the depths of people's hearts."

Now let us hear the general story of *La Nouvelle Héloïse*:

In the house of Baron d'Étange, a nobleman in the canton of Vaud, lives St-Preux, who is employed as an educator for the nobleman's daughter, Julie. He is a young man, born a citizen, whose character represents young Rousseau. St-Preux disobeys the laws of his class and falls in love with the aristocratic ward, Julie. He writes her a letter in which he reveals his love for her. He knows he has transgressed the prevailing morals and asks Julie to send him away. Needless to say, Julie wants him to stay. St-Preux replies that he cannot stay and be scoffed at, and threatens to commit suicide. Julie has no other choice and admits that she is in love with him, too, "Didn't I say something already? And didn't you understand me well?" She kisses him for the first time, in front of her friend Claire, and later seduces him in a chalet—this time Claire is, of course, absent.

St-Preux is seduced similar to Rousseau. He does not seduce Julie of his own accord, which is faithful to the passive, masochistic approach to sexuality. (Voltaire observed that it should not be said that St-Preux seduced Julie.) Julie represents the type of mistress Rousseau has always required. A dominant person who would exercise control over him. He says to her, "My Julie, you are predestined to rule . . . your spirit is crushing me. I am nothing in your presence."

Julie dominates St-Preux (Rousseau) but is herself ruled by a father who is also dominant and wants to prevent the marriage of his daughter to a burgher. He even beats his daughter who then, as a result of the beating, miscarries the child conceived with St-Preux. Julie forgives her father and reconciles with him. She deserts her lover and agrees to marry the aristocrat Wolmar, who was chosen by her father. She becomes an ideal wife and mother of her children despite the fact that she does not love Wolmar although she does revere him. She carries out her duties, is a faithful Christian and regains her purity in this way. She lives with the atheist Wolmar who is an unemotional but honest husband.

After several years St-Preux comes back from exile and becomes the educator of their children. They all live happily in a small paradise on the shore of Lake Geneva. Everyone has his appointed place and function from which he does not move, for he lives in a society governed by order, nature, and reason.

One day Wolmar decides to test the faithfulness of his wife and leaves her alone with St-Preux for some time. St-Preux and Julie take a rowing trip by boat across the lake. A storm drives them to the rocky shores at Meillerie where they get on land. In the stormy night and surrounded by the impressive beauty of the Alps, Julie discovers her love of St-Preux is still alive but her moral purity prevails and she withstands the temptation.

The writer halted here and did not know how to continue. He was satisfied with what he had written so far. In the final version of the novel the heroine dies after attempting to save her drowning child from the lake. At one time Rousseau even contemplated the possibility that he could bring Julie and St-Preux together.

The final chapters were written in the winter of 1756–1757 on special paper with a golden border. Rousseau dried the ink with a blue-silver powder. Single sheets were bound with a blue ribbon. Rousseau came to enjoy reading passages from the work to other people and when he could not find listeners he made Thérèse and Mme Levasseur listen to him. Thérèse would allegedly be sighing and letting her emotions run away with her, whereas her old mother barely understood what was going on and would confine herself to occasional exclamations such as, "I say, this is very beautiful."

Another listener was Alexandre Deleyre, an unsuccessful writer who was indispensable to Rousseau because his visits kept him in touch with Diderot and he brought Rousseau novelties from Paris. Rousseau tolerated him in spite of the ironic way of writing Deleyre occasionally used (Rousseau's sense of humor was rather limited). In one letter Deleyre wrote wittily that destitution was Rousseau's glory.

Mme d'Épinay was not enthusiastic about the novel (nor was Diderot who did not like Julie). But she kept her opinion hidden just as Rousseau hid his opinion of her.

Toward the end of summer Rousseau experienced a new relapse of his illness; this time he complained about pains in his joints in early fall. It is almost certain that he did not suffer from genuine rheumatism. Mme d'Épinay sent him a flannel petticoat from Paris and Thérèse produced a waistcoat for Rousseau from it.

His friends tried to persuade Rousseau to spend the winter in Paris but Rousseau was intransigent. Though visited once by Diderot, Rousseau felt lonely through the long winter evenings. He wrote in one letter to Mme d'Épinay that he had spoiled his stomach when he attempted to live as a peasant, on cabbage and bacon.

During this winter Rousseau set out for Paris only once. He visited Papa Gauffecourt, who had suffered a stroke which had apparently resulted in damage to the left hemisphere as he spoke with difficulty and his memory was impaired as well.

Rousseau returned to Hermitage in early January 1757 and immediately came down with a cold. Thérèse and her mother were ill as well. Even Mme d'Épinay was ill and she decided to go to Geneva to be treated by Dr. Tronchin. She asked Rousseau if he would accompany her but he refused. Mme d'Épinay then decided to postpone the journey. This type of situation would occur again in the future and eventually resulted in Rousseau's break with his protectress.

In his letters to Dr. Tronchin, Rousseau again considers the idea of returning to Geneva. He was encouraged along these lines by Dr. Tronchin who even suggested that Rousseau could get the post of a librarian there. This was, of course, unacceptable to Rousseau because such work would restrict his personal freedom, and was therefore not suitable for him. He explained that the main reason for his decision not to move to Geneva was that he could not find any work there (which was not true) but he also did not know what to do with Thérèse's mother—Mme Levasseur—who was eighty and dependent on other people to care for her. Whenever he was faced with someone's suggestion to resettle in Geneva he had a series of ready-made arguments at hand that were designed to explain why this step was impossible.

At that time Mme d'Épinay was dependent on her friendship with Rousseau because her lover, Baron de Grimm, had become the secretary to Maréchal-Duc d'Estrées and had accompanied him on the campaign to Westphalia. Instead of going to Geneva, Mme d'Épinay returned to the country in February 1757 and Rousseau had lunch with her on Spy Tuesday, February 22.

He wrote in *Confessions* that Mme d'Épinay was restricting the freedom she had promised him by setting their meetings arbitrarily, which made it very difficult for him to concentrate on his work. It should be pointed out, however, that the *Confessions* were written much later and Rousseau might have projected other feelings of bitterness into the description of his quarrels with Mme d'Épinay.

In 1757 Mme d'Épinay mediated very prudently in the argument between Rousseau and Diderot that broke out after Rousseau found an embarrassing remark in the new play *Le Fils naturel* (The Natural Son) that Diderot had sent to him. One character of the play, Constance, says to another character, Dorval, who (similar to Rousseau) intends to live in seclusion: "Only the wicked man is alone." (This remark survived a remarkably long time—recently I read this paraphrase: "You are a wicked man. You live in solitude and need only books.")

Rousseau was very aggrieved by these words. He has always emphasized that he was "good" though he was not thoroughly "virtuous." In *La Nouvelle Héloïse* he expressed the view, "All really great passions arise in solitude . . . not in a world where no thing has enough time to leave behind a deeper impression and where a host of tendencies weaken the strength of feelings." Rousseau was also very insulted because Diderot mentioned "a woman of eighty."

There ensued a lengthy exchange of tearful letters and Rousseau forbade Diderot to enter Hermitage but thanks to the intervention of Mme d'Épinay and Deleyre a precarious reconciliation was reached. As a reaction to Rousseau's letter, Diderot apologized in the postscript of his letter although this apology is not mentioned in *Confessions*. In *Confessions* Rousseau wrote that this reconciliation was reached thanks to him because Diderot was in difficulties. At that time Diderot was attacked by the Church, following a critical article in *Encyclopédie,* and he also had to face the defamation that his play *Le Fils naturel* was a plagiarism of Goldoni's play, *Il Vero amico.*

Diderot visited Rousseau in Hermitage in early April even though the wounds were not yet healed. Concerning Diderot's innuendo about Mme Levasseur and her stay in Hermitage, (according to Diderot's daughter, Mme Levasseur got secret financial gifts from Diderot), this worry was certainly legitimate and was shared by other people in Paris as well. Hermitage was definitely not an appropriate place for an old woman to stay during winter though Rousseau assured everyone it was her decision to stay there. Rousseau's descriptions of Thérèse's mother in *Confessions* are conflicting. He wrote that sometimes he was glad she was in Hermitage but he sometimes laments over her parsimony, secretiveness and her prodding of Thérèse. In the end he felt a captive in his own house and had "only contempt" for his mother-in-law.

In May 1757, however, all arguments were forgotten as a result of something nobody could expect: Rousseau fell in love.

He had known Élisabeth-Sophie-Françoise, Comtesse d'Houdetot, for some time. When she was eighteen they had acted together in an amateur-play, *L'Engagement téméraire*, and he also knew her from his visits to the Château La Chevrette as she was Mme d'Épinay's stepdaughter. She was married to Claude-Constant-César d'Houdetot who was a descendant of old Norman aristocracy. She had never loved her husband but had three children with him by the age of twenty-six. Her lover was Rousseau's friend, Jean-François de St-Lambert.

Sophie was not beautiful: her face was pockmarked, her skin was coarse, she was nearsighted, and her eyes were rather round and bulging. But all this was offset by her glorious dark, wavy long hair reaching down to her knees. She emitted goodness and sweetness, which earned her the nickname *Le Parfait*, "the Perfect One." She was of small stature but had a firm bosom, distinguishing her from Mme d'Épinay who had none. We know that Rousseau loved women with well-developed bosoms. St-Preux wrote Julie that he is aroused when he sees her bosom. Rousseau liked the same things because he later emphasized to the illustrator of *Julie*, the novel which later was named *La Nouvelle Héloïse*, that his heroine must be represented with a full bosom.

Rousseau admitted that he fell in love with Sophie because he saw in her the imaginary Julie of his novel ("I saw my Julie in Mme d'Houdetot"). He felt no love for Mme d'Houdetot before he created Julie. The impact of his literary fantasies was fatal for Rousseau—his original man, created in his discourses, was good, not yet corrupted, and poor. The publication of his works forced Rousseau to imitate the life of a pure, unspoiled man who preserves his own personal freedom and is independent of others ("to put my life in agreement with my principles").

When he finished *Héloïse*, in which he portrayed himself as St-Preux, he found he was missing Julie, so he picked a woman from his environment who was most similar to her and decided to fall in love with her. The doubts about whether this was a spontaneous love are justifiable. It seems more likely that Rousseau was acting a new part here, for himself and for others—it is difficult to determine whether the emphasis was more on acting for himself or for others—and that his romantic flare-up was well calculated; though it cannot be ruled out that he started to believe in the authenticity of his emotion later and worked himself into it.

It is simply not true, as some say, that Rousseau used his passion for Mme d'Houdetot as a model for his most famous novel. On the contrary, his passion was a copy of his novel. He started writing the novel in summer 1756 and did not fall in love with Sophie until May 1757. It must be admitted, however, that the work on *Héloïse* was not yet finished at the time Rousseau fell in love and that his infatuation with Sophie did influence the style of the novel in its later stages.

The great love did not begin romantically at all: the lover of Mme d'Houdetot, St-Lambert, was drafted (similar to Grimm, the lover of Mme d'Épinay) and asked Sophie to visit Rousseau and inform him about Gauffecourt's health. Mme d'Houdetot set out to visit Rousseau in January 1757. Her coachman went astray and she had to wade through mud, arriving at Hermitage in a completely sodden but cheerful state, whereupon she had to change into Thérèse's dress. (Many years later, in *Confessions*, Rousseau confused this visit with the visit of Mme d'Houdetot in June 1756.) During her first visit Mme d'Houdetot had noticed Rousseau looking at her with interest and her letters began to acquire a seductive undertone. It was understandable for she felt lonely and Rousseau, though already forty-five, had considerable sex appeal as a literary celebrity, which was common in France in the eighteenth century. It is also possible that she wanted to irk her relative Mme d'Épinay who claimed to be the protectress of her "bear."

Mme d'Houdetot was born as Élisabeth-Sophie-Françoise Lalive de Bellegarde on December 18, 1730 and was a sister of Mme d'Épinay's brother. There was a certain jealousy and rivalry between both relatives, based partly on the fact that the marriage of the wealthier Mme d'Épinay led to a slight descent on the social ladder. She had married a rich burgher whereas her stepsister married up to noble, aristocratic circles. Mme d'Houdetot had, as a member of *nobless de race*, the right to be received at the court in Versailles even though she was not as rich as Mme d'Épinay. Even the lovers of Mme d'Épinay (Francueil and Grimm) were not considered to be particularly important, whereas the lover of Mme d'Houdetot, St-Lambert, was appreciated in society and in keeping with the rules of *ancien régime* had to be accepted even by her own husband.

In the spring of 1757 Mme d'Houdetot visited Rousseau for the second time. This time she arrived on horseback in male clothing from her residence in Eaubonne about ten kilometers from Hermitage. Rousseau wrote that he was overwhelmed with romantic love (Rousseau used the word "romantic" very seldom even though it was related with his name), the "first and only love of my life."

Mme d'Houdetot asked him to visit her in Eaubonne where Rousseau declared his love to her. "Confessed love is always more enduring." Even though Sophie spoke of her love for St-Lambert, she did not turn down his declaration. She even encouraged his glow and savored being admired by a renowned writer. Not that Rousseau would mind if she spoke of her love for St-Lambert—he luxuriated in triangle relationships and was accustomed to them. In fact, her love for St-Lambert did titillate him (see medical analysis in Part 2). "There was equal love on both sides, though it was never mutual. We were both intoxicated with love—hers for her lover, and mine for her . . . She . . . talked to me about nothing with so much pleasure as about the intimate and delightful trio we could form together once I had returned to my senses."

A love triangle corresponded to Rousseau's masochistic predisposition and also, similar to the hero in his book, the manly soldier, writer and seducer, St-Lambert, who represented the character of a macho man of his time, Rousseau could successfully play the role of a romantically devoted, soft and weeping lover who lets himself be fully dominated by his mistress. Such a character must have had—by contrast—a certain charm for women of that time, in which the early signs of a developing feminism were starting to emerge. Mme d'Houdetot continued her visits to Hermitage and Rousseau reciprocated with visits to Eaubonne. Sophie loved long walks like Rousseau and their conversation was always entertaining. The only thing Rousseau was afraid of was that Sophie might be making fun of him:

> I became pressing: the position was a delicate one. It is astonishing, perhaps even unique, that a woman who had gone so far as to bargain, should have got off so lightly. She refused me nothing that the tenderest friendship could grant. She granted me nothing that could make her unfaithful, and I had the humiliation of seeing that the fire her slight favors kindled in my senses did not convey the tini-

est spark to hers . . . I swear, that if ever I was betrayed by my senses and tried to make her unfaithful, *I never truly desired it (Confessions,* italics added).

It follows from these quotations that, though Rousseau and Sophie were oftentimes alone on their walks in the garden and even in a grove at night, sexual intercourse had never taken place. Rousseau even slept in Mme d'Houdetot's bedroom, "Yet even when our intoxication was at its most dangerous height she never forgot herself for a moment . . . I loved her too well to wish to posses her." As a masochist, Rousseau was not seriously interested in real sexual intercourse, nor was Mme d'Houdetot, for whom this was rather a playful flirtation. "What intoxicating tears I shed at her knees!" Rousseau must have been kneeling in front of Sophie and weeping. It is the same picture he had depicted in Turin. The text is interspersed with masochistic expressions about "humiliation . . . abasement," and "I experienced the shame of seeing myself humiliated."

There is no doubt, however, that Rousseau was sexually aroused. "In her company I felt only the irksomeness of an inexhaustible and always useless vigor . . . This state and, what was worse, its continuance over three months of ceaseless stimulation and privation threw me into exhaustion." Sexual caresses and "petting," at which Rousseau was probably very experienced, were obviously a significant part of their relationship. This we know directly from Thérèse. When she was later unfaithful to Rousseau with James Boswell, who regarded himself to be a better lover than the older Rousseau, he was told openly by Thérèse that his youthful strength did not make him a more desirable lover than Rousseau. She said that Boswell was virile but lacked the art *she* liked. She asked him whether he, as a traveled man, did not know all the things a man could achieve with his hands and instructed him in *arte amoris* that she learned as Rousseau's mistress (see David Buchanan 1971, 334–47). Thanks to this remark we know that Rousseau was able to gratify women, even though he did not have outright sexual intercourse with them, and it increases the plausibility of the supposition that Rousseau was himself masturbated (urethrally) by Thérèse returned the pleasure by masturbating her.

In his letters Rousseau gave his beloved the names "Sophie," "Julie" or "Mimi." Thérèse, who was as jealous as Mme d'Épinay, delivered the letters of both lovers and it cannot be ruled out that Mme d'Épinay was aware of at least some of the letters which Thérèse might have showed her. Rousseau wrote about Mme d'Épinay's jealousy: "Women have all the arts of concealing their anger, especially when it is strong. Mme d'Épinay, a violent but deliberate woman, possessed this power to an eminent degree. She pretended to see nothing, to suspect nothing."

The idyll and laughter ended on June 12 because Mme d'Houdetot's official lover, St-Lambert, turned up unexpectedly at the Château La Chevrette. Everybody was rooted to the ground and the atmosphere turned cold, as we know from a letter written by Mme d'Épinay. Rousseau left and sent Mme d'Houdetot a formal letter the next day informing her that he had to visit Diderot in Paris and apologized for not being able to come and embrace St-Lambert. He described everything to Diderot who recommended that Rousseau tell St-Lambert everything and leave his mistress in peace. Rousseau promised to do everything Diderot told him to do but he never kept his promise.

The love triangle met again at the Château La Chevrette for supper but because the mood was not very good, Mme d'Épinay excused herself, saying she did not feel well. Rousseau then read St-Lambert his letter to Voltaire but his listener fell asleep. Rousseau went on reading in spite of St-Lambert's snoring.

The whole scandal was obviously already known in Paris because Deleyre wrote openly in a letter of June 22, 1757 that there was a rumor going around Paris about a hermit who wandered from one château to another visiting all the nymphs in the region.

St-Lambert returned to the front in Germany in early August but the affectionate relationship between Sophie and Rousseau was over. Sophie asked Rousseau to give back to her the letters she had written to him, but she did not return his letters to him, declaring that she had burned them, which probably was not true. Rousseau and Sophie continued to see each other but only platonically and Rousseau again had more time for Mme d'Épinay whose admiration, however, was not as strong as before. In a letter to Grimm she described Rousseau as "a moral dwarf on stilts." Outwardly, however, they continued to be good friends.

Rousseau suffered again, this time with a rather short relapse of his illness in August 1757. Visiting Eaubonne in August Rousseau found Mme d'Houdetot in tears—apparently she had received an angry letter from St-Lambert. She said that St-Lambert had "wrong information." She added that they must part, or their contacts must be absolutely correct.

It was about that time that Thérèse informed Rousseau that Mme d'Épinay had tried to gain access to his letters. This caused further cooling of their mutual relations. On Wednesday, August 31, Rousseau and Mme d'Épinay exchanged as many as five letters in a single day. Rousseau accused Mme d'Épinay of indiscretion and she denied his accusations. According to her records, Rousseau visited her later at La Chevrette, knelt down at her feet and accused himself of having suspected her unjustly. After Mme d'Épinay described Rousseau's behavior in a letter to Grimm, he warned her to be cautious in her contacts with Rousseau "as you know that lunatics are dangerous."

Rousseau also wrote a letter to St-Lambert accusing him of destroying his friendship with Mme d'Houdetot based on false reports and that he was being forced out of human society day by day and his only friends were St-Lambert and Mme d'Houdetot. When even this friendship disappeared he would have to "die alone and deserted in solitude." This was certainly an overstatement because Rousseau was a frequent visitor at La Chevrette, taking part in various celebrations there and writing several minor musical compositions, thereby getting his mind off Sophie.

Mme d'Épinay's lover, Grimm, returned from the war at the end of September. He was even more arrogant than before. Rousseau had to move out of the bedroom he had had at his disposal at the Château La Chevrette, which was situated next door to Mme d'Épinay's bedroom. Rousseau was indignant about it, especially when it turned out the bedroom was given to Grimm. His antipathy toward Grimm grew stronger. He wrote that Grimm was bluntly ignoring him. In addition, Grimm spent long hours manicuring his hands and was a hypocrite (according to Rousseau, Grimm was even able to weep deliberately at appropriate times in public). He told Mme d'Épinay he refused to have anything to do with Grimm. In *Confessions* Rousseau extensively described numerous defects in Grimm's character, as well as Grimm's hostile behavior toward him.

Eventually, however, Rousseau made peace with Grimm, again at Mme d'Épinay's insistence, which pleased Mme d'Houdetot as well. She wrote Rousseau that he was not made for a life without his friends: "They deserve you and you deserve them." Sophie and Rousseau met again at a celebration held in honor of Mme d'Épinay which was also attended by Mme d'Épinay's husband who could not have been in a good mood, having recently learned he was going to lose his lucrative tax collector post and, additionally, finding that his château was increasingly governed by his wife's lover, Grimm.

After the celebration Rousseau wrote Mme d'Houdetot a long letter in which he still addressed her with "*tu*" in the first paragraphs, although he later changed the address to the formal "*vous*." This emotional letter was not mailed and Rousseau replaced it with a more restrained one. St-Lambert's reply to Rousseau's letter was cordial (although he said to Diderot at that time that the only reply to such a letter should be a cane) and the friendship of the trio appeared to be all right again. Soon afterward, St-Lambert fell sick (he was stricken with paralysis at the age of forty-one) and the lover became a patient who needed care.

The mutual reconciliation was marred by Rousseau's row with Mme d'Épinay that eventually led to a complete break. As before, at the beginning of the year, Mme d'Épinay wanted to depart for Geneva in October and undergo treatment under the personal supervision of Dr. Tronchin. Rousseau learned the true reason for her trip to Geneva from Thérèse who in turn was informed by Mme d'Épinay's servants. Mme d'Épinay was allegedly pregnant by Grimm. This assumption was false because we know that Mme d'Épinay was genuinely sick.

She asked Rousseau to accompany her to Geneva, but for reasons that are difficult to understand, Rousseau resisted her request, which was supported by everybody—all of his as well as Mme d'Épinay's friends including Diderot—and refused to accompany her to Geneva. There could have been several different reasons why Rousseau refused to go. Perhaps he did not want to desert Mme d'Houdetot; perhaps he did not feel well in the approaching winter (he said he had to use the chamber pot every five minutes); perhaps he thought it was Grimm's duty as Mme d'Épinay's official lover to accompany her. It is most likely, however, that Rousseau could not forgive Mme d'Épinay for compelling Thérèse to show her the correspondence between Rousseau and Mme d'Houdetot, and then informing St-Lambert of their content, which had put an end to their love affair.

She knew that her stepsister would always prefer St-Lambert to Rousseau. Her demand that Rousseau accompany her to Geneva was probably motivated by jealousy. She wanted to foil further contacts between Rousseau and Mme d'Houdetot. Rousseau was well aware of this behind-the-scenes scheming. He knew about Mme d'Épinay's jealousy, he knew that it was she who had caused the end of the greatest amorous flare-up of his life, but he could not tell any of his friends about it.

Of course, this meant his friends could not understand why Rousseau did not want to accompany his benefactress to Geneva. In the rather extensive exchange of letters between Diderot and Rousseau, Diderot points out that Rousseau had moral obligations and duties to Mme d'Épinay. Rousseau was furious because he could hardly find a friend who did not recommend that he accompany Mme d'Épinay to Geneva. He described his life at Hermitage as a life in slavery (although he wrote in a letter to Malesherbes several years later that he "did not live until the time when he came to Hermitage on April 9, 1756.")

The tension between Rousseau and Mme d'Épinay came to a head in October when Rousseau informed Sophie of his intention to leave Hermitage. She tried to persuade him to stay because she feared a scandal that could do damage to her relationship with St-Lambert. October 25 was set as the day of Mme d'Épinay's departure for Geneva but the departure had to be postponed because her son became ill.

As it turned out, her friend Grimm did not accompany her to Geneva although Rousseau was convinced that he should. He wrote Grimm a long letter in which he eloquently interpreted everything for his own good. Why were all his friends thinking that he should accompany Mme d'Épinay? Was he at fault or were all his friends bewitched? Why should he be obliged to accompany Mme d'Épinay? Should he do it out of friendship, gratitude, or altruism? What has she done for Rousseau? She allowed him to live in a nice cottage, which she got built. What has he done for her? At a time when he wanted to return to his native town she did everything she could to keep him back. She broke down his resistance with entreaties and intrigues. Out of friendship he did not obey the advice of his friends or even his own will, and allowed Mme d'Épinay to push him into Hermitage. He often sobbed in sorrow for not being a thousand miles away from this place. Mme d'Épinay did not want to stay alone at the château and that was why she settled him at Hermitage. As a matter of fact he lived there in slavery, which was contrasted by the noble discussions about freedom he had to listen to. He would not be of any use to her on the journey because he was sick; he would have to wade through mud and that would worsen his illness. He could not help her in Geneva, either. He concludes his letter with the impassioned declaration that he is resolved to find for himself another refuge where none of those barbaric tyrants who call themselves friends would find him. The letter elucidated Rousseau's character well.

Grimm's first reply to this explosive letter was rather moderate. He wrote that there was still time for Rousseau to join Mme d'Épinay. But Rousseau wrote a letter to Mme d'Épinay as well, in which he briefly mentioned the illness of her son and went on saying quite openly that he regarded her request that he accompany her to Geneva as a conspiracy in an atmosphere of intrigues and tyranny, and that she was behind it all. The end of the letter is again an impassioned one, in a way typical of Rousseau: he would never forget her kindness, and when she did not want to have him any more as her slave she could always count on him as her friend.

Grimm's reply to his long second letter was much harder. Grimm wrote that he could not understand Rousseau's monstrous system and asked him to forget about him and not to poison his soul any more. Such was the end of a friendship that had never been heartfelt, especially after Rousseau had learned that Grimm described him as a bad note copyist, an ability of which Rousseau was very proud.

Rousseau also presented all these resentments to Sophie during his visits to Eaubonne, and later, after Sophie had broken up her household at Eaubonne and moved to Paris, they recurred in their correspondence. Mme d'Houdetot had always tried to moderate Rousseau and prevent a scandal that could do damage to her as well. Because her friend St-Lambert withdrew to the further care of his family after his treatment and did not come to her to Paris, she was quite unhappy and had stomach trouble for which she even took opiates. Rousseau advised her medically and warned her not to give in, as a lonely woman in Paris, to the temptations of Parisian life and ironically advised her to remain faithful to her friend St-Lambert. In a letter he wrote to Sophie on November 10, 1757, Rousseau explains that Mme d'Épinay's attitude to him has changed as a consequence of her jealousy, and she had even sworn to separate them. "In this way she brought trouble and discord into my humble household where peace is the solace of poverty."

The correspondence between Mme d'Épinay and Rousseau grew ever frostier and in a letter from November 23, 1757, Rousseau wrote that the friendship between them was dead. He would like to leave Hermitage but his friends were advising him to stay till spring, which is what he planned to do if she would agree. Mme d'Épinay replied on December 1 that she felt only compassion for him after several years in which she had showed him friendship. Since he wished to leave Hermitage, he should do it, and she was surprised that his friends were dissuading him from it. She personally would never ask her friends to advise her in matters of duty.

This letter meant that she was giving him immediate notice and Rousseau did not know what to do. By sheer chance, he was offered a dilapidated cottage in Montlouis at the periphery of the small town Montmorency. Rousseau finally left Hermitage on December 15. The move was accomplished in only two days despite the snow and ice.

Diderot visited him before the move, which Rousseau described as congenial; however, Diderot's own account of this visit in his *Tablettes* is less favorable. Their friendship was cooling down and Diderot was never to return to Rousseau's house again. He added that the ultimate split was Rousseau's fault. Rousseau made Thérèse repeat in Diderot's presence what she had told him about the letters she handed over to Mme d'Épinay.

The old Mme Levasseur, however, denied her account. Rousseau rejected her for this reason and did not take her to the new refuge in Montlouis. Instead, she was seated into a carriage, given some money, clothing and several pieces of furniture and sent to Paris in spite of Thérèse's protests. According to Mme d'Épinay, Mme Levasseur was deserted by Rousseau and supported financially by Grimm.

The house in Montmorency, which Rousseau rented from a native, Jacques-Joseph Mathas (a man employed as a tax assignee of Prince de Condé), was located about three kilometers from Hermitage and was in poor condition (it was rebuilt two years later and later became Rousseau's museum), but it was habitable. It was called Petit Montlouis because it had been built on the grounds of a bigger house called Montlouis at the periphery of Montmorency. It was more convenient for the visitors to reach this new house than was the case in Hermitage. He paid fifty livres a year for it. This was ten livres less than he had to pay the gardener in Hermitage, which was how he paid rent to Mme d'Épinay (although Rousseau paid the gardener in Hermitage in the form of advance payments; these were reimbursed to him by Mme d'Épinay).

He wrote to inform Mme d'Épinay of his departure from Hermitage on December 17, 1757 because she had refused to allow him to stay there till spring. It had allegedly been his fate to move there against his will and he had to leave it in the same way. It is a misfortune, continued Rousseau, when one errs in the choice of his friends and another still and no less bitter misfortune when one has to leave this sweet error. Mme d'Épinay's answer was conciliatory but Rousseau left her letter unanswered, in this way putting an end to their correspondence.

Petit Montlouis had a small garden, a terrace and a square turret called a *donjon* by Rousseau. He used it as his study though it could not be heated. Soon after he moved in, Rousseau suffered a severe relapse of urinary infection, and writes later, "No sooner was I established in my new home than violent and frequent attacks of my urinary retention were complicated by the fresh disability of a rupture, which had been bothering me for some time without my knowing what it was" (*Confessions*, 454). His symptoms were so severe that Rousseau overcame his aversion to all doctors and summoned "his old friend," Dr. Thierry, who unfortunately could do no more for him than to recommend catheterization and bandages. All this reminded him painfully that a young heart cannot beat scot-free in an old body. His health did not improve even when spring came. "I spent the entire year of 1758 languishing." He awaited death impatiently as the moment of his liberation and redemption from his enemies.

In spite of the cold, and his pains and discomfort, Rousseau continued to work. During his last visit to Hermitage, Diderot had informed him about the article on Geneva for *Encyclopédie* written by d'Alembert and the corresponding volume was delivered to Rousseau after his move to Petit Montlouis. D'Alembert's article had allegedly been reviewed by Genevan authorities and should have been instrumental in introducing theatre in Geneva. As a reply to this article, Rousseau wrote his well known *Lettre à Monsieur d'Alembert sur les spectacles* (Letter to Monsieur d'Alembert on the Theatre), which is noteworthy for its refined eloquence. Its contents are also of interest as a historical document. D'Alembert had written, at Diderot's instigation, an article for the entry "*Genève*" in the seventh volume of *Encyclopédie*. Rousseau was probably annoyed that Diderot did not choose him, a native Genevan, for the contribution on Geneva.

On the whole Rousseau agreed with d'Alembert's article, except for two things by which he was so aggrieved that he wrote a letter that was ten times longer than d'Alembert's article. He wrote the letter with the intention of having it published. He set about writing it with gusto in the bitter cold of his *donjon*, "with no protection from the wind and snow, with no other fire but that in my heart." He completed it within three weeks. It was undoubtedly quite cold in the *donjon*, but the account itself is overblown and attempts to show the writer as a suffering man who withstands personal sacrifices for truth.

The first thing Rousseau did not like in d'Alembert's article was the remark that the clergymen of Geneva had deserted Calvin's original teaching, so much so that Geneva was governed by Socinianism and had no real religion. (Fausto Socino reduced Christianity to deism.) A second remark provoked a still stronger opposition: D'Alembert proposed that a theatre be set up in Geneva to rectify the fact that theatre performances were banned there. He testified that the theatre would raise the morals and culture of the citizens and "would add Athenian urbanity to the rationality of Sparta."

D'Alembert dwelt in Geneva as part of the preparation of this article and was a guest in Voltaire's villa Les Délices. Rousseau suspected that these remarks were instigated by Voltaire, who wished to introduce theatre to Geneva so that his plays could be presented there. It is not entirely clear why Rousseau should be so outraged by the observation that the Genevan Church held more liberal Socinian views. It was the same liberalism of the Church that had made his conversion to Protestantism possible, and Rousseau's personal religious conviction was very liberal. He described it later in his *La Profession de foi du vicaire savoyard* that was embodied into *Émile*. This profession of faith was in its nature deistic though Rousseau's religious ideas were not identical with deism.

It would appear that Rousseau should not have had any serious objections to the introduction of theatre in Geneva. He himself wrote plays as well as operas. He liked to visit the theatre and his own opera *Le Devin du village* was staged in Carouge, a town in Savoy that is "outside the gates of Geneva," at nearly the same time as d'Alembert's article was printed. It is thus a paradox that Rousseau spent so much energy to prove that the institution of theatre in Geneva was bad and unsuitable for the city.

He did not agree with d'Alembert's view that the theatre could help to improve human morals for the better. He rejected the old argument that theatre gives vent to the passions and has thus a purging effect. According to him, only reason was a suitable means to purge evil passions—reason, however, has no influence in the theatre. People love theatre because it is a temple of illusions and make-believe. We cry more when we watch a disaster on the stage than when we see it happen in the real world: a theatrical disaster does not rouse fear in us. Theatre plays up emotions and its moral is exalted and illusory.

Rousseau regarded comedy to be even more dangerous than tragedy because comedies use ludicrousness which is the "shoulder of sin." Ancient authors wrote at least about heroic subjects. Contemporary authors wrote only about love. And in the theatre, Rousseau complained, love was very often sacrificed to duty so that innocent love presented on the stage could lead to sinful love in the real world. Here again the reader has to stop and ask why did Rousseau, with his character Julie, allow the heroine to desert her real love (St-Preux) and submit to the duty of a loveless marriage with Wolmar?

Actresses and actors were damned as well: a woman who sells herself on the stage would be tempted to do something similar when she leaves the stage. Rousseau painted a horrifying picture that he predicted would become the reality in Geneva should actresses begin to work there. Men would lie at their feet and elections would take place in the women's changing rooms. An actor pretends to be someone else, feigns passions which are not really experienced and his blood remains cool. Rousseau praises uncritically, as their opposite, the political speaker who is—in his eyes—as moral as the actor is corrupted.

Rousseau overlooks the fact that the psychology of a political speaker and that of an actor are similar. Both try to persuade their listeners about something in which they do not necessarily believe. Why is Rousseau trying to make such a distinction between actor and political speaker? This could be perhaps elucidated by the fact that Rousseau considered himself a moralist, a political activist and a reformer (he had just started his work on *Contract social*). He may have been moved to celebrate this vocation: he was glorifying himself.

On the other hand, however, Rousseau knew, or was at least dimly (subconsciously) aware, that his whole life very much resembled the appearance of an actor on the stage. His feelings were exalted and exaggerated, his morals were full of contradictions, and the attitude of his whole life served to disguise his inability to integrate into society. He fell in love in accordance with a script he wrote for himself and he tried to live up to models he had invented.

He does not condemn the theatre completely—it is necessary for a big and corrupted city such as Paris, but it is impossible in Geneva, a Republic with other interests. As an alternative, he recommended folklore, painting, singing and dancing. The Swiss national folklore was much better than similar entertainment in France (which he declared in the ninth promenade of his *Reveries of a Solitary Walker*). From what he remembered from his youth he recommends folk festivities, sports games and military parades that cultivate the feeling of solidarity: "The only true joy is the public joy."

Clubs for men and women's societies, too, are commendable facilities, with the sexes being separated. Women's presence makes men effeminate. He makes this last recommendation unaffected by the fact that he himself has always preferred women's company to that of men and moved in Parisian salons in the presence of both sexes praising, as has already been mentioned, the Parisiennes in particular.

Rousseau's ideal model of social life was and remained the ancient Sparta and he agreed with Plato's demand that no artists live in his ideal Republic.

Besides this he was writing ceaseless letters to Sophie and complained that her replies were not frequent enough. Sophie's feelings for Rousseau got visibly colder. Her main interest was to get a special copy of the novel *Julie,* from Rousseau which he was writing for her. Her letters from that time were nice and polite, but were in fact a mere façade.

The winter of that year was very cold and Rousseau, who worked in the unheated *donjon,* could not get rid of his urinary tract infections. He wrote numerous letters to Sophie but could not mail them because Mme d'Houdetot's husband was in Paris. The letters piled on his table. In them Rousseau celebrates the victory of chaste virtue over passion in their relationship and assures Sophie that his blind passion for her produced thousands of pure feelings which made him realize his duty to love her for his whole life. He mentions the happy moments when they were sitting under an oak, holding hands, and her eyes, fixed softly in his own, were wetted by tears as immaculate as the rain falling from heaven. He mentions those beautiful days of the charming summer, so short and so unforgettable.

Though the six letters were never mailed, they were not lost because they were revealed to the apostate Catholic priest in Rousseau's *Le Vicaire savoyard,* and included in the book *Émile.* At the time Rousseau wrote them, Sophie was not far off. She lived at her residence in Eaubonne, but did not come to visit him because her husband lived with her (although she continued to be unfaithful to him). She sent only one letter (February 22) in which she regretted she could not come and visit Rousseau. She asked him to write her about his health and to give her servant the next part of the text for his novel, *Julie.*

Rousseau's only visitor was Deleyre; according to him, Rousseau was in an appalling condition—he was sick, without means of support and in a depressed mood. It appeared that Rousseau thought in earnest that he would die: "I saw my last days draw near almost with eagerness." Instead of a will, Rousseau wrote a declaration suggesting that all of the contents of the cottage in Montlouis be given to his "maid Thérèse Levasseur," who had not been paid for thirteen years and whom he therefore owed 1,950 livres.

Rousseau refused to go with Thérèse to Geneva although his Genevan friend, Deluc, offered to pay for all his relocation costs. He felt too sick for a journey: "I suffer from my poor bladder, and I would only accept your offer if I thought that a golden catheter would help me piss better than the other ones."

In a letter to Dr. Thierry from late March, Rousseau wrote that the prescribed lemony water and milk did not produce any relief (here one can see the helplessness of medical science of that time). He continues, "A swelling developed in the lower body in the left groin. The swelling is in a straight line, in an oblique direction. One might take it for a continuation of the penis. It disappears when I lie down and reappears when I get up. It is not a hernia. It only produces the sort of dull, light pain which has been with me for years in that part of the body" (Cranston 1991, 127). The daily amount of urine was decreasing and urination was difficult. Only when his urine had the color of clear water did it drain a little bit more easily, but he always had to press on the lower part of his abdomen to be able to pass water at all. He stated in this letter that he was not expecting a remedy could be found to cure his complaints.

It follows from his description that his urinary organs, and probably his genitals, were affected by a severe, recurrent infection that sooner or later would necessarily ascend to the kidneys; Rousseau suffered from kidney infection in the years to come.

On March 9, Rousseau finished the letter to d'Alembert and offered it to Rey for publication. He asked to be paid thirty louis. He instructed Rey to hide the manuscript safely and not to show it to anybody. Since it was one of his favorite works he wanted to prevent its anonymous publication. He further wrote a letter to Diderot—in tears, according to Thérèse—and complained again about his remark that "Only the wicked man is alone," which must have offended him painfully.

At that time he was already considered a misanthrope. Like many people who turned their back on society, Rousseau took refuge in the company of animals. Animals offer lonely people the feeling of emotional certitude, which was what Rousseau lacked in contacts with people. According to Deleyre, Rousseau had pigeons, chickens, cats and a dog. The more he ceased to love people the deeper he was attracted into the company of animals (consider the aphorism: "The more I learn about people, the more I love my dog.") In March Mme d'Houdetot's official lover, St-Lambert, returned from Paris to live with Sophie again. She informed Rousseau of this in a letter from March 23 and added that she was happy again. She reminded him that she awaited the whole text of *Julie*. Their correspondence of that time was quite unpleasant and then ended abruptly.

St-Lambert learned from Diderot that Rousseau was in love with Sophie and that they had had a number of dates the previous summer. On May 6, 1758 Sophie wrote a letter in which she accused Rousseau of indiscretion; she accused him of disclosing his passion for her, which had never pleased her anyway. She announced to him that she was breaking off all contact with him.

Rousseau knew immediately that the affair had been revealed by Diderot because Diderot was the only person to whom he had confessed it. Diderot, for his part, defended himself. He said he had assumed that Rousseau had written a letter explaining everything to St-Lambert, as he had recommended. But several other sources make it obvious that Diderot knew Rousseau had not written any such letter. Diderot the friend turned into an enemy and Sophie reverted back to Mme d'Houdetot.

St-Lambert was magnanimous; he still considered Rousseau his friend and visited him twice in Montlouis. At his second visit Rousseau was not at home and St-Lambert chatted with Thérèse for two hours. He said to her that it was generally believed in Paris that Rousseau was Mme d'Épinay's lover. He was surprised when Thérèse categorically denied this. (One can believe she was telling the truth because Thérèse was well informed about Rousseau's sexual life.)

Rousseau's health improved in May. He now began to see the positive side of his new situation. He had rid himself of his tyrants. He had also freed himself of an intensive emotional involvement and had disentangled himself from its emotional chains. He wrote in *Confessions* that he had enough contacts to be able to enjoy pleasures offered by society without having to suffer from the loss of independence. In fact his social contacts were at that time rather limited.

One of the visitors to Montlouis was Giovanni-Giacomo Casanova, who visited Rousseau accompanied by his mistress, Mme d'Urfé. He brought some notes for copying. Casanova wrote in his memoirs that he was disappointed because Rousseau was neither an outstanding personality nor had an outstanding spirit; he was not nice and not very polite. In one of Rousseau's letters there is a remark that he had to wait for one of his visitors the whole day. If this visitor was Casanova it is no surprise that he was not received with kindness.

Rey notified Rousseau in May that he was going to print the *Letter to d'Alembert* and agreed to pay Rousseau the required thirty louis. Meanwhile Rousseau had become known to such an extent that Rey agreed to print anything Rousseau would write in the future. He promised to print *Letter* by the end of July (an unbelievably short time from today's perspective). Rousseau inserted one more passage into the foreword, in which he announced in a veiled form, though it was very clear to insiders, that he had parted with Diderot. This brought him criticism by some of his friends but on the whole contributed to the popularity of the book—particularly to the women readers who were curious to find out more about the secrets hidden behind such an announcement.

It was necessary to gain Malesherbe's permission as censor but this was not very difficult because Malesherbes admired Rousseau (which Rousseau did not initially realize), and the book was not targeting the Church or the state in any way. D'Alembert himself read the publication with delight and wrote to Malesherbes of his own free will to permit the book: "I read the book M. Rousseau wrote against me. I was very pleased. The public would no doubt enjoy it as well." D'Alembert also wrote to Rousseau, "I am far from being offended, monsieur, by your critique of my article "Geneva," on the contrary, I am flattered and honored that you have chosen it and written about it."

The first edition of *Letter* arrived in Geneva in August 1758. The rich patrician circles were largely Francophile and rather supported d'Alembert's view expressed in his article for *Encyclopédie*, stating that theatre should be introduced to Geneva. The Genevan theologians, on the other hand, agreed with Rousseau's arguments against the theatre. Rousseau sent the work to numerous Genevan representatives and also to his two cousins (Jean-François Rousseau, 1685–1763, son of Noè Rousseau, and Gabriel Rousseau, 1715–1780, son of David Rousseau).

The response in France itself was positive. After all, Rousseau had not claimed that Paris should not have theatre. His eloquent and elegant criticism was aimed only at the traditional French views on theatre and this aroused curiosity and attention. The Church had regained power and was not attacked by the publication.

To clarify the atmosphere of the period let us just add that Diderot was still being attacked by the Church as the editor of *Encyclopédie*, and Helvétius got into serious trouble after the publication of his materialistic work, *De l'Esprit*. Though being permitted by the censorship, Helvétius's book had to be withdrawn from sale following a campaign of the Church and Helvétius had to publicly abjure his views in order to avoid being criminally indicted.

Rousseau expressed his attitude to Helvétius in a letter to Deleyre: "M. Helvétius wrote a dangerous book and made a humiliating concession. But he renounced the career of tax collector, married an honest girl and made her happy, and often provided help to people in difficulties. My dear Deleyre, let us strive to earn such a reputation also for ourselves." Rousseau was spared being attacked by the Church and many Encyclopédistes believed his work contributed to a new reactionary wave and the sharpening of censorship in France during that time.

Voltaire in Geneva took *Letter* to be a direct attack on his person because he had been trying to get permission for a private theatre in Geneva. In a letter to d'Alembert, Voltaire called Rousseau "Diogenes barking from the depths of his barrel." Voltaire might also have interpreted Rousseau's *Letter* as an attempt to influence the Genevan government to expel him. Voltaire never did succeed in putting on his plays in his villa Les Délices, and his relations with the Republic's government were strained. This led him to buy the Châteaux Tournay and Ferney (known today as Ferney-Voltaire) north of Geneva but on French territory in 1758 and 1759.

Voltaire made Ferney his permanent residence and proudly showed visitors a stud farm, a manufacture and a factory that produced watches. When he moved to Ferney the area had only fifty inhabitants but this number rose to more then 1,200 by the time of his death in 1778. By virtue of the fact that he moved outside the city walls he could play what he desired in his private theatre. He wrote in his correspondence with Thieriot that he was not coming to Geneva but that Geneva was coming to him, in crowds.

Another critic of the *Letter* was the Genevan physician Dr. Theodore Tronchin who pointed to the fact that the Genevans' mores were far from being as pure as described by Rousseau. He disagreed also with the establishment of men's clubs. Geneva was not Greece. Geneva was a society of watchmakers and not of warriors, and Rousseau's proposal of a state education, physical body strengthening and military training was not appropriate for children who would later earn their living by trade and industry. This topic sparked a correspondence of some length in which Rousseau proclaimed that the status of a craftsman was the status into which he was born and he should have pursued it: that he deserted it had brought him only misfortune.

Rey, the publisher, was satisfied with the book's success and he started to put pressure on Rousseau to agree to the publication of his entire work. In the relative calm of Petit Montlouis, Rousseau could write undisturbed and without diversion. He worked on the final chapters and fates of *Julie*, (La Nouvelle Héloïse)which were finished in winter 1759. *Julie* was thus written between 1756 and 1759. He started writing the first chapters of *Émile* and compiled the *Dictionary of Music. Social Contract,* which was written in less than two years is actually a skeleton—he intended originally to write a more voluminous book that would bear the title *Political Institutions.*

Mme d'Houdetot's lover, St-Lambert, to whom Rousseau also sent the *Letter* took umbrage at Rousseau's public announcement of his parting with Diderot, and wrote him a *lettre de rupture.* He felt obligated to defend Diderot at a time when he was set upon from all sides. Rousseau's reply was short and contained, among other things, the announcement that he was going to copy a special edition of *Julie* for Mme d'Houdetot. It is possible that it was Mme d'Houdetot's suasion, since she had been trying for some time to get the whole copy of *Julie* from Rousseau, that in the end made St-Lambert rethink the whole thing.

On October 29, 1758 M. d'Épinay gave a supper at the Château La Chevrette at which they all met in the end: Dupins, Francueil, St-Lambert and Mme d'Houdetot. Rousseau was invited as well, and he accepted the invitation after a lengthy hesitation. He wrote in *Confessions* that his arrival (M. d'Épinay sent a carriage to bring him because of bad weather) caused a sensation which he was very pleased about, since everybody told him how they felt he badly needed social recognition. "None but the French have hearts capable of this kind of delicacy." Once again he saw, after a long time and with palpitating heart, Mme d'Houdetot. His conversation with St-Lambert was very friendly—so much so that Rousseau eventually thought more of St-Lambert than Mme d'Houdetot.

On December 12, 1758 Rousseau celebrated the so-called "Escalade" in Petit Montlouis, together with two compatriots, Lenieps and Coindet, and with the cottage's owner M. Mathas, a Genevan *fête national*. On this day in 1602 the Genevans warded off the conquest of Geneva by Savoy troops.

The cold winter and long hours spent in the unheated *donjon* caused another relapse of his illness.

On New Year's Day he was congratulated by Mme de Créqui on the success of his *Letter*: "You cannot write four lines without arousing a sensation." The congratulation was accompanied by four chickens, against which Rousseau protested indignantly. He mentioned in his reply that was thinking about education and invited her to convey her views on this topic but Mme de Créqui did not respond to his invitation.

The political situation in Paris continued to be bad even in January 1759. On January 23, the parlement of Paris condemned Diderot's *Encyclopédie* and his *Pénsées philosophiques* in spite of the fact that *Encyclopédie* had been permitted by the king. It was rumored that Malesherbes could lose his position as censor. The Encyclopédist La Condamine (1701–1774) who was in correspondence with Rousseau complained that his book *Mémoire* about vaccination against smallpox was met with such adversity that he decided to have the second edition published in Geneva.

In 1759, after five years, Rousseau's opera *Le Devin du village* was performed again at the Parisian opera and enjoyed a 52-night run. Rousseau was very annoyed because he was unable to gain any income from the new presentation.

In April Rousseau sent the final version of *Julie* to Rey. The book was named *Julie, ou la moderne Héloïse* but in subsequent editions it was renamed *La Nouvelle Héloïse*. Rousseau wished that the book could be illustrated by Boucher in the style of erotic rococo but feared his financial requirements.

In his seclusion at Petit Montlouis he was visited, among others, by his old friends from the time of his diplomatic work in Venice, M. Le Blond, the French consul in Venice, François-Xavier de Carrio, former secretary of the Spanish embassy in Venice who was elevated to peerage as Chevalier de Carrión and was now employed at the Spanish embassy in Versailles, and the French envoy in Geneva, François Chaillou de Jonville. It was typical of Rousseau that he was unable to maintain these friendships. He was always using favors offered to him by his friends but forgot to repay them. Social life is based on mutual exchange of altruisms, even though this exchange may sometimes involve only altruistic emotions.

In the spring of 1759 Rousseau could not receive any guests because the ceiling of the house fell in and the refuge became uninhabitable. Rousseau was helped at this critical time by a happy coincidence; a prominent French magnate, Charles-François-Fréderic de Montmorency-Luxembourg (born in 1702, a close friend of the king and one of the king's major military advisors, particularly during the time of the so-called Seven Years' War that was then raging), was visiting the valley at Easter. The duke of Luxembourg and maréchal de France was the head of an old family in Montmorency where he had a beautiful château that was built according to plans designed by Crozat le Cadet and Le Notre. As soon as the duke heard that Rousseau lived at the border of his domain he sent a servant to him several times to invite Rousseau for supper because he highly esteemed writers and philosophers.

Rousseau assumed that the invitation was motivated by curiosity and feared that he would have to sit at the servants' table, and did not accept it. He refused a second invitation as well. Finally Chevalier de Lorenzy, from the company of the duchess, was sent to Rousseau to try to induce him to accept the invitation. Rousseau was not influenced even by this. One day, quite unexpectedly, the duke himself appeared in Petit Montlouis accompanied by the duchess and a group of friends. Rousseau could not decline when invited personally by the duke.

Allegedly Rousseau was most afraid of the duchess whom he had met in the salon of Mme Dupin twelve years earlier. At that time she had been a shining, youthful beauty but was said to be malicious. In her first marriage she had a reputation of a *grande horizontale* and was incorrigibly unfaithful to her first husband Duc de Bouffleurs. Her affairs were considered scandalous even by the standards of Versailles of that time. As a young widow in 1750, she married her main lover, the Maréchal de Luxembourg, who was a widower as well. (His first wife was Marie-Sophie Colbert de Seignelay.)

When she met Rousseau for the second time, the duchess was still a tall, beautiful, elegant woman with full bosom, which Rousseau had always admired, and she could still easily charm men. According to Rousseau she had a "charm that withstood time" and Rousseau immediately became her slave although she was more than fifty. Once the ice was broken by a pleasant conversation, Rousseau could not refuse the invitation to the château where he later spent time in the company of the duke and his family as well as other prominent people such as Comtesse de Bouffleurs, Duc de Villeroy, Prince de Tingry, Marquis d'Armentieres and Comtesse de Valentinois.

Grimm said with malice that Rousseau replaced the society of the men of letters with the society of women. The fact is that Rousseau got into a much higher society than the society meeting at La Chevrette. Mme de Luxembourg, who certainly was not inexperienced with men, valued Rousseau's sincerity, frankness, and his occasional "brutal righteousness." She also admired his books.

But Rousseau preferred the company of the duke who represented a nostalgic anachronism from feudal times now broken by the absolutist monarchy. He was an exceptional man and in this he corresponded to Rousseau's own cup of tea—Rousseau regarded himself to be exceptional as well and thus in a sense allied with the eminent French aristocrat, whom he saw as a representative of a lost world as much as a representative of the world of the future. He did not mind the duke's wealth. If, however, the latter were a rich burgher he would not have gained Rousseau's friendship.

Petit Montlouis was definitely uninhabitable, therefore the duke and duchess offered Rousseau the opportunity to stay in a smallish but lovely manor in the garden of their château. The manor had four furnished flats. Rousseau decided to stay in the simple flat decorated in a blue and white color scheme, with a glorious view. He felt as if he were in a paradise, and there is where he wrote the fifth book of *Émile*. He lived with Thérèse, his dog and a cat. During the month of July 1759 he visited the duchess and duke daily.

The correspondence between Rousseau and the duke and duchess reveals how happy Rousseau felt in Petit Château. He loved the parks and the lake, fed the carp as he had done before in the Lake of Geneva. In one of his letters he defends his yearning for solitude: "Solitary personalities have romantic natures. Why should I attempt to cure my sweet folly when it makes me so happy? Men of the world and of the royal court—do not think that you are wiser than I am: we have only different illusions."

Rousseau's tendency to a lonely life (although he never lived in absolute seclusion) must have appeared incomprehensible to his contemporaries. One such remark led to his break with Dr. Tronchin. In a letter from March 1759, Dr. Tronchin asks how is it possible that "a friend of humanity stops being a friend of people?" He touched a sensitive spot, reminiscent of Diderot's statement which had offended Rousseau earlier, "Only the wicked man is alone."

The duke and duchess promised to respect his privacy. They did not interfere with his finances and abstained from giving him any presents because they knew his touchiness in this respect. When they lived at the château Rousseau could visit them and he consequently forgot about his resolution to live as a hermit. He spent whole days with them, usually coming in the morning to wait on the duchess and staying for lunch. After lunch he strolled and chatted with the duke, leaving in late afternoon because he feared the presence of a bigger crowd of people at supper.

He was still afraid of the duchess—he had never been able to understand her and the uneasiness of his contacts with her lasted till they parted. Since he knew that women liked to be entertained and that they would rather tolerate an affront than boredom he suggested to the duchess that he would read passages from *Julie* to her each morning. He usually came at ten o'clock every morning, settled with the duchess in her bedroom and read for her till she showed signs of readiness to get up.

Rousseau recalls that the success of his reading surpassed all his expectations. The duchess was fascinated by *Julie* and her author; she spoke incessantly of him, hugged him, and reserved a place for him at the table next to her seat. As the duchess knew that Rousseau copied *Julie* for Mme d'Houdetot she asked him to copy it for her also, on the same terms.

Though Rousseau was very pleased by all this he still preferred being in the company of the duke. In the summertime the duke and duchess also visited Rousseau in Petit Château. Their friendship went so far that they exchanged portraits. Rousseau donated to his patrons his pastel painted by La Tour and they gave him a miniature double-portrait.

When he finished the reading of *Julie* he started to read from *Émile*, which, however, was not to the duchess's taste and she was bored by it. According to Rousseau she suggested, of her own free will, to take care of the publication of *Émile* to ensure that Rousseau had more profit from it. He agreed but only under the proviso that *Émile* would not be printed in France. The duchess herself did not see any reasons why *Émile* should not be printed in France and she convinced Malesherbes about her view. Malesherbes sent Rousseau a long, personal letter in which he wrote that even *La Profession de foi du vicaire savoyard* could be published in France. But Rousseau insisted that the book be printed in the Netherlands because of his "extraordinary doubts," but agreed that it be given to a French publisher who would be in charge of its sale.

Having agreed to this with the duchess, Rousseau submitted the handwritten copy of *Émile* to her.

His old friend Deleyre had abandoned journalism and later worked at the French embassy in Wien. He wanted to marry Mlle Loiseau and visited Rousseau with her. Rousseau, who did not like her at all, discouraged Deleyre from marrying her. One of his letters to Deleyre reveals Rousseau's views on love: "I see that love makes children of philosophers as it does of everyone else... Ah, for heaven's sake remember that love is only an illusion and that one never sees things as they are when one loves. When you have just a little reason left, do not do anything without having consulted your parents." Deleyre had read the manuscript of *Julie* and he probably understood Rousseau's advice to consult his parents, but could hardly understand Rousseau's words about love.

Rousseau's views that he expressed in the letter reflected his true conviction. We must not forget that Rousseau wrote *Julie* with the intention of writing a successful novel that would captivate women's souls. Since he spent more time in the society of women than in the society of men he knew very accurately what he had to write and how to present it. He knew what women wanted to hear and he knew their way of thinking. He knew that women did not mind paradoxes and logical inconsistencies in romantic novels.

The repair of the cottage in Montlouis was finished and Rousseau prepared to move back. His supporters invited him to stay at Petit Château as long as he wished. Rousseau could not resist and kept the keys to the flat, using it from time to time. They also invited him to their spacious palace in Paris. The duchess wrote to him to come only when her husband would be present in the palace because she knew that Rousseau felt more at ease with the duke than with her. She added, "At my age one has no sex. What I was left is my heart and that will always lean toward you and in which you will always find attachment."

Rousseau replied, "How cruel is your kindness. Why does it disturb the peace of a hermit who renounced all pleasures of life because he wanted to evade its wearisomeness? He spent many days in a futile search for a lasting relationship and failed in attempting to form it in a social environment to which he belongs. Should I now try to find it in your circles? Ah, how I detest titles and how I pity you for having them. You deserve the sweetness of a private life."

Rousseau shows why he withdrew into solitude: he had not found his place in society emotionally and could not do so, though he was certainly trying. But this rhetorical confession is at the same time false. Rousseau had never endeavored to form any lasting relationships in the environment to which he belonged, that is in the society of artisans (which he considered to be his own environment). He had always tried to form lasting emotional relationships solely in the society of aristocrats, which he constantly frequented but to which he did not belong.

In spite of his promise that he would never again enter Paris, he paid several short visits to the Hôtel de Luxembourg near Montmartre. According to him, he did not break any promise because the carriage in which he traveled pulled into the garden of the duke's palace and he did not have to touch the streets of Paris with his feet. He was free to visit his small room in the palace anytime. He thus had at his disposal the cottage at Montlouis, Petit Château and one more retreat in Paris!

The cottage in Montlouis was completed and even the *donjon* in the garden was fitted with windows and a fireplace (a gift from the duke of Luxembourg). In the garden, lounging chairs and a table were placed, providing a nice place for the guests to sit around. Rousseau tamed and fed various birds and entertained his guests with them.

When Rey, his publisher, got the second part of *Julie* he was willing to pay 400 livres for it and the 2,160 livres by the end of the year.

The third part of *Julie* had been sent off on September 5 and the fourth at the end of October. Rousseau had not yet finished the copy of *Julie* for Mme d'Houdetot, who kept reminding him to complete it. We know this from a letter to the duchess of Luxembourg to whom he had promised a copy as well. In this letter he confessed that he had not started yet because there was someone else ahead of her.

With the approaching winter, Rousseau again complained about his health and the cold weather but the weather improved after several months and with it Rousseau's illness. He exchanged letters with the duke and duchess quite often and both sides assured each other emphatically of love, attachment, regard and a desire to meet personally again. Though Rousseau earned his living mainly as a writer he still carried on with his "profession"—note copying. But he had become choosy. When he was asked by Coindet to produce some copies for him Rousseau replied that he did not wish to be sent any French music that "hurt his eyes and ears."

Vernes from Geneva asked him to send him some of his compositions and Rousseau answered: "God, dear Vernes, what are you talking about? I do not have any music apart from the songs of nightingales; owls in the forest replace the Parisian opera. Now I derive pleasure only from nature and despise the pleasures of the city." In this letter he was intentionally not telling the truth because he assured Vernes of not having anything in press though *Julie* had already been sent to the publisher. He feared that Vernes would talk to Voltaire. The letter ends: "I sing one old Genevan tune with a weak voice and sign off crying about my homeland."

Having returned to Montlouis, Rousseau began to meet with a friend of Mme d'Houdetot, Marquise de Verdelin (Marie-Madeleine de Brémond d'Ars). Marquise de Verdelin, 1728–1810, came from a family which traced its roots back to the crusaders. She was married at the age of twenty-two to Charles de Brémond, Comte d'Ars, who was forty-four years older. Rousseau refers to him in *Confessions* using only the worst expressions which, however, he did not use in 1759. The marquise had a lover, Seigner de Margency. Rousseau had not paid much attention to her, despite the fact that she came from an old family and was prettier than Sophie d'Houdetot. But Mme de Verdelin lived next to Sophie in Margency and loaned Sophie the keys so she and Rousseau could get into her garden and use it for their favorite stroll near Mont Olympe.

Mme de Verdelin had moved from Margency to Soisy and desired to meet Rousseau. In his *Confessions* Rousseau does not mention this acquaintanceship favorably but without a doubt he liked meeting her and appreciated her affection in 1759. They both had their own problems that they confided to each other and this brought them closer together. "Nothing binds two hearts together as much as the pleasure of shedding tears together," wrote Rousseau, fully in keeping with the style of his time.

The marquise poured her heart out to Rousseau because her official lover was deserting her and was ever more turning to his new love—religion. Rousseau sent his first letter to the marquise on November 18, 1759 and complained in it how sad he was in his solitude after she went away, and that he could not avoid reproaching her for being the cause of his feeling lonely. We have to admit that Rousseau knew what women wanted to hear and consequently what he had to write to women in his letters.

Marquise's friend, Margency, offered Rousseau the excellent, well-paid job of a literary journalist for the *Journal de Savans* (Journal of Learning), for which he would write abstracts from historical, philosophical books and works of literature. He was offered eight hundred livres for eight days' work. This offer was evidently the work of Malesherbes. It was an extremely profitable job, which would certainly take financial worries off Rousseau's hands. After lengthy deliberation Rousseau refused this attractive offer because of the "unendurable constrains" he would be subject to: he would be unable to work according to his liking and he would be "a slave to time" (these formulations are characteristic of the literary style of masochists). In addition to that he was sure that he would carry out the work poorly. Those were the reasons which made him refuse a job for which he, according to his own word, was not born.

Thanks to the letters of Mme de Verdelin, Rousseau was notified of all the novelties in Paris. He learned that his intimate enemy, Grimm, got a position representing the French in Frankfurt (In Ratisbon, according to the marquise, incorrectly). The marquise's letters came in with such frequency that Rousseau felt unable to reply to them. Mme de Verdelin even started writing to Thérèse.

Rousseau and the atmosphere that surrounded him were described by two Genevan visitors, the businessman François Favre and one of the De Tournes' brothers. Favre recorded that Rousseau's best friend was his dog and, among people, the duke of Luxembourg. He wrote that Rousseau was in a good mood in spite of suffering incessant pain from his urinary retention. He concludes with admiration for Rousseau, considering him a great man, without any affectation or pretense. Favre suggested that some pride could be discovered in Rousseau's manners and thinking, but probably he was not aware of it because our pride is always so clever as to know how to take cover behind the notion of noble emotions.

In a letter to a Genevan priest, Moultou—who had recommended Favre to Rousseau—wrote a fierce attack against Voltaire, whose popularity was also mentioned by Moultou. Rousseau reproaches Moultou with indignation and asks why "he soiled the paper by remarking about Voltaire" whom he "would hate more when he did not hold him in such a contempt." Voltaire's talent and wealth served only the perversity of his heart. The citizens of Geneva would pay dearly for having provided him a harbor and would eventually end up as his victims. Already now, wrote Rousseau, Geneva was corrupted and his words in the *Letter to d'Alembert* were no longer valid. The city's illness was incurable and theatre was one of the palliative agents to be used.

The duchess of Luxembourg asked him in a letter from mid-January 1760, from Paris, not to forget about the copy of *Julie* he had promised to her. Rousseau replied that he had spent three years working on the copy for Mme d'Houdetot and that he had been working on the copy for her for only two months, but he promised to send her the first part in a week's time.

Rousseau kept his promise and sent her the first part. The duchess thanked him in an enthusiastic letter. She wrote that nothing as good and moving had ever been written and that she was dying of her desire to see him. She predicted a huge success for *Julie* and she was not mistaken. The work on the press dragged on all year and was accompanied by an incessant correspondence between Rousseau and his publisher Rey.

Rousseau himself was split in his attitude about *Julie*. On the one hand he was ashamed (because it was a romantic novel) and was also concerned about its reception, especially in Geneva. He indicated that the novel was a confabulation of a fever-stricken brain full of clear intellectual contradictions. But he did not take any precautions to eliminate them. On the other hand, he scrupulously strove to make sure that the edition was perfect in every respect. Even as late as January 18 he sent to his publisher an extensive list of amendments, the longest and most significant of which he put into Julie's mouth: it emphasized tellingly that "love purges sex."

Some readers accepted this romantic idea with enthusiasm but others were horrified by it because it made the eroticism of the novel even stronger. We know from a correspondence between Rousseau and Mme de Verdelin that Rousseau suffered from nosebleed in the first months of 1760 and that he worked long hours and got so little sleep that his friends were concerned about his health. But we can assume he did not suffer any more serious health problems at that time. In one letter to Mme de Verdelin, Rousseau wrote that since he had hardened his heart, did not love anybody and called humanity his enemy, he had become as fat as a pig. He could not recommend a better recipe for good health than callousness. Mme de Verdelin did not share this cynical recommendation that was rather typical of Rousseau.

In early March Rousseau received a letter of thanks from the duchess for the second part of *Julie*, in which she dismissed the suspicion of having sent him presents of a capon, a truffle and an almond cake (the presents were probably sent by Mme de Verdelin). The Easter of that year was not as pleasant as the year before. The duke was exhausted by his duties at the court and the duchess was not feeling well. Rey received the last, sixth part of *Julie* at the end of January but he could not commence printing because the canals in Amsterdam had become ice-bound and the paper could not be shipped to the printing house. The correspondence between Rousseau and his publisher at the beginning of that year was extensive. As opposed to other books where the author was designated "Jean-Jacques Rousseau, citizen of Geneva," here the designation was "editor" with the name Jean- Jacques Rousseau attached to it, this time without the addition of "citizen of Geneva."

When his health had improved, Rousseau visited the duke and duchess in their Parisian palace (he was still getting off the carriage only in the courtyard of the palace). He dedicated to the duchess a manuscript of an appendix to *Julie* that was not to be printed: *Les Aventures de Milord Édouard*. This appendix contained the description of rather intricate and, for today's literary taste, impossible amatory liaisons of an English lord to an Italian marquise and to the prostitute, Laura. Following a series of fantastic plots, the unfaithful *marchesa* reforms and Laura ends up in a convent.

The duchess was probably not pleased by this present. Out of politeness she did not say what she thought of it. She might have seen herself in the character of the unfaithful *marchesa* thinking of her first marriage. Rousseau remarks that the duchess did not compliment him on his present as he had expected. The friendly relations with the duke and duchess continued, however, and Rousseau visited them in Paris again on May 28.

The extensive correspondence between Rousseau and Rey, the publisher, often filled with irritation, reveals that Rousseau suffered "a terrible migraine" when he corrected the proofs of *Julie* and was barely able to open his eyes and read the text.

Rousseau's letter to Voltaire about "providence" was published in Berlin in June 1760, although Rousseau was not notified in advance. Nor had he given his permission to the publication. Rousseau entrusted Rey with the task to find out how it was possible that the letter got published when this was not intended by him (which probably was not true). The publication of the letter compelled Rousseau to write Voltaire a letter explaining that he himself had nothing to do with the publication.

In actual fact, Voltaire's friends published the letter. Rousseau had to force himself to write the letter to Voltaire because Voltaire had set up his own cultural empire in Geneva. Besides his villa in Geneva and a summer residence in Lausanne he possessed two châteaus, Tournay and Ferney (located in French territory). But he was still living in his villa Les Délices to which he had added several outbuildings. He staged *Tancrede* and *Mahomet*, theatre plays in which the citizens of Geneva appeared as actors, at the Château Tournay. He organized several festivities attended by nationals from France, Burgundy and Geneva, which Rousseau regarded as scandalous deportment.

It is no wonder that Rousseau ended his letter to Voltaire with unusual coarseness and hostility. Rousseau lets Voltaire know that he hates him because he had destroyed Geneva, the place which had offered him asylum. Further, he had taught Genevan citizens to hate Rousseau, therefore making Rousseau's stay in Geneva impossible. It was Voltaire who had forced him to live in a foreign country. For all the formerly positive feelings he had had for Voltaire, only respect for his undeniable genius remained in his heart. Voltaire left this aggressive letter unanswered and remarked later in a letter to Mme d'Épinay that Jean-Jacques must have gone crazy because he had contended that Voltaire destroyed Geneva.

At the beginning of summer 1760 Rousseau was visited in Montlouis by Comtesse de Bouffleurs. She admired Rousseau and this may have prompted him to realize her beauty. She was thirty-five, and she was both pretty and refined. She had been the official mistress of Prince de Conti for eight years and had tried to marry him to get into the royal family's circle. Rousseau wrote in *Confessions* that he nearly became a rival of Prince de Conti. Her relationship to Prince de Conti did not hinder the countess from looking for other interesting partners. She was loyal, though not faithful to her lover, in the same way as he was not faithful to her.

At that time Rousseau was fifty. Perhaps he was still thinking of Mme d'Houdetot and trying to forswear love till the end of life. Perhaps he feared the jealousy of the duchess of Luxembourg and wanted to preserve peace with Thérèse on whom he was dependent. The countess loved discussions about literature, philosophy, morals and virtue and found in Rousseau an understanding partner for discussion. Mme Du Deffand, one of the countess's critics, declared that the countess's principles had never impeded her pleasures. Philosophers had a special appeal to the countess. It is a known fact that Hume did not resist her several years later.

Because of the political situation in 1760, the duke of Luxembourg could not spend his usual summertime at the château. The Seven Years' War was not developing favorably for France and the provinces resisted the imposed war tax. The duke was in full swing to avert the possibility of uprisings. Petit Château, however, was nevertheless put to use. Rousseau received a noble visitor there, prince de Conti (Louis-Françoise Bourbon, 1717–76), in a setting that was appropriate to his visitor's status. The exact date of this visit is not recorded but it probably took place in August.

The second visit of the prince to Montlouis, with Comtesse de Bouffleurs in autumn, is described in *Confessions*. The prince asked Rousseau if he would do him the honor of playing chess with him. Rousseau agreed, and, disregarding the gesticulations of the courtiers that he should let the prince win, he won both games. The prince, who was notorious for his liberal views and hated subservience, was not annoyed. According to Rousseau, he appreciated being treated as a man. Following the visit, the prince sent Rousseau a present of some wild game he had hunted down, to which Rousseau reacted indignantly in a letter sent to Comtesse de Bouffleurs: "No present remains without effect. When someone starts accepting anything he ends up accepting everything."

He later regretted having written the letter, perhaps because he willingly accepted partridges when sent as a present by the duchess. He explained this in a letter of thanks where he wrote that the duke had always been an exception in his eyes (he had to write this postscript because he knew that Comtesse de Bouffleurs was a close friend of the duke and the duchess).

Correspondence between Rousseau and Rey concerning the publication of *Julie* continued. The title of the novel should have read: *Lettres de deux amants. Habitans d'une petite ville au pied des Alpes.* First editions appeared with this title and the name "Jean-Jacques Rousseau, editor." Malesherbes received the whole manuscript before publication for appraisal. Rousseau wrote to him that the book did not deserve a place in his library but that some of the letters could please his wife, Mme de Malesherbes. This and other remarks make it obvious that Rousseau wrote *Julie* mainly for women and that he himself did not think much of it. One of his major concerns was to prevent the book from getting into the hands of unauthorized publishers. He wanted no pirate publications.

The advance copy of *Julie* was read by Charles Duclos, who was asked by Rousseau to attach his critical observations. Duclos was the only man of letters in Paris with whom Rousseau kept up friendly contacts. Their friendship was based on mutual respect and trust. Duclos praised the book although his comments were not weighty. He recommended that Rousseau add one more volume to the novel so that the book would have a clear conclusion. He warned that the character of Wolmar depicted by Rousseau as an honest atheist could arouse the displeasure of the Church. He did not recommend that Rousseau write in the foreword that the novel was unsuitable for young girls. Rousseau replied that the novel was dangerous and a warning was therefore justified.

So we read in the foreword: "Theatres are a necessity in big cities and novels are necessary for corrupted people. As a witness to my time I had published these letters. I wish I would live in an age in which it would be possible to throw them into fire . . . This is not a book to be read by the general public. No innocent girl should read novels . . . The one that in defiance of the title (*Lettres de deux amants*) dares to read only a single page of it is a lost girl." In the second foreword—*Préface dialoguée*—Rousseau elaborates on this subject in still greater detail. It is not clear whether Rousseau really believed what he wrote, or whether everything was only a calculated smart move to increase the curiosity and interest of the readers. It could be rather difficult to find a woman who would not want to read about things against which she had been warned, especially when the title of the book suggests that it deals with a love affair.

Rousseau wished for *Julie* to be illustrated by François Boucher but he could not to raise the price requested by this fashionable painter. Coindet then recommended Gravelot to illustrate the book, which he was hired to do. Rousseau, as a former engraver's apprentice, was preoccupied with the illustrations. The main characters of the novel should definitely be graphically portrayed with appropriate personalities and character. Wolmar was to be depicted as "cold and haughty"; St-Preux as "sincere" and the character of the prostitute should be "immoral without being naked." Rousseau even noticed that Julie's right eye was drawn smaller than the left eye. As for the drawings of Julie and Claire, Rousseau complained that both of them had small bosoms, which, although they were trendy in Paris of that time, were not appropriate for Swiss women who were endowed with the ample bosoms that Rousseau preferred.

The first six packages of *Julie* left Amsterdam on November 22, 1760. The fact that the consignment arrived in Paris with delay meant that *Julie* was sold there several weeks later than in London. Rousseau wrote that it bored the ladies in London instead of boring the ladies in Paris.

All Paris was curious and impatient to see the book. Duclos, as a permanent secretary at the Academy, praised it in a public address at an Academy meeting. But even as late as December 22 there were only two copies of the novel in Paris, devoured by those who had them and the reason for many a sleepless night, as we learn from a letter from Lorenzy to Rousseau. Since Rousseau could not send his friends complimentary copies, he sent them, at least, cards with an apology.

He also sent a card to Sophie d'Houdetot. She thanked with a letter written in her own hand, but in the third person, rather coldly testifying to an ever increasing estrangement between the former "lovers." Sophie reminded Rousseau he had not sent her the remaining part of the manuscript yet, which he was copying for her. She asked him to send her also a copy of the manuscript of *Émile* and to allow St-Lambert to read it to the Polish king. Rousseau sent the last part of the copy to Mme d'Houdetot but we do not know whether he sent her the copy of *Émile*.

The last letters between Sophie and Rousseau were exchanged in December 1760. It should be added that the reason for Rousseau not emphasizing his relationship with her in *Confessions* was the fact that she was still living when he wrote his memoirs. When *Julie* was published, Mme d'Houdetot savored her fame as a romantic heroine. She lived to be quite old and died in 1813 (St-Lambert died in 1803). The Irish writer, Maria Engelworth, visited her in 1803 when Sophie was 73. She described her as a small woman, ugly and squint-eyed, and clad in a black dress.

Asked about Rousseau and whether he had ever showed gratitude to her for the favors she granted him, Mme d'Houdetot answered that Rousseau was ungrateful. He had a lot of bad traits but she paid attention only to his genius and the good he rendered to humanity. Similar to Mme de Warens, it was thanks to Rousseau that Mme d'Houdetot entered history. It seems, however, that unlike Mme de Warens, Mme d'Houdetot was a calculating person who took advantage of Rousseau's passion.

Another friend to receive Rousseau's letter with the promise that a copy of *Julie* would follow was Lenieps. Rousseau wrote about *Julie* as a "bad and stupid novel" that was written for women. He recommends that he give *Julie* first to his married daughter, Mme de Lambert, because he knows that he himself will hate the book. Rousseau warns also that the book must not be read by the young English Mlle Barton, a friend of Lenieps's daughter, under any circumstances, for the reasons that are dealt with in the foreword.

He assured Lenieps again that he had renounced writing books. He said that as an author he had yet to expiate his sin (here he hints to the children he had sent to a foundling home). This atonement consisted of the work he was doing on *Émile*, a book that was originally intended to be a manual for parents raising their children, something he himself had not done. *Émile* thus contains a veiled message: a man who cannot do justice to his fatherly duties has no right to have children. Poverty, opinions of others or his own interests cannot be used as an excuse. Who neglects these sacred duties will shed bitter tears for his fault and will never find solace.

Fame and Fall

1761 was the year of *Julie*. Cranston put it correctly when he wrote that *Julie* transformed the famous author to a cult figure.

From the perspective of the eighteenth century, the publication of the novel was indeed a literary revolution that had a profound impact on peoples' behavior and thinking. It should be stressed that Rousseau knew about the success of novels that were written as a series of letters, such as those by Samuel Richardson and other English writers translated into French. If it were not for the novel *Pamela*, or *Virtue Rewarded* and particularly *Clarissa Harlowe*, a novel published in successive volumes between 1747 and 1748, there would not have to be any *Héloïse*, at least not in this presentation. The success of this novel seems to be rather difficult to understand from today's perspective, at least at first sight. Rousseau, who spent most of his life in women's society, knew as a "big child" what women desired and what they wanted to hear.

Unlike most of his contemporaries he had no ambition to dominate women. On the contrary, he felt better when women dominated him. His masochism became part of his daily activities. The style of his conversation and his written expressions resembled female speech with its indulgence in exaggeration, ill fate, confused emotions, inaccuracies and willingness to pick up emotional and moral themes, to accentuate duties and tragic endings. A steady emotional and moral environment guaranteed that a woman could live in the stable relationships that are important for every woman, enabling her to fulfill her generative functions and provide the necessary protection of her role in society. Emancipated women would be hardly fond of *Julie* but they would probably read it in secret. *Julie* was a modern woman's novel, the prototype of novels for women and girls that, adapted to our time, are and will be consumed incessantly. The numerous television series for women, whether in Europe, the United States or in Spanish-speaking countries, are a variety of *Julie*. The Czech author, Karel Čapek, would probably say that *Julie* was the first novel for servants *(Marsyas)*.

There was no woman who was not convinced that the story was a real one because they believed no one would be able to write about such love if he himself had not experienced it. Rousseau emphasized in *Confessions* that the novel's success with women was based on their conviction that it was his autobiography. He pointed out that his imagination was so strong that it enabled him to describe a passion even in the absence of a real experience. His childhood memories as well as those concerned with Mme d'Houdetot were of great help to him. He admitted it was his intention to keep the readers in suspense, wondering whether they were reading fiction or a real story: "A rigorous moralist could say it was my duty to be frank and tell the truth but I think that in doing so I would demonstrate stupidity rather than sincerity." This sentence might raise doubts about Rousseau's moral views. The remark shows that his position as a known moralist was rather a pose that he used according to the situation in which he found himself. (As already mentioned, Mme d'Épinay said Rousseau was a moral dwarf on stilts.) Rousseau put his finger correctly on the psychologically confirmed fact: the original is always valued more than its copy.

In the same way, unconsciously, Rousseau has cogently described another characteristic attribute of big literature, *distance*. He tells the story but, as the author, makes no judgments and leaves it entirely up to the reader to make his or her own judgment. Julie's father forces his daughter to marry a person she is not in love with and she obeys him. Some critics (abbé Cahagne) held it against Rousseau that he defended the patriarchal tyranny of the father. In fact, no such claim was possible because Rousseau did not make any such judgment in the novel. He described the conflict of a woman who was faced with a decision between two possible relationships. Such a situation is certainly faced by most women and that is why the women readers could easily identify with Julie.

An anecdote described in *Confessions* shows what the reaction of most women would have been to Julie: A certain lady of the world who was about to depart for a fancy-dress ball, and who was already dressed up, started to read *Julie*. Her servants informed her that the carriage was already waiting but she replied it should wait further. At two o'clock she was still submerged in the book. At four o'clock in the morning she ordered the servants to unhorse the carriage and stretched out in her bed to finish reading the book. We can thus see that the soul of a woman does not change very much.

One of my friends watched a Spanish series on American television for two hours every evening though she did not understand a single Spanish word and regretted on our leaving the United States that she would not be able to follow the whole series so she would know how the story ended. The more sad and lachrymose the story was, the more beautiful it appeared. The number of dead characters increased the value of the series.

Julie was successful because Rousseau put his finger exactly on what women required. "It is to the favor of women that I owe their conviction that I have described the real story of my life and that I am a hero of the novel." All his readers believed that no one could describe the feelings so vividly if he had not experienced them himself. No one could imagine how Rousseau's fantasy could possibly have described so passionately what were, in fact, fictional characters. Rousseau shrewdly let his readers continue in their uncertainty. "I had no intention of destroying or reinforcing a mistake that was of so great an advantage for me." Even a segment of the male readership accepted the book quite well (though not with as much enthusiasm as the women), bearing witness to the influence of women on the public opinion of France in the eighteenth century.

The opinion of writers varied. The duchess of Luxembourg (who knew the story already from Rousseau's reading) expressed the general attitude toward the book quire correctly: "your *Julie* is the most beautiful book in the world: there is no other soul like yours that could create something similar." Today the most successful novels are written by women. Rousseau was a man who possessed a high degree of "feminization." The book was the biggest financial success of the century although Rousseau got but little. The book was most successful in France, especially at the French royal court, and its success was lowest in Switzerland.

Because the Holland edition of *Julie* was delayed, Robin published a second edition in Paris, with Malesherbes' agreement, that appeared on the market sooner then the first edition and pirate editions were soon sold in the provinces. It was as late as January 17, 1761 that Rey notified Rousseau the shipment of the first edition had arrived in Paris. The list of persons to receive complimentary copies reveals those who belonged to the circle of Rousseau's acquaintances and friends. We read here the names of the duke and duchess of Luxembourg, Comtesse de Bouffleurs and Prince de Conti, Lorenzy, Mme de Verdelin, Mme d'Houdetot, Mme de Créquie, Mme Dupin, Mme Sellon, Mme de Chenonceaux, Duclos, Lenieps, Lalive, Gauffecourt, Roguin, Carrión, Guérin, Watelet, Blondel d'Azaincourt, Sevelinge, La Tour, d'Alembert, Loyseau de Mauléon, Francueil, and Coindet. Rousseau sent one copy to M. d'Épinay with a distinctly written *"monsieur"* but not *"madame."* No copy was sent to his old friend Alexandre Deleyre because Rousseau could not forgive his marrying Caroline-Alexandrine Louiseau against Rousseau's advice.

The second edition was also accompanied by Rousseau's numerous objections regarding the illustrations. According to Rousseau, Wolmar had resembled an old druggist, Claire had the cheeks of a fat maid with a duster, and the dead Julie looked like a rag-and-bone woman. According to Rousseau's instructions, Wolmar's dress had to be improved to be more elegant and Claire received a decent *déshabillé*. Rousseau was especially concerned that the clothes of the characters clearly and accurately express their social status. Rousseau was not satisfied with the second edition of *Julie* because some passages were left out without his knowing.

The third edition was being prepared in February 1761, this time censored by the Jesuit abbé de Graves and the new chief censor, the rigorous Christophe Picquet. This edition was to be published by Guérin. In this edition fifty changes and improvements had to be made.

The Genevan priest, Moulton, asked Rousseau to send him a copy of *Julie* which Rousseau was not enthusiastic about doing because he knew that the book was not written for Genevan clerical dignitaries. The publication of *Julie* led to a flood of correspondence and caused a constant stream of visitors, leaving Rousseau without a moment of rest. The letter from Mme de Polignac exemplifies the impact *Julie* had on women. She wrote to Mme de Verdelin that she had never felt the desire to get to know Rousseau as a philosopher. But Rousseau as Julie's lover was something quite different. Having read the book she wanted to saddle a horse and drive to Montmorency to made his acquaintance at all costs. She wanted to say to him how elevated he was above other men in his awareness. She wanted him to show her Julie's portrait, in front of which she could kneel down and admire this magnificent woman.

Mme de Verdelin showed this by no means isolated letter to Rousseau. He had already started a collection of *courrier des admiratrices* that consisted of the letters sent to him by Parisian ladies. Their enthusiasm for his novel helped Rousseau to correct the view he had of women's character. The flood of letters that were sent to Rousseau from all of Europe contained many curiosities: an anonymous man cursed Rousseau because his mistress refused to sleep with him after she had read *Julie* though they already had a child together. She wanted to be as chaste as the novel's heroine.

Even in Geneva the book was received with enthusiasm and was condemned only by theologians. The Genevan consistory marked the book as very dangerous to morality and the *Petit Conseil* prohibited it to be loaned in public libraries. But *Julie* was not banned from sale because it would be futile to ban a book that could be bought everywhere.

As expected, the greatest criticism of *Julie* came from Voltaire. He described it as a stupid, bourgeois, shameless and annoying book and declared that it would become "the disgrace of this country." He wrote a sharp criticism under the pseudonym Marquis de Ximénès entitled "*Quatre Lettres sur La Nouvelle Héloïse,*" but it targeted more the author than the novel itself. In a letter to d'Alembert, Voltaire called Rousseau "a cunning lunatic." Voltaire's criticism actually did more damage to himself than to Rousseau. It is necessary to add in explanation that d'Alembert defended Rousseau. He wrote of him that he was a sick man with huge intellectual powers.

But other Genevan citizens assured Rousseau they were proud that Rousseau came from Geneva. Rousseau's Genevan friend, the banker Daniel Roguin, who lived in Parisian exile, wrote to Rousseau that he had not met anybody so far whom Rousseau would not charm. The opinion of the Genevan theologian Moulton was critical though polite: the seducer is described as a philosopher and Julie, who was deceiving the men, is described as a paragon of chastity. He regarded *Julie* as a book that was written for Paris and not for Geneva. Rousseau should write about more serious problems that would be worthy of his pen, for example, why the Genevans have lost their republican virtues.

The second foreword to *Julie*, entitled "*Préface dialoguée,*" was published by Guérin in the form of a pamphlet on Monday, February 16, 1761. This foreword contains approximately 10,000 words and describes a dialogue between the author-editor and a fictitious critic. By this pamphlet Rousseau wanted to preempt the expected criticisms. He could be reproached that what he wrote in it contradicted his views expressed in *Letter to d'Alembert*. Rousseau replies to the imaginary critic that he wrote the book to be read by the educated and not by "innocent" readers. People corrupted by art could be cured by art. Those who knew immoral literature could be introduced to virtues by moral literature. For him, however, moral literature was not identical with the sermons preached by various moralists to whom nobody listened anyway. His *Julie* offered the vision of a better world in the small setting of Clarens where people lived tolerantly, honestly and in love. He sent this pamphlet to a number of his friends as well, but this time it was explicitly meant to be read by men of letters and not by women.

At that time the publication of *Émile* came to the fore. As we know, Mme de Luxembourg was concerned with the publication from the outset and even interceded with Malesherbes to allow the book to be printed. As part of her correspondence with Malesherbes it is very interesting to consider the latter's comment on Rousseau's psychology. According to him *Rousseau was motivated by a perverse wish to be unhappy and poor.* As it is well known that Rousseau could have attained a well-paid position many times in his life and that he had always refused it, his "wish to be poor" can be looked upon as a variation of a masochistic disposition.

Looked upon from this perspective, the observation of a Hungarian count, Joseph Teleki de Szek, could also be of interest. He visited Rousseau and recorded some very interesting details of Rousseau's psychology. We learn from his account that Rousseau wore old worn-out clothes and his shoes had wooden soles with cut-out holes, perhaps because he suffered from deformities of his toes (hallux valgus). Teleki continued that Rousseau was forty-five (in fact he was forty-nine), was rather thin and round-shouldered, and his speech was hurried and animated. He was very intelligent and endowed with the French *esprit*. His thoughts were clear and he expressed them with ease. His conversation was not boring and though he spoke a lot one could not describe him as a chatterer.

The count's observations and the style of his speech are bizarre, but Rousseau himself was probably still more bizarre. He claimed, for example, that he slept less then one hour at night which was very difficult for the count to believe because Rousseau made an alert impression and had "clear, broad eyes." The count was surprised by the simplicity of Rousseau's environment. He found the *donjon* quite appealing with a portrait of Frederick II on the wall.

The meal was served in the kitchen's dining area; it was not overly rich but quite tasty: soup, veal and rabbit in gravy, pâté and grapes. A woman who was simultaneously a cook, maid and housewife waited on the guests. She was not handsome enough to be suspected to be something more for Rousseau. Teleki's description of Thérèse concurred with the description provided by other visitors, but he was mistaken with respect to her other roles.

While visiting Petit Château the count saw Indian arrows because Rousseau occasionally amused himself with archery. (It is difficult to say whether Rousseau believed that imitating a savage using a bow would make a better man of him, or whether he wanted to manifest that he was better because he lived as a primitive man.) The visitor noticed correctly that Rousseau wanted to be original at all costs and poor because he liked to show off his poverty—it contributed to his originality and exceptionality. This view was rife even during Rousseau's lifetime.

At Easter 1761 Rousseau visited the château at Montmorency where he was introduced to an important man of this epoch, Duc de Choiseul, who was foreign minister and dominated the government of France for twelve years (1758–1770) and was famous for rebuilding the French military power after the Seven Years' War (1756–1763), in which French troops were defeated. Duc de Choiseul favored Rousseau and went so far as to offer him a post in diplomatic service. Rousseau did not accept this favorable post, as he had turned down many posts before, though he respected de Choiseul and took his side in a controversy with Mme de Pompadour that was underway at the court at that time. At this Easter gathering, Rousseau noticed a certain chilliness in his contacts with the duchess (he lost his privileged place at the table next to her seat, for instance), but the duke continued to pay friendly attention to him.

Another prominent guest and admirer whom Rousseau was pleased to see at Montlouis was the Swiss banker, François Necker, the future minister of finance in the government of King Louis XV. Necker said that the six volumes of *Julie* "contained a delicacy that did not float metaphysically in the clouds but forced people to attain the peaks of daily virtue without dissuading them from following this path."

As a result of the success of *Julie*, Rousseau had little time to work on the abstract to Saint-Pierre's *"Jugement sur le project de paix perpetuelle"* (Project for Eternal Peace) though its publication was quite timely—the Seven Years' War ended by the Treaty of Paris in 1763. Its main result was a defeat suffered by the French in America. Perhaps Rousseau was one of the first to realized that the Seven Years' War differed from the typical dynastic wars of the past to which Saint-Pierre's proposal to form a confederation of individual states, representing the rulers of the states, might have applied.

The Seven Years' War was a new type of war, with the focus chiefly on the overseas' colonies. According to Rousseau's views, which he imparted to his Genevan compatriots Favre and De Tournes, the only possibility of peace was to ban territorial gains. Rousseau had never published this view and in *Confessions* he later considered himself lucky not to have done so since England struggled to push out Spain and was beginning to build a worldwide colonial and mercantile power, attempting at the same time to prevent France from succeeding in something similar. For this reason Rousseau did not share the opinion of many representatives of the French Enlightenment who regarded England as the "mirror of freedom."

His political conception differed also from Montesquieu's constitutional liberalism and Voltaire's Enlightenment absolutism. He himself espoused the *thése républicaine*, which he explained in the book *On the Social Contract, or the Principles of Political Law*. Rousseau offered this book to Rey for publication at the end of 1761. Though he told his Genevan visitors, "You will see a revolution soon," he was not predicting the course of events of 1789 and cannot be held responsible for the revolution of 1789. As a matter of fact, nobody had a greater aversion than he for "revolutions and leagues of all kinds." He was only "the painter of nature and the historian of the human heart."

The idea of a republican state was by no means Rousseau's original discovery as is often depicted. He came from "republican" Geneva and had always maintained that this system was the best.

The reception of the abstract to "Project for Eternal Peace" by his friends was favorable, especially by Duclos and Deleyre. The letter sent to Rousseau by the Genevan pastor, Vernes, was more reserved. Vernes wrote that he suspected French music would survive in spite of Rousseau's critical treatise, science would continue to prosper in spite of Rousseau's *Discours* and wars would keep occurring in spite of Rousseau's *Jugement sur le project de paix perpetuelle*. In this letter Vernes also comes back to *Julie* and says that he does not understand what made Rousseau make Wolmar an atheist when he was such a good man. Rousseau replied that it was not his ambition to teach philosophers that someone could believe in God without being a hypocrite, and that someone could be an atheist without being a villain.

At that time Rousseau had a disagreement with Mme de Bouffleur. As he wrote in *Confessions,* he always had bad luck with women who entertained literary ambitions. The countess had written a tragedy and the work was praised in the circles around Prince de Conti when it was read in public. Rousseau declared it was an imitation of an English model. Their dispute was settled at a joint dinner in Saint-Denis. In spite of the fact that he had offended the countess, not only as a woman but also as an author, as Rousseau admits in *Confessions* (and hated her intensively afterwards), the countess's behavior to him remained incomprehensibly friendly.

In the spring and summer of 1761 Rousseau suffered a serious reoccurrence of his urinary tract infection. He refused any medical attendance, did not leave his bed and assumed (as so often before) that he would die soon.

His conscience was still tormented by the memory of having sent his children to a foundling home. In a letter to Mme de Luxembourg, he described how he regrets that he will die without having corrected this sin. He confesses to her that the children sprang from his bond with Thérèse (which was common knowledge) and explains that he could not marry Thérèse "because we have different religious faiths." This was not true because at the time when the first child was born, which was during the winter of 1746, Rousseau was still a Roman Catholic and his conversion to Protestantism took place eight years later (1754), after more than ten years of coexistence with Thérèse. He asked the duchess whether she would help him find out about the fate of the first child, who was marked with a certain sign, the duplicate of which Rousseau still had. He concluded his letter protesting that his heart was beating only for the duke and the duchess, and for the poor girl (Thérèse), and may death come at any hour it would find him thinking of them.

The duchess, who allegedly wanted to adopt Rousseau's child, sent her steward La Roche to search for the child. The duchess, however, soon informed Rousseau that the fate of the girl could not be tracked down (here we first learn the gender of the firstborn child) and Rousseau asked her to stop the search. The version presented in *Confessions* is somewhat different: Rousseau did not write anything about his letter in which he asked the duchess to stop the search. He wrote only that the search was not successful ant that it was perhaps better so. He had no certainty that the child was really his own and he knew it would be very difficult to establish a true parental tie with the child, which should have been done when the child was quite young.

Out of fear that he could die soon, Rousseau also turned to the Genevan pastor Moultou and asked him if he would take over, in case of his disability or death, the publication of his collected works. This was to be done on the condition that his works must not be adapted (he adds a remark that *Julie* is not to be included in the edition). He did not want the task to be committed to a Frenchman. After some hesitation, Moultou agreed.

In mid-June 1761, when the duke and duchess returned to Château Montmorency, Rousseau's illness worsened so much that he had to move into Petit Château where his noble patrons could provide better care for him and visit him daily. They convinced Rousseau to agree to summon a known surgeon, Frère Côme, to carry out an operation, at which the duke was present. Rousseau described the operation as "long and painful" (the introduction of the probe lasted two hours despite Côme's dexterity) but Rousseau had to control his complaints in order to ease the suffering of the sensitive duke.

Frère Côme performed a catheterization of the urethra, which had been scarred following the previous inflammations, using a thin urinary probe, which is a difficult and very painful procedure. The surgeon Morand had not succeeded in his attempt to insert a probe ten years previously. These difficulties were the consequence of a pronounced cicatrisation and deformation of Rousseau's urethra. The surgeon could not find any stone in the urinary bladder. He found, however, a cirrhotic and enlarged prostate; this could be established by a rectal examination upon insertion of a finger into the rectum in the same way as it is performed today.

Frère Côme examined Rousseau four times. When examining Rousseau for the first time he suspected the presence of a large urinary calculus in the bladder, which could not be confirmed by subsequent examinations. The surgeon informed Rousseau that he would continue to suffer from his complaints all his life but that he would live for a long time. Rousseau was relieved to hear that his illness was incurable but not lethal and that there was no stone. According to *Confessions* this treatment and examinations took place during Easter 1762 (?) and Rousseau wrote that the examinations were performed in his house in the presence of the duke.

The relevant book of *Confessions* that relates to this period—1762—contains the account of the medical procedures carried out by Frère Côme. When assured by the surgeon that he would live for a long time the patient calmed down: "I was finally informed that my complaint was incurable although not mortal, and would last for the rest of my days. My imagination was restrained by this information and no longer showed me the prospect of a cruel death in the agonies of stone. I ceased to fear that the end of a catheter, which had broken in my urethra a long time ago had formed a nodule of a stone. Delivered from the imaginary ills crueler than my real ones, I endured the latter more patiently."

Rousseau's health had never been good while he lived in Montmorency. "I had been living at Montmorency for more than four years without enjoying a single day's good heath." In early winter his health suffered a severe blow— an unpleasant complication occurred. In a letter to Moultou Rousseau explained that a small piece of the end of a urinary catheter, which he had to have introduced for some time to be able to pass water at all, broke away and remained lodged in the urethra, which made the drainage of urine even more difficult. It remains unclear when exactly this complication occurred because Rousseau wrote—describing the probing performed by Frère Côme—that the catheter tip had broken away "a long time ago." He wrote: "As you know, foreign bodies in these parts do not remain in an unchanged condition but change their position and form the core for the developing stones." It is also possible that the catheter tip broke away during the masturbation practices, which have been previously mentioned.

The news about his misadventure spread very quickly. Rousseau had maintained a large correspondence, even including people he never met personally. Two of his anonymous admirers, signing as "Julie" and "Claire" (their real names were Marie-Anna Alissan de La Tour and Marie-Madeleine Bernardoni), corresponded with him in a flirtatiously jocular style, in "Julie's" case for as long as fifteen years.

It was Mme Bernardoni who started the correspondence as "Claire" with the announcement that "*Julie*" did not die but that she lives and loves him. She asked him to send his reply to Versailles to Marquise de Solar (who was a member of the Solaro family where Rousseau had been employed in Turin in 1729). Rousseau wrote in his reply that he decided not to write for the public any more but that this decision did not apply to his personal correspondence and that the letter he received stirred a desire in him to meet the lady. Rousseau was always ready to go out of his way to write letters and it seems that he needed this kind of safe, noncommittal flirtation and was even satisfied by it in some way.

"Julie" who had meanwhile given in to Rousseau's insistence and revealed her true name, Marie-Anne Alissan de La Tour, beseeched him to consult the surgeon M. Sarbourg whom she described as much more competent than Frère Côme, though he was not so well-known. Rousseau must have felt very bad because he agreed to follow her advice but on the condition that he would be only examined and not treated. He had very unfavorable views about medical treatment and said repeatedly that these confounded doctors were only killing him by bleeding him. He could do more for himself when he gargled and put his feet in hot water. He informed "Julie" in a letter that his illness "originated in some deformity" from which he had suffered since his birth.

Also, his second pen pal, "Claire" (Mme Bernardoni—in her case Rousseau did not want to know her identity), joined "Julie's" appeal. Mme Bernardoni wrote Rousseau several days later that his "Julie" fell sick, too, but made a rapid recovery after the enemas she received. It is interesting to note that the people of the eighteenth century spoke so frankly of their private ailments. It is perhaps an extension of the attitude of the Middle Ages continuing on, where even very private matters such as sexual intercourse or dying were accessible to others.

It is remarkable that the duke of Luxembourg cared so much for the sick Rousseau, especially since his own family was pursued by several tragic deaths. His sister, Duchess de Villeroy, died in December 1759, his daughter, Princess de Robecq, died in June 1760 and in a two-week period in June 1761, he lost his only son, the duke of Montmorency (who died while in military service) and his grandson, the count of Luxembourg who was to become the captain of the royal guard. Rousseau believed that the boy died through the fault of the attending physician, Dr. Bordeu, and that his life could have been saved if the family would have followed his advice and brought the boy to Montlouis. Here Thérèse would have fed him and he would not have been stuffed with all the medicines. This shows once again how deeply Rousseau mistrusted the doctors, and it should be added that his mistrust was certainly justified.

The June issue of *Journal encyclopédique* published a defense of Rousseau's

Julie, which had been criticized in the previous issue. Rousseau had ascribed the criticism to Voltaire but its real author was Charles Borde. The advocates of the novel were joined also by Charles Panckouke, a publisher from Amsterdam, who made Rousseau an offer to become an author in his publishing house. Panckouke had to turn to Amsterdam for publication of erotic literature. He also offered to publish Rousseau's collected works in a magnificent edition. Rousseau refused both his offers. It was not until after Rousseau's death that Panckouke published the first six volumes of *Confessions*.

Rousseau notified Rey that he could publish *Social Contract* provided that it would be printed on good quality paper (he said it was the last book he intended to write) and that it would appear before the printing of *Émile* that was to be "born" in France. Rey set the publication deadline for *Social Contract* at March 1762.

The reclusive Rousseau was very distraught at the death of his dog, Turc, whose original name of Duke had been changed after Rousseau met the duke of Luxembourg because he did not want the duke to take offence. Turc had been with him since the first days of his stay in Hermitage and had advanced to the honored place of Rousseau's friend and companion. Rousseau valued Turc for his friendly nature and loyalty. It was just a dog, wrote Rousseau in a letter to the duke, but, "it loved me, was responsive, impartial . . . one has many so-called friends who have none of such qualities." It is not unusual that lonely people, especially when they do not understand the rules governing emotional life in human society, find consolation and emotional certitude in the company of animals. From the viewpoint of the period it might be of interest to describe the immense response caused in society by the death of Rousseau's dog. Rousseau received emotional letters from the duke and duchess of Luxembourg, from Lorenzy, and from Comtesse de Bouffleurs who informed him that Prince de Conti would be pleased to give Rousseau a new dog if he would accepted it.

In a letter from June 20, 1761, Rousseau complains to the duchess of frequent vomiting which had improved but had left him feeling depressed and unable to concentrate, even on reading novels. He sent a letter also to Lenieps notifying him of his illness. It is noteworthy that in spite of his state of health Rousseau has never stopped writing letters. He maintained extensive correspondence, which linked him with the society, because his other social contacts were very limited. For Rousseau the correspondence was obviously much less of a burden than direct personal contacts; the correspondence served as a substitute for the latter and showed that Rousseau in fact needed society even though he saw himself as a hermit.

He required an exchange of letters especially from his backers, the duke and duchess of Luxembourg, who had to assure him incessantly of their love and respect. Whenever it seemed that they were falling behind with their letters (which was inevitable in view of their social and political obligations) Rousseau's emotional protests resulted. Rousseau remained a big child who needed its share of love and attachment. He had even suggested that the duke send him a blank sheet to save time. When, however, the duke complied and sent him several blank sheets, Rousseau reacted with irony verging on insult: "I am never, monsieur, tired of reading your letters even if I read them repeatedly. What luxuriance! What an elocution! No, monsieur de Maréchal, Montesquieu, Pascal or Tacitus has never said so many things with so little words."

The letters quelled his hunger for love and friendship. He tried to reduce his visitation, however, to a select group of persons. One of them was the Swiss pastor from Zürich, Leonhard Usteri, recommended to Rousseau by Moultou. Rousseau invited him to a visit along with the English traveler, Le Roux, who brought the English translation of *Julie* though Rousseau could not read it because he did not speak English. He gave it to Comtesse de Bouffleurs for assessment. Pastor Usteri left Montmorency with a copy of the manuscript of *Émile* to assess. The opinion of the rigorous pastor was very critical. He stressed in particular that an educator must not use artifice and tricks as part of education because he would teach the pupil to answer cunning with cunning.

In the fall of 1761 Rousseau's illness got somewhat better. In October he received a letter from Jean Ribotte who wrote that an upsurge of religious persecution and fanaticism was spreading in southwest France (that was to sweep Rousseau a year later as well). A Protestant pastor—François Rochette—had been jailed in Toulouse because he transgressed the ban imposed on religious rallies. Along with him, three lawyers were put into jail, the Grenin Brothers, who tried to achieve his release. Ribotte entreated Rousseau to intervene with the governor of the province, Duc de Richelieu, which was inexpedient, according to Rousseau, who declined to help in any way. Rousseau referred Ribotte to the Bible that determined that the laws must be obeyed. An attempt to free from prison even those who were innocent was, according to Rousseau, a clear example of a rebellion that can never be justified and which the government had the right to punish. He recommended that Ribotte turn to Voltaire, but at the same time voiced his doubt that Voltaire would have enough volition to help.

Here he did injustice to Voltaire. The persecution of Protestants in Toulouse stirred Voltaire, a Catholic, to a significant activity that contributed to his fame not only as a great writer but also as a champion of freedom. He could not save pastor Rochette and the Grenin Brothers. They were executed several weeks later. This case nevertheless prompted Voltaire to take several active steps that benefited the French Protestants. Compared to Voltaire, Rousseau seems to have behaved in a fearful and uncaring manner. But his situation was that of an exile and a Protestant in Catholic France at that time, whereas Voltaire as a Catholic and Frenchman enjoyed the privileges of his Genevan retreat.

In November Rousseau sent two manuscripts to the publishers that were soon to completely transform his life. *Social Contract* was to be published in Amsterdam by Rey and *Émile* in France by Duchesne. Rey received the manuscript of *Du Contract social* in mid-November 1761. He thanked Rousseau that he could publish his book again and regretted that he was not entrusted also with the publication of *Émile* that was to be published by Duchesne.

Émile brought quite a few difficulties even before its publication. As was usual for Rousseau, he complained that the publishers did not publish his book speedily enough. He fabricated a false theory explaining the delayed publication of the book, which led to an extensive correspondence between Duchesne, Malesherbes, the duke and duchess of Luxembourg and others. Rousseau claimed that the manuscript was intercepted by the Jesuits (the scholastic educational methods of whom were mentioned critically in *Émile*), who allegedly wanted to delay its publication and, according to Rousseau, it could not be ruled out that they might succeed in their efforts to bar its publication for good. Rousseau was convinced that they would not allow *Émile* to be published before his death and would later adapt the work so that it suited their wishes.

Rousseau's assumptions were erroneous. It was exactly at that time that the Jesuits were being persecuted in France and on November 18, 1761, when Rousseau wrote the said letter to Malesherbes in which he described the Jesuit conspiracy against *Émile*, a decree was signed ordering their deportation from

France following the affair with Father Lavalett. The verdict of the parlement of Paris was subsequently confirmed by a royal decree in 1764.

This development came as a surprise to Rousseau. He admits, in a letter of apology sent to Malesherbes, that his seclusion was detrimental, something he had fiercely denied so far: "Ah, it is very cruel for a sad and lonely invalid to have a deranged imagination and not to know anything about things that should concern him."

Rousseau had enemies but he was usually unable to recognize them, just as he was unable to recognize his friends. The patience of the people around him, even those in high positions, is therefore surprising. Malesherbes and others tried to placate and assure him that his *Émile* would not suffer any changes. Duchesne assured Rousseau that the book was supposed to be published in March 1762, or perhaps even in February.

But Rousseau returned to his suspicion against the Jesuits again, as late as December 1761, and proclaimed it in his letters that went everywhere, and did not apologize till the end of December. Malesherbes wrote in his reply to Rousseau's apology about his friend's great sensitivity, deep sadness and the habit of seeing things in the darkest colors. These were further aggravated by his loneliness and the way of life he had chosen. In a letter to Mme de Luxembourg, Malesherbes wrote that there was in the unhappy Jean-Jacques a mixture of grandeur, honesty, melancholy and occasional ecstasy, all of which caused his suffering in life but was also the source of his work.

Rousseau was increasingly concerned with Thérèse's future (which bears witness to the important role she played in his life). This led him to accept Rey's offer to pay Thérèse a lifelong pension of three hundred French francs annually. Rousseau saw it as a great help and relief, but he personally—as he assures us in *Confessions*—received no advantages from it. He allegedly said to Thérèse, "What is mine is ours, and what is yours is yours." The pension was not enough to satisfy Thérèse's livelihood demands and Rousseau always had to contribute some additional money. As he said quite realistically, "We were neither of us born ever to be rich, and I certainly do not reckon that among my misfortunes."

His Swiss friend, Daniel Roguin, moved to Yverdon and invited him to visit, which Rousseau rejected at first. The visit did take place soon, although under different circumstances.

The correspondence between Rousseau and Roguin reveals more medically significant information. Rousseau wrote that his teeth are the worst ever seen in a human being; however, his teeth were probably just the teeth of a person unattended and not repaired by a dentist, and not the result of a congenital deformity of dentition.

Jean Ribotte wrote him about a new and more severe outbreak of persecution of Protestants in Toulouse. The Protestant Calas was accused of having murdered his son, who had wanted to convert to Catholicism. Ribotte implored that he write something in favor of Calas but Rousseau hesitated as usual. Even Voltaire, who became famous as *l'homme de Calas,* acted only when it was too late. Calas was put on the wheel and executed. These events should have warned Rousseau as they warned Duclos, who was a good judge of society at that time. Rousseau perceived the disorganization of France following the lost war, and he experienced fears to which he had been sensitive since his youth. He contemplated leaving for Touraine after the publication of *Émile.*

His true friend—Malesherbes—who took an interest in his nature and character, asked Rousseau to describe the experiences of his life. In January 1762 Rousseau started writing a series of letters to Malesherbes, describing his life, and these letters (four altogether) later became the core of his *Confessions.*

The first letter is of psychological interest. In it, Rousseau tries to deny the accusation that his departure from Parisian society was caused by his misanthropic tendencies. According to his own words he was born "with a love of solitude" (in fact he was brought up in solitude and felt safe when alone). He was allegedly happier when he dwelt in the company of the characters he had created in his imagination than in that of real people around him. When in society, mainly in Paris, he was tormented by a melancholy—as can be seen in the literary production of that time—that did not oppress him in solitude. Even his literary works "from loneliness" are different. They reflect peace and lucidity of mind.

He attributed his failure in society to timidity; according to him timidity also led to his failure "to attain the place in the world I think I deserve." When he attained literary fame, when the whole world was courting him, he took an even greater dislike to society. As an unsociable individualist he later withdraw into loneliness and gained society's recognition through his literary work, owing to his steadfast ambition and conviction of his own exceptionality.

He explained his love of solitude as a result of his "irresistible spirit for freedom" that even inhibited the accepting of presents. ("A good deed obligates," says Hobbes.) His freedom made it possible for him to do what he wanted. He added a statement which was characteristic of his concept of freedom: he would be happy even in the Bastille where he would have nothing else to do except stay in prison (similar views are typical of masochists). His social isolation (actually never complete) was a kind of prison where he had to feel happy. The exchange of presents and emotions that is characteristic for social life fell away, and Rousseau always found such exchanges difficult. In his childhood he lacked the social education necessary for life in society. But as an isolated individualist he was convinced of his uniqueness and exceptionality: he wrote in the beginning of *Confessions*: "I am made unlike anyone I have ever met . . . I am like no one in the whole world; I may be no better, but at least I am different." Even here his conviction of his superiority is typical of all people who are not integrated in society and who use this attitude to explain their dissimilarity.

In the second letter, Rousseau described his ignorance regarding the real world: "I thought in my youth that I would meet in my life the sort of people I have read about in the books . . . but I was looking for something that did not exist and I was slowly despairing that I would ever find what I was looking for." In normal life Rousseau could hardly meet the celebrated personalities described by his favorite author Plutarch. In this letter Rousseau also described his "revelation" on his journey to Vincennes in summer, 1749; the actual events were much less dramatic than his description. Rousseau wrote also that his cardinal work consisted of both the Discourses and Émile.

The third letter was written on January 26, 1762. Rousseau described in it the happiness he found in Montmorency though it was disrupted by painful and incurable illness which had begun in his childhood. He implied in *Confessions* that he was born with a congenital defect (but he is silent on urinary tract illnesses in the descriptions of his youth and this story of a congenital defect is obviously not true).

In the fourth letter, Rousseau returned the justifications for his solitary way of life: people living in the country are more useful to society than the parasitic idlers who are babbling in the Academy. He had also to serve his home country—Geneva—by warnings about Voltaire, which he could not have done if he lived in Geneva itself. He did what he could to serve society.

He admits that he nearly abandoned his solitude out of love for M. and

Mme de Luxembourg, who saved his life when he was dying of melancholy. He loved them in spite of his aversion to aristocracy in general. Despite the fact that Malesherbes was an aristocrat, Rousseau wrote to him that he hated aristocracy. He hated it because of its position, hardness, prejudices and small-mindedness, and because of their sins. Having in mind all Rousseau said about aristocracy, one can hardly understand why Rousseau's friends were mainly its members. It is possible that he wanted to demonstrate that not only did he belong among those who were "superior" and had been "chosen" but that, unlike them, he was also "good."

Rousseau's illness got worse in the first weeks of 1762. He said in a letter to Duchesne that his last day will be his luckiest one. His friends pressed him to seek medical advice but Rousseau refused. His state of mind was made worse by the persisting arguments with both of his publishers, Rey and Duchesne. He wrote in a letter to Moultou that his health was getting worse hour by hour and that he suffered pain at night as well as by day. He also informed Moultou, for the first time, that *Du Contract social* was in print, the work that he allegedly started writing in a pithy form a long time ago but from which he now wanted to publish only selected parts. He informed Mme de Verdelin that he was so sick he was surprised he was still alive. Because of his illness he neglected the correspondence with his admirers "Julie" and "Claire." "Julie," (Mme Alissan de La Tour), rebuked him for this negligence and offered to terminate their correspondence if he wished.

At this time the proofs of *Contract* and *Émile* from both Duchesne and Rey started to arrive. In a letter to Rey, Rousseau described his ordeal caused by the remainder of the catheter that remained in his urethra, which he did not want to have removed. His bladder was in such bad condition that he would not survive the operation and he would prefer to die any other death than a death like this. The proofs of *Social Contract* proceeded smoothly and Rousseau was very obliged to Rey because of Rey's promise to pay Thérèse an annual pension (he informed Malesherbes about Rey's generosity, which was not usual among publishers).

Then the publication of *Émile* got into difficulties. Parts of the book were printed in the Netherlands by Néaulme. Rousseau fought back furiously when he was criticized with accusations that his French contained too many of the less frequently used words. He declared he had no desire to care for those who did not understand the language. He would not explain things that were clear.

His health improved in February.

He received a letter from Moultou in Geneva, to whom he had sent the manuscript of *Émile* for assessment. Moultou was terrified by the "Profession of Faith" and wrote "My God, I shake in your place." He was of the opinion that Rousseau would face persecution and condemnation not only in Geneva but also in France, where he would be criticized not only by Catholics but also by atheists. Especially the denial of divine revelation was heresy for which he could not be forgiven.

Rousseau, who was unable to discern the signs of his time, dismissed his warning and felt safe under the protection of Malesherbes and the Luxembourgs. Perhaps he was firmly convinced that he would die anyway, given the state of health he was in at the time. Rousseau needed more rationale than simply the courage to express truths that were good for humanity (again the conviction of his messianic mission). He said about the French that they were humane and hospitable by nature. Why would they persecute a wretch who stood in no one's way and preached only peace and honesty? As long as Helvétius, the author of *De l'Esprit*, could live in France, there was no danger for Rousseau, he reasoned.

Rousseau was badly mistaken. Helvétius had to recant his book, humbly, in public and Malesherbes could preserve his position only through the sacrifice of Teveire who was in charge of Helvétius's book as a censor. In Toulouse, again, several Protestants were tortured and executed. It is obvious that Rousseau had totally overestimated the French tolerance. But he had at least changed his mind and decided that it would be better indeed after only the first two volumes of *Émile* were published in France that the subsequent volumes containing the "Profession of Faith" published in the Netherlands by Néaulme. He replaced his previous conviction that it was the Jesuits who were plotting against the publication of *Émile* by guessing that it was the Jansenists, who controlled the municipal parlements, who were obstructing its publication.

In the first months of 1762 Rousseau wrote letters mainly to his publishers, Malesherbes and the duchess of Luxembourg, whose interventions with Malesherbes and perhaps also a financial intervention with Duchesne, who paid Rousseau an honorarium for *Émile*, facilitated the publication of the book.

With the approaching date of the publication of *Émile*, Malesherbes showed increasing signs of nervousness, as did Néaulme in Amsterdam whose nervousness changed into panic after he belatedly read what he was about to print and what was, according to Rousseau, the most important part of the whole book, the "Profession of Faith." In his letter to Rousseau of May 22, 1762, Néaulme wrote that he had assumed the author would propagate only "natural religion." He found out, however, that the author was denying the "revelation" as such, which could preclude the publication of the book in Holland.

According to Rousseau's views, everybody can believe in what they want to believe, it is a matter of their inner convictions and no church has the right to determine for them which religious dogma was correct or not. In *Social Contract* Rousseau called this type of faith *religion de l'homme* (people's religion). It is religion without temples, altars and ceremonies, and it remains restricted only to the inward cult of the highest God and of an "eternal duty of morality." It is a religion of a pure and simple Gospel, of true faith in God; it is what one might call the divine natural right. In addition to that there exists what Rousseau called *la religion du citoyen* (citizen's religion), that can vary between individual national states and is closely associated with the laws of the state. The most bizarre form of religion is *la religion du prêtre* (priest's religion) in which the believer serves two masters and the citizen is subject to contradictory duties (see *Social Contract*, Book Four: On Civic Religion).

To present religious ideas of this kind in the eighteenth century was the greatest imaginable provocation, and society's retaliation was not long in coming.

Moultou wrote Rousseau another letter from Geneva and asked Rousseau to think over once more whether the publication of "Profession of Faith" in *Émile* was the right thing to do. Rousseau's thoughts in this work were admittedly still concerned with Christianity but this differed from the true Christianity in that it was justifying the faith by giving rational reasons for it whereas all true Christians believed that the faith came from heaven. Moultou pointed out that there was a real distinction between enlightened Christians, such as Rousseau himself, and ordinary people who believed in miracles as the foundation of their faith. He expressed his conviction that the book was playing into the hands of Rousseau's enemies in Geneva, which turned out to be true, as soon as the pirate copies reached Geneva from Lyon.

But Rousseau replied to Moultou that it was already too late and he could do nothing about the book. He doubted, as he wrote, that the influence of the book on the believers in Geneva would be so bad. He admitted that *Émile* would not please his enemies in Geneva—this was allegedly the reason why he did not want to enter Geneva—"I love my country so much that I could not bear to see how hated I was there. It is better to live and die in exile."

In mid-April Rey sent the shipment with *Contract* to Paris where it was to be sold in mid-May. Rey's wife was pregnant and Rey asked Rousseau whether he would like to become the child's godfather. Rousseau agreed and became the godfather of a daughter born on May 2, 1762. The duke and duchess of Luxembourg spent Easter as usual at the château in Montmorency and Rousseau, who spent most of his time with them, had not much time left to answer the letters of his "Julie" who sent him letter after letter irrespective of her previous suggestion to discontinue their correspondence. Rousseau sent her a gruff letter in which he stipulated the right to answer her letters only when he wanted.

In a letter from April 22, 1762, Rousseau explained his remarkable thesis concerning the influence of knowledge on human virtues to the Swiss Vincent-Bernard Tscharner, governor in Aubonne on Bernese territory. He wrote that books had no meaning and influence in this respect. Has France changed for the better following the publication of Montesquieu's and Mirabeau's works? Though the writer's works can be of interest to people, they cannot make them happier or better. One has to ask why then did Rousseau write books at all when they were of no use?

Following the publication of *Contract*, which got to France with difficulties, Rousseau grew more optimistic with respect to the publication of *Émile*. He gave the publisher, Duchesne, a list of persons who should be sent author's copies. The list contained the names of the same people who had been sent the copies of *Julie* although, according to Rousseau's own words, *Julie* was written for "corrupted" people whereas *Émile* was addressed to the "wise."

The response of his friends to the author's copies not as enthusiastic as Rousseau had expected. He himself judged both publications differently several years later. According to the view expressed in *Confessions*, *Émile* was the most important and best of his books. In a letter to Dom Dechamps from May 22, 1762, however, Rousseau mentioned two publications that were to be brought out soon (*Émile* and *Contract*) and wrote that both of them were very inferior compared to his earlier works.

Rousseau was offended right from the beginning because the reception of the two books was not as enthusiastic as that following his works published so far: "The publication of *Émile* was not greeted with the burst of applause which had followed that of my previous works." Further alarming hints came also from his friends. The duke and duchess of Luxembourg asked Rousseau to send all their letters containing any mention of *Émile* back to them.

After Rousseau's death these requests were explained away as attempts to hide letters that contained private matters which should not have got leaked, but this was hardly the main reason. Malesherbes obviously discussed *Émile* with his father, the chancellor Lamoignon de Malesherbes, and it is most likely that his father warned him that the book could cause troubles. *Contract* was to be barred from publication in France. All these signs and hints of approaching danger did not alarm Rousseau, who underestimated the political development in France of that time.

He reassured the publisher, Rey, not to be concerned about his safety. Néaulme in Amsterdam decided to publish *Émile* but he wanted to share the impending danger with Rey, who was to publish *Émile* in "duodecimo edition," whereas he himself reserved the right to publish the "octavo edition." Mme de Bouffleurs praised *Émile* but she asked Rousseau to return her letter to her after he had read it. D'Alembert did not sign his letter of approval. Duclos abstained from any written comment on the copy sent to him. Mathas, Rousseau's landlord, loaned the copy sent to him to the parlement councilor de Blaire, who let him know it was an extraordinarily beautiful book which would be talked about soon, more than the author would have wished.

But Rousseau (mistakenly) assumed that he personally was safe and intended to withdraw into seclusion "after all persons who were envious of me have been destroyed and the highest triumph has been attained." He was confident that Mme de Luxembourg had taken care of the publication of *Émile*; he had always demanded that *Émile* be printed in Holland, and apart from that Malesherbes was informed of the book as the main censor.

But the domestic political situation changed. The Jansenist parlements (courts of justice) that had supported and put across the expulsion of Jesuits did not want to create the impression that they condoned heresy of any kind. In this situation, the influence of the Luxembourgs was of no help. On the contrary, it was probable that when imprisoned, the chicken-hearted Rousseau could confess during questioning that Mme de Luxembourg had helped to publish *Émile*, which would thus compromise her. Rousseau himself admits he had always been against lying at the court, whatever the result might be.

Jansenism was a specifically French reform movement inside the Catholic Church, named after the Flemish theologian, Cornelius Jansen. The movement was related to Protestant thoughts. Orthodox Catholics acknowledged the authority of the pope, and their recognition of the Crown's right to participate in decision-making concerning the ecclesiastical matters of the Church (Gallicanism) was only lukewarm. They emphasized the hierarchical position of the bishops as well as the importance of "Christian works." Jansenists, on the other hand, stressed inward religiousness as a sign of the "grace of God," according to the model of early Christians. They accepted the influence of the state in all secular aspects of the Church. But they refused to obey the state when it interfered with the questions of faith. After the death of the "Roi Soleil" (Louis XIV), Jansenists became very influential politically in the parlements as judges and lawyers. As a matter of fact they forced the ban of Jesuits from the government and the king had to sign it.

It was about the spring of 1762 that Rousseau acquired the first of his famous "Armenian costumes" which were made for him by an Armenian tailor who had come to visit his relatives in Montmorency. The material for the costume was procured for him by La Roche, the valet of the duchess of Luxembourg. The duchess encouraged him to wear the caftan, which, according to Rousseau, had the advantage that he did not have to wear trousers and could therefore better manipulate the urinary catheters—otherwise he would have to stay in the bedroom and be forced to use the chamber pot. It is likely that the urine that was continually dripping from the catheter had to be drained into some sort of container, which he could empty later.

Émile appeared on May 24, only to be forbidden in Paris on May 31. This was followed by an order to confiscate all copies. Rousseau was not overly disturbed by it, and his main concern was to prevent the occurrence of private copies. On June 1, Malesherbes personally signed the paperwork ordering the syndic of all Parisian publishers, Charles Saillant, to act immediately and confiscate all copies of *Émile*. He nevertheless managed to inform Duchesne about this order so that the latter could move his copies to safety. Malesherbes rendered similar services also to Diderot when he officially banned his books, even going so far as to conceal Diderot's books in his own house.

In a letter to the publisher, Néaulme, Rousseau insisted he would not change anything he had written because "he had done what was his duty." He wrote that he heard the parlement of Paris wanted to persecute him, but added that he doubted that such an enlightened institution would lend itself to such foolishness. Malesherbes, who knew the parlement better, was aware of the mortal danger Rousseau was facing—the condemnation of *Émile* could be followed by the condemnation of its author. As he could not warn Rousseau directly without compromising himself, he sent an intermediary to him who brought Rousseau a coded message saying he should leave France as soon as possible.

Even "Julie," with whom he was still corresponding, was anxious about Rousseau's fate because there were rumors flying around Paris. Rousseau sent "Julie" a coquettish letter and invited her to visit him at Montmorency where she could meet the Luxembourgs ("Ah, you must consider my bad health, the gray beard, and not overwhelm me with your seductive charm"). Mme Alissan declined the invitation and asked Rousseau not to divulge her identity under any circumstances—for good reasons—which Rousseau promised to her.

Rousseau started to notice the impending dangers because he asked Moultou, in a letter dated June 7, 1762, not to be worried about the rumors circulating about him in Paris. According to Rousseau, the actions of the parlement of Paris against dissidents were attempts to justify the expulsion of Jesuits and mentioned that "the only man in France who believes in God should become the victim of these defenders of Christianity." He continued that others were advising him to leave but he thought the dangers described by them were exaggerated. He, Jean-Jacques, had not learned to hide. As a citizen of Geneva he could not be held accountable to the parlement of Paris for a book that was published in Holland with the permission of Dutch authorities. Defending himself in front of the parlement of Paris he would tell only the truth. This claim is strange because in the letters to his friends Rousseau wrote that *Émile* was published in Holland, which was only a half-truth; the first two volumes were published in France.

One of the persons warning him was Mme de Créqui who wrote him, full of terror, on May 8: "In the name of God—disappear! . . . A man always has to act according to the circumstances." Also Comtesse de Bouffleurs, who knew of the activities of Prince de Conti at court, tried to persuade Rousseau to leave France and take refuge in England. She wanted to introduce him to David Hume. She made it clear to him that his possible arrest would compromise Mme de Luxembourg. But Rousseau refused the prospect of a stay in England because he did not like England or Englishmen. He felt safe under the protection of Mme de Luxembourg. According to him, it was she who was responsible for the publication of *Émile* in France.

The rumor circulating in Paris had it that the Parisian parlement did not want to burn only the book but also its author. Coindet, who fell into disgrace with Rousseau, made himself heard again and offered to accompany Rousseau into exile. He knew that Rousseau had been invited by his friend Roguin to visit him, and he suggested that Rousseau accept the invitation now.

Rousseau became alarmed for the first time when he was asked by M. de Luxembourg whether he had written in *Émile* or *Contract* something inimical to the first minister de Choiseul. Rousseau replied that he wrote only commendatory things about the minister. The duke wrote Rousseau another letter suggesting that it would have been better if Rousseau had expressed himself more clearly in the book because De Choiseul interpreted the praise as a hidden offence. The minister's conviction was further strengthened by Voltaire.

According to Rousseau, Mme de Luxembourg herself was at that time undisturbed, happy, and always had a smile on her face, which set his mind at rest. Rousseau received a direct warning from Pierre Guy who had information that Rousseau's case was going to be discussed by the parlement of Paris during its session on June 9. But even this did not disturb Rousseau very much and he spent the day before this session on a trip with several of his friends (Frère Alammani and Frère Mandard) where they ate with healthy appetites and savored good wine, which they drank with drinking straws because they forgot to take glasses with them.

During the night of June 8-9 the turn of events became quite dramatic. Rousseau was awakened by Mme de Luxembourg's valet, La Roche, who brought a letter the duchess had received from Prince de Conti. The latter informed her that the authorities decided—in spite of his efforts—to take very strict action against Rousseau. The warrant for Rousseau's arrest would be issued at seven o'clock the next morning. The prince was able to achieve the promise that Rousseau would not be pursued.

Rousseau wrote in *Confessions* that he arrived at the château at night and saw that Mme de Luxembourg was more terrified by the prospect of what might happen to her when he was arrested, than being genuinely concerned about his fate. He realized he could not become a martyr for his views without compromising her at the same time, and decided to sacrifice his reputation so she could calm down. He was disappointed that the duchess did not realize that he, in saving himself, was in fact sacrificing himself for her (he is once more the "victim" of a woman). Rousseau had always excelled in being able to justify the decisions he took in ways that invariably shed a good light on him.

The duke had allegedly offered Rousseau the use of a hiding place in the château, which Rousseau refused. He decided instead to make use of the invitation he had received from Roguin and go to Yverdon. His first idea had been to go to Geneva but he dismissed this foolishness after a short deliberation. He decided to go to Switzerland where he could wait close to Geneva and see how the whole affair developed. La Roche brought him his clothes and papers from Montlouis. Rousseau and the duke sorted the documents and those Rousseau did not take with him the duke put under lock and key in a special room. Thérèse arrived as well, flung her arms around his neck with hue and cry and wanted to leave with him. But Rousseau promised her that he would come back to her as soon as possible. The duke lent him a cabriolet and horses for the first leg of the journey and the ladies said good-bye to him with tears in their eyes (though the embrace of the duchess was allegedly colder than those of two or three years ago). Rousseau described the departure as the bitterest moment of his life.

The session of parlement which took place on the morning of June 9 was under the chairmanship of the hostile Malupeou. The chief prosecutor and chief lawyer (the brothers Omer and Guillame Joly de Fleury) declared that *Émile* was a book that subverted religion, morality and decency, and was pernicious in general. The parlement agreed with this declaration and ordered the imprisonment of the author in Conciergerie and the burning of all copies of the book. Rousseau should have been imprisoned by ten o'clock in the morning but the police arrived as late as four o'clock in the afternoon. On the journey, between Montmorency and La Barre, Rousseau looked out from his cabriolet to see four men in black suits who saluted him when the vehicles passed.

Mme de Luxembourg informed him later in a letter that the police arrived about one hour after his departure and that he must have met them on his way. The burning of *Émile* was carried out on June 11 and caused outrage in many countries—Holland, for example. In Geneva itself not only *Émile* but also *Contract* was banned and a warrant for the arrest of the defamatory author was issued. That was why Rousseau avoided the Genevan territory on his flight, and got to Switzerland via Pontalier after he had crossed the Jura Mountains.

On his way to Yverdon, Rousseau decided to write a poem in prose about

Levit from Ephraim. The work did not appear until after Rousseau's death, but Rousseau liked it and declared that though it was not his best it was his dearest work. From Roguin's villa, located on the shores of Lake Neuchâtel, Rousseau sent a letter to Mme de Luxembourg, writing that he had reached the country of freedom and justice which he would never abandon. He was mistaken in that. Rousseau's life as a hermit ended and he entered a new path of his life—he had become a refugee. John Locke wrote around 1690 that no one who has violated the mores and opinions of his environment would escape the punishment of criticism and enmity.

Both books, the publication of which forced Rousseau to leave France, are world-famous but at the same time are irrelevant from today's perspective. This applies especially to *Émile*. The *Social Contract* is an obligatory book in the study of political philosophy. Even in our time it is a fertile field for interpretations of all sorts.

Both books are based on faulty premises and therefore reach incorrect conclusions. Their faulty premises originate in Rousseau's style of thinking and in his views which, of course, developed partly as a result of his abnormal upbringing, including a lack of appropriate social life. This premise will certainly incur the displeasure of many readers, who have learned from the textbooks that Rousseau was a great philosopher, but most have not read these books and it is therefore necessary to outline their contents. Both books reflect and at the same time illustrate and explain Rousseau's nature. The reaction to his books serves as a window into the society of the eighteenth century. From today's perspective the response to them is hardly comprehensible.

The symptoms and behavior of a patient enable us understand his illness. In other words, the book is a mirror reflecting its author.

Émile

Rousseau gave his essay the title *Émile, ou de l'éducation* (the original title of the book was *Ou de l'éducation*) which provided Rousseau with an entry into history as an education theorist. Surprisingly, however, he denied his book dealt with education and looked upon it as a philosophical tract. Also, he did not dedicate it to parents but to *"les sages,"* unlike *Julie*, which was dedicated to "the corrupted." The role of parents in *Émile* has been reduced to the child's conception. The educator in charge of the boy (Rousseau did not write about education of girls) starts his work quite early and continues up to the boy's adulthood when the latter is allowed to meet the opposite sex. Once the author has reached this point, the character of the book changes abruptly and the philosophical tract becomes a philosophical novel.

The underlying thesis of the work is expressed in the introductory sentence of Book One, which reads: "All things that spring from the hands of God are good: all things become corrupt in human hands. When the people we see around are corrupt, it is society which is to blame for their corruption." As children are born innocent Rousseau recommends keeping them away from society and its pernicious influence as long as possible and to "follow nature." This is what is called "negative education." It is only after good educational results have been achieved that the child can be exposed to the bad culture.

Rousseau thus recommended what he had experienced in his own childhood: an education in isolation, without the influence of society. He was probably still convinced he had preserved his own innocence and goodness, in addition to his exceptionality, only because he had been brought up in this way. An education without societal influences, without contacts with other children and strangers, has only one result—the development of a personality which is unprepared for life in society and must fail in real life. Because he himself did not attend school, he recommended that the "education of a man" take place only as a private education at home. He also mentioned the "education of a citizen" who, however, could be educated only in a republican setting. It is interesting that he did not here recommend the Genevan system of school education, which he mentioned with praise elsewhere.

The second underlying premise expressed in *Émile* is faulty as well. Rousseau assumed man was born without any innate characteristics and that his nature and abilities were determined only by his sensory perception after birth. It is essentially the view expressed by Locke in his *Essay Concerning Human Understanding*, which Rousseau knew either from the French translation by Pierre Coste or from his discussions with Locke's French disciple Condillac, whom he met in Lyon. Rousseau must also have known Locke's essay *Thoughts on Education*. Rousseau taught accordingly that a child must be educated by example and not by words.

This second thesis, too, is regarded as incorrect from the perspective of modern science. The child is born with a wide-ranging spectrum of genetically determined characteristics that are later supplemented by those that develop during the child's intrauterine life (for example the influence of hormones on the development of the brain).

Rousseau observed quite correctly that the child passes through certain developmental stages that are analogous to the development of the human race, which Rousseau described in his *Second Discourse* (Upon the Origin of Inequality). The first state the child must pass through is the "natural state," *amour de soi*, in which it is naïve, similar to uncivilized man. It does not know the concept of social ethics; it is egocentric and can only have a nature that has not yet been transformed to *amour propre*. The child differs from a savage, however, by its dependence on others, especially on its mother. A child must always show respect for its mother, and a child that refuses to do so must be "strangled as soon as possible as a monster." Accordingly, Rousseau called upon all mothers to breast-feed their children, which was rather exceptional at that time. Children of rich people were fed by a wet-nurse and infant mortality was very high: 50 percent of the children died before the age of three.

Rousseau also did not recommend the tight swaddling of infants which was usual at that time. These advanced views had a significant effect in Rousseau's time, the *ancien régime*, and breast-feeding suddenly became popular. Parents should love their child but should not spoil it, and should not become the slaves of the child because egoistic tendencies emerge at an early age, though they are not innate. Many of the children's "wrongs" are not wrongs at all. The destructiveness of children is just a sign of superfluous energy.

Children should be brought up in a Spartan way (again his old passion for Sparta). They should not be fed regularly, must learn to endure cold, and be able to walk barefoot, even in winter, and tolerate thirst and fatigue. They must not, however, be punished physically because in this way someone else's will is imposed upon them, which reduces their chances to acquire a proper sense of freedom. If the child harms itself while playing that is good because the child learns from experience in this way.

Book Two of *Émile* deals with the child between five and twelve years of age. At this age the child is given into the care of the educator for further upbringing. In this book, Rousseau stopped talking of children in general. He created the character of a pupil, Émile, a rich orphan. Needless to say, Émile lives at a château surrounded by numerous servants. His ideal, superhuman educator, with whom Rousseau identified (but let us remember Rousseau's own failures as educator!), demands that Émile obey only him, which is his principal condition of education.

The educator completely dominates Émile but he must respect the pupil's freedom because: "The happiness of children, similar to all people, consists in exercising their freedom." Obviously, we are soon faced with this paradox: how can a child feel free when it is constrained by the imperative of absolute obedience? Rousseau proposed his own solution to this contradiction: to make Émile *believe* he is free in his decisions even though he is in fact being guided by his educator. Dissimulation and tricks are thus incorporated into the system of education, which was criticized by many of Rousseau's contemporaries.

Rousseau rejected Locke's recommendation that the educator discuss matters with his pupil. In the "natural state," designated by Rousseau in the first manuscript as a period extending from birth to the age of twelve, the child is allegedly unable to use its reason. This view would be unacceptable today. Émile learns science by observing natural phenomena and carrying out simple experiments.

The really negative part of education (rather a pernicious one) is what Rousseau himself called "negative education": Émile must spend most of his time in solitude and should not see other children or the servants. It is curious that Rousseau did not recommend that the child read books, with the exception of one book, his favorite, *Robinson Crusoe*, which allegedly teaches the pupil how to live without dependence on other people! Here again, Rousseau's defective education in his own childhood becomes apparent. It is not lack of intelligence that precludes Rousseau from realizing the basic fact that man is a social being and that it is only in society that his nature can fully develop.

Émile should carry out physical exercises in open nature and develop a strong body nourished by proper diet. It is best to reject the physicians as well as vaccinations because the best medicine is "purity." It is necessary to endure occasional illnesses as part of the natural education in suffering. Life in cities should be condemned because the more the people live together the more corrupted they are. Study of history, geography and Latin should be postponed. It was incomprehensible in his time, and for some of his readers even terrifying, that Émile should not be instructed in religion till the age of twelve.

Rousseau's recommendations as to the education by example are sometimes more cruel than the physical punishments that he condemns. For example: the sense of property that should be developed prior to the sense of freedom should be elucidated to the pupil by means of the following example: the teacher encourages his pupil to plant a line of beans; then they jointly water them and enjoy the sight of their growth, in which Rousseau agreed with Locke, who regarded the property right as given by the work invested in the property. The gardener is then clandestinely ordered to pull out the beans because the land belongs to him and he wanted to plant melons there. This should teach Émile that he is not allowed to use the property of the legitimate owner without his permission.

In spite of all this, we read that the educator says to Émile: "The man must be happy, dear Émile. This is the ultimate endeavor of all sentient creatures."

The next period of development begins at the age of twelve, when the child becomes capable of comparing things and thinking of them. It learns to appreciate the value of usefulness and useful activity even though it does not yet have any idea of social relationships or the moral options that always accompany social relationships. The ideal is again Robinson Crusoe who could always manage himself. The necessity of human cooperation remained unknown to Rousseau, or was highly objectionable. Émile should, of course, learn some occupation (rejected occupations are actor, artist, writer and musician). The most suitable is trade, probably because it enables man to work alone (Rousseau always stressed that he was born in the family of an artisan), and so Rousseau chose the trade of a carpenter.

At the age of fifteen Émile is "reborn." He becomes a man. So far, he was concerned only with himself, but now he has to learn that other people are important for him as well. Social relationships will determine his whole life and that is why he must study them. His egoistic *amour de soi* must be transformed into *amour propre*. But it is good to slow down the transformation of the boy to man.

As far as sexual education is concerned one should not lie and explanations should be provided in simple way and without smiles. The pupil's inquisitiveness should not be encouraged. Rousseau agreed with the explanation of a mother who replied to her son's question about how children come to the world: "they are peed by mothers in pains and often cost them their lives." (*Les femmes les pissent avec des douleurs qui les coûtent quelquefois leur vie.*) Here Rousseau probably thought of his own mother and his personal problems when urinating.

It is necessary for the pupil to get to know the value of friendship before getting to know the value of love. Rousseau linked the human longing for friendship with human weakness: "It is our common suffering that makes the human heart lean to humanity." Sympathy, as the first social emotion in the human evolution from savage to civilization, emerges in adolescence. Émile should be sensitive to the suffering of others, but if he sees too much human misery his heart might harden.

It is only at the age of eighteen that Émile can receive instruction in "moral sciences." He can study history, which is a dangerous science because it portrays the bad things in man and not the good in him. Only cunning men can attain glory. A good man will be forgotten, or becomes ridiculous. History, similar to philosophy, vilifies the human race. Historians describe history but insert in it their own prejudices. It is better to study more of the older history than the modern one. The best way to teach history is to read biographies, possibly those written by Plutarch (also a favorite book of Rousseau's). It is only at this age that the pupil can understand fables and their hidden messages.

Rousseau offered an extraordinary justification for his educational methods: the customary education, where the pupil must learn "speculative disciplines" at an age when he is in the prime of his activity, results in the pupil entering the world unprepared and without any practical knowledge of it. "He is being trained for life in society as if he were to spend his life in a monastery," wrote Rousseau. In contrast, Rousseau affirmed that his method teaches Émile how to become integrated into the world, how to live a successful life, how to earn his living and how to get along with people. But his method actually recommended that children be raised in isolation, or semi-isolation. Every child, from an early age, needs to learn the principles of human coexistence, both in its family and in daily contacts with other children. Isolation invariably results in a more or less obvious deformation of character.

It is only as an adult that Émile can study nature and society and be initiated into the secrets of religion. Instruction in religion at early age would result in the child forming an incorrect conception of the nature of God and it is therefore better to have no idea at all than to develop a distorted one. Here, in Book Four, Rousseau inserted *"La Profession de foi du vicaire savoyard "* (the biggest stumbling block of the whole book for society of that time), a message conveyed by a Catholic theologian, and not commented on by the educator. It is left up to Émile to chose his religion, or a religious sect—it is one of the few possibilities where he can make his own decision.

When the young man reaches the age of twenty, "the age of love" or "the age of reason" begins, as Rousseau designated it in the first version of the book. But Émile must not get lost to it immediately and unprepared, though Rousseau allowed him to have a mate. He must calm down by performing intensive exercises and the recommended form of sport is hunting, not carried out for the pleasure derived from killing but because hunting diverts attention from dangerous tendencies, by which Rousseau meant sex. The choice of a partner is not entrusted to Émile alone. The mate for the youth is chosen by the educator according to his own consideration; the educator uses various artifices again to make his pupil believe that the choice was his own.

Before he gets to know his love (or better, before he is introduced to her) he should spend one year in Paris where he will live as a refined city-dweller but preserving his simplicity and modesty. He will meet literary authors, will read their books, visit the salons, and will even visit the theatre, "not to study morality but to refine his taste." But he will certainly not find his ideal woman in Paris. This woman lives in the country; she was born into a family of a provincial nobility. The educator will describe for his pupil an ideal picture of her and will even tell him her name—she will be called Sophie, a suitable and fortunate name. It was not until *Confessions* was published that the readers discovered why Sophie was a suitable name for an ideal woman.

What should Sophie be like? She should have a responsive heart and a lively imagination. She is by no means ravishingly beautiful but is nevertheless attractive and charming, which she does not show off. She dresses smartly yet in a simple way. She can handle all the works of a good housewife and is anxiously clean. She is well read and intelligent, her religion is a simple one and her chief passion (like Julie) is the love of virtue. Unlike Julie, however, she can freely choose her husband. But she does not find him in society.

The encounter of both candidates of marriage is "the work of coincidence" and here the book becomes a novel: On a trip together, the educator and Émile get lost and are offered hospitality. When they have supper the daughter of the house owner is introduced to them. Her name is Sophie. Hearing this name, Émile recognizes that he has found his dreamed-up idol.

In *Émile* we also find most of Rousseau's opinions about both sexes, their mutual relationships, and about family. According to Rousseau, who expressed his views already in the discourse, family was not something provided by nature, as assumed by Locke, or the philosophers of the Enlightenment. In the primordial state of savagery, women were just as independent as men, they lived and reared their progeny in isolation. According to Rousseau, there were countless women in the forests (in the natural state) and so men had no difficulties in selecting a woman. This is the reason for the weaker sexual tendencies observed in men. (This is probably an expression of Rousseau's masochism—Rousseau did not indulge in male sex.) This idea must have appeared absurd even to the readers of that time.

It was only when people moved to caves and huts and started to live together (Rousseau did not explain why this developmental change occurred), that marital and parental love developed, which Rousseau considered a fortunate evolution even though it meant the end of sexual freedom. It was "the golden age" corrupted only by later evolution. Sexual instincts were weak in this primordial state. It took some time before further evolution caused sex to play a dominant role so that romantic love could emerge, which gave rise to enormous pleasure but also to jealousy. Sex that played just a secondary role in the natural state started to fulfill, since the development of civilization, the function of an interpersonal bond binding people together but also dividing them in bitter rivalry.

Women support love because it is their instrument to achieve their purposes. Since women got weaker as a result of their role in the family (they were strong in the natural state), and became dependent on men, they must use certain tricks and artifices to bind the men to them. Every woman must obtain a man who would love and protect her. Women must make the man (men) dependent on her so they must employ various strategies, maneuvers and manipulations to achieve this goal because they lack manly power. Sexual relationships have thus been "political" since the very beginning, i.e. they rest on power relationships.

This is certainly a correct observation, and no less correct is Rousseau's finding that, to understand the relationships of both sexes, it is necessary to stress the differences between them, and not to claim that they were actually nonexistent as did Mme Dupin, a feminist of the eighteenth century. Similar arguments are used by less-educated feminists even today.

Rousseau acknowledged the existence of sexual differences and does not regret this fact. But he regretted that women had emerged as a crucial and powerful factor in society and he explained how this unfortunate state of affairs came about: since the sexual lust of men is inferior to that of women (this view is probably the expression of Rousseau's personal experience because he himself had never excelled in matters of sexual appetite and was, in addition to that, often confronted with women whose sexual appetite was strong), the woman must stimulate it, which she accomplishes by hiding her sexual charms or pretending that they can be obtained only with difficulty. She surrounds herself with various mysteries that should attract men.

This strategy benefits both sides. Women become more humble, which inhibits their "predatory" sexual tendencies, and men are protected against being "driven to death" by the women's sexual whims. *Men become more civilized and try to gratify women and women in turn try to gratify men.* This sentence, again, expresses Rousseau's personal experience.

As a masochist, Rousseau knew how intensive a gratification a woman can produce in man when she employs practices other than direct sex (see the thesis about urethral masturbation carried out by Thérèse on Rousseau). We also know, from certain allusions made by Thérèse, that Rousseau was able to make a woman experience orgasm by manual stimulation, which he probably practiced not only with Thérèse but also with Sophie d'Houdetot; he declared that he had never had sexual intercourse with her (in this he was similar to President Clinton who tried to justify his sexual affairs by claiming that oral sex was not sexual intercourse and therefore not infidelity).

"The law of nature makes man dependent on the wishes of a woman, which he seeks to satisfy, so that she makes him believe that he is stronger," wrote Rousseau. The woman was not modest in the primordial society. According to Rousseau, the women in civilized society use artificial decency to transform man's weak sexual desire into strong love. Decency and modesty are by no means natural traits of women. These traits are only used by women, together with bashfulness, as weapons to "arm the weak to enslave the strong." It is difficult, for the same reason, for a woman to stay pure, and even religion cannot be of much help for her. When seeing that "the whole world lies at her feet, a woman triumphs over all and over herself." The motive for this behavior is a woman's desire to dominate man and the whole world. He regretted by his Genevan republican disposition (in the foreword to the *Second Discourse*, Rousseau eloquently praises the women of Geneva) that the values of ancient Sparta and Rome had disappeared and that the kingdom of France had created a sexual uniformity where men were as effeminate as women. Men had become the slaves of women in society and the slaves of a despot in the state.

Rousseau regarded politics as an activity for which women are unsuitable because politicians have always to deal with war and women are much too valuable as mothers and educators to wage wars and use weapons. The political skills of a woman are more sophisticated and indirect; she uses personal contacts. The politics in public requires an impersonal, rational approach based on legislation, which is a task to be carried out by men. Rousseau represented two completely different and mutually exclusive attitudes to the "reign" of sexes. According to one thesis, the woman should rule in the family but man should rule the state; according to another thesis, the woman must obey in both the family and state.

Similar contradictory views are typical of Rousseau, and many of Rousseau's quotations must be taken with a pinch of salt because it is not uncommon that one can find two quotations with opposite meanings.

But still, women are very important for men. Mothers determine the decisive stage of a man's education and therefore have a decisive influence on the characteristics, passions, and taste of the future man; they decide about his future pleasures and determine whether he will attain happiness.

Rousseau spent most of his life in the society of women and he was what can be called a "feminized" type, dependent on women. According to him, the whole education of women should concentrate on man: she must be taught how to make him happy, how to please, love and respect him, how to advise and console him. These are a woman's tasks for all time and she must be instructed in them from an early age.

Rousseau observed that little girls took an interest in clothes and played with dolls, and that these activities could not be observed in boys. He thus recommended that these interests of little girls be encouraged—also they must be able to sew. They should also be good at arithmetic because they will be responsible for housekeeping later. Cunning and deviousness are natural attributes of women's character, and because everything springing from nature is good, this inborn cunning of little girls must also be refined and educated. As women are more gifted for the arts than men, they should be instructed in dance, music and singing.

At the same time, however, one must never forget about the moral characteristics belonging to their sex: modesty, docility and delicacy. They must always feel they are being overseen; here Rousseau makes a distinction with respect to Émile's education: Émile must not realize, under any circumstances, that his free will in decisions is being limited.

Each girl should have the same religion as her mother (Julie's children are Catholic though her husband—Wolmar—is an atheist). Every woman should have the religion of her husband. As opposed to boys, the instruction of girls in religion must start very early because they can never understand the essence of religion and religion teaches them to obey.

It is just as impossible that women would understand philosophy or seek abstract truths and universal rules. A woman, via observation, understands much better the hearts of members of her family. Women can discover "experimental ethics" that are reduced to a system by men. "Women observe, men reason." It is not necessary to accompany every opinion expressed by Rousseau with a commentary regarding its correctness or incorrectness from our point of view today, but it is worthwhile to make an exception here. Rousseau saw correctly that women are specialists of interpersonal relationships and concrete things whereas men tend to make generalizations.

Let us return to Émile and Sophie. They fell happily in love—Émile instructed her in music and dance (as did Rousseau with his numerous pupils). On their walks in the country he introduces her to the basics of natural science and awakens her love for neighbors, especially when these are in need. He also continues to pursue his artisan profession and Sophie is moved when she observes that a lettered man is able to work with his hands.

But Émile's teacher has another surprise for his pupil. He forbids marriage for the time being because Émile is still inexperienced at the age of twenty-two. He surprises Émile by asking him what he would do if he learned that Sophie had died. Émile is scared to death and pops his eyes out at his tutor but is assured that Sophie is hale and healthy. He allows Émile to marry her only after he spends two years traveling across Europe where he has to depend upon his own resources because his educator does not accompany him.

It is only after all of this that Émile and Sophie get the educator's blessing, but also a warning to guard themselves against romantic love which can become too cold; instead they should let the sweet habit of friendship replace their passion. With this recommendation, the tutor leaves the scene and hands over the care of Émile to Sophie despite Émile's entreaties to stay because they both still have so much to learn from him and will certainly need his advice till the end of their lives. Here *Émile* ends, but this end is not a definite one.

Similar to *Julie,* where Rousseau wrote a still-unpublished addendum to the novel describing the adventures of an English lord in Italy (the manuscript was given only to the duchess of Luxembourg), Rousseau added, after some time, a fictional installment to *Émile* (similar to *Julie* in letter form), with the title *Les Solitaires*, which reveals the subsequent fates of Émile and Sophie. This installment is Rousseau's most controversial work. It shows that Émile, who has been brought up according to his propositions, and the carefully chosen Sophie *fail* in the test of life and do not attain the happiness for which they have long prepared. The reader may judge this for himself:

Émile takes Sophie to a capital city (probably Paris), where both succumb to this highly corrupted environment. Émile pursues trade and enjoys the pleasures of the city, and neglects Sophie and their two small children. Sophie comes under the bad influence of ladies of society who teach her that, in polite society, husband and wife must treat each other with friendliness and social correctness but they can afford sexual pleasures with other partners. Their small daughter dies and Émile tries to regain the affection of his wife. She informs him, however, that she is pregnant with another man's child. Émile despairs, deserts his family and job, and lives in the country as a carpenter. Sophie finds out where he is living but leaves again for fear that he would keep their son. Émile cannot acquiesce in the thought that he should accept a strange child as his own and therefore moves further away from Sophie. When he sails on a ship in Mediterranean Sea he is captured by pirates and is sold into slavery in Algeria. He survives thanks to his education. He is tough and stoical. He feels free even when he is shackled (here again Rousseau's masochistic tendencies come to the fore): "He who knows what is determined by necessity is the most free because he is never forced to do what he does not want to." His abilities help him to become the personal slave of a bey.

The novel remains unfinished though Rousseau wanted, according to his friends, to make the novel end happily. But this does not change the fact that Rousseau conceded that even the best education is of no avail and that Émile excels only in the role of a slave. It is possible that the added installment also expressed Rousseau's personal pessimistic view. Even the best education is not enough to make people immune against the pernicious influence of civilization. Perhaps this influence was expressed symbolically by the chains fettering

Émile. The only way to escape the chains is self-deceit, when he can succeed in convincing himself that he is free. Rousseau's next work, *Du Social Contract*, also opens with the same image: "Man is born free but he is everywhere in chains." More about this work later.

A person's religion is a mirror of his or her psychology. Everybody creates a religion that is more or less personal and this religion cleaves, sometimes tightly, sometimes relatively loosely, to some of the individual churches. People who are well integrated into human society usually have religious views that are in agreement with common social conceptions, i.e. the most prevalent churches. The greater the individualism of a society the more variegated the range of available churches responding to society's needs. The offer of an individualist society will be broader, and narrower in collectivist societies (see the number of religious denominations in the United States compared to Germany).

Individuals who failed in their attempts to integrate into social life, or who were prevented from succeeding in this process as a result of deprivation or semi-deprivation, have no other choice than to create their own individual religious/ideological ideas that are best suited to their psychology. At present it is not very difficult as long as these non-integrated or only partially integrated individuals respect the rules set by society, i.e. to the extent to which they respect laws and morality.

Rousseau, as a poorly integrated individual who rejected society as a source of corruption, developed religious ideas that were quite dissimilar to those of society and suited his subjective psychology. These ideas became fateful for him because he lived in the eighteenth century, in an era of lingering religious fanaticism that became even stronger in France around the middle of this century. His *Émile* was dismissed and he himself was persecuted, not for his educational views, but for his religious views that were revealed in Book Four of *Émile* by a Catholic chaplain and entered history under the title, "*La Profession de foi du vicaire savoyard*." Rousseau called this priest M. Mallarede and put in the priest's mouth *his* religious views, which must have been obvious to his readers.

The model for the priest was partly abbé Gaime. Rousseau met him during his stay in Turin, when he converted to Catholicism at the age of sixteen; the abbé was employed as a tutor in the Mallarede family in Turin. "The Profession of Faith" was used as part of the belated religious education of

Émile but God did not play any role in the subsequent life of the hero. Émile finds comfort in stoical philosophy in his misfortunes, rather than the faith of the Savoyard vicar. As we are interested in Rousseau's psychological profile, and as this passage of the book had a great impact on Rousseau's subsequent life, it will be described in more detail.

Rousseau believed in God and his Savoyard vicar, right from the start, argues against the atheistic metaphysics of Holbach. The universe cannot move by itself. The movement must be caused by some external power. Without *cause motrice* the universe would be unmoved. The external power can be also the Creator's will. "I believe because the world is steered by a powerful and mighty will. I see it, or rather I feel it." The entity that governs the world and moves it is called God. The highest being is also gracious, despite the natural catastrophes that it can visit upon the world (the earthquake in Lisbon in 1755) and man has to believe in this graciousness. Rousseau said to Voltaire: "I have suffered too much to be able to live without faith." What cannot be grasped cannot be denied. It is not possible to imagine that a being endowed with reason could die and that is why its immortality must be assumed.

Whoever seeks to live a virtuous life becomes the instrument of God. Conscience is God's voice in each individual and whoever obeys Him can rest assured that he walks along the right path. Reason itself is not condemned because it is a godsend. It helps to uncover the divine will and to recognize man's duties. Reason is not tied up with any ecclesiastical authority; it is not tied up with priests, prophets, and not even with the Bible. Rousseau revealed, through the mouth of his vicar, that he did not pray. He (the vicar) immerses all his powers into the Supreme Being; he is stunned by it. He thanks God for His offerings but he does not pray to Him. What should he tell him? Should he pray that He change the course of nature and let miracles happen? God gave him everything and determines everything—why, then, should one ask for anything?

In Rousseau's conception, Jesus is compared with Socrates. Both were wise men. But the Savoyard priest does not refer to Jesus as Savior. Rousseau did not believe in original sin and therefore did not see why anything should be redeemed or expiated. On another occasion, Rousseau referred to Jesus as the wisest and most loved of all mortals, as a teacher of love. We also know that Rousseau regarded himself as God's prophet; he identified with various prophets and felt himself to be the Son of God. He adopted an attitude of skeptical respect toward the doctrine of Divine Revelation that was regarded as very important by most churches of that time—but this attitude was more suggestive of a rejection than of respect.

The dogmas of the Church are superfluous. They defile divinity, result in absurd contradictions and make people intolerant and cruel. Miracles are also reprehensible. God does not need to point to his essence by violating laws that He had created. The Savoyard vicar respects the Bible but admits that it is filled with unbelievable and impossible things that are incomprehensible and unacceptable for a sensitive man. The Bible is just a book written by humans. The Savoyard vicar rejects the priesthood as well. He says that the priests are as corrupted as other people. For someone to believe in God, no intermediary is necessary: "There are too many people between me and God!" he complains.

The only thing that remains, according to the vicar, Rousseau's mouthpiece, is "nature religion." This is his real, subjective view of religion and he explains and defends it with his typical eloquence: "What am I to be blamed for when I minister to God according to the enlightenment that He gave my reason and feeling, that inspired my heart? . . . Show me what you can add to enhance God's glory, the well being of society and my own advantage, to the duties that have already been prescribed by the law of nature . . . The loftiest divine thoughts come from reason alone. Observe the theatre of nature. Listen to your inner voice. Did not God already reveal the message about everything to our eyes, our consciousness, or our decisions? What else can people say to us?" What Rousseau called nature religion is connected with nature indeed. He saw the divine in the grandeur of the mountains—replacing cathedrals for him—in forests and the whole of nature. In his loneliness Rousseau created a divine family: nature was his mother reigned over by God, his father, and he was their son and prophet in one person. Therefore, he did not need any church. Nature spoke to him directly. He declared that nature religion was the real, true religion, true Christianity. He himself was its prophet enjoying a privileged position. He was convinced of his exclusivity.

His religious ideas did not imply that state churches are unnecessary. They were necessary in spite of their teachings because they helped to maintain social order. This lead Rousseau to emphasize that people should belong to an established church. No one has the right to form his own cult. He still respected the principle: *cuius regio eius religio.*

For Rousseau the political needs of the state ranked higher than a person's denomination. The Christianity of the Bible was for him the true religion but this religion did not make people into good republican citizens. Like Machiavelli, Rousseau preferred the religion of the state and damned the religion of the Bible. He explicitly warned against "pious believers" (dogmatists). There is nothing more dangerous than their company. They must either rule or destroy themselves. In the same way Rousseau warned against philosophers who are "furious missionaries of atheism and arrogant dogmatists tolerating only with rage that someone does things differently."

Rousseau appears here as the harbinger of tolerance, with thoughts such as those which had emerged in the seventeenth century. Different people proclaimed tolerance for different reasons. Locke required tolerance only for various Protestant movements. According to him, tolerance could not be applied to Catholics and atheists. Lord Ashton required tolerance because it benefited trade.

Rousseau required tolerance primarily for his personal, egoistic reasons. He was aware of the fact that his political as well as religious views and his literary works differed from the prevalent views of the society of his time. The fear of persecution made him require tolerance—mainly and exclusively for his own person. Other, less important people did not need tolerance: the French Protestants had disobeyed the laws by holding conjoint services and must therefore be punished.

The impact of "The Profession of Faith" on French Catholicism, but also on Genevan Protestantism can be hardly imagined today. Even though Rousseau wrote that the Church was necessary for the state, his personal confession was a heresy that was bound to have repercussions. Rousseau recalled that he read from *Proffesion de foi* to Charles Duclos who came to visit him at the time when *Émile* was in print. When he finished reading, Duclos asked him whether this book was going to be printed in Paris, and when Rousseau said that it was Duclos said, "I agree, but do not tell anybody that you have read it to me, please." *Émile* was a book that made a runaway of Rousseau. The second book, which also contributed to this fate, was *On Social Contract*.

On Social Contract

The unabridged title of the book reads: *Du Contract social: Ou principes du droit politique. Par J.J. Rousseau, citoyen de Genève.* Rousseau's name has always been associated with the idea of a social contract in which people undertake to coexist in society. Rousseau did not consider society to be something that existed naturally and did not believe that society can ever achieve peaceful coexistence. He did not regard people to be social beings and described them as having an innate tendency to "radical individualism." This underlying conception no doubt reflected his own individualism, which foiled all his attempts to arrive at an objective appreciation of social reality. Unlike Hobbes, Rousseau maintained that the original state of humans was a peaceful one and that it was only after man had become part of a society that a government had to be formed to deal with conflicts that emerged as a result of property holdings and divisions of labor.

The idyllic primitive society, which he called the "golden middle" between the laziness of the original state and the touchy activity of modern pride, had been replaced by "the most horrible state of war." People were being "denatured" by society. Society changed their healthy, instinctive, self-defensive self-love that was derived directly from nature—*amour de soi même* into a desire to surpass others and attain recognition by them, *amour-propre*. Everybody became a slave to others' opinions. In the natural state also the passions of people were weaker, including sexual instincts (in fact the exact opposite is true—the development of civilization is accompanied by the development of emotional management—see N. Elias: *On the Process of Civilization*).

Rousseau's *Contract* deals with a contract between people, disclosing *how it should function* to guarantee them peaceful coexistence while retaining a free will for everyone. The new freedom for everyone would bring people also a new form of equality. It was an idea of a new beginning. Rousseau did not realize that liberty and equality do not go together very well as long as liberty is not defined as a recognized necessity and therefore as a kind of prison.

The first sentence of the book starts with a sensational sentence any present-day advertising agency would be proud of: "Man is born free but everywhere he lies in chains." This gloomy diagnosis is followed by an assurance to the readers that things could change if only humanity followed his recipe. People would get a new and better kind of liberty, republican liberty. To obey self-prescribed law is liberty.

This brings us to a complicated concept of liberty, in which Hobbes and Rousseau differ. Hobbes understood the concept of freedom as defined by the absence of any ban. Everything is allowed provided laws do not prohibit it, which, at present, is best exemplified by the American law. Rousseau disagreed with the underlying view, i.e. that law and liberty are split into two separate and mutually exclusive concepts. Where people themselves are the creator of laws there is no such contradiction of law and liberty. In Hobbes's system the laws are set by a sovereign, in Rousseau's system the people alone are sovereign (we shall see that this is not the case).

Cranston pointed out that Rousseau's concept of freedom was susceptible to many difficulties. To start with, man as a separate individual has will and his own concept of freedom. A group of people, however, consists of individuals who can have different opinions, and also their will, i.e. their concept of freedom, can differ. If, for example, 60 percent of the members of a society decide in favor of a certain solution and the remaining 40 percent are of a different opinion, it is very difficult to declare that 40 percent of the group have free will. Rousseau solved this problem by the means of an old simile; namely, that people unite and create an "artificial person" (the most famous example being Hobbes's Leviathan). This artificial person has one collective will, called by Rousseau *volonté générale*. In this aspect of his argument, Rousseau resembles Hobbes. In creating the social contract, individual members "misappropriate" their personal rights in favor of society. Rousseau saw this process as a form of exchange. Human "natural" rights are exchanged for "civil rights." Once all rights have been expropriated, a complete restitution of rights has been attained but on a different, higher level. The rights renounced by the people were based on power. The rights they obtained rested on laws.

Rousseau's views could be regarded as a kind of democratic thinking. Democracy, though, is a word Rousseau himself used very seldom and only in a special context. That is to say Rousseau distinguished very strictly between legislation on the one hand, which must stay in the citizens' hands and underlies their sovereignty; on the other hand, and opposed to it, stands the executive—interpretation and implementation of laws in the hands of magistrates, or ministers. Rousseau sometimes referred to the leading representative of the executive power as "prince," having in mind, however, rather the Roman republican "princeps" and not a member of monarchy, in Locke's or Montesquieu's sense.

Rousseau admitted that his political views are borrowed from Locke, but his way of thinking was actually quite the reverse of Locke: people renounce their natural rights so they can create a social contract, whereas according to Locke, people accept the contract so they can preserve their rights. According to Locke, people brought their natural rights with them to the new society and the ruler should be endowed with sufficient power to preserve and defend their rights. In Rousseau, natural rights are replaced by civil rights, people remain sovereign and the contract gives rise to the state. This, however, results in an aporia admitting various interpretations. The formation of a state is based on a contract but this legal act itself presupposes the existence of a legal condition.

Locke advocated a representative government. Rousseau categorically condemned the principle of representation: "The English deem themselves to be free. This is a big mistake. They are free only when they elect the members of their parliament. As soon as the election is over the citizens are enslaved." Legislation must be determined at meetings where everyone is present and can also vote. The participation at these meetings was of course limited—only adult men could take part, as was the case in certain Swiss cantons until quite recently. Rousseau did not recommend the pure form of democracy because: "If there were a nation of gods, it would govern itself democratically. A government so perfect is not suited to men." Rousseau wanted the democracy only to legislate but he rejected a democratically-elected government; in view of this it is best to refer to him as republican. In his passion for a republican form of government (which is by no means his invention) Rousseau leans on the republicanism of ancient Greece, especially Sparta, Rome and his native Geneva.

Rousseau had no democratic leanings because he did not put any trust in the wisdom of the general public. Though the people have complete sovereignty (they can create and revoke laws which extend to the social contract itself) they are unable to formulate their own fundamental law—*loi fondamentale*. This required the character of a "lawgiver," endowed with nearly divine powers, who reveals to them the laws that are necessary. Here Rousseau had in mind historic lawgivers such as Solon, Moses and Lycurgus. An analogous character in *Émile* is the "educator" with whom Rousseau identified, and when reading *Contract* one just cannot stop thinking that it is Rousseau himself who would play the role of the divine lawgiver. In any case, the sovereign, i.e. the people themselves, are unable to formulate the fundamental law. Theoretically, then, it is open to every dictator to refer to Rousseau and claim that he himself is the lawgiver and then pass any laws he needs.

It must be said here that the lawgiver makes his appearance at the beginning of a new social order and then disappears. The people become unified "humanity" and govern themselves. The government should be an aristocratic one, in the original sense of the word, i.e. a government of the best, which represents "the best form of government." Traditional hereditary aristocracy is reprehensible because it represents "the worst form of government." Rousseau emphasized also the necessity of the existence of an authority that must be distinguished from mere power and he regarded authority as something compatible with the concept of liberty. A man can thus be *forced to freedom* when he transgresses the spirit of the laws, or *volonté générale*. In punishing the transgressor the society rectifies him and helps him to overcome his own passions. At the same time the society guards against those who want to transgress the laws.

Rousseau adduced the example of the inscription *Libertas* on the gate of the jail in Genoa. Rousseau assured the reader that "the use of this motto is excellent and correct." The real law described in *Contract* is something entirely different compared to the laws that are in force, which only help the strong to oppress the weak. Real laws arise through decisions made by the majority and are absolutely obligatory. The liberty under the laws that are in force is only a seeming one and the laws help to hide the interests of the wealthy, who benefit from this "liberty," but are deleterious to the poor—the best solution would be when each one has something and no one has too much. One could perhaps agree with the first half of the requirement but not with the second: the role of the state should be to forestall poverty but it must not prevent anyone from being able to become rich.

Everyone who accepts the social contract agrees that he will respect the decisions made by the majority. Not even the private conscience, the voice of soul as it is called in "The Profession of Faith," has meaning where it is necessary to respect the common will. Rousseau's state obtains virtually immense powers and the opportunity to enforce them, which is dangerous to the freedom of an individual. This makes it obvious why Rousseau was so popular with all dictators and why many researches regard Rousseau as a theorist of totalitarianism (see for example J. L. Talmon: *The Rise of Totalitarian Democracy*). Aporias and inaccuracies of his argumentation also allow interpretations which are quite opposed to totalitarianism: some researchers regard Rousseau as a theorist of liberalism (see for example B. F. Haymann and J. W. Chapman: *Rousseau—Totalitarian or Liberal?*)

Rousseau's contemporaries found it difficult to understand his ideas about religion and so it was this part of *Contract* that made many people his enemies. Looked upon from the perspective of our time it is perhaps the best part of the book. His recommendation is not an original one because it was used in India, and is used even today, in the United States and in those democracies where the constitution basically plays the role of civil religion. Rousseau declared, to the consternation of his contemporaries, that Christianity was the true religion but that it was totally unfit to be a civil religion. The real world of Christians is not this world but the life that begins only after death. The fundamental purpose of each Christian was to get to paradise. Compared to that, all worldly things are of secondary importance. A Christian, to be sure, does meet his duties, but he meets them with a deep nonchalance regarding success or failure of his conduct.

Though Rousseau did not quote Machiavelli explicitly, he repeated his views about Christianity which teach monkish humbleness and meekness instead of the qualities required by the Republic: courage, patriotism, virility, love of glory and the ability to sacrifice for the state.

The civil religion should be a patriotic cult limiting its theological component to a minimum, making it possible that people become tolerant and support the republican virtues that are restricted by Christianity. Rousseau divided the theology contained in civil religion into the following four positive norms: 1) faith in the existence of an almighty God; 2) faith in the after-life and the happiness of the just; 3) punishment of the bad; and 4) sanctity of social contract and laws. There is only one negative dogma: intolerance. Tolerance is absolutely inadmissible in both of its interrelated forms, i.e. as religious and civil intolerance. Rousseau liked to dramatize, which made him write the familiar sentence: "When someone acknowledges these dogmas in public and then behaves as if he does not believe in them, he should be punished by death." (Compare another of his requirements expressed in *Émile*—a child who does not respect his mother should be strangled).

It is important for the state that every citizen should have a religion prescribing that he should love his duties. The state cares for the dogmas of this religion only as long as they teach the citizens to respect morals and duties, which they should obey in relation to others. Once this has been done everyone can espouse views and opinions according to his liking and the sovereign need not know about them. By this Rousseau meant the individual religious ideas of each citizen, especially his own. He called these individual religious ideas the religion of people (*religion de l'homme*). It was the only real religion, not like the religion prevailing during his time, but the religion of the Gospel in which all are brothers, and their communion is not dissolved by death.

Through his religious views, Rousseau participates in a trend of thinking of his time that could be called "reduction of transcendence." The state frees itself of the transcendental concerns and claims of the Church to participate in the government. The emphasis shifts more and more to the concerns of life in this world. The influence and appeal of life after death was being reduced, and totally abolished in atheism.

Calvin was still using the transcendence as a means to make people diligent and interested in success in this world: those people who have attained affluence should see in it a "sign of God's grace" and a promise that they will be saved. In contrast to that, Rousseau's civil religion contained only minimum religiousness and stressed tolerance instead. Calvin's system, on the other hand, contains extensive theological dogmatics that are used as a civil religion, whereas tolerance is not yet included.

Contract corresponds also to another significant trend, which was the then increasing power of the bourgeoisie that struggled to get rid of the limitations imposed on it. It also had to get rid of the aristocracy because it hampered it in its economic expansion. It is questionable whether Rousseau realized this because he hated the bourgeoisie, but the new class certainly did not mind picking out from Rousseau's work those parts that were useful for the future revolution.

Finally, *Contract* is an expression of the weakening power of state and the increasing impoverishment of the population. The state should become stronger and push forward with its interests but this is possible only after the legitimacy of executive power has changed. Rousseau himself had always preferred the preservation of the existing order to liberty (see his letter in which he wrote about the religious persecutions in Toulouse).

It is not unimportant that Rousseau's spiritual predecessors had experienced the terrors of war and the ensuing misery directly. Rousseau did not invent anything that would be fundamentally new but he radicalized the ideas of his predecessors in this field. These men should be briefly mentioned. As opposed to Rousseau, who was an amateur and not very educated in political theory, all these men were well educated. Jean Bodin (born 1529 or 1530) who survived the Massacre of Saint Bartholomew's Day had coined the concept of the sovereignty of the state and demanded a strong but tolerant kingdom. Hugo Grotius (born 1583) was called the father of international law and lived through the war in which the Netherlands gained independence, as well as the Thirty Years' War. Thomas Hobbes (born 1588) lived much of his long life at the time of the English Civil War in almost constant fear ("My mother brought twins into the world—me and fear"); the same war was experienced also by John Locke (born 1632). Samuel Pufendorf (born 1632) was born during the Thirty Years' War. Montesquieu (born 1689) was the only man from this list of thinkers who did not have to live in exile, but he lived in the weakening kingdom following the War of Spanish Succession fought also by France.

As with so many of Rousseau's works that were begun with optimism and ended with pessimism, *Contract* ends on a pessimistic note. He predicted that the prince and the magistrates who were concerned with the executive would naturally tend to penetrate into the domain of legislation as well, and would decide issues that should be decided by the sovereignty of people. Governments always tend to extend their power. The magistrates would usurp legislative power and a situation would ensue in which the laws enslave the people again.

Here Rousseau depended on his knowledge of the development of his native Geneva, where the hereditary patriciate that was originally concerned with the executive began to dominate the legislative and preserved Calvin's Republic only on paper. It is therefore not surprising that the reception of *Contract* by the Genevan authorities was hostile and his work was banned, together with *Émile*.

Chapter Five

Exile: Years in Switzerland and England—Back to France

> Here begins the work of darkness in which I have been
> entombed. *Confessions*, Book Twelve.

Rousseau starts the description of this period of his life with a typically masochistic formulation.

Rousseau's flight from France opened a new chapter of his life, a period as a social runaway that would last till his death. Society, into which he had never been able to integrate and in which he could not attain the place "he deserved," and from which he voluntarily withdrew into partial isolation, banished him completely in the end (after massive literary provocation caused by his works).

The authorities of the eighteenth century saw his works as a manifestation of an antisocial mentality that differed substantially from the general view of the time. Further, they viewed the contents of these works as dangerous to the ruling classes. Rousseau suggested radical political change and this affected the interests of both Catholic and Protestant governments. Even after the "reduction of transcendence," the Church and Christian religion were still an important ideological instrument of governments across Europe, and Rousseau's attacks on the Church potentiated political radicalism.

The dangerousness of Rousseau's views to the ruling classes was soon revealed in the form of the political situation in Geneva and, after Rousseau's death, in the explosion of the French Revolution. From time immemorial all societies have punished nonconformist individuals either by condemnation, expulsion from society, which was tantamount to death in primitive societies, or by directly killing the antisocial individual. Needless to say, Rousseau was unable to understand this fact. He tried to vindicate himself and to explain his motives, which he did in his *Confessions* which he began to write in this period of his life.

On June 14, 1762, shortly before his fiftieth birthday, Rousseau arrived in

Yverdon and was warmly received by his old friend and compatriot, former Parisian banker Daniel Roguin. He lived with his nieces and great-nieces, his "Roguinerie" as he called them. All vied in attempts to help him. Rousseau was offered a pavilion to live in that belonged to the villa, and Roguin's niece Julianne, a widow of the late merchant from Lyon, Pierre Boy de La Tour, offered to take care of Rousseau's limited finances. The fifteen-year-old Madeleine-Catherine became Rousseau's favorite, for whom he later wrote the *Lettres sur la botanique*. It is interesting that Rousseau was partial to young girls at his age. When he lived in Montmorency he became acquainted with the twelve-year-old granddaughter of Mme de Luxembourg, Mlle de Boufleurs (the later Duchess de Luzun) whom he was allowed to kiss several times. But once he kissed her in secret, which was at variance with the principles of his *Émile* that he had himself read to the duchess and she did not overlook the chance to remind him of that.

In the eighteenth century Yverdon was a small town with 22,000 inhabitants, it had mineral springs and was built at the site of a former Roman settlement. It formally belonged to the canton Vaud but was in fact a French-speaking province of Bern, which was primarily German-speaking. It was impossible that his stay in such a small place would remain undisclosed for long and it soon became an open secret.

Rousseau's gouvernante, Thérèse, remained in France and when we take into consideration what we have previously revealed about the origin of Rousseau's urinary tract disease, it is not surprising that Rousseau's health during this period was "surprisingly" good, which is verified in his correspondence with the Luxembourgs.

Rousseau wrote Thérèse a letter and gave her a choice of staying in France or accompanying him into exile; he was not sure what her reply would be. He mentions in *Confessions* he had observed for some time that she was drifting apart from him, which he ascribed to the fact he had stopped having sexual intercourse with her for three or four years, for fear she would become pregnant again. He also noticed that having sexual intercourse only made his symptoms worse. Interruption of sexual intercourse cools off the emotional attitude of most women, which Rousseau had already experienced with Maman. Thérèse's attachment to Rousseau was not caused by her love but by a sense of duty.

Rousseau considered masturbation to be less dangerous for his health and continued to practice it: "The compensatory vice, of which I have never been able entirely to cure myself, seemed to me less deleterious." It should be added here that, as we know, Rousseau regarded women as generally more possessed with sexual desire than men; this view was in accord with medieval ideas. Psychological research proves the opposite, i.e. women use sex as a means to keep the chosen man and generally emphasize sex less than "love," i.e. a permanent relationship.

But Thérèse replied immediately—she wrote her letter at four o'clock in the morning, and described in it how much she loved him and her desire to come as soon as possible. She informed him that Mme de Bouffleurs had done her a great favor and introduced her to Prince de Conti. Fortunately, Rousseau did not forget to sent him a letter of thanks for his warning that made it possible for him escape being arrested by the parlement of Paris.

D'Alembert informed him about the situation in Paris in a letter assuring him that people there disapproved of his being persecuted and that, if he returned, he would find a great many open hearts. But he did not expect him to return. Instead he advised him quite reasonably that he take refuge in nearby Neuchâtel, which was located in the territory belonging to the Prussian king, Frederick II, and whose governor, Earl Marischal Keith, would receive him with pleasure. It is symptomatic, however, that d'Alembert did not sign his letter and posted it from the château in Montmorency, which led Rousseau to surmise that d'Alembert now occupied Rousseau's former position with the duke and duchess of Luxembourg.

Mme de Bouffleurs reproached him in her letter for forgetting about her and not writing to her. Rousseau had no love affair with Mme de Bouffleurs, although she would not have been against it. Their behavior to each other was that of ex-lovers who were bickering but cared for each other. Mme de Bouffleurs repeated her offer for him to go into English exile, and suggested in another letter that he go to Germany and stay with Mme de La Marck at the Château Schleiden in the Rhine valley. She further recommended that he should moderate his hatred of the parlement of Paris because it was only doing its duty. She asked him to make his stay in Switzerland public because there was a rumor going around in Paris that he was hiding at the château in Montmorency under the protection of the duke of Luxembourg, or at the l'Isle Adam with the knowledge of Prince de Conti, which compromised both of his benefactors.

But Rousseau could never forgive the parlement of Paris. The parlement's judgment and the grounds for it, detailing the reasons why *Émile* was banned, was printed and spread abroad, which led to *Émile* being banned in other countries as well. Rousseau was accused of questioning the veracity of the Bible and the divine nature of Jesus; he was also accused of blasphemy and other lapses. He was allegedly educating people toward skepticism and tolerance.

Moultou notified Rousseau from Geneva that the *petit conseil* was debating *Émile* at its meeting on June 18, where *Contract* was on the agenda as well. It was decided that both books should be burned. Though the meeting was held behind closed doors the notes taken at it were found later and make it obvious that the *conseil* also discussed the punishment of the author. A resolution was chosen, from several alternatives, ordering that the author be jailed as soon as and whenever he arrived in Geneva.

Whereas the outrage in France centered mainly on *Émile* as a religious heresy, in Geneva it was *Contract*, regarded by the government as more dangerous because of its political brisance. Rousseau described in the book how the magistrates usurp, in the name of the people's Republic, more and more political rights, changing the Republic into a despotic regime.

The Genevan *petit conseil* consisted of twenty-five members, from patrician families, who recognized that *Contract* was leveled against them. In a way the condemnation of *Émile* for religious reasons made it possible to condemn *Contract* for the same reasons. As Moultou put it, *Émile* was the torch that ignited *Contract*.

The procurator general of Geneva, Robert Tronchin, argued that Rousseau actually was not a legal citizen of Geneva because the procedures of his conversion to Calvinism in 1754 were not quite correct. He maintained later that he only wanted to protect Rousseau: if Rousseau was not citizen of Geneva, he could not be arrested.

In a letter from June 22, 1762, Rousseau informed Moultou he did not feel well (probably as a result of the news regarding the fate of his books), and felt the pains that usually preceded the recurrence of his illness. He thanked him for defending him in Geneva but asked him to heed his own security. Moultou himself was not a common priest and was not a Genevan citizen by birth. He was born in Montpellier and his father, a rich French Protestant *émigré*, brought him to Geneva as a child. In 1762 Moultou was thirty-seven, and was married to Marianne Cayla, who came from an old Genevan family and moved in upper Genevan society.

He was not alone in his efforts to defend Rousseau. In Geneva the old conflict between the patrician *petit conseil* and a group of citizens who tried to preserve the legislative sovereignty of the *grand conseil*, to which all Genevan citizens belonged, was still smoldering. The conflict sparked a civil war that ended through a French "mediation" in 1737. *Contract* thus became helpful to the Genevan opposition, which had never been completely stifled, because it supported their cause.

On June 22, Charles Pictet, a former colonel and a member of the Two Hundred (a two hundred-member council, which had only formal executive powers) and a known Genevan citizen, wrote a letter to the bookseller Duvillard. In the letter Pictet expressed partial criticism about *Contract* but at the same time protested against the way in which the *petit conseil* treated the author of the book. The letter was copied and circulated with Pictet's tacit consent in Geneva. Pictet was punished but his punishment only stirred up the old controversy between the patrician aristocracy and the liberal advocates of civil rights.

Mme de Bouffleurs received a letter from Hume, who wrote her from Edinburgh that Rousseau could live in England and expressed a hope that Rousseau would get a pension from the King Georg III. Yet he also expressed some doubts as to whether Rousseau would be willing to stay in England because he did not speak English. At the same time Hume wrote directly to Rousseau, also in English.

Leonhard Usteri suggested to Rousseau that he accept "secure refuge" in the wise republic of Zürich and the king of Prussia, Frederick II, was asked to grant Rousseau asylum at his territory in Neuchâtel.

Visitors soon followed the letters. One of the people to visit Rousseau in Yverdon was the physician Samuel-André Tissot, whose medical and public health views were quite unorthodox. He agreed with Rousseau's views expressed in *Émile*, particularly those about vaccination and onanism. He himself wrote a bestseller of his time, the book *L'Onanisme*, which was translated into numerous languages. According to the book, the impacts of masturbation were far worse than those of syphilis.

In *Émile* Rousseau condemned masturbation as a "disgusting practice." He wrote in the book: "As soon as your pupil learns to use this dangerous instrument, he is as good as forlorn—he will bear the sad effects of this habit till the end of his life, which is the most deleterious of all habits a young man can become addicted to." Here Rousseau probably speaks from his own experience. He must have realized that the masturbation of urethra that he probably practiced (presumably with Thérèse's assistance) was usually followed, sooner or later, by urinary tract infection, in most cases accompanied by extreme difficulties and pain. In *Confessions,* however, Rousseau admits that he had used this "supplement" for his whole life because it made it possible for him as a man with a strong imagination to obtain in his fantasy as many women as he wished. But, in spite of that, he congratulated Dr. Tissot on his book and they became friends.

On June 20, Rousseau formally asked, through the mediation of the prefect of Yverdon, M. de Moiry (who supported his request), to be allowed to stay on Bernese territory. One Bernese newspaper, *Gazette De Berne,* by publishing the full text of the condemnation of *Émile* by the parlement of Paris, reduced the chances of a positive response to his request. Geneva also informed the Bernese authorities that both subversive books were being sold in Nyon. It appears that even Voltaire, who hated Rousseau, was involved in these Genevan interventions in Bern.

Julie von Bondeli wrote that the first blow came from Geneva and that the cabal from the Château Ferney (which belonged to Voltaire) reached even Bern. This news also hit Paris and people there were surprised that Voltaire, an advocate of tolerance and the persecuted, participated in Rousseau's persecution. Voltaire denied the accusations and went so far as to declare in front of d'Alembert that he had offered Rousseau a safe haven after the latter's condemnation by the parlement of Paris.

Another Genevan citizen, Charles Bonnet informed the famous Bernese biologist Albrecht von Haller, in a letter from June 18, about Rousseau's indictment in Geneva, and expressed his hope that the Bernese senate would proceed equally against the opponent of religion and government. He even wrote, in a subsequent letter, that Rousseau would have been burned in Geneva two hundred years ago but that now only his books were being burned.

Rousseau was convinced by the end of June that he would be allowed to stay on Bernese territory in Yverdon—in the meantime Thérèse set out for Yverdon, as we know from a letter sent to Rousseau by Mme de Verdelin, who cared for his cat, Minette. Mme de Luxembourg wrote him that the wagon with his belongings was already on the way and to take care of everything he wished. On July 1, 1762, however, devastating news arrived in Yverdon. The senate of Bern had not only banned the sale of *Émile* but had also ordered that the author be ousted from the Bernese territory.

Contract was not mentioned. Bern, too, regarded religion as more important than the possible political implications of *Contract*. Bern had an overtly aristocratic constitution and the ruling aristocracy did not have to resort to the pretext of a democratic authorization. The few patrician families that dominated Bern held hereditary rights to govern. But the Protestant dogmatics were a political link between the French-speaking canton Vaud and the German-speaking Bern. This was also the reason that the prefect of Yverdon was informed that Rousseau had to leave Yverdon within several days. Even the intervention of Vincent-Bernard Tscharner, who had visited Rousseau in Montmorency and offered him membership in the *Société Économique de Berne*, did not help. The request by the prefect of Yverdon was turned down as well: "His excellency cannot revoke the decision from July1." The only delay permitted would be if Rousseau were sick, and his departure could be postponed one or two weeks at the most.

When the prefect imparted this decision to Rousseau, the latter allegedly had tears in his eyes. But he stated that these were tears of joy to have met the prefect. His Bernese admirer, Julie von Bondeli, said, "He left as a sage but not as a stoic because was shedding tears." Rousseau decided to leave immediately, but he had to decide first where to go. After a lengthy hesitation, Rousseau decided to take refuge in the territory of the Prussian king, Frederick II. Personally, he hated Frederick II as a tyrant and warrior. His "courage to extradite himself to the king's mercy" was apparently aided by the offer of Roguin's niece, Mme de Boy. She suggested that Rousseau could use an empty, dilapidated house that she owned in nearby Môtiers as a refuge. Rousseau agreed, on the condition that he would pay rent to her. This was set at thirty francs annually. Mme de Boy later objected that the rent was too high and that she was glad just to have the house inhabited. She suggested that Rousseau furnish the house at her expense, according to his taste.

The village Môtiers is situated in the Val de Travers on the other side of a mountain ridge. As the wagon had to make a detour to get into this valley, Rousseau decided to walk to Môtiers. Colonel Roguin accompanied him. They left on July 9, 1762. Consequently, Rousseau did not spend even a whole month in Yverdon. Within a relatively short time Rousseau had been expelled from two states and professed to be a criminal in a third state—his native Geneva. The travelers stayed for a night in an inn and reached Môtiers the next morning. Rousseau was enchanted by the natural beauty of the mountain range.

The Val de Travers extends from Pontalier to the hills surrounding the city of Neuchâtel situated on the shores of a lake. In the eighteenth century, Môtiers, which is located approximately in the middle of the valley, had only four hundred inhabitants who primarily worked in the local asphalt mines or as small manufacturers rather than in agriculture, which of course could not find Rousseau's approval. Colonel Roguin introduced Rousseau to Mme Boy's relative, Major Girardier. The major received Rousseau amicably and Rousseau boarded at his house, at a cost of six écu blancs a month, till Thérèse's arrival.

In actual fact, the major could not have been very enthusiastic about Rousseau's presence because he had been using the house, which was to be inhabited by Rousseau, without having to pay for it. Immediately after his arrival, Rousseau wrote thank-you letters to Mme Boy, M. de Moiry and, the most important letter, to the governor of the territory, Lord Keith. In this letter he introduced himself as a runaway expelled from three states because he expressed what he deemed useful and true. He begged that his fate be considered. He would leave when told to leave, though he did not know where he would go.

The dignified and experienced Lord Keith liked his petition. Keith, the last Earl Marischal of Scotland (the title was hereditary in the family), was also living in exile. He was born at the Château Inverugie in the county of Kinkardine, on April 2, 1693, and died in Potsdam on May 25, 1778, the same year as Voltaire and Rousseau. He participated as a young man in the Jacobites' rebellion in 1715, after which he lost his Scottish domain, then he served in the Spanish army, became the Prussian envoy of Frederick II at the court in Paris (1751–1754) and became the king's friend, with whom he shared an interest in literature.

The governorship of Neuchâtel was actually his pension. As he grew older, he partially lost his enthusiasm for the Jacobites and was granted amnesty by King George III. His Scottish property was restored to him in 1760. Though he contemplated returning to Scotland, he preferred to stay in Switzerland at the age of seventy-six to serve Frederick II, with whom he shared the same anticlerical and skeptical views as he did with his friend, David Hume.

His brother, James, became known as the field marshal of Frederick II. He distinguished himself in the Seven Years' War. He was killed in action on October 14, 1758 at Hochkirch.

Since Lord Keith was an exile as well, he was understanding toward Rousseau and replied immediately to his letter. He did not conceal that he had written to the king to ask for instructions. But Rousseau was welcome. He invited him to visit at his residence, Château Colombier near Neuchâtel. He even offered to send a carriage for him and added that when Rousseau arrived he would find an old man who was a little bit of a savage, too, though somewhat corrupted by the company of civilized barbarians (his remark makes it obvious that Rousseau's views were common knowledge in the educated circles of that time).

Rousseau also wrote a letter to Frederick II, in which he confessed he had occasionally spoken in cross words about him. Fortunately he did not post this letter. Frederick II replied to Lord Keith in a letter from the battlefield at Ditmansdorf and consented to the asylum for "the unhappy Rousseau." In another letter, several weeks later, the king offered to grant Rousseau a small pension of one hundred écu that was to be paid in kind (wood, coal) because he knew Rousseau would not accept money. He continued that if he had not been ruined by the war, he would have ordered that a hermitage with a garden be built for Rousseau, in which he could live up to his ideas about the way of life of our ancestors. He wrote further that he believed the morals of our savage were as pure as his mind was savage (natural).

Lord Keith interpreted the royal offer to Rousseau diplomatically, so that Rousseau was convinced that Frederick II, in offering him a house, was his protector and benefactor. So it happened that after only two days in Môtiers, Rousseau was brought in a carriage to the château in Colombier, where both men became friends. Rousseau found in the lord a fatherly figure who replaced the duke of Luxembourg. He even called him *"mon père"* and the lord called him *"mon fils."* Rousseau later visited the lord regularly and walked to Colombier several times. The lord once spent two days visiting Rousseau in Môtiers. Rousseau regarded Lord Keith as a wise man who possessed some human imperfections.

Moultou, in Geneva, wanted initially to write a pamphlet defending

Rousseau and *Émile*. But his friends warned him against this and the publication of the pamphlet was subsequently cancelled, one reason being the fact that the married priest, Moultou, fell in love with a beautiful young widow (twenty-two years old), Anne-Germaine Vermenoux.

Rousseau took steps to become involved in the local Protestant church. Unlike the liberal king, Frederick II, the inhabitants of Neuchâtel were bigoted and the city clergy belonged to the most parochial and intolerant Calvinists. The situation of that time can be best elucidated by the case of a pastor from Ponts, Ferdinand-Olivier Petitpierre, who was accused of having denied in a sermon in 1758 that the punishment of sinners would last for all eternity. The *vénérable classe*—a board of local clergy and clerks—called on him to discontinue preaching such heretical views in public. Yet Petitpierre disobeyed and had to be asked to step down. His parishioners supported him and the local authorities were at a loss regarding the best course of action to take—they could not reach any agreement.

King Frederick II commented on the dispute in a way typical of him, "When these pederasts wish to burn in hell for all eternity, it is not my business to prevent them from doing so." To restore order, the king summoned Lord Keith, who took up his office in Colombier in February 1762, six months before Rousseau arrived. Lord Keith, ever a judicious diplomat, sent a letter to the intendant of Môtiers asking him to help Rousseau enter into a good relationship with the local pastor—a move that would calm the *vénérable classe*.

The local pastor was named Frédéric-Guillaume de Montmollin, but he dubbed himself pretentiously *"Le Professeur de Montmollin."* He was a bigoted and conceited intellectual snob and belonged to the most rigorous of Petitpierre's persecutors. On the other hand, he was thrilled by the prospect of becoming a friend of such a famous author, in spite of the fact that Rousseau's views as expressed in *Émile* were much more sinful than those of Petitpierre. He therefore welcomed Rousseau as a participant in the services and as communicant of Holy Communion, according to Calvinist rite. Rousseau gladly accepted. Among others, active membership of the Neuchâtel Calvinist Church hampered his excommunication by the Genevan Church. Besides Moultou, Rousseau also had other friends in the Genevan theologian circles. One of them was Antoine-Jacques Roustan whose friendly criticism was not leveled so much against *Émile* as against *Contract*, mainly because of Rousseau's claim that Christianity was not feasible in a republican state.

Thérèse arrived in Môtiers on July 20, 1762. Her journey took nine days and just like in 1754, on her journey to Geneva, she was sexually molested. (On her future journey to London in 1766, she will be seduced by James Bosvell, or rather she will seduce Bosvell.) Rousseau described her arrival in *Confessions* passionately: "How violent was our first embrace! Oh, how sweet are the tears of joy and affection, and how my heart feasts on them!"

They had been separated for less than two months but it was their first separation after almost seventeen years. At the age of forty-one, Thérèse did not give the impression of being Rousseau's mistress. She looked more like a housewife and nurse taking care of Rousseau's recurrent urinary problems and performing the catheterizations which were so often needed. In fact, she gave the impression of being one of the servants because she was not always allowed to eat at the table, as we know from the reports of some of Rousseau's visitors.

Initially she was received well in Môtiers. She was even offered the use of professor de Montmollin's private carriage so she could attend Catholic services nearby. After Thérèse arrived, the house was furnished modestly and she started to cook.

Rousseau maintained correspondence with the duke and duchess of Luxembourg and with Mme de Bouffleurs, who kept recommending that he go to England. The attention of the authorities in France turned first to *Émile*—the book was banned as heretical, and now the government turned against *Contract* because it criticized the monarchy.

Among the first visitors, who came mainly from the German-speaking Swiss cantons, especially from Zürich and Bern, were Samuel Engel, the president of *Société Économique de Berne* and Rousseau's friends, Jan-Rodolphe Tschiffeli, Nicolas-Antoine Kirchberger, Daniel Fellenberg, Carolus Sturler, Vincent-Bernard Tscharner and Baron von Liebersdorf. Rousseau's most devoted admirer was *"das Haupt der Sekte von Rousseaus Bewunderern,"* Julia von Bondeli, whose salon was visited by the crème of Bernese society. But she met Rousseau only after a long correspondence.

Rousseau's Maman, Mme de Warens, died in absolute destitution in Chambéry on July 29, 1762. In *Confessions* Rousseau wrote at the occasion of her death that she was "the best woman and mother" and that he hoped to meet her in the other world. Mme Boy, who had hired out the house to Rousseau, visited him on August 20. She also took care of his finances—from his investment of 3,000 francs, Rousseau got 5 percent annually from her bank in Lyon. She also offered him her rustic house in Pierrenod where he could live for the summer. Rousseau obviously fell in love platonically with her daughter, *la petit blonde* Madeleine-Catherine and it is possible that several letters he wrote in summer 1762, that bore the title "To Sara," might have been sent to her (see the remark about Rousseau's weakness for young girls). But in real life he continued to correspond with staid ladies such as the duchess of Luxembourg and Mme Alissan—his admirer, "Julie."

Lord Keith informed him on August 16, 1762 that Frederick II was pleased he could grant asylum to this "persecuted personality." But this message contained the condition that Rousseau would stop writing about controversial matters that could excite the minds in Neuchâtel and cause differences among the theologians who indulged in discussions and were full of fanaticism. It is necessary to say that Rousseau did not feel obligated to firmly observe this condition. He began to see Frederick II as his protector; he was devoted to the king and took an interest in his successes though he regarded them as undeserved in the past.

Rousseau celebrated the peace treaty with a festive illumination of his house but because he found out that the king was not disarming after the war had ended, he wrote him a letter in which he admonished and rebuked him (this was the second of his letters to the king—his last letter was posted from Wooton, England on March 30, 1766). The king left his letter unanswered and when Lord Keith asked the king at his visit in Berlin about the letter's contents, Frederick II replied that Rousseau "had bawled him out properly." In *Confessions* Rousseau admits that he may not have chosen the correct tone but that he complied with the feelings "that forced the pen into his hand."

Initially, Rousseau abstained from meddling in the politics of Geneva, where Voltaire's last publication appeared, the anticlerical work, "*Le Serment des cinquante*." Rousseau remarked that it was strange the Genevan authorities should tolerate this atheistic publication but were at the same time disinclined to tolerate his religious views that simply differed from theirs. But experience tells that the Church does not regard a real atheist to be as dangerous as a religious heretic.

Rousseau outwardly demonstrated his harmlessness in political and religious matters with the display of a unique new pastime. He learned to make bobbin lace and produce silken ribbons, carrying his newly acquired activity with him, whether he was sitting on the balcony of the landlady's house, or even in front of it. He could not earn his living with copying notes in Môtiers. On August 29, he joined in Protestant communion at his own written request, which flattered Montmollin. It was a clever move since more than two hundred copies of his written request got to Geneva where it pleased his backers.

D'Alembert, however, sent a letter to Voltaire in which he described Rousseau's declaration as a hypocritical masquerade. The simple explanation of all this was that Rousseau experienced his urge to write and provoke again.

His Armenian caftan arrived from Yverdon and Rousseau wore it to services and while producing the silken ribbons. *He described himself as a half-woman in a letter sent to Mme de Verdelin and regretted not having been born as a woman completely* (see the feminine features of masochists described in Part 2). He donated a few of the ribbons he produced to the brides of Môtiers as wedding presents—they had promised him they would breast-feed their babies. But others, for example the French Mme Sandoz, daughter of Count de Chaumont, did not approve of his hobby. She had a literary salon in Neuchâtel.

Rousseau wore his Armenian caftan and a turban also when he attended a supper given by Lord Keith. The old man liked the costume and greeted Rousseau with the Arab *"Salamleki."* One of the guests this evening, Mme Sturler, described Rousseau's appearance at the supper in a letter to Julie von Bondeli. She wrote that Rousseau's behavior was very unusual—during the conversation he was allegedly shouting, gesticulating and trying fanatically to persuade others that money was worthless, and preaching on moral simplicity. He criticized contemporary morals, particularly those of contemporary women, so that everybody laughed and admitted he was right.

At that time Rousseau was planning to publish his collected works, he was working on his *Dictionary of Music,* and he had contemplated publishing a volume with critical articles concerning the novel *Julie.* He dropped this last project, but he did not dismiss the idea of writing his biography as an introduction to his collected works. Let me remind the reader that he had made the first step of this project by having written four autobiographical letters to Malesherbes. It should be added perhaps that Rousseau was never passive or bored, even at times when he was not working on a specific project, because, as he wrote, "My imagination can fill all voids, and is in itself enough to occupy me."

Other visitors, both new friends and old, came to visit Rousseau in

Môitiers. One of the visitors was Claude-Henri Watelet, a former tax collector. He was accompanied by Marguerite Le Comte who had broken with her husband and lived with Watelet. The visitors from Zürich came more often, among them a young professor of Hebrew, Caspar Hess, who spent most of his honeymoon there, accompanied by philosophical discussions. Although it seems rather strange, it documents the deep impact of Rousseau's novel *La Nouvelle Héloïse* on his contemporaries. According to Byron, to visit Rousseau was to visit "the birthplace of love."

Hess was neither the first nor the last to visit Rousseau with his bride. Rousseau used to warn these visitors against romantic love that could never last forever. According to his advice, the only sound base of marriage was friendship.

The visitors from Zürich suggested that Rousseau could live there because Zwingli's Protestantism was not as fanatical and the mercantile oligarchy of Zürich was not as strict as the hereditary Bernese aristocracy. The heretical pastor, Petitpierre, who had found refuge in England recommended Rousseau do the same and wrote that *Émile* was a commercial success in England. But he also warned Rousseau that the cost of living was quite high in England and one had to have a minimum of two hundred pounds a year.

Lord Keith, who intended to return to Scotland, offered Rousseau "lodging in Keith Hall." He wrote in a letter to Hume that Rousseau was persecuted even in Switzerland and that "Tho' it be to me a very great pleasure to converse with the honest savage, yet I advise him to go to England where he will enjoy *placidam sub libertate qiuetem.*"

Lord Keith tried to help Rousseau financially as well. Since he knew that Rousseau would not accept such help from him he wanted to create an impression that Frederick II was offering him a pension. But he did not choose the best time for his help because Frederick II had just obtained Silesia, which provoked Rousseau's resistance. Rousseau wrote another reproachful letter to the king who was granting him asylum. Lord Keith promised to deliver the letter in Berlin without expressing his opinion about it. He also offered to move Rousseau to Colombier over the winter, where he would find a warmer place.

The winters in the Jura Mountains were usually very cold and Rousseau was afraid of them. He even started to bake his own bread, for which he had to pay one écu blanc to the local baker. He tried to educate some of the local children in music. His philosophy of simple life and happiness among simple people did not work in reality at all. The people of Môtiers were rather dull, Rousseau grew depressive, and even his old illness reappeared, probably partly due to the care of his "nurse" Thérèse.

He wrote in a letter to Rey, his publisher: "*Je suis froid, je suis triste, je pisse mall.*" Rousseau's declaration, written on the occasion of his communion in Môtiers, in which he called himself a Christian, got to Geneva where it not only pleased his backers but also provoked a sharp response from the Genevan clergy. A distant relative of Rousseau's friend, Pastor Jean Sarasin (1703–1778), wrote the local pastor in Môtiers—Montmollin—a sharp letter asking the pastor to explain why he had admitted Rousseau to communion.

Montmollin showed this letter to Rousseau and asked him to help with a reply. Even Rousseau's old friend, who once helped Rousseau regain his Genevan rights in 1754, Jacques-François Deluc, was outraged and shocked that Rousseau had refused, in *Émile*, belief in miracles and revelation and he stopped corresponding with Rousseau. The two of them became friends again later, after Deluc read a copy of Rousseau's letter to Montmollin, and Rousseau invited him to a visit in Môtiers.

On October 1, Rousseau was visited by three Genevans: the young pastor, Antoine Roustan, with his companion, a pastor as well, and Rousseau's relative, Pierre Mouchon. They stayed in Môtiers for eight days, living at a local inn. Pierre Mouchon described the nature of his celebrated kinsman to his wife enthusiastically. He wrote how winsome Rousseau was, about his nice manners, lively gesticulation and sparkling eyes.

Most people thought that Rousseau was a faultfinder and censor, that he was invariably in a bad mood, but in fact he was a man who liked to tease others and laughed with them; he talked with children and joked with his housekeeper, Mlle Levasseur. He accompanied his visitors on several perambulations and trips. During a nightly barbecue in his kitchen he declaimed the fairy tale *La Reine fantasque* to them, which he had written in 1756 (a queen christened her son "Whim" and her daughter "Reason," but she found out later the children's names did not match their characters).

The visitors were introduced to pastor Montmollin who invited them to preach in the local church. Two Genevan theologians requested copies of Montmollin's letter to Sarasin so they could circulate it in Geneva. Sarasin, when he learned of it, wrote a second letter to Montmollin, this time more polite. He still demanded, however, that Rousseau publicly recant his heretical views, which had probably crept into his works "contrary to his will." After they had left, all three Genevan visitors wrote Rousseau as well as Montmollin letters of thanks and Mouchon even opined that the visit was "an epoch of his life."

We know that Rousseau usually behaved bluntly and sourly toward his visitors; however, it appears that his unusually agreeable and friendly behavior to his Genevan visitors, and the establishment of their acquaintance with Pastor Montmollin, were very clever moves. Rousseau was trying to find additional friends in Geneva so they would help to mobilize the weakening sympathies of Genevans, and he succeeded to a certain extent.

It should also be mentioned that Rousseau was an attractive figure to be used as a notice board for the political opposition in Geneva, which tried to curb the influence of the *petit conseil* and avert reelection of the procurator general Robert Tronchin, who was regarded as responsible for the banning of *Émile* and *Social Contract*. Deluc, who also belonged to this opposition, visited Rousseau in Môtiers to consult with him about political strategy against Tronchin. Unfortunately, Deluc got sick in Môtiers.

Another Genevan oppositionist who tried to involve Rousseau in Genevan politics was the businessman François-Henri d'Ivernois. But the bid of the Genevan opposition failed. Robert Tronchin was reelected on November 21. Rousseau was very disappointed about his election; he lost interest in Geneva and returned to his defense of *Émile*, in spite of King Frederick's condition that he must not write about controversial things.

He wrote a defensive pamphlet, addressed to the archbishop of Paris, Christophe de Beaumont, who had condemned *Émile*. Rousseau demonstrated again that he was an eloquent writer of pamphlets and a brilliant polemicist. He maintained that a book by a Protestant author, published in a Protestant country, could not be banned by the parlement of Paris in the first place. He pointed out that books by atheists such as Spinosa were being sold freely in Paris.

As far as he was concerned, he was a pupil, but not of the priests—he was a pupil of Jesus Christ. He raised the questions: how was it possible that all people were punished for the sins of their ancestors, and why should Christians believe that God was so unjust as to punish mankind for sins it had not committed. Having rejected the doctrine of original sin, Rousseau got to the central subject of his writings—that man was good by nature but was being corrupted by human society. The innocent, original *amour de soi* becomes corrupted in contact with others and develops into the malicious *amour de propre* that was at the heart of all conflicts.

He informed Rey in a letter dated November 16 that, though he was sick, he had no other choice and had to take up his pen again to write a defense of *Émile*. He had been working on the manuscript for two months and thought it could be ready within six weeks. Rey replied by letter in December 1762, and assured Rousseau he would print anything Rousseau sent to him. Moreover, he added that the money he had promised to pay Thérèse was going to be transferred for the entire year 1763 to the account of his agent in Neuchâtel. Rey received the manuscript in early 1763 and the letter was printed in April of the same year. As Rey expected, the pamphlet only increased the ranks of Rousseau's enemies.

Rousseau received letters from his old Parisian friends. Mme de Bouffleurs was concerned about his finances and his isolation. Mme de Chenonceaux, who had the banned copy of *Contract* circulated in Paris, congratulated him on his being in Switzerland because he would otherwise be stoned in France. Mme de Verdelin wrote Rousseau in late December. She was let down because her lover Adrien de Margency had deserted her. She wrote that she consoled herself over this loss somewhat by reading *Émile*, but especially by reading *Julie*. She voiced her concern about Rousseau's health in the rough highland winter.

The winter of 1762–1763 was the worst of the century. The Seine and Thames rivers froze. There was as much snow in the plains of Switzerland as in the Alps. Rousseau got sick in late December and reported to Moultou in Geneva that he got a cold that was joined by fever and "that he believed his old urinary bladder would get totally blocked." His sickness was serious indeed. He supposed he would die and started researching if, according to the Neuchâtel law, Thérèse could inherit all his belongings. Lord Keith suggested that Rousseau write a simple will and testament. But Rousseau wrote a more detailed one. He made Thérèse, his "housewife," his universal heir. She should inherit all his property and all his books, including those that were being printed. He regretted he could not pay her for the twenty years she had spent taking care of him without any pay. He excluded all his relatives from the testament. He bequeathed only the nominal sum of five sols to both his aunt, Susanne Concerut, and his cousin, Gabriel Rousseau, which he did only to satisfy the laws of the country in which he lived.

The testament demonstrates very clearly that Thérèse was much more than "a housekeeper." As a semi-literate and primitive person she was obviously gratifying his masochistic sexual needs through performing urethral masturbation on him (he had always separated these needs from the concept of love) and, as a result of inflammatory consequences of urethral masturbation, she had gradually become indispensable for him because she had to introduce bougies into his urethra. In this way, the sexual component combined with nursing.

It is a fact encountered commonly in medical practice that the scars forming in the urethra gradually result in the development of very complicated and tortuous strictures. Only a person who knows the ins and outs of such a highly "individual urethra" can catheterize it based on experience with the catheterization of the same person on daily basis. It is otherwise very difficult to explain why Rousseau should have been almost obsessed with the primitive Thérèse, and why he tried to secure her financially in contrast to his beloved Maman, Mme de Warens.

In his last will, Rousseau also demanded that a postmortem be carried out after his death that would show the real cause of his "strange illness that was bothering him for so many years." In the conclusion of the testament, Rousseau recorded the following details about his illness:

1) He was tormented by urinary retention for twenty years, which was diagnosed as due to a urinary stone, until Frère Côme found out that the stone did not exist.

2) That he had never been able to pass water completely freely and was experiencing, at the same time, a permanent urgency to urinate. He was afraid that the stream of urine that was becoming thinner and thinner would sooner or later disappear completely.

3) That his urethra was blocked and that the bougies of M. Daran (usually used to treat venereal diseases—which led to the assumption that Rousseau suffered from venereal disease) proved to be ineffective.

4) That the obstruction spread and affected also the urinary bladder in the course of time.

5) That baths and diuretics only further increased his pains, that the method of bleeding did not produce any relief and that physicians as well as surgeons had failed to establish the cause of his illness and find a cure.

6) That Frère Côme diagnosed a swollen and scirrhotic prostate so that the cause of the illness must have been connected with the prostate, the neck of the urinary bladder or the urethra—probably with all three of these organs.

7) That the illness was not caused by a venereal infection because he had never contracted it.

Rousseau signed his last will on January 29, 1763, when his illness culminated. His health improved in February. His *"notes sur la maladie"* are interesting from a medical point of view. As opposed to some of his previous assertions (that he suffered from urinary retention since his early childhood, that the cause was a "congenital defect, and that he had survived only thanks to the care of his foster mothers) he now wrote that his illness began in his thirties when he came to Paris and got together with Thérèse. His description of the symptoms corresponds to the consequences of urethral masturbation. At a time when bacterial infections were still unrecognized, he probably did not realize that his illness might have been related to urethral masturbation. This can be clearly seen in his wish that a postmortem be carried out after his death so the cause of his illness could be found.

At the request of the duke of Luxembourg, Rousseau described in two letters his new residence in the Val de Travers. In contrast to the *Letter to d'Alembert* written five years earlier, in which he wrote about unspoiled highlanders, Rousseau criticized his neighbors and wrote about their love of money, their avarice, obstinacy, jealousy and love of titles. Though they had some morality they lacked principles. Their Christianity was limited to church visits on Sundays. They did not love their neighbors. They received him by banning his books. Out of love of money, the highlanders became soldiers and the money had corrupted their character. The Protestant refugees from France had brought industry to the region and local people left their fields in exchange for the money earned in the manufactories. The clergy of Neuchâtel was bigoted and cantankerous.

In his second letter to the duke, Rousseau described the beautiful country surrounding the Val de Travers. He also wrote a friendly letter to David Hume (as a reply to his letter from July, which he had received as late as February). In it, he described his present situation. He wrote that he hopes his health would make it possible for him to get to Scotland one day, and mentioned Lord Keith, who offered him not only a refuge but also "Scotland in Switzerland."

He began to write courteous letters to his admirer, Mme Alissan. He asked her about her appearance and age, and quoted Italian poets. He was playing with fire, for he must have known that Mme Alissan loved him. She revealed that she was thirty-two and asked Rousseau whether he did not know of a house close to his own that could be purchased. But she was afraid because she was a Catholic she would not be allowed to buy a house in a Protestant canton. She also asked whether he would allow her to address him as *"mon ami"* instead of *"monsieur."* Rousseau wrote her that his greatest love was older than thirty, which was not true (Sophie d'Houdetot was twenty-six in 1726). Mme Alissan also revealed that her first name was Marianne and added that she intended to send him a copy of her portrait. But Rousseau apparently did not take their correspondence seriously, even though he addressed his letters to "Ravishing Marianne" or "Sweet Marianne."

In Geneva he was losing his old friend Moultou, who tended more and more to Voltaire. Moultou, but also Deluc, exhorted Rousseau to write and send to Geneva a statement regarding his religious views, which Rousseau stringently refused. Rousseau's pamphlet *"Letter to the Archbishop Beaumont"* was published in April and was immediately banned from printing by the Genevan *petit conseil*. Rousseau replied by renouncing his Genevan citizenship. He could venture this step because he had nothing to fear—Lord Keith had assured him he was going to get the citizenship of Neuchâtel. Also Couvet, a village in the Val de Travers, included Rousseau into the list of its residents, which was not the case in Môtiers where Rousseau was not overly popular. He wrote to his friends in Geneva that he would never stop loving Geneva even though he would not live there. That is to say, he loved a certain picture of Geneva but felt an aversion to the government and inhabitants of that time.

According to his own account in *Confessions,* Rousseau felt good in Môtiers at that time and assumed he would stay there till his death. But he had no regular income and life in Môtiers was allegedly quite expensive. His small financial reserve was diminishing. He hoped that his works would gradually catch on and the governments of various countries would permit the publication of his books. Before this happened he planned to live on his financial reserves. But he seemingly did not believe it himself and returned to his work on a music lexicon.

He also started to sort the letters sent to him by the duke of Luxembourg because he intended to use them for the work on his *Confessions*. He found out, however, that part of the letters had disappeared, together with the draft of *Sensitive Moral* and *Adventures of Lord Eduard*. At first he suspected Mme de Luxembourg because he had always believed the duke and had his doubts regarding the duchess. In the end, however, he suspected that d'Alembert stole the papers (he also suspected that d'Alembert was copying down his thoughts about music and wanted to use them in his own article for *Encyclopédie*).

In the spring of 1763 the young Magyar Baron de Sauttern visited Rousseau in Môtiers with the intention of staying for some time as Rousseau's pupil. His French was poor and as Rousseau did not speak Hungarian or German, the two of them tried to make themselves understood in Latin. Rousseau took to his new friend because they shared a love of hiking in the mountains. They became inseparable, and went together to visit Lord Keith. Rousseau mentioned Sauttern very favorably in *Confessions*.

His Genevan friends warned Rousseau against the baron, whom they suspected of being a French spy, which was not true. But it must be said that not everything Sauttern said about himself was true either. Lord Keith described this man as a kind of impostor. Sauttern himself later admitted he had not always told the truth. Rousseau forgave him, not only because he took to him but also because he recalled his own youth, when he pretended to be "Vaussore de Villeneuve" and "Mr. Dudding." He wrote in *Confessions* that Sauttern stayed in Môtiers for two years, but it was, in fact, only five months.

Another visitor to Môtiers was Moultou, who returned to Geneva with a letter written by Rousseau that later became known under the name "An Appeal for Uprising." According to the Genevan constitution, five to six citizens could form a *représentation* in case they disagreed with a governmental decision. This clause had never been used but Rousseau hoped the citizens would use it and form a *représentation* on his behalf. Deluc, who headed the Genevan opposition, informed Rousseau that forty citizens had indeed handed in a *représentation* on his behalf. Deluc and his allies pointed out in it that the action against Rousseau was illegal on the grounds that the *petit conseil* was not entitled to decide matters of religious disputes. This task was, according to Article 88 of the Constitution, exclusively in the competence of the consistory. But the *petit conseil* brusquely rejected this objection. Rousseau's letter only further sharpened the political situation in Geneva.

Rousseau continued to receive letters from the duke of Luxembourg, who wrote quite often despite bad health and his considerable duties at the court.

The duchess fell silent. Letters continued to come also from Mme de Verdelin and Mme de Chenonceaux (her husband was still in the jailhouse for debtors). Mme de Verdelin wrote that Rousseau's previous place of refuge in Montlouis was still in good repair, and Thérèse's mother in Deuil was enjoying good health and was not without means of support. This shows that Rousseau continued to send her financial support.

In summer of that year, Baron Sauttern suddenly left Môtiers because the maidservant in the inn in which he was staying got pregnant. He pretended he had to leave immediately for Hungary, but he actually left for Strasbourg where he seduced a married woman. Rousseau knew everything about his friend's behavior but because he liked the baron he looked on with benevolence.

In early August Rousseau became sick again and this time his pains were so severe that he contemplated suicide, which he indicated in a letter to Duclos. This letter also shows clearly how dependent Rousseau was on Thérèse. He praises her faithfulness, patience and compassion, and declares that Thérèse has "a heart like my own." He asked Duclos to force the publisher Duchesne—in case he died—to give Thérèse the fifty louis that the publisher had promised to give him.

Thérèse was obviously the only human being able to carry out the catheterization of Rousseau's cicatricial and tortuous urethra, thereby draining the urine and alleviating the pain. His suicidal thoughts disappeared as soon as his condition improved. We learn from a letter to Mme Boy that he was unable to spend the summertime in her cottage in Pierrenod, which he genuinely regretted because he had grown to hate Môtiers and its inhabitants, and considered it the worst and most annoying place, as he wrote with unusually brutal frankness.

It is difficult to identify the cause of such a rapid worsening of his attitude toward the inhabitants of Môtiers. Perhaps the main reason was Thérèse, whom the Protestants highlanders hated (she was Catholic), and she, for her part, had only words of contempt for them. Since most women usually repeat their views daily, she could have inoculated Rousseau with her antipathies which would not have been difficult in view of Rousseau's dependence on her.

Although Daniel Roguin had promised to take Thérèse into his family in case Rousseau should die, Rousseau assumed that the religious differences would make it impossible for Thérèse to ever feel happy in Switzerland. That was why he tried to make sure that she could stay at abbé Grumet's in Ambérieu. This was the same clergyman with whom Thérèse had traveled from Montmorency to Switzerland, and who had safeguarded her against seduction.

Rousseau's mood improved with his health. Lord Keith left for Scotland and Rousseau lost a friend and protector. But Lord Keith did not stay in Scotland for long and returned to be with King Frederick II in Berlin, though he never met personally with Rousseau again.

The leader of the Genevan opposition, Deluc, asked Rousseau to come to Geneva to fight for the law but Rousseau refused. Following the dismissal of the first *représentation,* signed by four hundred citizens, the opposition formed a second *représentation* that had already been signed by six hundred people. But even this was turned down without any official reaction. A third *représentation,* formed on August 20, went so far as to ask that the laws in Geneva be expounded by the *grand conseil* and not by the currently ruling *petit conseil.* The *petit conseil* replied to this requirement with an interpretation of *droit négativ,* which allowed them to decide whether a *représentation* was permissible or not.

The political situation in Geneva escalated and public opinion was split into two major groups—*Répresentants* who used Rousseau as their notice board and were led by Duclos, and *Négativs* who supported the *petit conseil* and had in their ranks the procurator general Robert Tronchin. Tronchin wrote a defense in the form of a pamphlet in September, known as *Lettres de la campagne* (Letters from the Country). Deluc asked Rousseau to write a reply to this letter and Rousseau started his work on *"Lettres de la montagne"* (Letters from the Mountain).

He was already looking forward to winter because in the summer he had to receive visitors from France and Switzerland who were annoying to him. His correspondence with the Luxembourgs was declining and he corresponded only with Mme de Verdelin and Mme de Bouffleurs. She persisted in her efforts to convince Rousseau that an asylum in England was the best solution for him. But England did not attract Rousseau.

He revealed in a letter to Mme de Verdelin that he wished to move to France where he had spent the best years of his life. He revealed the real reason to one of his Swiss visitors: he would prefer to die in a Catholic country than in a Protestant one because while the Catholics preached intolerance the Protestants were practicing it.

He did not like the portrait of Mme Alissan and sent it back to her, together with a coldly respectful letter, and *"trés bonne Marianne"* of his previous letters became *"madame"* again.

Rousseau tried to show in "Letters from the Mountain" that his writings did not undermine government or religion and that the ruling elite of Geneva was systematically violating the Republic's constitution. He did not use his *Du Contract social* as a criterion for his criticism because its principles did not apply to the real situation of Geneva. Genevan citizens formed only a privileged minority which included less than a third of all the inhabitants of Geneva, unlike in his *Contract* where *each* society member was a citizen. Another difference was that, while in *Contract* Rousseau had argued against a division of power balanced between several political bodies, in "Letters from the Mountain" he defended the same arrangement.

He did not criticize Geneva on the grounds of not living up to the standards presented in *Social Contract*, but rather because Geneva did not adhere to its own constitution. The division of power introduced historically in 1738 followed the outbreak of civil unrest in Geneva. He adduced in *Letters* the example of England, as a country in which the power was successfully balanced. (Let us recall that in his *Social Contract* Rousseau wrote that Englishmen deemed themselves to be free, which was a mistake. They are free only on election day. As soon as the election is over they are enslaved.)

It is obvious that Rousseau's attitude toward Geneva had changed dramatically. In the dedication to his *Discours sur l'inégalité* in 1755, Rousseau still saw Geneva as the paragon of a system of government with happy and free citizens. Now he maintained that the citizens of Geneva were being suppressed by their own government and he tried to support them. Geneva of the fifteenth century still had its legislative body, the *conseil général*. But the power of this body disappeared and was replaced by the license of twenty-five despots. Rousseau's *Letters* are pithier than *Social Contract* and became very useful for the Genevan opposition.

The publication of Tronchin's "Letters from the Country" had significantly weakened the influence of Genevan opposition and its members anxiously awaited Rousseau's "Letters from the Mountain." The work on it was kept secret and it was never mentioned directly. Its code name—used in the letters—was "Melody of the Mandolin."

At the beginning of 1764 *Imitation théatrale*, a short essay by Rousseau was published (Voltaire wrote his bookseller asking him to send Rousseau's latest "vomits" about the theatre). Duchesne and Guy published an anthology of his works. One of the author's copies was sent to Mme Alissan, which was received as a gesture of reconciliation, and *"Chère Marianne"* and *"Mon cher Jean-Jacques"* returned into their correspondence.

While the visits died down the following winter, the correspondence was carefully upheld. A new correspondent was Prince Louis of Württenberg, who admired Rousseau and attempted to educate his daughter in accordance with the principles of *Émile,* but found out that the education described in the book was intended only for boys. Rousseau ordered that, similar to the boys, he educate his daughter using the Spartan way of cold baths, thin clothing and walking without shoes or boots, even in snow. The prince obeyed blindly, saying that his wife was called Sophie, his daughter was named Sophie as well, and *Émile's* tutor was his teacher and friend. The prince disobeyed the advice of Dr. Tissot and the small Sophie paid dearly for it—she died at the age of twelve. This historical illustration shows the real extent of Rousseau's influence on some of his contemporaries.

"Letters from the Mountain" should have been published originally in Avingon, but the local inquisitor forbade the publication. In July 1764 Rousseau sent the manuscript to Rey who promised to publish it in November, despite Rousseau's warning that it will make many Genevans into his enemies.

Further information about Rousseau, his character and his stay in Môtiers, comes from the somewhat inaccurate memoirs of a young aristocrat from Neuchâtel (and future count of the Holy Roman Empire), François-Louis d'Escherny. He visited Rousseau and the two made music together and went on mountain hikes.

Other valuable sources regarding Rousseau at that time are the letters of Jakob-Heinrich Meister, written to his father. Meister was to become the collaborator and follower of Grimm in his *Correspondance littéraire.* But at the time of his first meeting with Rousseau, Meister was an eighteen-year-old youth and a chaplain in Zürich. As he spent only the summertime in Môtiers, when Rousseau's health was better, he described him as a man with strong health. He described his exterior, his eloquence (especially when enthused over something), his dark complexion and black eyes.

He remembered what Rousseau told him about books, namely that they did more wrong than good; books insulted those who did not understand them and were useless for those who understood them. The secret of his literary style was allegedly his belief in what he wrote. That is, according to Rousseau, he was able to believe in it even when it was not true. He revealed to his visitors that he loved Italian poets and despised their French counterparts. His favorite authors were Plutarch, Tacitus and Homer, and among the recent authors he admired Buffon, Montesquieu and Gessner. Meister wrote that his voice was charming and harmonious.

He took the young men on several mountain trips, getting them into a proper sweat. Once they even lost their way and one of them said flatteringly how good it was to get lost with the famous Rousseau. Rousseau allegedly replied not to compliment him, would he not prefer to get lost with a pretty girl?

In summer 1764 one of Rousseau's most faithful friends died, the duke of Luxembourg, who had done many good things for Rousseau. As the duke was very sick and unable to write to Rousseau in the last months of his life, Rousseau assumed that the duke had forgotten about him, and his letter of condolence to the duchess was formulated ungratefully and reproachfully. After her modest response, Rousseau formulated his subsequent letter more politely but their old friendship was never restored.

In *Confessions* Rousseau accused the doctors of the duke's death: "The first of them was M. de Luxembourg, who after suffering long torment from the doctors at last fell a victim to them. For they treated his gout, which they refused to recognize, as a disease which they could cure."

Rousseau could not complain about lack of friends in this period of his life. He made the acquaintance of a Neuchâtel patrician, colonel Abraham de Pury who had a chalet north of Môtiers—"Molési"—where a society of men gathered. They called themselves the "*salon de philosophes.*" It was here that Rousseau first met Jean-Antoine d'Ivernois, a physician and botanist, who later became his teacher in this discipline. Botany was to become Rousseau's passion.

Another and still more important of Rousseau's friends was Pierre-Alexandre Du Peyrou, whom Rousseau called "the American" because he came from a Huguenot family that had once settled in Dutch Guyana. He was a swarthy, reticent man who had become rich as a slave trader. He was deaf and suffered from gout. At one time he had proposed to Mme de Pury, but she preferred the colonel. Out of love for the mother, the forty-year-old Du Peyrou later married her eighteen-year-old daughter, Henriette. In spite of his afflu-ence (let us remember that Rousseau announced that affluence was the reason of his hatred for Baron Holbach), Rousseau grew fond of him and admitted that wealth did not have to hinder friendship.

With these and other friends Rousseau went on trips to the surroundings, for example to Mont Chasseron, from the peak of which one can overlook seven Swiss lakes. The trips were organized with military strictness: the colonel, as the navigator, was equipped with a compass; provender, blankets and a rich supply of wine were transported on a mule. Both d'Escherny and Meister have recorded that Rousseau was in good physical shape; he climbed "as a goat." They spent the nights in barns, on grass, and Rousseau's reply to the customary question in the morning "Did you sleep well?" was invariably that he did not sleep at all. Colonel Pury stopped him and said he had heard him snoring all night and that it was he who did not close his eyes.

In June, Rousseau and François-Henri d'Ivernois (a Genevan business-man—not to be confused with the physician, Jean-Antoine d'Ivernois), one of the leaders of the Genevan opposition, went on several days' hike to Yverdon, Goumoüens and environs. Rousseau did not mention his companion very flat-teringly in *Confessions* (when he wrote this chapter he was desolate and saw everything in dark colors), although he spoke of him very amicably in his let-ters from that time. François-Henri d'Ivernois helped to publish and distribute the *Letters* in Geneva and rendered multifarious services to Rousseau. Rousseau also accepted gifts from him and perhaps reciprocated by getting him peerage, with the help of Lord Keith.

Rousseau's trips to the surroundings of Môtiers were motivated by a desire to escape from intrusive visitors. They also provided a good opportuni-ty to find a new sanctuary because both he and Thérèse started to detest Môtiers and its inhabitants.

In August 1764 Rousseau went to the spa, Aix-les-Bains, because he was plagued by sciatica and while there he used the opportunity to visit his old friends, Conzié, in nearby Chambéry in Les Charmettes, and Gauffecourt in Lyon. In Thonon, on the Savoy side of Lake Geneva, he had a political ren-dezvous with a group of Genevan oppositionists—*Répresentants*. Rousseau stipulated that no women be present. At that time he had already completed his work on "Letters from the Mountain" though he did not reveal anything from his work at the meeting.

In spite of his efforts to keep the work a secret, its contents got leaked to the public in France before publication. Though Rousseau had concrete suspicions, he did not want to betray them in *Confessions*. At the end of the meeting, Rousseau got sick during a spell of bad weather and returned to Môtiers.

Mme de Verdelin wanted to send him some money, which almost resulted in a bitter parting of these two good friends. Mme de Verdelin's annual income after the death of her husband was 20,000 francs and, because she had moved to a smaller flat and kept only four servants, she could live on it with her daughter quite comfortably. (By comparison, Voltaire set the annual income of his mistress, Mme Denis, at 20,000 francs.)

Rousseau was not short of money at that time because he got paid by Rey and his Parisian publishers, as we learn from a letter sent to Mme de Bouffleurs. He wrote to her about his new love, botany, which was the right occupation for an "active body and lazy soul." Mme de Bouffleurs had also lost her husband. But she regretted more the loss of her influential lover, Prince de Conti, who did not marry her, as she had expected, but became the prior of the Knights of Malta.

In early fall 1763 Rousseau stayed for a week with Thérèse in the chalet Champ-de-Moulin near Brot. In his favorite pub, La Couronne, owned by the Sandoz family (who were obliged to him for an intercession with Lord Keith), Rousseau met the count Charles von Zinzendorf, an imperial valet from Vienna who planned to visit him in Môtiers. Rousseau received the count courteously and, as Zinzendorf himself recorded, rewarded, or rather, punished, the count by taking him for a long and difficult trip around Gorges de l'Arleuse, about which the count wrote that "I had to skip from one boulder to another as a goat." A short lunch was followed by still another trip to a peak overlooking the abyss La Clusette. Pastor Montmollin recompensed the count for these hardships with anecdotes about his prominent parishioner.

Matteo Buttafoco, a Corsican officer, visited Rousseau at that time, and Rousseau was pleased by his visit. Buttafoco asked Rousseau if he would prepare a draft of a new constitution for Corsica, which had obtained a de facto independence from Genoa some time before. Rousseau wrote in the *Social Contract* that a wise man would teach good people how they could preserve their freedom and was therefore enthused by the proposal of the Corsican captain. The captain promised to send Rousseau all necessary materials about the history and laws of Corsica. Rousseau wrote openly about this project in his letters and the news became public in no time, so much so that the *Gazette de Bern* announced that Rousseau had been invited to go to Corsica as a governor.

In the fall of that year Samuel Fauche, a bookseller from Neuchâtel, approached Rousseau and offered to publish his collected works. Rousseau reckoned the profit of the bookseller and publisher would amount to roughly 100,000 francs, of which the author usually got one quarter. But he was not sure if such a profit was possible in Neuchâtel. Du Peyrou offered to sponsor this project and Rousseau gratefully accepted, but he refused to accept Du Peyrou's offer to move to a small house near the latter's residence in Bellevue. Rousseau also asked Du Peyrou to act as his representative in dealings with publishers in Neuchâtel.

Rey sent the copies of "Letters from the Mountain" to Paris, and the list of persons to be sent author's copies informs us about the circle of Rousseau's friends of that time. Among the women were the duchess of Luxembourg, Comtesse de Bouffleurs, Marquise de Verdelin, Marquise de Créquie, Mme Alissan, and Mme de Chenonceaux. Among the men were Watelet, Duclos, d'Alembert, Panckouke (the publisher), the painter La Tour (held in high esteem by Rousseau), Coindet, Lorenzi and the banker, Rougemont, who helped to transfer Rousseau's income to Môtiers.

Apparing on the scene at the time was the "colorful bird" James Boswell, a twenty-four-year-old adventurer who enraptured Rousseau by a mixture of charm and impudence (let us remember how often Rousseau fell for similar adventurers and how often he himself acted in a similar manner). Boswell wanted to get to know the famous philosopher and introduced himself as a Scottish laird from an old Scottish family (at other times he gave himself the title Baron Boswell d'Auchinleck), who had the reference of Lord Keith which he had unfortunately lost. In a letter to Rousseau, he introduced himself as a man of extraordinary merits. He wrote that he had got into a peculiar situation and needed advice. His strategy was effective and Rousseau asked him to come for a visit.

Thanks to Boswell's notes we are informed about their conversations, and also about some interesting details of Rousseau's daily life. Boswell's records also contain a description of Thérèse, whom he wooed at first and later seduced on the way to England, or should we rather say that she willingly agreed with the seduction? When the dressed-up Boswell arrived for his first visit, Thérèse received him at the door. He wrote about her that she was "a little, lively, neat French girl and did not increase my fear [nervousness]." At that time Thérèse was forty-two, could have been his mother, and was obviously used by Boswell as the instrument to gain access to Rousseau.

Their first conversation shifted to Lord Keith and King Frederick II. Rousseau criticized the clergy, attacked Frenchmen and spoke favorably of Scotsmen. He did not forget to tell Boswell that he had been asked to write a draft of the Corsican constitution. Boswell's manners were very relaxed; he held Rousseau's hand and patted Rousseau on the shoulder.

At a second visit, which was mediated by Thérèse, the conversation turned to abbé Saint-Pierre and his Project for Eternal Peace; Boswell told Rousseau that he had converted to Catholicism and wanted to take an order, which Rousseau dismissed as stupidity. Boswell admitted he had a gloomy nature and asked Rousseau if he had it too. He also asked Rousseau if he was a Christian and would he like to become his spiritual leader. Rousseau refused, referring to the fact that he was a sick man suffering from pains, and told him that "I need the chamber pot every minute" (apparently Rousseau developed ischuria paradoxa—see the medical analysis in Part 2). The conversation was held in bad but intelligible French.

In a letter written after his departure—he sent it to Rousseau through Thérèse—Boswell described his amorous adventures in Scotland where he got involved with a married woman. Rousseau recommended that Boswell discontinue this relationship immediately. In another discussion Boswell confessed that he would like to have thirty women, as was usual in the Orient. Rousseau objected that these women were slaves. Boswell replied that polygamy was not forbidden, even in the Old Testament, but Rousseau insisted that we must respect the laws of the country in which we live.

Finally Boswell was asked to come for lunch (if he would not be too hungry, as Rousseau told him). Boswell came willingly and ahead of time, allegedly to help Thérèse cook the soup. He must have flirted with her because they went together to the village where they distributed goods to the needy. Boswell's account reveals that a lunch at Rousseau's at that time was quite luxurious compared to our time: excellent soup, cooked beef and veal, mixed vegetables, cold pork, preserved trout and a bowl of something Boswell forgot, and as a dessert, peas and walnuts. They drank white and red wines. Boswell behaved attentively to Thérèse in spite of Rousseau's presence. Before he left, he promised to write to her from time to time and asked what he should buy her as a present in Geneva. Thérèse expressed a desire for a necklace of garnets which later she actually received. Boswell allegedly said, "You have treated me with great kindness, but I deserve it." To which Rousseau allegedly replied, "Yes, you are a rogue, but a nice rogue. A rogue that I like."

The copies of "Letters from the Mountain" were smuggled into Geneva where their effect resembled that of "fire in a powder magazine"; these words were used by François d'Ivernois in a letter to Rousseau. The stance of *petit conseil* was surprisingly temporizing and cautious. The government was not interested in anything that would further escalate the political situation. Voltaire's reaction was quite indignant and he demanded that the "blasphemous insurgent" be punished "with the whole strength of the law." Though Voltaire always pretended, particularly to his friends, that he was Rousseau's friend and that he even protected him, in fact he hated him—the reason for this hatred remains obscure.

Rousseau supplied his Genevan allies with advice as to how to organize their political resistance and the results were not long in coming. On New Year's Day the election of the new municipal syndic was held and the most liberal of all the candidates, Jean Jallabert, a known scientist who knew Rousseau, was elected. Perhaps this was the reason why the *petit conseil*, which was sliding into the defensive, did not take any steps against Rousseau.

Voltaire, however, was determined to pillory Rousseau and published a pamphlet attacking him, written in the style of a Calvinist pastor: "*Le Sentiments de citoyens*." In it, Rousseau was accused of being a hypocrite and Antichrist, carrying the omen of his debauchery, dragging with him his pitiful wife whose mother he had killed and whose children he abandoned in front of the gates of a foundling home. He had renounced all natural feelings and had the effrontery to advise his fellow citizens and speak about the duties of society. The effect of this cruel criticism on Rousseau was terrible. He assumed at first that the pamphlet had been written by Jacob Vernet.

Rousseau's friends from Geneva and Bern praised his "Letters from the Mountain"—although Paris was not particularly interested in the politics of the remote Geneva. The publication was rejected by abbé de Mably, an early theorist of socialism and communism.

But the impact of the work and Voltaire's pamphlet was most serious in Môtiers. Pastor Montmollin was pleased to have received the copy of "Letters" but found it contained the same unorthodox religious ideas as *Émile*. "*Le*

Sentiments de citoyens" shed a new light on Thérèse, who was already unpopular in the village.

Rousseau contemplated writing a response to Voltaire's pamphlet and was already corresponding with Duchesne and Guy, but then changed his mind. He knew all too well that the malevolent pamphlet contained facts that he could not easily deny and that he could not exonerate himself. He said to Charles Duclos that he intended to write the story of his whole life, to be published after his death. It should not be his memoirs but a confession of his life. Voltaire's pamphlet certainly was one of the reasons for his writing *Confessions* (Rousseau died on July 2, 1778 and *Confessions* was published in 1781).

Meanwhile he spent the winter months learning more about botany. He painted the flora of the Jura Mountains and also used a microscope, although he did not pursue it as a scientific activity but as a hobby, helping him to forget his personal troubles. His "Letters from the Mountain" were banned and burned in Paris, Bern and in The Hague.

He did not feel safe in Môtiers any more and mentioned in his letters to Lord Keith that he had thought of other possible places where he could stay. One of the places he wanted to go was Italy, which had a better climate than England. Lord Keith recommended that Rousseau apply for asylum in Germany. During this difficult time he tried to keep up the correspondence with his friends. He started writing again to "beloved Marianne" and Mme de Verdelin.

As late as the first weeks of 1765 Rousseau advised his Genevan friends how they should proceed (he recommended proceeding peacefully, not to vilify the *petit conseil*, and to abstain from aggression). In early February, however, the *petit conseil* resorted to a courageous political move that was to thwart all political ambitions of the opposition. Nineteen of the twenty-five magistrates threatened to step down collectively if they did not receive the confidence of Genevan citizens. A significant majority of the citizens surrendered and declared themselves loyal to the government.

Rousseau was disgusted and caught unawares by this development, the more so as the *petit conseil* forced the citizens to declare they condemned Rousseau's publication "Letters from the Mountain" as a libelous collection and as an unworthy and false attack on religion. The *petit conseil* linked this with a promise to fulfill all reasonable demands of the citizens. Rousseau lost all power with the Genevan opposition and he himself announced, in a letter to Lenieps, he was giving up any interference with Genevan politics because all his love of truth and justice resulted only in evil. He did not want to hear anything about Geneva. The "Letters from the Mountain" were publicly burned in Paris on March 19, 1765, together with Voltaire's *Philosophical Dictionary.*

On February 13, 1765 the clergy of Neuchâtel demanded that "Letters from the Mountain," as well as the planned publication of Rousseau's collected works, be banned. The municipal drummer of Neuchâtel was sent to the streets of Neuchâtel to announce to everybody that none of Rousseau's books was allowed to be sold in town. Lord Keith advised Rousseau to leave because the king enjoyed only a limited authority in Neuchâtel. It was certainly a reasonable piece of advice. But Rousseau's friends in Neuchâtel asked him to stay and Rousseau decided to fight the local clergy.

As in Geneva, Rousseau was suddenly embroiled in municipal politics; he stood on the side of the king's representatives who struggled with local clergy and the scum of the city—canaille who were exploited by the clergy. The *conseil d'état* consisted of the king's representatives, joined by patricians who had their own political plans and different ideas of the form of government. The monarchists and philosophers belonged to Rousseau's supporters.

Unlike Geneva, where the procurator general Tronchin was opposed to Rousseau, the procurator general of Neuchâtel, Samuel Meuron (1703–1777), adhered to the decree of the king that promised Rousseau safety and support and acknowledged tolerance. Also on Rousseau's side were two retired colonels, Jean-Frédéric Chaillet and Abraham de Pury, together with Du Peyrou.

The local pastor in Môtiers, Montmollin, who up until now had not expressed his disapproval of "Letters from the Mountain," of a sudden recommended that Rousseau not attend the Easter Communion in the church and warned him against excommunication. Rousseau sent a letter to Meuron and informed him about this. He tried to placate Montmollin by a declaration in which he promised not to write about religious issues any more.

Lord Keith, who was in Berlin, was unable to obtain permission for the publication of Rousseau's collected works in Neuchâtel, but succeeded only in obtaining the promise that the "Letters from the Mountain" would not be banned there. He repeated his advice that Rousseau leave and offered him fifty louis in case he did not have enough money. He asked the British *chargé d'af-*

faires in Potsdam, Alexander Burnett, to help ensure that the persecuted Rousseau would be granted asylum in England. His backers in Neuchâtel approached him again and asked him not to satisfy the hopes of the city clergy because they wanted him to stay.

The *vénérable classe* decided in its session in March that Rousseau would be summoned to appear in front of the parochial consistory to answer for his religious views. The commission included both sides—the followers of the clergy and pastor Montmollin, who, as Rousseau reported, tried to influence them with wine from his own cellar, and the followers of Rousseau.

Rousseau was very upset about the summons because he would be allegedly unable to speak freely in front of the gathering. He drew up his speech and memorized it, which earned him the ridicule of Thérèse. In the morning, however, he had completely forgotten his memorized defense. He did not appear in front of the commission and used his bad health as an excuse.

Only two of the five commission members present voted with Montmollin and the remaining three turned to the *conseil d'état* with an inquiry: Was the commission even authorized to investigate in matters of religion and faith? The *conseil* notified the consistory that they could investigate only in matters of morality but not in those of faith. On the whole, Rousseau prevailed and Montmollin lost.

The dispute partially calmed down the whole situation around Rousseau but it was becoming increasingly clear that Rousseau could not stay in Môtiers for good. Conzié was offering him a refuge in Les Charmettes in Savoy but warned him that he would not be able to wear his Armenian caftan and would have to remain incognito. The invitation to Berlin was also not reliable. Lord Keith repeated his offer of England but without any concrete invitation. England was recommended also by Mme de Verdelin, although she now admitted she regarded Englishmen more critically. This applied also to David Hume who had the reputation of a favorite of all pretty women and was therefore not her favorite.

She promised Rousseau she would arrange a permit for him that would allow him a safe passage through France, and sent him 1,000 francs to pay for the transport to England. Rousseau sent the money back but did not rule out possibly needing it later. He gratefully accepted the *laissez-passer*. Rodolphe de Vautravers offered him the invitation to stay at his residence "Rockhall" near Biel (Bienne). De Vautravers was, like many of the people to whom Rousseau was attracted, a little bit of a charlatan who got rich as an antiquarian book-seller in England, where he even became a member of the Royal Society in London after he published a treatise on earthquakes. Biel was an enclave under the jurisdiction of the prince-bishop of Basel and was independent of Bern, from where Rousseau had already been expelled when in Yverdon.

Rousseau's health got better again and he made trips to inspect the loca-tions which had been offered to him as possible refuges. In the pub, La Couronne, he met his faithful Bernese admirer, Julie von Bondeli, who described her two meetings with Rousseau in letters to Usteri. At that time Rousseau enjoyed excellent health; he wrote to Du Peyrou that the excursion to Biel was good for both his body and soul.

Rousseau's correspondence with his Parisian publishers, Duchesne and Guy (Duchesne died later that year and the publishing house was then head-ed by Guy), was concerned mainly with the edition of the *Dictionary of Music* for which he was to receive yearly annuities of three hundred francs (in *Confessions* the sum is mentioned as three hundred thalers) and one hundred louisidors in cash.

He had been working for some time on *Confessions,* which was to be pub-lished after his death. He admitted, however, he was unable to keep his mem-ories in order as he would have liked, and did not observe the chronological order of the described events. In addition to that, he also contemplated the publication of his collected works. Since he was not writing anything new, he feared his financial reserves could get depleted. We have to realize that Rousseau was the first writer who lived solely on writing books, if we disre-gard note copying.

He often left Môtiers, where he did not feel well, to undertake longer trips and also to escape the many unwelcome visitors, inter alia his English transla-tor William Kenrick. He visited Daniel Roguin and his niece, Mme Boy, who was then sick in Yverdon. In Pierrenod he met François d'Ivernois (who hoped Rousseau would help him obtain—via Lord Keith—a peerage from the king of Prussia, similar to Colonel de Pury, who had gotten the appointment of *con-seiller d'état*). D'Ivernois briefed Rousseau on interesting news from Geneva: Voltaire was allegedly telling people in Geneva that in his youth Rousseau was employed at the Venetian embassy, not as a secretary to the ambassador but as his servant.

When Rousseau returned to Môtiers on June 9, he once more got involved with clerical dignitaries. Since spring, pastor Montmollin had been regularly preaching at church against nonbelievers and Antichrists. He did not mention Rousseau directly but it was an open secret that Rousseau was the target of the pastor's criticism. On May 22, King Frederick expressed his disapproval of the sermons that were disrupting the peace, but this was not of any great help.

Montmollin suspected Rousseau was the author of a pamphlet attacking the pastor. But the pamphlet, which became known as "Lettre de Goa," originated from Du Peyrou. Montmollin wrote a reply in which he stated that in his "Letters from the Mountain" Rousseau continued to express the heretical views contained in *Émile* and was, moreover, attacking the Protestant clergy (particularly the clergy of Geneva).

This publication moved Rousseau to write a sharp rejoinder (thereby breaking his promise not to write about religious issues any more). He described his contacts with Montmollin from the very beginning, and held his hypocrisy against him as well as his incessant inciting of people in his sermons. In these sermons Montmollin called his parishioners *la canaille* and women *les caillettes*. Rousseau's letter was printed in October and in it he called the inhabitants of Môtiers wild beasts.

It is understandable that Rousseau was always very glad when he could escape from Môtiers. He undertook a botanical expedition to La Ferrière together with the French officer Feins. But he could not enjoy the expedition because he got a cold, suffered from fever and could not pursue botany at all. His next trip led Rousseau to the isle of St-Pierre in Lake Biel. He described this trip in a letter to Du Peyrou, who could not travel with him because of an attack of gout. Here Rousseau mentioned for the first time that he started his work on *Confessions*, his principal work.

In a letter to François d'Ivernois, Rousseau wrote that he spent eight or ten glad days at the isle though unwelcome visitors surrounded him. But the visit of M. de Graffenried, the prefect in Nidau, was not unwelcome. Karl Emmanuel von Graffenried (1732–1780) was a member of a noble Bernese family, the same family from which also Mlle de Graffenried came. As a youth, Rousseau had spent one unforgettable day with her in a cherry orchard in Thônes. M. de Graffenried greeted Rousseau on the Bernese territory and assured him that he was welcome there. Rousseau took his words for granted, overestimating the prefect's influence.

Pierre Guy managed the publishing house after the late Duchesne in his widow's behalf (la Veuve Duchesne). As a capable businessman, he started to collect Rousseau's letters and excerpts from his writings under the title "*Esprit, Maximes et Principes de M. Jean-Jacques Rousseau de Genève.*" He also added material to *Rousseau's Collected Works* which was being published by La Porte. The publication of *Rousseau's Collected Works* was forbidden in France. But the work was printed in the Netherlands and smuggled into France.

The demand for Rousseau's banned works was huge and already thirteen pirate editions of *Social Contract* had been brought out since Rousseau left France in 1762. The publishers made great profit on his books and it is therefore no wonder that Guy, who was offered the publication of Du Peyrou's "*Lettre de Goa*" and Rousseau's subsequent replies to it, replied that he would happily accept and publish anything sent to him by Rousseau. He sent Thérèse some presents and Rousseau several books on botany. In August 1765 Mme Boy visited Rousseau, accompanied by her daughter, Madelon, and Colonel Chaiellet from Colombiere. Rousseau invited the colonel to dinner and played chess with him.

In early September Rousseau received another visitor, Mme de Verdelin, with her daughter. The journey that the marquise had to make to reach the Val de Travers was certainly very difficult. She had to travel in a narrow carriage that would allow her to pass through the valley on her way from Pontalier. This testifies to the genuineness of her friendship. In their correspondence they invariably addressed each other as "*mon voisin*" and "*ma voisin*," in reminiscence of their neighborhood in Montmorency. The daughter and servants stayed in a local inn and the marquise slept in the "salon" of Rousseau's house.

On Sunday, after one of the impassioned sermons of pastor Montmollin, the marquise witnessed how the inflamed parishioners attacked Rousseau in spite of her presence and how several rocks hit Rousseau's house at night. The marquise abstained from any comments, probably out of politeness, much to Rousseau's disappointment. She reminded him of Hume's offer that he could live in England. Mme de Verdelin left on September 3 to resume her stay in the spa of Bourbonne. The same day, Rousseau undertook a walk in his Armenian costume and was again attacked, and this time weapons were used.

On Friday, September 6, an annual fair took place in Môtiers and drunken citizens, as they returned to their homes that night, threw rocks at Rousseau's house. In a letter to Pierre Guy, Rousseau wrote that the raging *canaille* damaged the door of his house, broke several windows, and that a rock as big as a head landed in his bedroom. The case was investigated and the outcome was a recommendation that Rousseau leave Môtiers.

Pastor Montmollin was safe. Two of his cousins were members of the *conseil d'état* and some of his wife's relatives were employed as clerks. To defend the pastor, a legend was circulated that it could have been Thérèse herself who threw the rock through the window, and that she gathered rocks on the balcony of their house because she wanted Rousseau to leave Môtiers.

Other testimonies, however, make it much more probable that it was indeed the intoxicated rabble who attacked the house of the "Antichrist." Rousseau was simply too different, and what was worse, he stressed his dissimilarity by wearing grotesque clothing, which irritated local people. He had different religious views and lived in a household with a woman whose faith was altogether different. Consequently, there were many reasons to provoke an outbreak of intolerance.

The inhabitants of Môtiers were living evidence of the incorrectness of Rousseau's theory that the simple highlanders were better than a refined society. Rousseau never realized that the degree of primitiveness of a society correlated with the degree of intolerance that could be found in it. Tolerance can develop only after people have learned to appreciate the relativity of truth.

According to an agreement that was reached after the nighttime attack, Rousseau was to leave immediately, whereas Thérèse was to stay and a guard was sent to her assistance to protect the house. It is perhaps interesting to mention that Rousseau was visited by a group of citizens from a nearby village, Couvet, who came to offer him a new shelter (Rousseau had previously been granted citizenship of Couvet). But he refused because Couvet was situated too close to Môtiers.

Mme de Verdelin wrote from Paris that Lord Walpole wanted to offer Rousseau a sanctuary on his estate in England and mentioned some particulars of his stay. Lord Keith asked him to follow him to Potsdam and live with him, and Rousseau was inclined to accept this offer because Frederick II had also expressed an "invitation of a kind." The account in *Confessions* stresses Rousseau's love of Switzerland that made him decide to stay in the end.

The first night following the incident, Rousseau slept in the house of his friend, Du Peyrou, who was tolerated in Neuchâtel mainly because of his wealth. The next day, Monday, September 9, Rousseau settled with his dog Sultan at the isle of St-Pierre in Lake Biel which he had visited on one of his previous trips. The isle was once occupied by monks and was part of a Bernese spital (the hospital standing there today is still called "Inselspital"). In Neuchâtel the island was called Mothe. The only inhabitants of the island, the Engel family, accommodated Rousseau in a large room, which has been preserved up to this day.

The island has barely changed since Rousseau's time. Here he felt peaceful and safe, as he wrote to Mme Boy. He said he would like to stay here till the end of his life. The choice of the island corresponded to his desire to be alone.

He felt secure financially. He agreed to be paid a pension of six hundred francs offered to him by Lord Keith, although he obstinately refused to accept financial gifts from other people; he was being paid three hundred francs from Guy for his *Dictionary of Music,* and also some money from Du Peyrou for the publishing rights to his works after his death.

He described the island not only in *Confessions,* on which he was writing at the time, but also in *Rêveries,* written toward the end of his life when he devoted an entire chapter to the island—"the fifth stroll." He asked himself what the quintessence of happiness was and his answer read: idleness—*far niente*— and solitude. But in his real life Rousseau was not inactive and was seldom totally isolated.

He worked on *Confessions* and on "Project of Corsican Constitution" the draft of which he had promised to Captain Buttafoco. The underlying idea of the project was a recommendation, somewhat paradoxical in his situation, that Corsica should imitate Switzerland. After his bad experiences in Geneva he clearly could not recommend this city, or the rich Bern, but he suggested that Corsica imitate the more agricultural cantons in eastern Switzerland (Glarus, Uri, Schwyz, Appenzell, Unterwalden). These had simple agricultural social systems, which Rousseau, however, did not know from his own experience.

He condemned industry and maintained that every society should be self-sufficient, that money should be replaced by barter of goods. This would make money irrelevant and it would not divide people into rich and poor any more. Also public servants should be paid in kind and citizens should not pay taxes, rendering the state various services instead. Every man should be called into the army and become a soldier. Private property is allowed but it should be limited to amounts as small as possible, whereas the property of the state should be considerable. He recommended direct democracy where the laws are determined by the citizens themselves and the formation of hereditary aristocracy must be prevented under all circumstances. All should be equal from the time of their birth. The project was never completed—Captain Buttafoco never received it. Rousseau handed the incomplete manuscript to Moultou shortly before his death and it was not published until 1861.

In addition to writing, Rousseau pursued botany and intended to publish a collection of the entire flora of the island, *Flora Petriinsularis*. In *Confessions* Rousseau expressed his enthusiasm about the island's nature which represented mother for him: "O Nature! O my Mother! Here am I under thy sole protection: here no cunning, two-faced man can come between us." He often enjoyed being cradled by the waves in the boat (to the displeasure of his dog, Sultan), or visiting a second, small, uninhabited islet where he felt like Robinson Crusoe. He pompously set out a colony of rabbits on the islet that he had brought in by boat, which was recorded in a picture by the painter Monsiaux. The picture also shows Thérèse on the boat—she came to the island on Monday, September 23.

One day Rousseau was picking apples and was surprised by his young Bernese friend, Nicolas-Antoine Kirchberger; other visitors came as well, from Bienne and surrounding locations. An important visitor was the director of a Bernese hospital, Friedrich Zehender (October 15). Rousseau tried to make a good impression on him but soon, on October 16, he was informed by the prefect Graffenried that the latter had received orders that Rousseau must leave the island.

Rousseau was stupefied because he had no idea where to go. But in fact he was quite familiar with the relentlessness of Bernese authorities and must have expected he would be expelled. One can easily imagine that his stay on the island was in fact a provocation. The deportation made a martyr and persecuted prophet of him, before the eyes of the whole world, which certainly suited his masochistic disposition. He even contemplated going to Corsica for which he was to write the draft of a new constitution. He was advised against it by his friends and probably had nothing against dropping this plan himself. He presents several objections against the journey to Corsica in *Confessions*.

In a letter to Mme de Verdelin from October 18, 1765 (who had found her lost enthusiasm for Hume again), Rousseau wrote about his deportation by Bernese authorities that allegedly passed the senate only because the body voted at a time when most politicians were outside of Bern. He was mistaken in that. His deportation was decided by the secret council of Bern and the senate, in which nineteen of the twenty-seven deputies were present, upheld this decision unanimously. Graffenried's appeal to postpone the deportation so that Rousseau could complete the necessary preparations for departure was resolutely rejected. A new order from October 21 allowed him to stay only until the following Saturday.

Rousseau was thus packing up once more. He decided to go to England, "the only country where at least some freedom still remained." Hume assured him that he would be safe in England and started preparing to receive Rousseau with the help of his distant relative John Steward.

Rousseau was very concerned about his manuscripts as well as the letters and documents Thérèse brought from Môtiers. He decided to leave them with his friend Du Peyrou in Neuchâtel. Among the manuscripts were also the first chapters of *Confessions,* which contained the memories of his youth up to his arrival in Paris.

After the order to leave the territory of Bern, Alexander Wildremet offered to let Rousseau settle in the "free town" Bienne (Biel) which was an enclave under the jurisdiction of the bishop of Basel and was independent of Bern. But he spent only several days in Bienne, because Kirchberg informed him some of the city's magistrates were against his stay. The departure from Bienne is the last event described in *Confessions.* Rousseau assumed he would travel to Berlin, but he ended up in England. *Confessions* was not published until after his death but as we learn from the last page of this work, Rousseau used to read from it to aristocratic society during his lifetime.

Rousseau left Bienne on October 27 and reached Basel "in fever, with a sore throat, his dog Sultan" and "death in heart." His friend, the businessman Jean-Jacques de Luze, found a wagon for him and Rousseau left Switzerland on Thursday, October 31, never to see this country again. He continued to Strasbourg. Prefect Graffenried equipped him with a passport designated *"Pour aller en Allemagne."*

He arrived in Strasbourg on Saturday, November 2, and took lodging in the inn La Fleur. He wrote to Thérèse that the journey was horrible. But he was in fact happy to have left Switzerland and its inhabitants, "simple peasants, uncorrupted by civilization," and reach France, the world of marquises and counts, whom he despised, but whose refinement, friendship and help he made use of so willingly.

Strasbourg was a French garrison city where the city's elite spoke French and the common Alsatians spoke German. At first Rousseau wanted to preserve anonymity and remain incognito but was soon surprised by a friendly reception. He was actually glorified and enjoyed this after his experiences in Môtiers. He wrote to Colonel Chaillet that it was sweet to find oneself among human beings after such a long time spent among wolves. Both the commander of the province, Maréchal-Duc de Contades, and the commander of the city, Marquis de Nanclas, a relative of Mme de Verdelin, told him he was welcome in Strasbourg. He was invited into the homes of most of the leading families of the city and was welcomed everywhere with admiration and grace.

His first letters were full of enthusiasm. It took three weeks before he announced for the first time that he was tired of the endless social obligations and that he should become a "bear" again, which was a term he used for himself in winter when he should, as a bear, leave society and "hibernate."

But contrary to his own words, Rousseau did not "hibernate" in Strasbourg. He became involved with theatre. The director of the French theatre, Villeneuve, asked Rousseau for permission to stage his opera *Le Devin du village*, which was also being performed in Paris. The gala performance in Strasbourg was to be attended by the notables of the city. Rousseau feared that the quality of the performance would not be as good as it was in Paris and we know, thanks to the record of an anonymous witness, that he attended the rehearsal of the opera personally, at two o'clock on November 9. Rousseau insisted that even the smallest errors be corrected and that the music be as simple and sweet as the songs of simple people.

The opera was performed the next day and was a huge success. The theatre was full and the box offices had to return the entrance fee to those who could not get into the theatre. Rousseau was very pleased, not only at the success of the play but also when he was asked to permit the performance of his other plays as well, starting with *Narcisse*. Rousseau wrote to Du Peyrou to ask him to send the texts of *Pygmalion* and *L'Engagement téméraire* and to bring them personally when possible. He asked him also to bring Thérèse.

Du Peyrou, who was not very fond of Thérèse, apologized and used his old mother as an excuse. Also, he had to oversee the work on his new house. He sent the requested materials by mail. He also reassured Rousseau, who was worried about Thérèse. Meanwhile, in Strasbourg, *Narcisse* was being rehearsed, a play which Rousseau had declared was a bad play fourteen years previously.

Whereas the situation in Neuchâtel developed well for Pastor Montmollin—together with the local clergy he gained control over the *conseil d'état* and the old order could be restored—in Geneva it was Rousseau's friends who could chalk up dramatic successes. Their party successfully rejected the candidates of the *petit conseil*. Rousseau learned this news from Guillaume-Antoine Deluc and François d'Ivernois, who wrote to him that "the philosopher had inspired the citizens."

Even Voltaire changed his attitude and suddenly became a supporter of the civic party, probably because the *petit conseil* ordered the incineration of his *Dictionaire philosophique*. Voltaire used to receive representatives of the opposition at his Château Ferney and advised them on political strategy. We know that Rousseau explicitly approved of it. In this respect he did not regard his personal feud with Voltaire as important. The decisive question for him was whether Voltaire could help the civic party in Geneva. Though Lenieps asked Rousseau to become involved in Genevan politics once more and even described his ideas as to how to establish a government in Geneva that would correspond to the primary principles of the city, he refused. One reason, among others, was with respect to Versailles, where he was already suspected of provoking unrest by his writings, and which was in a region where France wished to preserve peace and neutrality.

Mme de Boufleurs managed to convince Prince de Conti to offer Rousseau asylum in the Temple of the Knights of Malta which had its own jurisdiction, independent of both Versailles and the parlement of Paris, but this offer came too late. Rousseau had already accepted the offer from Pierre Guy to settle in the house of the widow of the late publisher, Duchesne. Rey, too, offered to take care of him in Amsterdam but Rousseau was not inclined to spend the winter there.

He informed Du Peyrou, in a letter on November 30, 1765, he had decided to go to England, and he wrote to Hume on December 4 (Hume was living in Paris) that he hoped to embrace him in his arms within five or six days. He left Strasbourg only reluctantly and it is actually unclear why he left at all—everybody assured him how welcome he was there. Meanwhile Thérèse remained at the island St-Pierre.

It is important to record, from the medical point of view, that Rousseau was sick only one or two days in the last week of his stay in Strasbourg. The cause of his illness remains unclear but it obviously was not anything serious.

It becomes clear once more that he did not need Thérèse as a nurse (at that time) and that his urinary problem did not occur in her absence. We also know from a remark in a letter from Mme Boy that he had put on weight because he found the belts too short at that time.

Rousseau set out for Paris in a coach on December 9, 1765 at seven o'clock in the morning, accompanied by his dog and taking with him part of his luggage. He refused to travel in a private carriage. On the evening before his departure the theatre performed *Narcisse*. Rousseau thanked the theatre company but did not attend the play and used his departure in the early morning hours next day as an excuse.

The coach arrived in Paris toward the evening on December 16. Rousseau took lodging in the house of the widow Duchesne. He claimed he wanted to remain incognito, as he assured de Lutz, and informed Mme de Verdelin that he would need only two or three days' rest before he could leave the house. In spite of this he promenaded with Sultan in his Armenian costume in the Luxembourg Gardens on the next day, clearly revealing his presence to the public.

On the third day of his stay Rousseau was invited to visit Prince de Conti who arranged for Rousseau to be moved to the elegant Hôtel de St-Simon, after which there was no interruption in the stream of visitors. Among those who came to visit him were de Lutz, Mme de Verdelin and Mme de Bouffleurs.

Prince de Conti invited Rousseau to stay permanently at his château in Trye but Rousseau refused because of "unacceptable terms"—he was probably asked to change his name. Rousseau was soon to meet Hume who was very popular in Paris.

Hume was a fat, clumsy man whose informal behavior was regarded as frankness. Although his French was bad, he had undeniable personal charm and wittiness of spirit. He was a Scotsman, not an Englishman—and he was simply *le bon David* to everyone. In the Seven Years' War, France had lost Canada and India, which became part of the English Empire, and one can understand the French enthusiasm for England was rather limited. Hume was not admired in Paris for his philosophical but rather for his historical works, especially for his *History of England*. In Versailles he was introduced to three sons of the dauphin who were reading passages from his books. The ladies of Paris who vied for influence in political and social matters, which they partially achieved by personal interventions, were united in their admiration for Hume. Mme Geoffrin treated him as her son, Mlle Lespinasse as her father.

Mme de Bouffleurs tried to take possession of Hume as she had done once with Rousseau—her efforts there had not cooled off until after the death of her husband when she entertained hopes she could marry Prince de Conti and become a member of the royal family. But Prince de Conti chose just Hume as his confidant, and asked him to talk her out of this dream as gently as possible.

The diplomatic career of Hume was not exactly clear. He was sent to Paris as the British *chargé d'affaires* but was discharged after several months, in December 1765. Hume saw that Rousseau was not very popular among philosophers. He also knew two of Rousseau's greatest adversaries, Grimm and Holbach. Hume looked critically upon French philosophers—as a skeptic he did not regard their dogmatism as correct, whether it was their dogmatic atheism, political radicalism, or materialistic philosophy.

There were of course similarities as well as differences between Hume and Rousseau. Both were well aware of their exceptionality. But Rousseau was extremely emotional, showing his feelings without restraint; he wept in public and embraced his friends. He was also demanding, tactless and honest. Hume, on the other hand, was very disciplined and did not show any great emotion. Rousseau regarded friendship as a kind of love, whereas for Hume it was a kind of mutually advantageous, friendly relationship.

When Hume and Rousseau met for the first time they agreed that they would travel to England together, and Hume spoke of Rousseau in favorable terms as we learn from a letter he wrote to professor of philosophy Blair in Edinburgh. He wrote that Rousseau was a small man who could almost be described as ugly if it were not for his delicate physiognomy. He was gentle, modest and cheerful. His speech and writing were impulsive and he sometimes gave the impression of being inspired by a direct contact with deity. Sometimes he fell into ecstasy.

Hume wrote that Rousseau's popularity in Paris was enormous. He did not know any other person who would command as much attention as Rousseau; no other nation valued their geniuses more than Frenchmen. Compared to that, neither Voltaire nor others got so much attention. Hume even admitted that his importance in France had risen since he became Rousseau's friend. Even Thérèse got more attention than the princess of Monaco, or the duchess of Egmont, despite her simple nature and rather hideous looks. His dog was known worldwide. We learn from another letter that Rousseau was nearsighted at that time and that the constant stream of visitors made him tired and rather annoyed.

After he moved into the Temple, Rousseau seldom left his asylum. He probably was in no danger of being imprisoned by the agents of the parlement of Paris because these were obviously ordered to cast a blind eye on him. Rousseau was just fleeing its visitors. Invited visitors were granted audience and their selection was overseen by Mme de Bouffleurs who lived in a nearby house. She took care of Rousseau's social life in Paris as well, encouraged the appropriate people to visit Rousseau, and basked in the reflected glory of being his friend.

At that time Rousseau's opera, *Les Muses galantes,* was performed in Prince Conti's private theatre and musical evenings were given in the sumptuous auditorium of the Temple (it was in this auditorium that a young boy named Mozart gave his concerts shortly afterwards but by then Rousseau had already left). Rousseau was most bothered by "ladies of the world" for he had always held their morals in contempt.

Among Rousseau's oldest friends to visit him was the duchess of Luxembourg, but in spite of his presents—Rousseau gave her "Letters from the Mountain" and some Swiss cheese—their friendship still remained as cold as it had been since the death of the duke. Mme de Verdelin was probably the closest of his friends, but she had lost her father, Duke Brémont d'Ars, and she had therefore not much time for her *"cher voisin."* His "epistolary" love, Marianne Alissan, learned of his presence from newspapers and wrote him a reproachful letter but assured him of her lasting love. Rousseau confined himself to a short letter—he expressed his annoyance over her "incessant reproaches"; Marianne wrote him another letter but this time she brought it personally to the Hôtel de St-Simon. Here they met for the first time and, after this, their correspondence returned to the previous *"Mon cher Jean-Jacques"* and *"Chère Marianne."*

Men visited him also: Malesherbes, Morellet and Turgot. It was even rumored that Rousseau reconciled with Diderot. We know from Diderot's letter to Sophie Volland (December 20), that Diderot would have welcomed their meeting, but he did not expect Rousseau to make the first step in which "he would explain his behavior." He, Diderot, would also not make the first step because it was he who had been offended. Madame de Buffon convinced Hume to bring Rousseau to a dinner she gave. Mme Helvétius also tried to invite Rousseau, but to no avail.

He discussed the political situation in Geneva with Lenieps. Lenieps was leaning toward the political radicalism that was expressed by Rousseau in his "Letters from the Mountain." The letters from François d'Ivernois show that he recommended Rousseau employ a rather more moderate approach that should ensure freedom and peace to the citizens. The French diplomacy was not interested in any radicalization of the political situation in Geneva, it sided with the authority of the *petit conseil*. Lenieps himself was later imprisoned in Bastille.

But not all Parisians were Rousseau's friends. Many of them wished that he would leave as soon as possible. One of these, who had neither read Rousseau's works nor had met him, was Horace Walpole who was told, perhaps from Holbach, that Rousseau actually *enjoyed being persecuted*. He wrote Rousseau a fictitious letter—probably for fun and without any intention to harm him—written as if King Frederick II were offering to persecute Rousseau as he wished.

The thought that Rousseau actually felt good if persecuted might appear absurd but it was not mistaken. Rousseau did not require suffering only from sexual masochism, he was also a moral masochist! As a persecuted campaigner for the "truths" and "virtues" he had discovered, he might have felt himself to be the stoned prophet (he regarded himself as a prophet at several occasions), who stood above the slow-witted barbarians and the society as a whole that he was attempting to reform because he was unable to identify with it and adjust to it as a result of his semi-deprived childhood. His attitude was well known during his lifetime and it was only later, as a result of the process of the idealization of Rousseau as a great philosopher, that the veil of oblivion covered it.

The imaginary letter to Rousseau was to play an important role in his subsequent life and it is therefore worthwhile becoming acquainted with it. Horace Walpole wrote:

My dear Jean-Jacques.

You have renounced Geneva, your homeland: you have yourself driven out of Switzerland, a place much praised in your writings; the French have issued a warrant for your arrest; so come to me. I admire your talents; I am amused by your reveries, on which, incidentally, you dwell too much and too long. In the end, you must be wise and happy. You have excited enough talk by singularities that hardly become a truly great man. Show your enemies that you sometimes have common sense. That will annoy them and do you no harm. My states offer you a peaceful refuge. I wish you well and will treat you well if you wish me to. But if you persist in rejecting my help, believe me, I shall tell no one. If you go racking your brains to find new misfortunes, choose what you will. I am King and can provide you with as much suffering as you desire and—something you will not obtain from your enemies—I shall continue persecuting you when you cease to seek glory in being persecuted.

Your good friend,

Frederick

Walpole showed the letter to Helvétius and Duke de Nivernais who revamped Walpole's French and soon the copies of the letter circulated in Paris and were read in the salons. Rousseau himself read it several weeks later when he had already left Paris. The letter was meant to be a joke but those who knew how overly sensitive Rousseau was no doubt knew he would not laugh at it and would see it in only one possible way—as an attack on his person.

Prince de Conti, Mme de Luxembourg, and Mme de Bouffleurs reproached Walpole for his "letter" that they regarded as more cruel than witty. Hume could have known about the letter because he lived under one roof with Walpole in the Hôtel du Parc Royal. Rousseau later concluded that Hume was the co-author of this derisive missive.

But at the time of Rousseau's stay in Paris the relationship between Rousseau and Hume was harmonious. Hume called Rousseau his "pupil" though he was only one year older. On Friday, January 3, 1766, Hume returned from a visit at Holbach's and discussed with his "pupil" and Mme de Bouffleurs their departure from Paris that was set for the following day. According to the testimony of Morellet, Baron Holbach warned Hume against Rousseau. Baron said: "I am sorry to dispel the hopes and illusions that flatter you, but I tell you that it will be long before you are undeceived. You do not know your man. I tell you plainly that you are nursing a viper on your bosom."

As late as on January 3, Rousseau wrote a letter to Mme de Créqui (she was almost ninety) apologizing that he could not visit her. It was only necessity, the cruel necessity always ruling our lives, that thwarted his desire to see her.

Rousseau set out on his journey to England in cruel winter but in a good mood at eleven o'clock in the morning on January 4, 1766. He traveled together with Hume, de Luze and his dog, Sultan. In a letter written several years later, Rousseau said that one night on the way to Calais, Hume cried out in his sleep, "I've got Jean-Jacques Rousseau" (*Je tiens Jean-Jacques Rousseau*). Rousseau says that he was scared but had to laugh over his horror at the same time. Everything was forgotten on the next day, and it was only much later that Rousseau recalled this episode.

The journey went through Arras and St-Omer to Calais, where they had to wait for two days because of bad weather. Here Hume raised the question whether Rousseau would possibly accept a pension from the king of England, George III, if it was offered to him. Rousseau knew that he was not in the best financial situation and that the cost of living in England was high, and was therefore inclined not to hesitate and to accept the offer if it was made to him. But he could not express this openly because he had refused the offer of both the French and Prussian kings before. So he replied diplomatically that if his "father," Lord Keith, would agree with it he would answer "yes" to the offer.

We know about this dialogue from Hume's letter to Mme de Bouffleurs. He also wrote in it that he had encouraged Rousseau to write his memoirs. Rousseau disclosed to him that he was already working on them and continued that, in fact, no one knew the true Rousseau. But he would change this and describe himself in his memoirs so openly that everyone would learn the truth about Rousseau. Hume added that he really believed Rousseau wanted to describe himself in the colors he himself believed to be true, but "at the same time I think that no one knew oneself less than he." The skeptical Hume was right about this.

The weather was still very stormy on the day of their embarkation and Hume was surprised at how well Rousseau tolerated the journey and how tough he was. He wrote to Mme de Bouffleurs that Rousseau was one of the most robust men he had ever known. He remained on the deck for ten hours in frosty weather and suffered not in the least by it. This observation shows that without Thérèse, Rousseau's health remained pretty good; the relapses of his urinary tract infection did not occur, which was probably in connection with Thérèse's absence—she could not, as his "nurse," induce new infections with catheterization. Rousseau even tolerated the winter weather which normally worsened his condition. Thérèse was still on the island of St-Pierre and Rousseau sent her letters from Paris through Du Peyrou.

Upon landing in Dover, Rousseau embraced his friend, covered his face with kisses and watered it with tears of gratitude. The skeptic Hume probably could no longer be surprised by Rousseau's behavior.

They got to London on Monday, January 13, and their arrival was recorded as a social event by several newspapers. Rousseau took lodging in the house of John Steward on Buckingham street. He learned with displeasure about the presence in London of Louis-François Tronchin, the son of his Genevan enemy, the procurator Théodore Tronchin. Rousseau aroused attention in the street with his Armenian costume, which Hume thought at first was just one of the whims of his friend. But Rousseau told him that he needed the chamber pot every minute and trousers were therefore not the right clothing for him. These words show once more that at that time Rousseau already suffered from ischuria paradoxa (see medical information in Part 2).

Rousseau's first days in London passed peacefully. Rousseau did not visit anybody but received a series of personalities. He was visited by the duke of York (incognito), Charles William Ferdinand of Brunswick, Prince Héritier, and a friend of Lord Keith, the Reverend Richard Penneck, who was then director of the Reading room of the British Museum. Rousseau was visited also by his cousin, Jean Rousseau, and others. Chevalier d'Eon, the French *chargé d'affaires* (who dressed as a woman), sent Rousseau a brief letter but abstained from visiting him personally.

David Garrick invited Rousseau to accompany him to a gala theatre performance attended by the royal couple. The theatre visit was almost cancelled because Rousseau's dog Sultan started howling and Rousseau did not want to leave him alone in the flat. The theatre was bursting with spectators and, as the newspaper recorded, many visitors lost parts of their clothing in the crowd. Rousseau's box was opposite the royal box. Hume recorded that the king and queen paid more attention to Rousseau than to the plays. The plays of the evening were the tragedy, *Zara,* and the comedy, *Lethe,* by Garrick. Rousseau cried politely during the tragedy and laughed during the comedy though he did not understand the English text. Eventually he was so excited that Garrick had to hold him by the caftan lest he should fall out of the box. Following the performance, Rousseau was introduced to several writers.

Soon Rousseau became tired of London and longed for life in the country. The search for a permanent residence was not easy. The room in Fullham offered to him by Stewart was dirty, and, worse, was occupied by another man confined to bed by illness.

Hume did what he could. Meanwhile Rousseau lived in Chiswick, a London suburb, in expectation of further developments. It was at that time that Rousseau started experiencing obsessive thoughts of being persecuted. During a botanical outing with Prof. John Walker on the shores of the Thames, a group of young sailors disembarked on the bank. Rousseau became suspicious and thought they wanted to imprison and deport him, and he took to flight in panic. Prof. Walker caught up with him only with difficulty and reassured him. Rousseau also suspected other writers of not wishing him success, which was partially true. Rousseau did not like Edmund Burke who later criticized Rousseau in his work *Reflections on the Revolution in France* (1790) as "a founder of a philosophy of conceited vanity." Also, Dr. Johnson was expressing sharp criticism of Rousseau's stay in England.

Thérèse arrived in England, accompanied by Boswell, with whom she had had an affair during the journey. She claimed that Boswell seduced her but it cannot be ruled out that the opposite was true. We know that she secretely ran off and spent eleven days in bed with him on the road between Paris and London. Her arrival did not make Rousseau's situation easier. Her position precluded Rousseau from finding a suitable residence because he insisted obstinately that she must dine together with him, though he spoke of her as his housemaid. In England at that time it was regarded as correct for a gentleman to dine with his mistress, but to sit at a table with one's housemaid was unacceptable.

De Lutz described Thérèse to Hume as malevolent, cantankerous and slanderous, and added that she had been the main reason why Rousseau had to leave Neuchâtel. We know also that later on Thérèse was the main reason for Rousseau's departure from England, or at least sped it up. Hume was to record that she was "so dull that she never knows in what year of the Lord she is, nor in what month of the year, nor in what day of the month or week: she can never learn the different value of the pieces of money in any country," but *"she governs him as absolutely as a nurse does a child."* His observations and those of other contemporaries were obviously correct. Rousseau liked to be treated in a masochistic way, not only physically, but he felt blissful when he could experience mental humiliation by a woman as well. The fact that he, a famous personality, was governed and humiliated by the primitive Thérèse could only have increased his masochistic feelings. Humiliation at the hands of a rude, primitive person attracted the masochistic "philosopher" much more than humiliation by a cultivated woman would. It is otherwise very difficult to explain their relationship. In spite of her obtuseness, Thérèse must have come to realize this. She knew that Rousseau was more dependent on her mentally than physically, that he was unable to deny anything to her, and she behaved accordingly.

When Thérèse arrived, Rousseau lived in Dorkinng, in Daniel Malthuse's house, who he knew from Switzerland. Malthuse's son, Thomas Robert Malthuse, became known later as the author of *Essay on Population*. When the famous Allan Ramsey worked on Rousseau's portrait, for which Rousseau sat in his Armenian costume (Rousseau did not like the painting), Rousseau was introduced to the rich Richard Davenport, who offered that he could live in his house, Wootton Hall, on the border between Staffordshire and Derbyshire. The house was situated in a park built on an undulating piece of land. Davenport had been forewarned by Hume that Rousseau would not want to stay for free—this would offend him. For this reason, a symbolic rent of thirty pounds a year was set. Davenport munificently put his own carriage at Rousseau's disposal to bring him to his new home and had to pretend that it was returning empty.

On March 17, two days before their departure, Hume invited Rousseau and Thérèse to his flat on Lisle Street. He also invited the secretary of state, General Seymour Convay, with whom he had talked about a pension for Rousseau, and Lady Aylesbury. Rousseau apologized for his ailment and he also asked them to excuse Mademoiselle Levasseur because she was not accustomed to moving in high society. He visited Hume on the evening before his departure to thank him but also to reproach him because he had a hunch that everything had been set up so he would not have to pay for the conveyance to Wootton Hall. Hume objected, which was followed by the most emotional scene Hume had ever experienced. He described it in a letter to his friend, Dr. Hugh Blair: All of a sudden, Rousseau sat on his knees, started embracing and kissing him, crying and asking for forgiveness. At the same time, he assured

Hume of how he loved and respected him, and that he—in spite of his foolish behavior—had a heart worthy of Hume's friendship.

After the arrival in Wootton Hall, everything seemed to be all right. Rousseau liked the house. The weather was bad but the surroundings were beautiful. Rousseau undertook botanical outings and resumed his work on *Confessions*. The servants greeted them cordially and Rousseau was even called on by a few neighbors.

But this peaceful situation could not last for long. All of a sudden Rousseau's relationship to Hume changed. The reason was the already mentioned mocking letter written by Walpole, which was published in the *St. James Chronicle* on April 1, 1776, in French, and in an English translation on the next day.

Rousseau was already informed about the letter and by now he had begun to fabricate his own hypothesis about its origins, according to which the co-author of the letter was Hume. Hume and Walpole were friends, the letter was published in a newspaper published by Walpole, and Louis-François Tronchin, son of his enemy from Geneva, lived in the same house as Walpole. Based on all this, Rousseau came to the erroneous conclusion that Hume was trying to demolish him and notified him in a rigorous letter that he was discontinuing their friendship. The completely stupefied Hume replied with a letter asking for an explanation. Rousseau replied in a long letter accusing Hume of a conspiracy against him. He wrote that he knew only what he felt. He reproached Hume because his interest in him had declined, as had the interest of others, and that his friendship had turned into derision.

Rousseau's delusions of persecution took Hume by surprise. He enumerated everything he had done for him, and he told Rousseau he was trying to obtain a pension for him (which he carried on with magnanimously, notwithstanding their quarrel). Hume succeeded in May—Rousseau was granted a royal annuity although he was wavering about whether or not to accept, and then Hume wrote Rousseau adieu—forever.

In his righteous embitterment, Hume decided to publish the correspondence from the time of their quarrel, though many of his friends, mainly his friends in Paris, tried to talk him out of it. In a letter to Dr. Blair, he described Rousseau as the greatest rogue under the sun and said that he was ashamed of everything good he had ever written about him. The pamphlet was printed in October in French, and in November in English, and was entitled, "*A Concise and Genuine Account of the Dispute between Mr. Hume and Mr. Rousseau."* All lovers of defamation in London and Paris read the pamphlet with delight. Especially pleased was Voltaire because the impostor had been exposed at last. According to him it was about time, too! Rousseau remained silent.

In Wootton, Rousseau rubbed shoulders mainly with his French-speaking neighbor, Bernard Granville, who was frequently visited by noblewomen. These showed a lively interest in the picturesque Rousseau: Especially the duchess of Portland, who accompanied Rousseau frequently during his botanical perambulations. Rousseau liked Granville's twenty-year-old niece, Mary Dewes.

Rousseau's opera, *Le Devin du village* was adapted for the English public and was staged under the title, *"The Cunning Man,"* in Garrick's theatre Drury Lane on November 31. But the performance was a failure and the second half of it was booed off the stage. It is not likely that Hume would have hired people to boo the opera. But it cannot be ruled out that Hume's pamphlet ridiculed Rousseau in the eyes of the public and that his mockery induced the hostile reception of the opera.

Thanks to Thérèse, the situation in Wootton got worse at the end of 1767. She found the stay there increasingly boring and she started quarreling with the servants. They refused to receive orders from a person they knew was stupid or half-witted, and who was actually in a class below themselves. Thérèse had never had a good record with respect to servants. In the eighteenth century, the domestic staff did not expect their masters to have high moral codes, but upper classes knew how to behave. Thérèse was coarse and ignorant and her behavior gave away her origin.

The feud came to a head in April when, following a servant's quarrel with Thérèse, Rousseau was dished up soup in which he found cinder and ash. He wrote an indignant letter to Davenport informing him that he was leaving the house. He left the letter in the guestroom where it stayed unheeded and Davenport did not learn of Rousseau's departure till around May 20.

Rousseau left for Spalding in Lincolnshire, two hundred miles away from his previous residence, and his reasons for having chosen this place remain unclear. It is obvious that his unstable mental condition continued to deteriorate—we know that Rousseau asked the Lord Chancellor Camden, in a letter from May 5, 1767, to give him a personal guardian to escort him to Dover. The lord replied that Rousseau would enjoy the same safety as any of the employees of the Post.

Rousseau decided to leave England definitely and arrived in Dover as soon as several days later. He posted a letter from there addressed to General Conway. The letter was shown also to Hume, who said it was the craziest letter he had ever seen. Rousseau assumed in it that he was a prisoner of the state, held by the generals, and he felt his life was in danger. His reputation in England that was destroyed in his lifetime would be restored only after his death.

Hume thought the best solution would be to let Rousseau live in France for some time, in some quiet asylum, under tactful supervision. The weather in Dover was again bad and Rousseau had to wait. He was tormented by constant delusions that he was about to be arrested. During supper, to which one local citizen invited him, Rousseau repeatedly sprang from the table to look from the window to find out about the weather. He even ran away from the supper to the ship and hid in his cabin from which he had to be brought back by an angry Thérèse. Then he allegedly calmed down and continued his conversation with his host for the rest of the evening.

During these years Rousseau gradually moved from the idea of degradation and humiliation to that of active persecution: he began to stress the element of mystery and subterfuge in the plot (Grimsley 1969, 204). "Black vapors" were arising everywhere to choke him, he got the idea of "subterranean" hostility, his enemies were "moles burrowing underground." He was terrified by the "unnatural" behavior of his enemies, since it is "not in nature" for men to be so cruel. He was overcome by a panic-stricken sense of helplessness.

These delusions of persecution are usually interpreted as symptomatic of paranoid disorders. This disastrous mental deterioration could have also been caused by progressive uremia that potentiated and increasingly distorted his masochistic fantasies. The expressions he used to describe his being persecuted made use of masochistic repertoire. The persecutors were identified with various kinds of animals and birds (depersonalizations) who took an almost sadistic pleasure in tormenting their helpless victim. There were "tigers . . . wolves," even "rooks." His enemies were sometimes devilish creatures. The savagery of their attacks assumes "infernal" proportions. His enemies remained hidden, intent upon surrounding him with an air of mystery, secrecy and silence. They were frequently "underground" or engaged in "subterranean maneuvers . . . moles . . . spies," malevolent and watchful, working continually in the dark and all the more dangerous for being "unseen." They kept their victim in ignorance not only of their real activities but also of the reason for their hatred: they were engaged in casting a "net" around him and trapping him within their "meshes."

Grimsley (1969, 207–208) noted that at times Rousseau's imagery assumed an almost Kafkaesque note of nightmarish fear with its emphasis on the "work of darkness" and the inexplicable animosity of these hidden forces. Kafka is known as a classic example of a literary masochist.

On May 21, 1767 Rousseau sailed off to France at last, where he was pompously received in Amiens four days later. He arrived under his own name. After being warned by Prince de Conti that he was at risk of imprisonment, he left secretly during the night of June 3 for the prince's Château Tyre in Normandy, where he spent one year. He hoped to find peace there but this was not to be. Here, as in Wootton, the servants could not get along, mainly with Thérèse, and Rousseau again felt persecuted and surrounded by enemies and spies who were plotting against him. The prince tried to calm him but his efforts were of no avail.

Rousseau contemplated giving himself up to the authorities. He would either be exonerated or imprisoned in Bastille, where he would be safe. In November his old friend, Du Peyrou, visited Rousseau but, unfortunately, he suffered an acute attack of gout and shouted in a delirium that someone must have poisoned him. Rousseau was afraid he could be accused of having poisoned Du Peyrou and so he wrote a declaration that he had no stake in Du Peyrou's property and therefore had no reason to poison him. When his friend recovered he apologized to him and stayed till January 1768.

In Paris toward the end of 1767, Rousseau's *Dictionary of Music,* on which he had worked for so long, was published. He became increasingly restless at the château and wrote to Mme de Bouffleurs, asking her to help him find a new sanctuary. He also disobeyed the instructions of Prince de Conti and wrote a letter to the king's minister, Duke de Choiseul, and asked if he could live under his protection.

We do not know what the minister replied to Rousseau. In May Prince de Conti agreed that Rousseau should leave the château (where only Thérèse was to stay) and Rousseau was to live under the pseudonym Renou and keep out of the reach of the parlement of Paris. Rousseau, as M. Renou, arrived in the Parisian Temple on June 12. From there he continued to Lyon and Grenoble and even made a short stopover in Chambéry where he had a little cry at the grave of Mme de Warens.

He left Grenoble on August 12 and decided to marry Thérèse in the nearby town of Bourgoin. She arrived on August 26 and posed as M. Renou's sister. Rousseau told Thérèse nothing about the wedding and asked the mayor of the town and an artillery captain to come to the inn where he lived on August 30 to confirm their wedding, which was to have the form of a mutual agreement. Legal weddings between Catholics and Protestants were forbidden. After the exchange of marital vows, Rousseau delivered a speech about marital duties that was so emotional the guests wept. Rousseau explained he had decided to marry Thérèse as an expression of acknowledgement of her devotion. He said he had never met any duty with more delight or more freely because he had never aroused her expectation of a wedding and she did not know about his decision until two minutes before the wedding. As she did not want to live without him, he wanted her to follow him as a virtuous woman.

In August Rousseau was embroiled in a lawsuit with a workman, Nicola-Élie Thévenin, who demanded that Rousseau pay him nine francs he allegedly had owed him from some former time. It was a swindle but Rousseau had to wait for the trial till September 14. Though he won the lawsuit, this episode further confirmed his pathological conviction that he was being persecuted. The brief thoughts he wrote on the wall while waiting for the trial attest to the ability he still had to be witty as he formulated his erroneous ideas about his persecution. He described these thoughts in a letter sent to Madelon Delessert. All of these comments relate to his person—he painted a picture of himself as a suffering man, for example, "The municipalities hate me for the evil they have wrought on me . . . The Swiss will never forgive me the evil they have done to me . . . The philosophers whom I have exposed try to destroy me and they will succeed in it."

Rousseau considered going away to Minorca, Cyprus, and even to America. He thought about returning to Wootton as well. But because he was afraid that Walpole had conspired against him with the English ambassador in Paris, he decided to remain in France. On January 30, 1769 he moved from Bourgoin to the nearby Monquin, a small town situated higher in the Alps. In July he visited Prince de Conti at his summer residence in Pongues, close to Loire, and tried to move him to find him a new refuge, which the prince probably refused.

He did not heed the warnings of his friends and went to Paris on June 24, 1770, after having spent the two preceding months in Lyon at Mme Boy's. Here he was honored by the performances of his *Pygmalion* and *Le Devin du village*. On his way to Paris, Rousseau stopped in Dijon, where he discussed botany with Duke de Buffon and his assistant L.J.M. Daubenton. In Paris he settled in rue Plâtrière, the present-day rue Jean-Jacques Rousseau. The time of anonymity had passed and *Monsieur et Madame Rousseau* lived publicly under their own names.

Premier de Choiseul (1758–1770), during whose term in office the parlement of Paris issued the warrant of arrest for Rousseau, stepped down. Choiseul's resignation was brought about by the change of the king's favorite—this position had been occupied by Duchess du Barry (and the clique around her) since 1768. The duchess asserted herself against her rival, Madame de Pompadour, who was the king's mistress and adviser between 1745–1764 (she was opposed by the so-called devout party centered around the king's wife Marie Lescynska).

The wedding of the Dauphin, the grandson of Louis XV, who later became Louis XVI (he succeeded to the French throne after 1774), with Marie-Antoinette, was a favorable occasion for amnesty of all the politically persecuted. It was determined that Rousseau could live in Paris, but must not wear his Armenian costume, and could write books that would be published only after his death.

As so often before, Rousseau earned his living by note copying, received numerous visitors and was invited into society. In Paris he also wrote the last pages of *Confessions* and read extracts from them in Parisian salons; the reading often went on for fifteen to seventeen hours!

Confessions was meant to rehabilitate and exonerate him, but he feared at the same time that he revealed matters to his enemies which could be used against him. Many of Rousseau's acquaintances feared that *Confessions* contained intimate matters that should not get into public. It is a recorded fact that the police lieutenant of Paris ordered Rousseau to desist from these readings.

In 1770 Rousseau was asked by the Polish nobleman, Count Michel-Joseph Wielhorski, to write a draft of the constitution for the Polish parliament—Sejm. Rousseau was flattered by this request and started studying Polish history and the social situation from sources supplied by the count. In this way the *"Considérations sur le gouvernement de Pologne"* was created. Since Poland had eleven million inhabitants and was a big country, Rousseau's recommendations for a political system for Poland differed from those he wrote for Corsica. He regarded republicanism as suitable only for smaller states. But Poland was a populous country with a large territory. "Large population and extensive territories! This is the first and main reason for an unfortunate fate . . ." He suggested that Poland should cultivate patriotism, adapt the political and social system and introduce the federal system.

The Polish monarchy of that time was one of the weakest and most corrupt. The Sejm was an oligarchic establishment in which three hundred aristocratic families determined the fate of the state; each single member of the Sejm had the right of veto—liberum veto and everyone could therefore prevent a legislative change with a mere statement: "I do not agree" (nie pozwalan). This right was first used in 1652 and later extended so that the legislative work could be interrupted any time and the Sejm could be dissolved.

In such circumstances Poland fell an easy prey to its neighbors. Freedom is easily swallowed but to digest it is much more difficult and requires a strong stomach. According to Rousseau, Poland could not avert being swallowed by Russia but it had to be so resistant as not to be digested. The idea of a democratic Poland was not realistic. In Poland, the aristocracy was everything; bourgeoisie was nothing and peasantry "less than nothing." On that account the laws could not be binding for those who had not voted for them or did not send the representatives of their choice to vote on their behalf.

Rousseau did not recommend revolution, or any radical political changes. He did not believe in revolutions. The right liberum veto should be preserved, but limited to major laws only, which were included in the volonté génerale of his Social Contract. He rejected a permanent army lest it should become too powerful and recommended instead forming local militia patterned upon the situation in Switzerland. His projects for Poland were expressly conservative.

In 1772 Rousseau wrote "Lettres sur la botanique" for Mme Madelon Delessert, the most favorite of Mme Boy's daughters; it was published only after his death.

Last Years

In the last years of his life Rousseau's interest in his own person became even stronger. He felt, perhaps more than ever before, that his personality was split between the image of "the most loving of men" and the one who was "the horror of his fellow men." The good Jean-Jacques on the one side and the evil Jean-Jacques, created by the malevolent minds of his enemies, on the other. The result was the dialogue entitled *"Rousseau Juge de Jean-Jacques."* Rousseau's autobiographic literature is astonishingly voluminous and has been subject to the most variegated interpretation. Rousseau was not simply writing memoirs and descriptions of his life-stories. He wanted to ease his conscience as well and described some of the wrongs he had committed on others in his life, especially the part about sending his children to a foundling home.

But even this does not seem to have been the real motive for writing these autobiographical works. These poignant and disgraceful episodes were rather intended to arouse the impression that the author is unscrupulously honest in his criticism and does not forgive anything of himself. This authorized him to criticize others as well. The dialogues constitute a powerful defense and effort to exonerate himself.

It appears the main reason for Rousseau's never-ending need to demonstrate to others what he was actually like is to be found in the necessity to justify himself in the eyes of others. He was aware of the deep abyss gaping between him and society, that he was different, special and did not fit into society. He tried to show how, in spite of the dissimilarity caused by the educational semi-deprivation of his youth, which had left its irreversible mark on the whole of his subsequent life, including his views, philosophy and behavior, he was a "good" man. Why he was different and why he could not become an integral part of society was to remain a mystery to him.

The eighteenth century knew as little about the consequences of a defective education as it knew about antibiotics. He never felt good in society (nor could he ever have, for that matter). He fled into solitude where he could survive as a "good" man and condemned the "corrupted" society into which he was unable to integrate. This is the classic attitude of all reformers of human society.

Man is a social being and isolation represents the worst possible punishment for every normal person. Rousseau knew all this and even here he was able to rationalize this fact in a way highly typical of him: he turned to the signs of "good" and "evil." He wrote, "The hell of an evil man" is when he has to live with himself. But a life in isolation can also be "the paradise of good man." As with every social outcast, he desired society and he desired friendship, and it is this desire that underlies *Confessions* as its main motive: "It was my vocation to be the best friend that could ever be found. But he who could match me has yet to be born."

Rousseau was always convinced of his exceptionality. The same conviction, by its very nature, precluded that he would live in absolute isolation and separation. Such a conviction abhored solitude. He demanded that others *corroborate* his exceptionality. He lived alone yet he did not want and could not remain in total isolation. This is evidenced by the sheer amount of his correspondence and the stream of visitors which he so often complained about, but of which he was so fond.

The visits served the purpose of compensating him for (the otherwise lacking) normal social life, being at the same time conveniently noncommittal. The visitors stayed for a certain time and then disappeared. They came and experienced his exceptionality, his eloquence, but were unable to learn more about Rousseau as a man because of the short time they spent with him.

Knowledge disillusions. A philanthropist is a man who loves all people with the exception of those whom he knows well. Subconsciously, Rousseau knew that any formation of more lasting relationships, accompanied by permanent personal contact, would unveil his true nature of an egoistic masochist. That was why Rousseau did not want to form any lasting and firm emotional ties. Visiting the salons, he did not have to stay in contact with any person with which he was formally "befriended." Emotional ties, watered down in the guise of correspondence were easier to tolerate because of the lack of real interaction in person. Rousseau knew that what he needed was what could be called social ties.

He was impractical and, when left to his own resources, he was helpless. He remained a "big child" till the end of his life. He always needed protectors, who would offer him refuge and would intercede on his behalf. On the one hand, he proudly rejected even the smallest material or financial donations which could undermine his "independence," but he was reluctant, on the other hand, to realize that a recommendation on his behalf, the offer of a place to live, or a piece of advice, are all of the same nature as the tiny gifts that are meant to sustain friendship. Even though he lived on society's periphery he could never succeed in excluding them and the limitation he practiced was a pose, a theatrical demonstration of his views.

He could co-exist permanently only with his animals, a dog and cat that provided elementary emotions (they expressed pleasure, disapproval). Domestic animals provide emotional certitude and soothe mentally unstable people. Contact with people, for whom the socially acceptable degree of lying and pretence is a necessity, does not have a calming effect on psychopaths. Solitude is much more tolerable with animal companions. Thérèse, as a somewhat feebleminded person, was also emotionally unsophisticated. She gratified Rousseau sexually (probably with fatal consequences), did not bother him with complicated emotions, looked after him and conformed to his masochistic tendencies. Rousseau's solitude was therefore never an absolute and Rousseau had never desired it in earnest.

Rousseau's autobiographical writings were written during different time periods and reflect the author's varying mental states. His earliest autobiographical works are the manuscript *Mon portrait* and the already mentioned letters to Malesherbes from 1762. According to Rousseau, the first to come up with the idea that he should write *Confessions* was Rey, who, for strange reasons, pressed for him to write his memoirs. As he wrote, Rousseau complied, mainly to reveal his soul with absolute frankness.

Rousseau certainly was not the first to write memoirs. Many significant people before him had written their memoirs, for example Saint Augustine in 397, who described his sinful life and his conversion by the grace of God. As opposed to Saint Augustine, however, Rousseau tried to prove that he had *always* been a good man, though there were occasional misdemeanors, but these were caused by his innocence, tormented him and he wanted to confess them. He had doubts whether he would be forgiven. He had come to the conclusion that the world preferred secrecy to truth. "Polite society" was hypocritical, which was one more reason for him to despise it.

According to Rousseau, the autobiography written by Montaigne was "fraudulently sincere" in order to be more attractive for the readers. But is Rousseau's *Confessions* "truly sincere"? Does he say in it everything, without exception, for example regarding his sexual life with Thérèse?

He chose an epigram by Juvenal as the maxim of his life: *vitam impedere vero* (to dedicate life to truth). But to what truth did he dedicate his life? It had always been his subjective truth, the truth in which he believed at any given time. He did not acknowledge the relativity of truth, and the skepticism cultivated by Hume remained incomprehensible to him. That is why his requirement of tolerance was meant to apply to his own person in the first place: others should simply tolerate his views. He himself had never been tolerant of the views of others and often fulminated against atheists and philosophers. He was an ideological dogmatist and this fact explains his unceasing appeal to revolutionaries and dictators of every political shade. For example, Marx of the early 1840s bears and obvious, though largely unacknowledged, debt to Rousseau's moral vision of the world, a profound conceptual affinity.

In the last years of his life Rousseau wrote, *Rousseau Juge de Jean-Jacques* (1772–1776), (Rousseau, Judge of Jean-Jacques). It is known also under the title *Dialogues*. These dialogues are psychologically valuable, though the work does not stand out literarily. *Dialogues* bear witness to the progressive deterioration of his thinking, with delusions of persecution, which leave their mark on the last book of *Confessions* as well. It is possible, considering Rousseau's masochism with its typical indulgence in persecution, that the delusions of persecution from which he allegedly "suffered," could be interpreted as related to his hidden wishes. Or vice versa—to what extent did his wishes degenerate into delusions of persecution? "How frightful are the illusions of human life!" he wrote in *Confessions* (236).

In *Dialogues,* Rousseau's masochistic terminology and masochistic fantasies reappear: his enemies regarded him as "a monster . . . bear . . . serpent and reptile . . . a hypocrite," who is "the horror of the human race . . . the laughing stock . . . plaything of the mob," a veritable "scourge of humanity." He was being humiliated, he must suffer, was not considered human, and was depersonalized. His misfortunes began with the decision to be an author and the subsequent achievement of fame and glory. He was "without support" as a man absolutely "alone in the world." He was surrounded by "mystery" and "darkness." He was quite unable to locate the source of the attacks against him and break the barrier of silence and mystery; he realized with horror that he was shut in by "a triple wall of darkness," he was "buried alive among the living," terrified by the feeling of being constantly watched by unseen, sinister eyes. He was an object of contempt. His correspondence was meticulously examined by his enemies, his writings were seized and falsified. He *accepted* persecution and suffered as the objective guarantee of his innate goodness. He was good because others are wicked. He choose (consciously or unconsciously) to be persecuted.

Dialogues remains a most valuable document for the understanding of Rousseau's state of mind at this period of his life. The psychological starting point is similar to that of the previous *Confessions*. He was still obsessed by the need to destroy the false portrait which he believed to exist in the public's mind. He now admitted that *Confessions* had a similar purpose. *Dialogues* is dominated by the black and white antithesis between the false and the true Rousseau. In essence, he accused everybody of conspiring against him.

The motive of self-justification is here even more pronounced than in *Confessions*. Rousseau had not yet given up hope that he would succeed in showing people the true picture of himself and that he would then deserve to be accepted into human society.

The work is written in the form of a conversation between the person, Rousseau, a supposedly impartial observer who, though apparently eager to find out the truth about the Jean-Jacques case, is really benevolently disposed toward him, and "the Frenchman," who is at first extremely hostile toward Jean-Jacques. The Frenchman's animosity is converted to sympathy as he learns more about Jean-Jacques's true character.

In the first dialogue we have an elaborate account of the "wicked" Jean-Jacques who is the object of such universal persecution. The second refutes this black account by presenting the real Jean-Jacques, the innocent and good man. The third and last dialogue deals with Jean-Jacques, the writer. It finally appears that Jean-Jacques is the good man of his writings. Even then he has to account for the disquieting fact that, in spite of his goodness, he committed actions of which he is now ashamed. These lapses, he insists, can be explained quite simply by means of his temperament. His actions have always stemmed from his sensibility and not from his reason—from his "heart" and not from his "will."

Though he has always been good, he has not always been "virtuous"—if by "virtue" is meant a strong, rational will that is able, if necessary, to resist and overcome the needs of the heart. He will always admire virtue, while admitting his inability to practice it himself. His natural *paresse de penser* makes it impossible and also explains his tendency to allow himself to be subjugated by personalities stronger that his own. He saw himself as a man who no longer needed to be "virtuous." By an accident of birth he had been born with a temperament which absolved him from the necessity of striving for "virtuous" perfection which was—or should be—the object of other men's lives: his particular disposition had prevented him from being permanently corrupted by society and he had never really lost the pristine innocence of "the first forty years" (Grimsley 1969).

In the middle of the second dialogue, Rousseau wrote with eloquence on the *pleasures of imagination* (see Part 2).

Happy fictions take the place of a real happiness . . . Who, passing beyond the narrow prison of personal interest and petty earthly passion, rises on the wings of imagination above the mists of our atmosphere: he who without exhausting his strength and powers in struggling against fortune and fate, knows how to leap up into the ethereal regions, hover there and keep himself up by his sublime meditation, can in this way defy the onslaughts of fate and the mad judgments of men. He is beyond their attacks: he has no need of their approbation in order to be wise, or of their favor in order to be happy.

The *Dialogues*, then, along with the *Rêveries*, represent Rousseau's last effort to fix the main outlines of a personality, which he still felt to be Protéan and contradictory. He is driven on by an intense anxiety which seeks desperately to eliminate all contradictions. *Confessions* abandoned the final judgment to the reader himself, *Dialogues* aims at producing a definite and completely satisfactory answer to the problem of his life's meaning. On February 24, 1776 he decided to place the manuscript on the high altar of Nôtre-Dame but it was shut by an iron grill. In this exalted period, in April, Rousseau personally handed out the work with the heading: "To every Frenchman who still loves justice and truth," to strangers who were passing by who should later become witnesses in a lawsuit he prepared against his friends.

Dialogues should have shown that Rousseau's work followed the underlying idea, "Nature gratifies people and makes them good but society corrupts them." But this does not mean that the present society should be abolished and a "return to nature" should take place. It was impossible for human nature to return to the state of original innocence and equality once it had left it. Revolutions only encouraged false hopes and led to chaos and the "real" Rousseau was just a reformer who was trying to carry out reforms within the constitutional and conventional framework as this has developed in the course of evolution.

Later, the revolutionaries who referred to Rousseau had always to adapt his views so as to suit their purposes. He wrote his *Social Contract* for Geneva, for which the form recommended by him was suitable. But he warned explicitly that this form was not appropriate for large states. The solutions he proposed for Corsica and Poland were quite different.

The manic period of his thinking depicted in *Dialogues* was followed by a period that was rather serene. In this period he wrote his last work, *Les Rêveries du promeneur solitaire* (Reveries of a Solitary Walker) written from 1776 to 1778, which consists of ten promenades (walks) and is at the same time the epilogue to *Confessions*. The first promenade dates back to the end of summer 1776; he interrupted his work on the tenth, unfinished walk on April 12, less than three months before his death (July 2, 1778).

Rousseau resigns and explores his soul. He gives up worrying about what others might think of him, he accepts his fate of a social exile and is (seemingly) satisfied in his isolation because he can concentrate on his introspective observation undisturbed by anyone.

Rousseau still felt that all his efforts to find happiness were threatened by the relentless hostility of his "persecutors." The theme of persecution appears in the very first paragraph:

> Here am I, then, alone on the earth, having no brother, neighbor, friend or companion but myself. The most sociable and loving of human beings has been outlawed by a unanimous agreement. In the subtleties of their hatred they have sought what torment could be the most cruel for my sensitive soul, and they have violently broken all the bonds which tied me to them. I should have loved men in spite of themselves. They have been able to elude my affection only by ceasing to be men. There they are then, strangers, unknown persons, nothing to me since they have wished it thus.

In the eighth promenade the theme of persecution almost reaches the intensity of the *Dialogues* with the typical masochistic terminology. He cannot "escape from the cruel hands of men determined to torment me," he has now learned "to submit to my fate without kicking any more against necessity." The persecution forms "the most iniquitous and absurd system that the infernal spirit could ever have invented." He must submit to "the saddest fate ever suffered by a mortal," his condition is one which "perhaps no other man would be able to face without terror," he is "in the strangest situation in which a mortal has ever found himself . . . God wants me to suffer and He knows that I am innocent . . . As soon as I succeeded in seeing through the whole scale of the conspiracy I relinquished any thought that I could win over the public to my side in the course of my life . . . Even if the people wanted to persuade me to return to them they could never succeed in it. Their manner has robbed me of all respect for them."

In the state of reverie he imagined himself as "invisible and omnipotent as God." He "is self-sufficient like God" or he sees himself "as impassive as God Himself." Such remarks seem to illustrate that inclination to "omnipotence of thought" which Freud attributed to children, neurotics and primitive people and which marks a state of mind that abolishes all distinction between wish and reality: unable to find satisfaction in the everyday world, the self moves into a domain of fantastic wish-fulfillment and forgets the limitations of its real life (Grimsley 1969).

In the first promenade of *Rêveries,* Rousseau accepts his isolation with resignation, an isolation he had never sought or welcomed. He described himself as the most sociable human being and "the most loving of men" who has nevertheless been expelled from society. He must have forgotten that his ideal was Robinson Crusoe and that he himself always longed to live in solitude throughout his adult life, from Les Charmettes to isle St-Pierre. His words evince that he in fact *longed* to be incorporated into human society as its member, but owing to his education *had* to live in semi-isolation and solitude.

He entered history as reformer, but he had never really understood people, first and foremost himself. The only solace of his state is that he can freely converse with his soul. Unlike Montaigne, he does not want others to participate in his feelings—he does not describe his feelings for them. His reveries are determined only for him. This claim of his does not seem to be very credible.

In the subsequent promenades, Rousseau recalls various experiences of his life: botanical excursions, moments of humiliation, and the happiness which he felt on the isle St-Pierre in Lake Biel (this isle is now called "*Isle de Rousseau*"). In nature he forgets not only the attacks of his persecutors, but also the masochistic, oppressive influence of his own stifled sense of guilt and unworthiness.

In the third promenade, he goes back to his controversy with the *philosophes* of whom he speaks as missionaries of atheism and dogmatism; this attitude made it impossible for them to discover truths of the heart that are of much greater importance for life. They broke in him all certitude he had had before. He had nothing to face their arguments with, only the escape into solitude which he had freely chosen.

In *Rêveries* Rousseau coined and employed the term "generation": "The fate of my person and my reputation was determined by the entire contemporary generation." It is here that Rousseau, who was otherwise so convinced of his "truths" and principles, raises doubts for the first time. He knows that his views differ from those of the entire generation of his contemporaries: is he and he alone really right?

In the third promenade, in a short spell of clear consciousness in his otherwise pathological thinking, Rousseau asks the skeptical question, so atypical of the whole of his thinking: "Am I the only reasonable, the only enlightened among all mortals?" The question was to remain only an isolated flash of reason in his disrupted psyche.

In the eighth promenade he admits a state that was so typical of him and which is of psychological interest for us: he does not have pleasant memories of the brief moments of his prosperity. On the contrary, all the misfortunes of his life caused him to experience "sweet and delicate feelings that poured over his broken heart as a healing balsam," and always seemed to transform suffering into pleasures. Here Rousseau himself says what his contemporaries declared of him (see for example the counterfeit letter by Horace Walpole) and what he had indignantly resisted all his life: The hardships and humiliations of his life resulted in mental pleasure and that was why he looked for them.

His marked sexual masochism was just a complement to his social and moral masochism. It is interesting that Rousseau himself wrote that he acquired a "feminine nature" as a result of his early upbringing—extreme pampering and education in a "woman's isolation"—these are his own words.

It is only now that we can understand why Rousseau always declined promising careers offered to him, for example, in diplomatic service or as a clerk, why he refused to accept financial security—a pension offered to him by French and Prussian kings. Rousseau went in search of life failures; he selected the themes for his works in a way that was bound to arouse resistance and indignation, which was what he actually wanted and what his works were calculated to produce (the *First* and *Second Discourses*, the treatise on French music, *Émile, Social Contract*). The fact that his works were also admired can be explained by the social atmosphere of the eighteenth century. He regarded his most successful work, *Julie,* as a second-class literary novel written for women.

In the fourth promenade, Rousseau examines the problem of *lying.* He is conscious of having lied gratuitously on a number of occasions. At such times he had lied with *gaieté de coeur.* But again, he justified this with his innate nature. His "shy nature" overcomes "all his heart's wishes . . . Never did I lie for my interest," but only because of shame and embarrassment. His view that "to keep silent about a truth that one is not obliged to utter is not to lie," is basic to the understanding of all his admissions and confessions. In *Confessions,* he could have withheld (in spite of assurances to the contrary) many things; he would not have to mention them because he did not feel obliged to talk about them. This obviously applied also to his real relationship with Thérèse.

Truth-telling depends primarily on the question of utility. Even lying is possible: "To lie without profit or prejudice to oneself or others is not to lie: it is not lying but fiction . . . Never did duplicity dictate my lies, for they all came from weakness, but that will excuse me." As Grimsley (1969) observes, the desire to find out the truth about himself and the fear of facing it are strangely intermingled. In general, the pressure of anxiety is too great for him to be able to achieve full insight: truth can emerge only if he abandons the thought of himself as an "innocent man": but this is impossible.

He admits to having used fiction and fantasies in *Confessions.* He often lied against himself in order that he might not seem to be presenting himself in a too favorable light. If he had sometimes affirmed more than truth, it was simply because of *le délire de l´imagination*: these additions were not really lies. "I filled in the gaps with details which I imagined as a supplement to these memories, but which were never contrary to them . . . No! When I have spoken contrary to the truth which was known to me, it has always been in different matters and more from embarrassment at having to speak or for the pleasure of writing than for any motive of self-interest or of profit and loss to others." Masochists are cunning liars with a deep-seated desire to justify themselves.

Masochistic tendencies can be observed throughout *Confessions.* They underlie the inexorable descriptions of his weaknesses, misdemeanors and injustices he committed. Thereby he wanted to demean himself in his own eyes and still more in the eyes of the readers. Humiliation made him experience pleasure and delight. This pose is usually interpreted as a merciless confession of truth that started the tradition of modern autobiography and is valued as a token of the author's love of truth and frankness. His biographers have missed out on the medical and psychological foundations of such frankness. They do not write about the causes of Rousseau's flagellant, martyred "veracity" or about his mental masochistic tendencies that were as compulsive as his desire for sexual masochism.

Rousseau admitted that he often made himself appear worse than the reality. The punishment he deserved thereby was accordingly greater. This point of view enables us to interpret and understand his self-portrayal in the beginning of *Confessions*: "I am made unlike any one I have ever met . . . I am like no one in the whole world, I may be no better, but at least I am different." In other words, *Confessions* is true and can be trusted when it is concerned with emotional experiences because their storage in memory is better than that of the chronology of dates, or the emotional appraisal of human characters of minor importance (e.g. frequent discrepancies in assessment of certain persons in *Confessions* and letters; chronological inaccuracies).

Balancing the merits and shortcomings of his own personality as described in *Confessions*, we find that Rousseau always tried hard to show the world that his merits outweighed his shortcomings, which are often explained away as mistakes. His self-justification makes an unfavorable impression on those occasions where his behavior was unquestionably socially unacceptable, for example when he sent his children to a foundling home and justified his deed as removal of his children from education in family. The consequences of his semi-deprived childhood, i.e. his egoism and weakness, find the most vivid expression here. He did not want to become immortal by virtue of his genes but by virtue of his works.

His self-justification in *Confessions* is the necessary counterbalance of self-abasement and self-exposure. The conviction and claim of his being "good" and "exceptional," of being the savior of humanity, would otherwise be untenable. Rousseau assumed he could understand others only after he had known himself. Considering his own development, he could not have attained either. The exhibitionism of moral masochism represents a kind of infantile, childlike delight in showing off.

The tenth, unfinished promenade deals with Rousseau's memories of Mme de Warens, his Maman and mistress, who had awakened his heart. The date—April 12, 1778—is Palm Sunday and is the fiftieth anniversary of his first encounter with Mme de Warens. He could legitimately say that this short period of his life was filled with real life. He was looking for a friend of his heart and found her. For the rest of his life he was the victim of forces stronger then himself: he had been so "agitated, tossed about and torn by other people's passions" that he rarely had the feeling of being a free agent.

The attitude of Mme de Warens toward Rousseau was certainly different (no doubt more realistic). Later, he wrote, he was happy to be loved by Thérèse "a woman full of desire to render joy and delicacy" who put him in a position to do what he wanted to do and be what he wanted to be. These words are symptomatic and remarkable. The semi-feebleminded Thérèse was capable indeed "to render joy to him" and "do what he wanted." It is impossible to say exactly what Rousseau meant with these words but it is most likely that he described, in a veiled form, the masochistic delights rendered to him by Thérèse who made him into her slave, fully in agreement with his demands.

On June 20, 1778 Rousseau and Thérèse left Paris. Rousseau accepted the offer of his admirer, Marquis René-Louis de Giradin, to live in the house of a castellan on his estate in Ermenonville where several rooms were put at his disposal. Ermenonville lies about forty-eight kilometers north of Paris on the route to Soissons. Rousseau agreed, on the condition that he would "repay" by giving music lessons to the marquis's daughter and teaching his ten-year-old son botany. Rousseau had only few visitors at that time. In Ermenonville a young student of law, Maximillien Robespierre, visited him. In Paris, Voltaire died on May 30.

On June 28, Rousseau celebrated his sixty-sixth birthday. On July 2, 1778, six weeks after he left Paris, Rousseau died in Ermenonville during breakfast, after a morning walk.

Immediately after his death, Marquis de Giradin called on the sculptor, Jean Antoine Houdon, to make Rousseau's posthumous mask. According to Rousseau's last will, several surgeons carried out a postmortem of his body (July 3, 1778). The postmortem protocol records that the surgeons were unable to find any abnormalities on his urinary bladder, ureters, testicles or vas deferens.

He was buried on the Isle des Peupliers, a small island in the middle of the lake at Château Ermenonville. On his grave a simple epitaph was engraved: "Ici repose l'homme de la Nature et de la Vérité." Marquis de Giradin declared in a letter that Rousseau would be revered by men and bemoaned by women. The island became a pilgrimage site. One of the first visitors was the unhappy

Marie-Antoinette who arrived with a procession of princes and princesses and spent more than an hour meditating at Rousseau's grave under the tops of poplars.

Shortly after Rousseau's death, Thérèse became mistress of the marquise's valet. The Revolutionary government set her a pension in 1790 and this amount was even raised in 1794. Thérèse died in abandonment at the age of 81 (1801).

But Rousseau's death did not mean peace for Paris. His autobiographical works attracted more and more attention and his name became, at first clandestinely and later openly, the slogan of the French Revolution and his *Social Contract* its bible. On the playing cards from the period of the Revolution, Rousseau is depicted on the ace with his book in hand.

During the French Revolution, the National Assembly passed a decree that Rousseau's corpse be brought to Paris where it was to be buried with honor. At first Marquis de Giradin resisted this but after spending sixteen months in prison as an aristocrat, he agreed to the transfer. On the morning of October 9, 1794, Rousseau's mortal remains were brought to Paris. The musicians played melodies from his compositions, crowds of people in every small town greeted the procession; they laid flowers on the coffin, some remaining silent but some shouting, *"Vive la Republique! Vive la mémoire de Jean-Jacques Rousseau!"* On October 10, the procession got to Paris where it was greeted by large crowds with torches, and the following day Rousseau was buried in the Pantheon next to his opponent Voltaire, who had died a month earlier.

In Paris, Montmorency, Môtiers and Wootton, statues of him have been erected. The reigning council of Geneva, whose predecessors condemned the *Social Contract*, held a procession on the occasion of the anniversary of his birth, and they erected a monument to the memory of the famous son in his home city.

Chapter Six

Historical Review of Masochism

It is man's destiny to suffer in any time (*Émile*, Book One).

God wants me to suffer and He knows that I am innocent (*Rêveries*).

Nothing is better evidence of a man's true inclinations than the character of those whom he loves (*Confessions*, Book Seven, Introduction).

The proposition of this book is that Rousseau was a masochistic personality characterized by coexistence of particular types of masochism. The origin of his masochistic disposition has to be sought in the first years of his life. Deprivation, partial deprivation (semi-deprivation), or other abnormal influences can disturb this sensitive period of a child's development and lead to development of all sorts of character pathologies and disturbances in social and sexual behavior. Many authors have shown the great importance of undisturbed development during this early period. Let me particularly mention the experiments done by Harlow, the lifework of Matějček, and more recently the contributions by Shore, Lansky, Morrison and others.

Most people and many medical practitioners assume that masochism is a sexual deviation. Much less known is the fact that moral masochism usually represents a permanent character trait, which can—but by no means has to—evolve into sexual deviation. Rousseau's biographers and interpreters did not realize that Rousseau was, in the first place, a moral (social) masochist. This is reason enough for a detailed discussion and demonstration of the whole issue of masochism as a character deviation.

Even Jean Starobinsky, one of the best known experts on Rousseau, did not appreciate correctly the importance and scope of Rousseau's masochistic deviation. The chapter on Rousseau's diseases (Starobinsky 1977, 542–560) contains only two references to this deviation. "Psychoanalytically speaking it is a sadomasochistic structure," is the conclusion expressed when Starobinsky compares Rousseau's description of his own weakness and "the seed of suffering" at birth with Rousseau's demand expressed in *Émile* that sick infants be put to death.

His second reference concerning "the inclination to masochism" can be found in the following sentence: "Because of his own cynical courage to lay bare his wounds in such a way and because he fearlessly describes his foolish deeds and misdemeanors (a stolen ribbon, tendency to masochism, deserted children), we have no reason not to trust him in less offensive matters."

Grimsley (1969), who studied Rousseau's psychology in detail, also considered his sexual masochism to be only a passing deviation of early years. His opinion that Rousseau was an exhibitionist is not correct.

Masochism formed not only Rousseau's personality and his character, it also manifests itself in his literary work. It is obviously responsible for his diseases as well, leading ultimately to his death. Masochism literally ruined Rousseau; Rousseau sacrificed himself. But, of course, his "sacrifice" earned him historical immortality.

The wide field of masochism represents different forms of deviation, many of which can be found in our patient. The word *masochism* was coined by Richard von Krafft-Ebing (1840–1902), in his work *Psychopathia Sexualis* published in 1866. It was meant to characterize the sexual deviation of an Austrian writer, Knight Leopold von Sacher-Masoch (1836–1896), who wrote in his novel *Venus in Fur*: "I find unique pleasure in suffering: tyranny, cruelty and particularly unfaithfulness of a beautiful woman heighten my passion."

The heroine of the novel, *Wanda*, is the embodiment of the female ideal of male masochists, "mistress" or domina, and this name remains in use to this day referring to women who offer their services to male masochists. These days Rousseau would not experience any problems finding the right domina, contrary to the situation in his time. Sacher-Masoch was a professor of history in Gratz and as such knew only too well that the history of mankind was an endless series of sadomasochistic cruelties. Rousseau, too, spent considerable time reading historical books on Ancient Rome and Greece and admired them despite their inconceivable brutality.

Krafft-Ebing described masochism mainly from a sexual point of view. We find in his description, however, the term *"ideeler Masochismus,"* and in this form the source of pleasure is not the physical masochistic relationship, but the idea of dependency and enslavement. In the year of publication of *Psychopathia Sexualis*, 1866, (which subsequently had many more editions), Sacher-Masoch was given a triumphant reception in Paris as a great writer. Part of his throng of admirers included Ibsen, Zola and Hugo, and his work influenced Goethe and Flaubert, for example in *Salammbô*. Sacher-Masoch and his friends resisted the description of sexual perversion for the term "masochism."

Before this, Krafft-Ebing, Baudelaire and Schoppenhauer used a different term to describe what became later known as masochism, a term borrowed from the Greek comedy-writerMeandr (or Terence)—Heautontimotoumenos —The Self-Tormentor, which was supposed to describe a person who punishes himself for having infringed honor.

Freud, in his discourse *Economic Problem of Masochism* (1924), did not limit masochism only to sexuality. He distinguished: 1) an "erotogenic" type of masochism; 2) a "feminine" type, which he considered to be the expression of innate feminine passivity combined with a sense of necessity to be punished; and 3) "moral masochism" characterized by a predominating sense of mostly unconscious guilt and where every pleasure has to be atoned for with the greatest suffering possible (see Rousseau: "For ten months later I was born, a poor and sickly child, and cost my mother her life. So my birth was the first of my misfortunes" [*Confessions*, 19]). Freud wrote that in a special orientation this kind of masochism is the most important form. *(In gewisser Hinsicht wichtigste Erscheinungsform des Masochismus.)*

This is why masochists act in a way that provokes the desired punishment (see below). Instead of "moral masochism," Reik (1977) prefers the term "social masochism" as more suitable; according to him, the latter has developed from the sexual deviation as "all round" masochism. The term "moral masochism," however, is used more often.

Freud's pupil, Wilhelm Reich (1933), analyzed the masochistic character, the origin of which he considered to be inseparable from social influences. A given culture is responsible for its neuroses and consequently for masochism (see the higher prevalence of masochism in "violent" cultures, Noyes 1998).

Masochism occurs in individuals whose need of affection has been frustrated in their childhood or whose needs along these lines have not been satisfied. On the other side, spoiled or pampered children are also candidates for the development of masochism. A masochist's need for affection and love is thus too great and is impossible to satisfy in real life. Their strong longing for love originates from a fear of being deserted. Many of them develop a sense of being left alone in the world.

Reich (1973) lists the following characteristic traits of moral masochists: a constant feeling of suffering, which manifests itself in a tendency to complain incessantly (citations of this kind abound in Rousseau's biography), a tendency toward self-damaging activities and self-abasement, timidity when dealing with other people, and efforts to make oneself look small.

The origin of masochism is seen by Reich as early childhood, similar to other researchers in this field, and the development of specific forms depends, according to him, on the degree of restriction or suppression of impulses from the outer world and the phase of childhood development in which this restriction or suppression occurred (let us remember that as a child, Rousseau was not allowed to associate freely with other children until his father left Geneva in 1722). Reich states in the spirit of his time, "The ego emerges from the conflicts between the inner world of impulses and the outer world; when neurotic, the ego forms a more or less rigid defensive 'armor' resulting in substantial restriction of psychological movability of the personality as a whole." (*Aus den Konflikten zwischen Trieb- und Außenwelt geht das Ich hervor, das im neurotischen Falle einen mehr oder weniger starren "Panzer" bildet, der die psychische Beweglichkeit der Gesamtpersönlichkeit sehr einengt.*)

In contrast to Freud, Reich emphasizes that a masochist in fact desires pleasure but, based on his childhood development, reacts to any heightened pleasure with anxiety and panic. The masochist is afraid not only of sexuality but fears also spontaneity, expansion and healthy aggressiveness. He tries to provoke punishment for his wrongdoing. Reich views masochism as a deviation which is difficult to correct, and adds that the last word about its origin will not come from psychologists but from biologists.

Fromm (1942) was concerned with the problem of freedom. Masochists find freedom embarrassing. They are afraid of it and try to escape by means of various escape mechanisms, including submission to someone else's authority. The burden of freedom can be escaped by forming a neurotic relationship with another person. It is not necessary for this to be an actual person. The role of the controlling authority can be played by one's own consciousness; for example, conscience, or a sense of responsibility. Man can be governed by his own conscience with the same harshness as by an outer authority—outer authority is simply transformed into inner authority. Fromm describes masochists as endeavoring to express feelings of insignificance, inferiority and helplessness, but deeper analysis shows that they unconsciously cling to them, despite conscious complaints about such feelings. Suffering, both physical and moral, and being treated as a child, further deepen the feelings of insignificance.

The Danish writer Hans Scherfig described in his novel, *The Missing Clerk*, the character of a clerk, Theodor Amstedt, whose attitude toward freedom resembles Rousseau's. His hero is imprisoned and it is his own fault—he was convicted of a murder which he did not commit. In prison, he is pleased to have gained internal safety and does not wish to be independent any more. In prison, he is at home, in the solid haven of authority. Let us compare his feelings with the views of Rousseau, who declared repeatedly that the greatest freedom he can imagine is to be in prison (Bastille).

Berliner (1947, 459) wrote: "The analogy with the sexual perversions obscured the fact that moral masochism is the general and basic form that furnishes the ground, upon which, in a minority of persons and under certain circumstances in psychosexual development, the perversion may evolve."

It appears to be ever more likely that the masochistic character orientation is primary and that this "character neurosis" (Wurmser 1993) may, in certain patients, evolve into sexual deviation. On the other hand, Goedde (1983), observes correctly that the characteristics of moral/social/nonsexual masochism are the same as those of its sexual counterpart: voluntary and demonstrative giving in to foreign power, to foreign will. Both forms of masochism need submission and desire humiliation and suffering. Freud wrote:

> The suffering itself is the important thing: whether imposed by someone whom the masochist loves or from an indifferent person, is irrelevant, it can even be caused by personal powers or circumstances, the real masochist holds always his cheek out whenever there's a chance to receive a blow. *(Das Leiden selbst ist das, worauf es ankommt: ob es von einer geliebten oder gleichgültigen Person verhängt wird, spielt keine Rolle: es mag auch von persönlichen Mächten oder Verhältnissen verursacht sein, der richtige Masochist hält immer eine Wange hin, wo er Aussicht hat, einen Schlag zu bekommen)* (Freud 1924, 378).

Moral (social/nonsexual) masochism is obviously much more prevalent than we realize and may be hidden under diverse social descriptions as "normal" or "correct" behavior.

In every human being there slumbers greater or lesser portions of masochistic predisposition, which can but need not be activated. The real motives remain hidden both to the affected individual and to society. We know parents, especially mothers, whose feelings of "self-sacrifice" are accompanied by a sense of pleasure and satisfaction of one's own "correct" behavior; there is the "absolute delight" from asceticism, or religious, ideological and patriotic martyrdom, or self-sacrifice for various political ideals such as National Socialism or Communism, or possibly their opposite ideologies. Self-sacrifice enables the affected individual to get rid of his own fears and anxieties and helps him, at the same time, to become a hero and an "important" figure. During this process the masochistic tendency remains hidden and unconscious.

The following extract, which was also used by Wurmser (1993), is from the work of Václav Havel, *Dálkovy vyslech* (Long-distance Interrogation), and may be considered an example of móral masochism:

> . . . that I simply knew that there is a kind of invisible wall between me and my surroundings and that I—which may seem paradoxical—felt sort of lonely, inferior, lost, ridiculed . . .

> Sometimes I even say to myself, whether the origin of my writing and striving after something did not just serve the purpose of overcoming my basic experience of unseemliness, awkwardness, sense of being out of place, simply an absurdity or learning to be able to live with it.

> . . . I steadily doubt myself and every while blame and curse myself nearly masochistically for something . . .

> . . . indeed, I am actually afraid of something, and even my alleged courage and stamina originate in fear: that is in fear of my own conscience which takes such pleasure in tormenting me for failures, real and supposed!

Havel's words are very typical of the feelings of a moral masochist and nearly identical expressions can be found by Rousseau: he feels guilty, lonely and inferior; other people ridicule him and persecute him. He feels he does not fit completely into society, has irrational fears combined with feelings of shame and his own consciousness torments him. References to a "wall of darkness" can be found also in Rousseau, he is shut in by "a triple wall of darkness." (In his 1999 New Year's Address, Havel returned once again to "walls," which divided the society). The reader will know that Havel is a writer-dramatist (masochists like writing and dramatizing) and issues of morality, truth, civic virtues, honor and conscience are among his favorite themes. Conscience can develop into a brutal power, an implacable inner judge, who can exercise absolute totalitarian power and who forces the affected individuals to do things which will certainly bring them punishment from the ruling regime (see Havel's fate under Communism).

According to Wurmser (1997) the masochist seeks suffering, pain or humiliation in exchange for love and respect. He sabotages success. Wurmser differentiates the following four forms:

> 1) Outer masochism: the main relationships with others seem to reflect an incessant search for and clinging to tormenting and humiliating partners, a need to end up as the victim;
> 2) Inner or moral masochism: tormenting, berating and shaming are mostly carried by the conscience and directed against the self;
> 3) Sexual masochism, masochistic perversion: sexual gratification is bound to symbolic or concrete pain and humiliation;
> 4) Masochism covered by a sadistic-narcissistic facade: what appears as outwardly directed cruelty and selfishness has to hide the acting out of masochistic core fantasy.

According to Wurmser, there are no strict boundaries between these four forms. They usually occur in combination but with different emphases. But masochistic features are universal. Certain forms of masochism become pathological only after they have assumed a compulsive character. Just as there exists normal narcissism or normal aggressiveness, there exists normal masochism.

He does not consider sexual masochism to be the basic form, which is what gave this perversion its name. The latter seems to be rather a defense against moral masochism, against the weight and pressures of superego.

Conscience creates the greatest conflicts, feelings of guilt, conflicts of loyalty and conflicts between moral values. Wurmser agrees with Berliner's (1947) view that the basic form is moral masochism, which can, under certain circumstances, develop into psychosexual perversion. Masochists are dominated by a painful event, especially the absence of the mother. "They sometimes try hard to transform suffering into action or at least provocation; they can exhibit strong hatred, or jealousy.

Almost all masochists have split natures. They perceive the outer reality as perceived by others, but in addition construct, in their minds, a reality of their own, which denies their traumatic past and is primarily formed by the totalitarian superego. Collision of these two realities is bound to lead to conflicts between masochist and society. The masochist's conscience is his inner judge, who passes harsh judgments on other people as well. It is sadism under the veil of morality. The masochist can behave cruelly and arrogantly to the surrounding world (counter-masochism—Berliner 1947; Cooper 1988).

Freud noticed that moral masochists seemed to be impotent more often than not and fantasized about being tied and beaten. Various authors later modified Freud's ideas. Biber (1966) supplied a very good historical overview and concludes that sadism and masochism represent maladaptive pathological responses to feelings of being threatened. Freud considered masochism to be sadism turned against one's own person. He based this view on the experience that a man, governed by aggressive impulses which cannot be expressed, turns these ultimately against his own person. He looks at masochism as a strategy aimed at preservation of life. Fights between wolves or dogs have been used as examples of this. A dog that feels it could be lethally hurt and is weaker, lies on its back, stops defending and deliberately exposes its most vulnerable spot—its neck. This behavior has an immediate effect and curbs the aggressiveness of the opponent. In this case, of course, we cannot speak of maladaptive behavior. Masochistic behavior should thus have an adaptive meaning as well.

Initially, sexual orientation of any person is autoerotic. The following gradual reversal of the polarity of sexual impulses from one's own body toward others is an integral part of human development. In cases where this development is disturbed it results in sexual deviation, which can then assume all sorts of different forms. Masturbation, for instance, is considered to be a deviant form of autoeroticism only when permanently replacing coitus. Oral eroticism, anal eroticism, pleasurable feelings connected with urination, pleasure derived from rhythmic movements (cradle, carousel, swinging), skin eroticism (tickling, stroking) are all well-known in children. Transition from autoeroticism to alloeroticism begins at the end of the first year of life when the child starts to experience others as objects of its own pleasure. It demands caressing hands, bodily warmth, stroking, tickling, mother's kisses.

Borneman's Classification of Masochism

Borneman (1990) differentiates the following forms:

Nonsexual or mental masochism,

This is characterized by the desire to be defeated both in personal and social life, to be submissive in one's job, and/or to be humiliated and unsuccessful (this type corresponds to moral/social masochism—see above). These people enjoy feelings of suffering and guilt, and illusions of inferiority; they complain about the cruelty of their fate, which persecutes them and to which they fall victim; and they suffer from feelings of being persecuted or being conspired against. They accept bad treatment without any protest. Weakness, humiliation and fear of success are only feigned, because they constantly provoke their defeat without being aware of it. They often suffer from insufficient libido. Fear of coitus is explained away (rationalized) by chastity. The patient is unable to overcome his status of childhood submissiveness and even tries to restore it subconsciously to experience again the joys of childhood, preeminently the absence of any responsibility. The typical nonsexual masochist does not show any sexual practices. We know with certainty that Rousseau masturbated all his life. It is very probable that he performed urethra masturbation beginning at the time of his stay in Venice (see below).

The whole course of Rousseau's life offers many examples typical of nonsexual masochists. Rousseau resisted responsibility during his whole life (he didn't stick to any of his jobs; he gave his children to a foundling hospital) and rationalized his acts as longing for "freedom" and "independence." Whenever he felt he could be successful in a job he quickly put an end to it (see his stay in Turin and his appointment as secretary for Duke de Gouvon, his work in the offices in Chambéry, Venice and by Francueil in Paris).

This type of person seems to want to live in an extremely unpleasant environment, to make sacrifices, to practice undignified jobs (note copyist), and to wear ugly clothes (according to his contemporaries Rousseau wore conspicuously torn clothes and dressed badly, especially after his "conversion"). They refuse to live in accordance with their own aesthetic standards and mental capabilities. To their compulsive desires belong repentance, isolation, captivity, being stripped of freedom, and submission.

Rousseau himself wished to lead a secluded life in a small house. Hermitage, dedicated to him by Mme d'Épinay; the reader is made to believe, however, according to his own presentation in *Confessions* that Rousseau only fulfilled Mme d'Épinay's wishes by living in the house. His considerate hostess knew of his dislike of the presence of other people and suggested to him that she would let him know when she was alone so he could visit her without fear. Rousseau described this suggestion as coercion, yoke, fetters and dependence.

Let us recall that Rousseau wrote on several occasions about his desire to be imprisoned in Bastille. He regarded his lonely stay on the island St-Pierre as the happiest period of his life and wished "that the island be appropriated to him as eternal prison" *(Rêveries)*. His ideal was Robinson Crusoe, who was "imprisoned" on a desolate island.

Rousseau lived in destitute seclusion with the semi-feebleminded Thérèse, who knew that Rousseau liked to be controlled and tormented, and so she slowly became the person controlling Rousseau, not only physically (catheterization), but also psychologically. Rousseau would not hear a word against her and always looked after the financial security of his "governess."

He punished himself by living as a hermit. He stressed that he was always happy in bad material situations and that his sense of happiness regularly disappeared when his fate improved and poverty receded. His misfortunes began with his decision to be an author and his subsequent achievement of fame and glory. At the beginning of the eighth promenade he makes some observations on this seemingly curious paradox: "The various periods of my brief prosperities have left me almost no pleasant memory of the intimate and permanent manner in which they affected me, and, on the contrary, in all the troubles of my life, I constantly felt myself filled with tender, touching and delightful feelings, which, while pouring a wholesome balm on the wounds of my bleeding heart, seemed to transform pain into pleasure."

Sexual or conjunctive masochism.

This requires sexual interaction in conjunction with the infliction of pain and humiliation from the sexual partner. The personality of the sexual masochist may differ considerably from that of a nonsexual masochist. In everyday life, the nonsexual masochist gives the impression of a weakling. A sexual masochist, on the contrary, gives the impression of a strong personality with authority and successes in social life. He may be conspicuous through his hardness, purposefulness and domineering attitude. According to Borneman (1990) the mental masochist suffers from an unconscious fear of success. The sexual masochist is unconsciously ashamed of success and has to be punished for it in his sexual life.

This distinction between the characters of sexual and nonsexual masochists, however, does not seem to be universally valid and one can find mixed types.

The provocative behavior of a masochist asking for punishment from his mistress represents a certain kind of defiant love towards mother. Accordingly, a domina is usually older than her slave. The masochist tries to transfer responsibility for his fate to her; in this context, Sartre speaks of the paradox of "seeking a guardian." It is basically an escape from the reality of life.

In Rousseau's life there were many women who met these criteria. His ideal was a woman representing half-mistress and half-motherly relationships for him. "He loves Mlle Lamberciere as mother and perhaps more than mother." He loves Mme de Warens too; he calls her maman all his life and finds her care quite satisfactory. The care of Mme de Warens goes so far that she teaches him intercourse, which Rousseau, as a true masochist, did not desire and which was indeed not pleasurable for him. Rousseau complied with this "lesson" only to gratify his protectress. He knew that a refusal of intercourse offered by a woman is always deeply insulting. He did not desire sexual intercourse with Mme de Warens.

Since Mme de Warens never realized his masochistic orientation and Rousseau never plucked up the courage to disclose them to her, he felt at his best when he could enjoy being alone with his protectress and lie at her feet as he was once ordered to do by Signora Basile in Turin. Let us further recall his relationship with Mme de Larnage and a number of other protectresses in Paris (Mme de Besenval, Mme de Broglie, Mme Dupin, Mme d'Épinay, Mme de Luxembourg, Mme de Verdelin, Mme de Bouffleurs, Mme Boy, and others).

One form of humiliation a masochist seeks with pleasure is to be deceived by his partner or by his own wife. Rousseau parted with Diderot over one single sentence, "Only a wicked man is alone," but he forgave Gaffecourt his attempt to seduce Thérèse when they traveled to Geneva in 1754 and they continued to be good friends.

We can find plenty of triangle relationships in his life with Rousseau invariably playing the passive role. It is well known that female masochists prefer rather callous, uneducated and rude men and provoke them so they will be raped and humiliated. The same is true for male masochists. It explains the seemingly mysterious attraction Thérèse had for Rousseau. According to Stekel, masochism can be defined as an attempt of a man to make the difference between his sexual partner and himself as great as possible.

Perverse or compensation masochism

This is characterized by the need for physical pain and mental humiliation, which replace the desire for sexual intercourse. The sexual desire to be whipped by a woman does not serve the purpose of initiating a process leading to sexual intercourse but replaces it. Orgasm is achieved spontaneously or through masturbation, or the patient can lack the ability to achieve orgasm entirely, which further increases the need of masochistic practices. These compensate for the missing intercourse.

This development can begin with the masochist's choice of an especially repugnant partner (intelligent Rousseau selected the semi-feebleminded Thérèse). Repugnance replaces pain as an instrument of humiliation. In Sacher-Masoch's novel, four black women stab Severin with needles—the epitome of humiliation in the nineteenth century, because blacks were generally despised.

The masochist does disgusting services for his mistress. Let us recall the episode where Rousseau urges Mme de Warens to spit out chewed up food and then eats it. This behavior category includes also eating women's excrement: at the premiere of *Le Devin du village* (The Village Soothsayer), Rousseau was, as he wrote, *sexually* aroused because he imagined licking the tears of the moved women in the audience.

This episode was recorded by Dr. A. Haidenheim, who described Rousseau's behavior as masochistic (see the footnote in Grimsley 1969, 53); here Professor Sells, who considered Rousseau a masochist based on Krafft-Ebing's descriptions, is also mentioned. Rousseau's own description of sexual arousal (*volupté du sexe*) at the sight of crying women in the theatre was also noticed by Winwar (1961), who did not interpret this as masochistic behavior, however.

In masochists, different variants of secretion fetishism are known: licking of sweat, vaginal secretions, ear wax, nasal secretions, umbilical dirt.

To this category also belongs the incident, reported in *Confessions*, which has not been appreciated as a manifestation of masochism by any author: Mme de Warens prepared different ointments from herbs and these "disgusting" things had soiled her fingers. She wanted Jean-Jacques to taste her drugs. In spite of the revulsion he felt at these drugs, he could not resist, he had to open his mouth and lick her fingers (*Confessions*, Book Three, 1728–1732).

The symbolic character of such a threat does not necessarily result in inflicting pain. It is often limited to mere fear and humiliation. The masochist wants to be ill-treated in a particularly humiliating way.

Automasochism refers to sexual activity of a patient who inflicts pain to his own body without any external assistance. This group involves all sorts of self-damaging activities such as causing injury to one's genitalia, burning of skin, pulling of nails, cutting off of one's nose or ears (van Gogh). One can even encounter swallowing of foreign objects or pulling out of one's own tongue. The methods of self-maiming (autotomy) constitute an incredibly long array of unbelievably cruel activities. One of them is self-catheterization. The dangerousness of many automasochistic, self-damaging activities is such that they can lead to the death of the affected person. It is likely that some cases of suicide are in fact lethal automasochisms (see Litman 1997; Litman 1996).

To obtain gratification, the masochist has to experience pain in all his sexual activities. Instead of coitus, which he unconsciously avoids, the masochist performs painful interventions on his body, one of which is self-catheterization. Autotomy is the sacrifice of one's body aimed at obtaining pleasure. It is essentially part of some religious practices, the principle of a sacrifice (the word "*keex*," originating in the Yucatan denotes sacrifice, and, at the same time, an object of exchange). The worshipper does something, which causes him pain with the aim of getting something else. The highest sacrifice is one's life (masochist asks others to strangle, hang them, etc.); the second greatest sacrifice is mutilation of one's body. In his last will in 1763, Rousseau demands that his body be dissected—sacrificed to the dissection knife, since it was necessary to find out the truth about his illness.

Borderline Personality and Masochism

Masochism has many features of a borderline personality, and borderline personality disorder has some features of masochism. Self-defeating (masochistic) personalities overlap more than 50 percent with borderline, avoidant, and dependent disorders (Reich 1987, and Finell 1992, used a good term, a *masoborderline* patient). Sadomasochism shows complementarity in the interaction of the narcissistic and borderline personality type. One is exploitative, grandiose and dominant, forever seeking admiration and exhibiting an aggrandized self, the other experiences humiliation, neediness, helplessness and the terror of aloneness (Finell 1992).

Borderline personality disorders (BPD) patients frequently have a diagnosis of depressive disorder, panic disorder, social and specific phobia, post-traumatic stress disorder (PTSD), and obsessive-compulsive disorder (Zimmerman and Matia 1999). The core aspect of borderline personality is impulsiveness, which causes depressive symptoms. In BPD patients, depressive symptoms are modified by impulsiveness, masochism, vanity, despair and difficulty in interpersonal relationships (Machizawa 1994). Impulsivity is stable over time and highly predictive of borderline psychopathology. Borderline personality suffers from extreme feelings, destructiveness or self-destructiveness, fragmentation or "identitylessness," and victimization (Zamarini et al. 1998).

BPD has a high rate of completed suicides, especially those with admixture of antisocial elements, chronic hostility and affective instability with depressive and anxious features (Rothenhauser and Kapfhammer 1999). Self-mutilative behavior is significantly related to PTSD, intermittent explosive disorder, disassociation and child abuse. To the self-mutilative behavior also belong self-injurious skin picking by obsessive-compulsive personality disorders and borderline personality disorders. In some cases it may represent an attempt to regulate intense emotions (Wilhelm et al. 1999).

Sex and Masochism

It appears that women have more masochistic traits, although they remain primarily limited to mental masochism. This type also does not deviate into conjunctive, compensation masochism and automasochism as often as in men. Maria Marcus (1981), herself a sexual masochist, quotes a woman from a meeting of Germaine Greer, who declared that about three-fourths of all women are masochists. In this context, she relates observations from old Russia, where women complained their husbands did not love them when they did not receive beatings from them. (Compare the familiar statement of Nietsche: If you are going to a woman, don't forget your whip!)

Natalie Shainess (1997) is convinced that masochism occurs more often in women: "I emphasized that masochism is more frequent in women because of the very great social reinforcement, not the biological endowment." Even sexual intercourse itself must be perceived by women as a masochistic act. This comes to an end only after nine months and the delivery itself amounts to an orgy of masochistic pleasure (Helene Deutsch 1944).

Women and masochists have much in common, with respect to many of their (character) traits: respect for authority, search for a strong personality they can "lean" against, search for a protector, higher levels of emotionality and sensitivity, enjoyment of myth and fantasy, and the predominant role played by the right hemisphere in thinking and behavior. Let us remember that women are more stimulated by words, whereas men by images. It is interesting that many women authors write about masochism these days, and, for that matter, about depression. Every woman likes to read about in love affairs. It explains the success of the novel La Nouvelle Héloïse. The masochist fulfilled women's masochistic fantasies.

Compared with that, the prevalence in men of more pronounced sexual variations and automasochism, which can even lead to suicide, may be higher. It is characteristic that Krafft-Ebing (1866), in his *Psychopathia Sexualis*, mentions thirty-four cases of male masochism compared with only three cases in women.

Early American studies on sadomasochism assumed that it mostly concerned men. More recent work, however, shows that 20 to 30 percent of the cases are women. Both sexes are capable of playing either sadistic or masochistic roles.

Fifty percent of men and 21 percent of women knew of their deviation before the age of fourteen. According to these recent studies, the sexual orientation of these men was mostly heterosexual, whereas the women, for the most part, stated they were bisexual.

It is interesting that both sexes with this deviation had above-average intelligence and socioeconomic status. They intended to continue their sexual activity, which may well explain the generally low success of therapy in this field. In these men the fantasies were more concerned with sadistic actions, whereas the women's fantasies had a predominantly masochistic character. In the United States, masochism is regarded as the most prevalent paraphilia in women (Diamant and McAnulty 1995).

The American Psychiatric Association decided to change the masochism category in DSM-III to a category called "Self-Defeating Personality" and cancelled it completely in DSM-IV (American Psychiatric Association Diagnostic and Statistical Manual of Mental Disorders) in 1994. Sexual sadism and masochism have been labeled as "discrete disorders." Masochism and sadism do not meet the criteria required for clinical diagnosis, as most people gain pleasure and sustain no damage from these activities. These are mostly subclinical manifestations and borderline deviations.

There can be no doubt, however, that the term "masochism," used to denote a personality deviation on the whole well-circumscribed, persists. It even appears that masochism is increasing, in a society characterized by competition (Shainess 1997).

Forms of Masochism in Rousseau

The review up to this point leads inevitably to the conclusion that Rousseau's masochism was actually a combination of several forms, and, further, that these combinations underwent changes throughout his life. The basic form was nonsexual masochism (moral, social) and this form had a decisive formative influence on Rousseau's character.

In his adolescence, we observe the emergence of sexual masochism (sexual arousal following a thrashing given to him by Mlle Lambercier; masochistic play with Mlle Goton). This form was joined (probably during his stay in Venice) by automasochism: he masturbated by means of self-catheterization.

After he had met Thérèse, Rousseau obviously passed to another phase, sexual-conjunctive masochism, where the sexual intercourse was preceded by painful urethra masturbation delivered by Thérèse's hands, who was "docile." The experienced pain symbolized subjection and self-sacrifice and Rousseau used it to heighten his sexual experience. It is not certain whether Rousseau was interested in sexual intercourse following these masochistic practices or whether he engaged in it only to reward Thérèse for her services. He was well aware of the fact that every woman looks at sexual intercourse as a kind of mutual bond, which forms a necessary component of women's psychology. Besides, he was convinced that women, in comparison with men, were more active sexually.

The records of Boswell provide clear evidence that Rousseau masturbated with Thérèse prior to having sexual intercourse with her. In the next phase of his life, conjunctive masochism was replaced by compensation masochism and Thérèse performed painful urethra masturbation on him with fateful consequences. Infections, which developed during urethra masturbation, closed a vicious circle: ascending infection led to chronic nephritis and the resulting renal failure was obviously the real cause of Rousseau's death (uremia).

Part Two—The Patient Jean-Jacques Rousseau

Chapter Seven

Etiology of Masochism

There is general agreement that the basis of masochism and masochistic tendencies develop in the first years of life when the personality is formed. "Part of the personal history of every masochistic patient is an unhappy childhood, often to such an extent that we have to ask ourselves whether the development of a masochistic character does not serve as a defense against schizophrenia or depressive psychosis," wrote Berliner (1947, 461). Antecedents of masochism; i.e., types of damaging events, insults, and so forth in early life, which lead to the development of masochism, emphasize the role of the mother as the decisive person for personality development (see Sullivan 1953). Most authors stress disturbed relationships to the mother: "Every single case began life with a highly unsatisfactory relationship to the mother" (Millet 1959; or Doryan Lebe 1997). For a very good up-to-date review see: Shainess (1997).

Most explanations of character disturbances in the early phases of life have been provided by psychoanalysis. Real understanding of the development and disturbance of children's brains is possible only as part of an integration of psychology with neurobiology (Schore 1994).

Brain development takes place in critical periods influenced by social environment. From its weight at birth, 400 grams, the brain of a child increases to 1000 grams by the end of the first year. Cortical regions, which mature later, are especially sensitive to postnatal influences. The development of children's brains passes through certain phases, which induce its hierarchical organization. The genetic program for brain development is activated and influenced by the postnatal environment. The initiation and conclusion of sensitive developmental periods is based on the activation and expression of certain genes. In this context the role of the external environment is played mainly by the mother, who consequently acts as a hidden regulator of the child's endocrine and nervous systems. The mother's behavior (external

environment) changes during this development and thereby induces reor-
ganization of the cerebral structures.

Role of Right Hesmisphere in Brain Development in Children

Newer research makes it increasingly obvious that various adverse environmental influences may disturb the maturing process of a child's individual
brain centers, localized mainly in the right hemisphere. The right hemisphere
is particularly important for normal brain development, as it matures earlier
than the left hemisphere. Orbitofrontal parts of the brain and their connections
with the limbic system play a particularly significant roll. Disturbed development of the right hemisphere can result in disturbances during postnatal
processes of cerebral lateralization and sexual cerebral dimorphism. Right
hemisphere may require emotional stimulation from the environment in order
to develop properly.

This new theoretical concept suggests the direction future research
concerned with masochism could take. Masochism is particularly related to
disturbances of emotionality. Among others, attention should be drawn to
works by LeDoux (1996) and Goleman (1997) that deal with connections
between the limbic system and emotionality, especially the emotions of
fear. Effeminacy, the female character of masochists as their characteristic
feature, could be explained by a "female" organization of the masochist's
brain. As these are rather new insights, it is necessary to describe them in
more detail.

It appears likely that unfavorable development during the first years of a
child's life can disturb maturation of particular brain centers, especially those
responsible for emotions, sociability and aggressiveness and thus for inten-
tional behavior. These centers include, apart from the orbitofrontal areas in the
right hemisphere, various nuclei of the limbic system. Here, the amygdala
(nuclei amygdala), regio septalis (septal region) and hippocampal formation
are of particular importance.

These brain centers mature gradually and the child's development is critical at this stage. Defective social interaction (e.g., absence of the mother) can
result in severe mental disturbances, as demonstrated by the classical experiments by Harlow (1963, 1966). Normal maturation of individual cortical and
limbic system centers is necessary for normal development of psychosocial
relationships in later years.

Together with defective maturation of individual limbic system centers, disturbed brain lateralization could also play a role in the etiology of masochism. Only proper cooperation of both cerebral halves (hemispheres) guarantees appropriate social behavior. Normal emotionality depends on proper balancing of the activities of both the left and right hemispheres. Cases where one brain hemisphere develops predominance result in the development of character changes.

Studies in patients who suffered isolated damage to the right or left hemisphere provide information on different "character" qualities of both cerebral halves. In patients with isolated left hemisphere damage a catastrophic-depressive mood sets in, as an expression of right hemisphere dominance when the pessimism ceases to be corrected by the left hemisphere. On the other side, patients with right hemisphere damage react with euphoria and mania as a result of lacking input from the right hemisphere.

The right hemisphere is dominant in non-verbal communication, whereas the left hemisphere dominates speech functions. Man is probably the only primate whose higher brain functions are partly extremely lateralized. Differentiation of cerebral functions is genetically coded and postnatally trained, during a relatively plastic stage of development.

Lateralization processes take place at different maturation times. Cerebral lateralization and proper coordination must be completed at a certain time; no later correction is possible. Prosodic features of a language are a good example—the speech center, located in the right hemisphere, matures at about ten years of age. Individuals learning a foreign language after this age learn its grammatical components correctly (semantic repertoire of a language is stored in the left cerebral half); however, they do not learn the proper use of foreign language prosodic components, i.e., the speech never loses its foreign accent. Cerebral lateralization results in roughly double the increased brain capacity.

Sexual hormones play an important role in prenatal organization of cerebral functions and consequently in lateralization. Both cerebral halves have different capabilities and solve different tasks by different means. The capacity for problem solving may grow larger and so does the potential for the development of inner conflicts in the form of moral conflicts, phobias, moral convictions and ideologies.

There are different kinds of intelligence connected to specific brain regions, and each exceptional intelligence usually has its symptoms of insanity which leads to atrophy of other kinds of intelligence. Genius could be defined as one-sided hypertrophy of one kind of intelligence.

In children under the age of four or five years old, the connection between hemispheres and information sharing between both cerebral halves is incomplete, because corpus callosum, a bunch of fibers connecting both sides, is still insufficiently myelinized and therefore unable to transmit information precisely.

Even in adults, the exchange of information between hemispheres is not always optimal and it seems that a precise communication between both cerebral halves is not always necessary. For more detailed information see Miller, Cummings (1998) and Molfese and Segalowitz (1988).

It is probable that every adult person has his or her own "hemispheric reaction pattern," which can undergo certain changes even during later life. Functional lateralization is more pronounced in adult men than in adult women and in right-handed people versus left-handed. Functional asymmetry of a woman's brain, in comparison with a man's, is less pronounced; in men, prenatal fetal androgens organize the brain in a different way.

Because of the less pronounced cerebral lateralization in women, the role played by right-sided hemispheric functions in behavior is more conspicuous. Women respond in a more emotional manner, have a stronger tendency to fear experiences and are more cautious as well as pessimistic. They show more compassion for others, a tendency which is generally dangerous for one's psyche. Compassion can lead to feelings of shame and guilt which can in turn result in depression.

The left hemisphere is called dominant mainly because it contains speech centers (Broca's and Wernicke's areas), and because the awareness of one's ego and self-consciousness (self-esteem) are localized there. The latter fact could explain higher levels of self-esteem usually encountered in men. It is oriented towards cognitive strategies, employing logical and analytical approaches. Its moods tend to be optimistic and carefree.

The right hemisphere is specialized for visual-spatial and some musical functions and processes tasks rather globally. It is responsible for orientation, attention and emotional functions.

Emotional dominance makes it possible for the left hemisphere to recognize more easily the emotional meaning of facial expressions, gestures, non-verbal components of speech and social situations. It also controls communication of emotions, and their verbal as well as non-verbal expression.

Emotionality of the right cerebral half, and the expression of its emotions in a situation where their cognitive control by the left hemisphere is insufficient, gives the impression of "spontaneous" and "authentic" emotions, which are at the same time "cruel" and "culturally non-conformist." Such emotional expressions are typical for children, who say what they think and see, irrespective of the cultural correctness of such emotions (see Andersen's fairy tale *The Emperor's New Clothes*). It determines the individual's moods much better than the left hemisphere. It also controls tolerance of pain.

Experiments on pain tolerance demonstrated that the left half of the body (controlled by the right hemisphere) has lower pain tolerance in comparison with the right part (controlled by the left hemisphere). It obviously explains the higher sensory and emotional sensitivity of women in comparison with men.

The linguistic imagination of writers and highly differentiated imagery of language are developmentally young and their centers are located in later evolutionary regions of the cerebral cortex, in the prefrontal part of the frontal lobe and in the temporal lobe. It may be that the degree of lateralization of functions of the associative (integration) brain regions in neocortex increases with the "lateness" of emergence of the function in the course of human phylogenetic evolution. The right hemisphere seems to be responsible for emotional expression. It further controls responses by the autonomic nervous system to emotional stimulation and is probably responsible for vegetative functions. Patients who have suffered right hemisphere damage have insufficient excitability, which leads to "hypoarousal."

The right hemisphere is very active during REM stages of sleep and is therefore related to dreams as well as confabulations and mystical experiences. Dreams are usually cheerless and we tend to wake up soaked with perspiration and filled with horror, thankful that we have escaped the dream. It is probably the result of the pessimistic and gloomy mood of the right hemisphere.

It must be mentioned that, from an evolutionary point of view, the right hemisphere was more important earlier than at present and was therefore "dominant" because of its greater importance for our ancestors. It was able to better decode the meaning of gestures, facial expressions and emotional components of speech. Writing itself has developed from pictures.

In children, the right cerebral half seems to be more important and "dominant." Children act more emotionally and use the so-called pre-linguistic code in their information processing. Children's dreams, fears and emotional experiences are processed nonverbally by the limbic system and right hemisphere. In this phase, the child's psyche is very vulnerable (Langmeier and Matějček 1975).

The most important processing of emotional experiences takes place in the amygdala. According to experimental work by LeDoux (1996) the visual and acoustic information from regions surrounding the amygdala can reach the thalamus before it reaches the cortex and the amygdala react to these stimuli faster (than the cortex). In a dangerous situation every split second is important for survival and this explains why the amygdala receive this prompt information. When the situation is assessed as dangerous, vegetative defense response can be triggered immediately.

Emotional experiences produced by amygdaloid nuclei in response to relevant stimuli are stored in memory without the conscious participation of the cortex and can be activated unconsciously in similar situations at any time. In this way "cognitive unconsciousness" is formed. The amygdala is thus the site of all passion. When the fibers connecting amygdala with other cerebral parts are severed, the affected individual becomes unable to assess the meaning of emotional events and the result is "affective blindness" concerning all emotions.

Crying—formation of tears, too—is set off by the amygdala and a nearby region of cerebral cortex, the cingulate gyrus. The amygdala is responsible for the origin and coordination of an emotional reaction. Post-traumatic stress disorders (PTSD) are caused by incessant signals sent into the consciousness by irritated amygdala. The victims feel their suffering is not accidental and that they have been chosen on purpose. Their ideas of people's trustworthiness and the safety of interpersonal relationships deteriorate.

I have already mentioned that the left cerebral hemisphere tends to communicate positive emotions and the right hemisphere negative emotions. The left hemisphere is involved in "approach" maneuvers (Annäherungsemotionen), the right in separation or "avoidance" tendencies (Vermeidungsemotionen). People with higher activity of the left prefrontal lobe are more likely to be good-natured, they enjoy life and people more. People with relatively high activity of the right cerebral half tend toward negativism and bad moods. They are more easily engulfed by problematic life situations, are unable to solve them purposefully—they continue to suffer because they are not able to get rid of their sorrows and worries.

The right hemispheric orbitofrontal affect regulator performs functions that are essential to the adaptive moral functioning of the individual. This frontolimbic system is identical to the ego ideal, described in the psychoanalytic literature as a component of the superego that emerges at 18 months. In current revision of this theory, the superego is understood to modulate emotional expression and mood states, and the ego ideal functions to regulate self-esteem. The superego affect of shame arises when a self-monitoring system process evaluates that there has been a failure to meet ego ideal expectations (Shore 1994, 353–354).

The emotions of fear and disgust, to a lesser degree, show the strongest right hemispheric lateralization; most often they are considered to be located in the right temporal area. The right hemisphere signals immediately all unusual environmental events and irregularities. When a known environmental pattern appears disturbed, when something new and unexpected emerges, requiring implementation of unusual means to cope with the situation, feelings of fear arise. Emotions thus serve as a basis for moral standards and conformist behavior.

This explains much of women's behavior; women try not to offend the collective conscience or societal moral standards. Imperatives of moral behavior are expected to have a clear "binary" code. It should be exactly set out what is correct and what is not correct, what is fair–unfair, moral–immoral. Emotional memory, which mainly depends on normal amygdala function, can then cope with feelings of anxiety and rectify them. In cases where the connection between cerebral cortex and amygdaloid nuclei does not function properly or when the amygdala is itself irritated, feelings of fear can deepen.

For this reason women tend to be more religious. Women have no sympathy for paradoxes making many different "truths" possible. The world's relativity is man's business. Every woman is morally–emotionally convinced that what she does is "morally" correct. Adherence to moral codes represents adherence to conventional social relationships. Life is predictable and not filled with expected reversals.

For a woman, fear is synonymous with pain. It should prevent her from launching dangerous ventures associated with feelings of fear. Feelings of fear arise in women more easily; they are more intensive and often irrational in nature. Women cope with feelings of fear with more difficulty, which may explain the fact that they suffer from pathological feelings of fear more often than men do and are plagued by various phobias and depressions. The experience of stress by women is also more intensive. Women also tend to communicate their feelings willingly to other people, who are then more likely to respond with providing protection and help to "the weaker sex."

Women cry more often and crying serves the purpose of expressing that positive or negative emotions, or sensory impulses, are reaching levels which are too high. This higher emotional sensitivity is not sufficiently inhibited by the left hemisphere and is freely verbalized. This also gives rise to typical "women's speech," which contains more questions (isn't it true?), more expressions of doubt and more "intensifiers," words which intensify meaning: something is terribly sad, awfully beautiful, really interesting, endlessly long, incredibly sweet, extremely nice, etc. Women's speech is more fluent; it contains fewer pauses and grammatical mistakes, and the sentences are more complex. Women's aggressive actions are often verbal and aimed at inflicting mental pain.

Men and women prefer to talk about different things. Women attach more importance to personal relationships, intimate feelings, family, friendship, and questions of morality and virtue. They are susceptible to violations of morality and virtue, which explains their interest in scandals. Rousseau's literary style can serve as a good example of the way women talk, with innumerable baroque-style metaphors, rhetorical questions and copious, sentimental expressions. Being a masochist, he likes to use passive forms ("To submit henceforth to my fate, to persist no longer in struggling against it . . ." and another example, "Even though they torment me for the rest of my days, they will not prevent me from dying in peace.") His literary style was therefore very popular with women. Women like to hear emotional exaggerations.

The site which records feelings of pain, is thought to be the cingulate gyrus, which seems to be set up differently in the two sexes. Cingulum resting metabolic activity obtained by PET was found to be higher in women. Cingulate gyrus is probably also the site of cortical affective perception of pain. In intractable pain, severe depressions and severe anxiety states, cingulectomy (surgical excision) or cingulotomy (interruption of connecting fibers) is performed.

It is well known that women complain about pains and feel ill more often than men. Amygdaloid nuclei or at least some of their parts are associated with feelings of fear, embarrassment, feelings of guilt and pangs of conscience. It is assumed that people with these character traits (which typically occur in masochists) are born with a neuro-chemical arrangement of these centers that facilitates their arousal.

Significance of shame and feelings of guilt and fear

Oversensitive and scared children become fearful and shy adults. It is estimated that 15 to 20 percent of all children are "behaviorally inhibited." As adults they often seek seclusion, they fear performances in public and are reticent. The behavior of parents or educators can have a positive influence on children's timidity. Otherwise the increased irritability of amygdala remains unchanged, especially when mothers behave protectively and prevent exposure of their children to situations of daily life. A parent's opinion that the child has to "rub off the corners" strengthens the self-esteem of a fearful child.

Research on development of the *sense of shame* has shown the deep influence a mother can have on the mental development of a child in the first years after birth. A sense of shame always accompanies masochism, as do the feelings of fear, guilt and inferiority. The reasons for the strong correlation between shame and masochism are not yet known, as are the circumstances in which shame aids the development of masochism. It is very probable that this is the point where the "secret of masochism" will be broken, as suggested by Freud when he wrote: "All makeshift ideas in psychology are probably going to be anchored in organic structures one day." Freud himself stressed mainly guilt as the emotional state responsible for the genesis of various psychological pathologies. Freud occasionally mentioned also shame, but he probably never differentiated between guilt and shame. At present, the pathogenetic factor is thought to be shame and extensive research is attempting to find the difference between guilt and shame. Excessive shame is said to be the cause of alcoholism, drug abuse, antisocial behavior, "borderline personality," depression, bulimia and anorexia, pathologic narcissism, paranoia, hysteria, post-traumatic stress, sexual variations—paraphilias, excessive shyness and similar problems (review with bibliography, see Harder 1995).

Although shame and guilt often occur together, it appears that shame is the predecessor.

The nature of shame is "preverbal" and it evokes the feeling of social fear.

Feelings of guilt occur after the child has begun to use speech. Shame appears to be a devastating feeling of self-disgust and self-paralysis, together with the feeling of looking silly. The affected looks upon himself as a childish, stupid, humiliated, scared person, someone despised by others. Another often-encountered phenomenon is the attack of "rageful anger." The feeling of guilt is less destructive for one's consciousness as only certain acts are bad—guilt, however, can lead to feelings of self-hatred when it is seen as irreparable.

It is important to differentiate between *shame* and *shyness:* the latter can be seen in children as young as three months old. Shyness seems to be more a biological than a psychological phenomenon. It does not necessarily have the component of evaluation as some children show signs of shyness at birth.

Shame has been called the *hidden emotion* (Helene Lewis 1987) and a *sleeper in psychopathology,* or *the bedrock of psychopathology.* The sense of shame can be found in different mental disorders. For the person experiencing shame it is undesirable and can be controlled only with difficulty—it has its facial expression and inhibits specifically interest and pleasure. Feelings of fear and a sense of guilt are closely connected and invariably occur together. *The function of shame is to prevent and avert certain socially unacceptable actions.* With the increasing complexity of the brain, the sense of shame acquires the potential to influence more cerebral functions.

The sense of shame can have also positive effects, because its realization, together with fear, draws our attention to imminent danger and forces us to take defensive actions.

"Shame fits" resemble acute states of social phobias. A person plagued by different social phobias tends also to experience shame. Shame is accompanied by a desire to run away and hide—a desire which is also characteristic of social phobias. On the other hand, shame is connected with feelings of rage and wrath developing as its consequence. Many researchers have found that shame is accompanied by an increased tendency to rage; feelings of guilt, on the other hand, show no association with rage. Concealing shame behind expressions of indignation is a "face saving" strategy, typically used by men, where it becomes the source of violence. Bowlby (1973) entitled the second volume of his *Attachment Trilogy: Separation, Anxiety and Anger.*

PET scans obtained on persons experiencing feelings of fear and worry showed an increased metabolic activity of the right frontal lobe and basal ganglia on the same side—these are concerned with the processing and coordination of information. Another site with increased metabolism was the cerebellum, whose functions also include the storing of routine and often used patterns of both thought and movement. Other activated structures included the nuclei in *pons cerebri*, which control brain arousal.

The Role of Corticotrophin-Releasing Factor (CRF)

CRF (a peptide comprised of forty-one aminoacids) plays a role in depression and anxiety disorders and with high probability in masochism, too. CRF is a hypothalamic releasing factor which has a dual role in integrating hormonal and neural mechanisms by acting both as secretagogue for anterior pituitary hormones and as an extrapituitary peptide neurotransmitter. CRF acts as a neurotransmitter in the noradrenergic locus coeruleus (LC) to activate this system during stress. Endogenous CRF systems in the brain may have a role in mediating behavioral responses to stress. CRF neurons activate the locus coeruleus. Norepinephrine systems, emanating from locus coeruleus mediate behavioral constructs associated with alertness, arousal, and stress. This feed-forward system may be particularly important in situations where the organisms must mobilize not only the pituitary adrenal system but also the central nervous system.

Such feed-forward mechanisms in a fundamental brain-activating system may be particularly vulnerable to dysfunction and thus may be the key to a variety of pathologic conditions, such as anxiety, and affective disorders (Koob 1999; Manzaghi et al. 1993).

Stress, in particular *early-life stress*, has been associated with a *higher prevalence rate of affective and anxiety disorders in adulthood*. CRF is hypersecreted from hypothalamic as well as from extrahypothalamic neurons in depression, resulting in hyperactivity of the hypothalamic-pituitary-adrenal (HPA) axis (Aborelius et al. 1999). Chronic stress with permanent HPA axis activation and glukokortikoid (GC) hypersecretion has a detrimental effect on some brain structures. Chronic stress plays a role in several human pathologies. Glukokortikoid hypersecretion affects hippocampal function. In the brain, the hippocampus has the highest concentration of GC receptors. Chronic stress induces neuropathological alterations, such as dendritic atrophy in hippocampal neurons, which are paralleled by cognitive deficits (Raber 1998). Children with avoidance history have bad memories and cognitive abilities.

Psychological trauma is associated with dissociative phenomena and trauma-related distress (Gershuny and Thayer 1999). Dissociative symptoms include *flashbacks*, i.e., vivid scenic recollections of traumatic episodes in patients with borderline personality disorder. In Rousseau's life we have seen many such flashbacks (remember the accusation of his father that Jean-Jacques was the cause of his mother's death).

There is evidence suggesting changes in endogenous opioids by such patients. Naltrexone, an opioid receptor antagonist may reduce dissociative symptoms (Schmal et al. 1999; Bohus et al. 1999). These findings could answer the old question: Why are pain and humiliation sometimes connected with agreeable feelings? Changes in endogenous opioid secretion under stress conditions may be the explanation.

The Role Of Mother in Early Socialization

In children of less than two years of age, normal maturation and development of the brain requires the presence of contacts between the child and its mother. The mother's care has a direct influence on neuronal junctions in children's brain (Dawson 1994). Here again, the right hemisphere is dominant because it matures earlier than the left and collects socio-emotional information. It also controls the expression and regulation of more primitive emotions.

At this stage, visual contact between mother and child is decisive. For the child, the most important stimulus is the mother's facial expressions and the child accordingly shows great interest in the mother's face, especially her eyes. Eye contacts between mother and child represent their mutual dialogue, which takes place in milliseconds; eye contacts increase in the second and third trimesters of the first year when myelinization of the child's cortical visual areas in occipital parts of the brain takes place. Eye contacts between mother and child represent a social game characterized by rapidly and synchronously changing facial expressions of both partners and development of "interaffectivity." The human face is a unique stimulus—facial expressions communicate biologically important information. The developing love relationship or attachment also regulates internal arousal.

Visual stimulation affects the child's brain and represents a "protoconversation" between mother and child. This relationship forms the basis for the emerging emotions of a child. "Protoconversation" affects the levels of neurotransmitters in children's brain—dopamine and norepinephrine. Dopamine is associated with the arousal and expectation of reward and with processes leading to the feeling of pleasure. Another effect is elevation of CRF (corti-cotrophin-releasing factor) levels stimulating in turn higher adrenaline levels.

The mother's face has also been found to increase endorphin (endogenous opiate) levels in the developing brain. These induce feelings of pleasure from social interaction and social emotions.

Norepinephrine, dopamine and opioids function as trophic regulators of brain development. Studies in children show that they love and actively look for these eye dialogues. Normal eye conversation induces not only the development and maturation of prefrontal brain areas, which constitutes 30 percent of the total area of human cortex, but also maturation of connections between the cortex and limbic systems.

In this process, a central role is played by the orbital area of the prefrontal lobe "hidden" on the ventral and medial surface of the prefrontal lobe. For its rich connections with the limbic system, it is called the "association cortex" of the limbic formation. Interestingly, the critical period for the effects sexual steroids have on differentiation of orbitofrontal cortex falls into the first months after birth (Clark and Goldman-Rakic 1989, quotation according to Shore 1994, 262). Here again, the decisive role is played in the right cerebral half, which matures earlier than the left, and therefore can be more easily modified by early social experiences; its activity underlies the relationships of affection and love.

In early childhood, by the end of the first year, 90 percent of the mother's care consists of providing love, games, excitement and care. Later on, around the eighteenth month, the mother's behavior changes dramatically. The person who provided limitless care changes into the person who induces the child's socialization and starts to limit, more and more, the activities of the child. Socialization is indispensable to the development of shame and guilt. Socialization causes the child to care about the opinions of others, making the child want to follow social standards. It teaches the child about rules and standards for behavior, and endows particular standards with significance. In the "toddler" period, the expression on the mother's face disapproves and forbids every nine minutes, on average.

The mother has to convince the child that it must not give in to temper tantrums, that it is not allowed to inquire freely into everything and that it must control its bladder and bowel movements. Initially, the child's socialization thus includes the setting of limits to positive emotions.

Socialization can succeed only through developing a sense of shame, which becomes the "primary social emotion"; it develops at the age of fourteen to sixteen months. A child, accustomed in its contacts with its mother to encounter expressions of joy, starts to discover that the mother does not simply reflect its own feelings but sometimes dissatisfaction, an affect awakening stressful feelings of shame in the child. Expectations have not been met.

Disapproving facial expression represents a means of socialization which parents employ, although they are often unaware of it. For children, facial expressions of disapproval are very strong stimuli, because, at this stage, children are unable to control negative feelings automatically. Parasympathetic inhibition systems in the frontal lobes develop later than those in charge of excitation sympathetic processes.

According to Shore (1998), the child responds with stress reactions accompanied by increased corticosteroid levels and decreased levels of endogenous opiates and CRF. Whereas in the first year the "dialogues" with mother were followed by the ergotrophic, energy mobilizing influence of the sympathetic system, now the obvious disapproval in mother's face produces a *sense of shame, which is accompanied by parasympathetic arousal,* inhibiting activity and inducing the cheerless stress reaction. The parasympathetic arousal is mediated by the vagus nerve, the influence of which improves, according to recent findings, functions of memory. It is a common experience that we tend to remember stronger emotional experiences which lead to activation of the vagus nerve (dangerous life situations, dreadful experiences and so forth).

For the further development of a child, the decisive factor is the duration of this parasympathetic stress reaction.

When the expression of disapproval disappears quickly from mother's face and a pleasant mutual eye contact is established, shame is metabolized and controlled rapidly, and the previous relationship of love and affection is reestablished. From the point of view of affect regulation, the overcoming of stress in a child is necessary. This process was described as "disruption and repair." At eighteen months the child for the first time exhibits moral pro-social altruistic behavior in the form of conforming to—regulating the negative affect of—a distressed other. This other-oriented empathy is attained when the child is capable of reading its own negative as well as another's negative internal state. These formulations suggest that moral development begins earlier than previously thought, and is much more of a visual than a verbal process (Shore 1999, 354).

When a child is punished by derision, humiliation and rejection, it devel-

---

ops a sense of being unworthy of help. Humiliation, especially when associated with punishment, results in dysregulations accompanied by an increased parasympathetic system tone and a simultaneous increase of sympathetic system tone; these dysregulations can lead to a state called "shame rage." By itself, shame is not harmful. It can be harmful only when its autoregulation has not been successfully attained. Long-lasting periods of negative affective states inhibit the development of the limbic system (Shore 1998). Interpersonal relationships with others can become internally encoded ("internalized") and act as biological regulators controlling physiological processes.

Activation of orbitofrontal cortex activates the vagus-parasympathetic system, and induces internal inhibition and paralyses activity. The hypothalamic-pituitary-adrenal axis is also activated. In this way, the right hemisphere controls both physiological and endocrine functions, which are primarily controlled by subcortical centers. Centers influenced by this process include not only those controlling the gonads but also adrenals (Wittling and Pflüger 1990). In this connection it is worthwhile to remember that in depression, too, cortisol and cortisone levels are elevated and, in a longer-lasting depression, hypertrophy of adrenal cortex occurs; the latter can be reversed by successful therapy of depression.

In the right-hemispheric cortex, a vagus regulatory circuit for emotions, controlled by right-hemispheric orbitofrontal cortex, has been described (Porges, Doussard-Roosevelt and Maiti 1944, quoted in Shore 1988, 70).

Sufficient evidence has been accumulated to show that negative emotions activate the first (not left) hemisphere, by which they are afterwards modulated. This hemisphere contains the "nonverbal affect lexicon" for facial expressions. Even "primitive, biological" shame (Brouček 1982), which is the most painful and least easily tolerated negative emotion, originates in the right hemisphere. The words "shame" and "humiliation," when administered tachistoscopically to experimental subjects, activate specifically the right hemisphere.

Erikson's classical conception describes shame as a state in which an individual tries hard to conceal his face because of his belief that *others* are gazing at him. This state is also described by Rousseau, particularly in his later years. He feels he is incessantly watched by "strange, hidden eyes." (Hostility of another's gaze, and a feeling of being constantly watched by unseen, sinister eyes; his will is paralyzed by the "insulting . . . impudent . . . cruel . . . mocking," and "malevolent" looks of others; baleful looks make him feel he is an object of "contempt," etc.)

Apart from these negative effects of shame it must be stated that *expressed shame has the effect of appeasing other people,* who are then more willing to forgive and pardon the social transgressions of a person signaling his or her sense of shame. Those who are able to feign feelings of shame can count on society's support.

Generally speaking, women are much more "skilled in shame" than men and imitate with pleasure the behavior of small children, an activity that has a damping effect on social aggressions.

Those who internally reject shame following social transgressions, or cannot signal it, must be prepared to meet relentless and hard response from other people. Therefore, shame is also a defensive social strategy, which can stop imminent aggression by other members of society.

Masochists have the interesting ability to shame "internally" but, at the same time, do not always signal their feelings of shame to other people. By deliberate provocation and social transgressions, which can bear the labels of truth, justice, humanity, etc., moral masochists ask for societal punishment. A sexual masochist consciously violates orders issued by his mistress in order to obtain punishment. The masochist lacks the "appeasing" function of shame. Rousseau knew only too well that his writings must provoke society. Despite that, he never revealed his feelings of shame and always defended his opinions as "true." Only when *Émile* and *Contract social* had been published did he succeed in escalating social provocation to such a degree that he earned a punishing societal response, for which he secretly wished.

Where the ability to *overcome* the feelings of shame does not develop in an individual, passive coping mechanisms, governed by the parasympathetic nervous system, occur even in later life and are expressed in immobility, feelings of surrender, submission and seeking a refuge, where the affected could hide, to prevent other people from looking at him. The problem-focused coping behavior, trying to solve social problems by active, purposeful action, is exchanged for emotion-focused coping, trying to limit the stressful social impact.

Women prefer emotional coping mechanisms, as they think more with the right hemisphere and have thus a higher incidence of depression, shame, social phobia, apprehension, "life masochism" and pessimism.

"Germinal" masochism, therefore, similar to shame, could evolve as early as in the first two years of life where, in the absence of a mother, disturbed socialization processes probably occur. These processes do not result in shame removal, but in its persistence, accompanied by permanent activation of right hemisphere and limbic system. In masochists, the right cortico-limbic system appears to be not only hypertrophied but also dysfunctional. It should furthermore be clear that shame and masochism have much in common, even though their mutual (causal?) interconnection has not yet been clarified.

In Rousseau's life, we find typical features of both the presence of extreme shame and masochism. Rousseau's social life is inactive, marked by submissiveness; he surrenders easily, seeks escape from oppressive reality in fantasies and seclusion. He sees society as the source of evil and suffering. He can, however, suppress feelings of shame when his purpose is to obtain social punishment. Punishment, humiliation and abasement bring new and probably more intensive feelings of shame.

The reader who read these lines attentively and compared them with masochists' character traits, will easily recognize that masochists behave and think like women, i.e., more with the right hemisphere, and that the organization of their amygdaloid nuclei is more sensitive and has a reaction mode similar to that of women.

This new insight can possibly shed light on the "mystery" of masochism. Freud maintained that masochism is intimately related to femininity and, indeed, the behavior of a male masochist exhibits many features justifying this statement. Of course, being a man, the masochist cannot exhibit pure feminine features. Reik (1977) remarked that a masochist always distorts his feminine character. It is interesting, as far as sexual masochism is concerned, that this deviation occurs in women less frequently than in men.

The deviation of cerebral lateralization in masochists could occur prenatally, during the phase of brain "masculinization" or in the early postnatal period. "As a species, human beings have a basic ambisexualism of the brain and its imagery. However, hormonal history prenatally, in interaction with gender history postnatally, usually resolves the ambisexualism into unisexualism . . ." (Money et al. 1984).

Women and masochists are more emotionally minded, they tend to be near to tears (function of amygdala): In his literary work, Rousseau described on countless occasions how he wept in somebody's hands, shed bitter tears of pain or joy, etc. The behavior of women and masochists is similar—they behave "submissively" and seemingly non-aggressively, they respect authority and

tend to conform, they like to speak of morality, and are more skilled at concealing their feelings (Shainess speaks of chameleon behavior, which is almost "as
sweet as saccharine" and, in the same tenor, Rousseau describes himself as
being more changeable than an amoeba, or a chameleon—self-portrait in
Persifleur), they have a flair for dramatization and take pleasure in tragic events.

According to H. Walpole, life is a comedy for those who think and a
tragedy for those who feel. The literary work of Rousseau does not spark any
single sparklet of humor and Rousseau himself had no sense of humor. He also
lacked Voltaire's sharp irony.

The Role of Memory in Future Interpersonal Relations

Interpersonal experiences directly influence how we mentally construct
reality. The brain constructs internal reality as it interacts with the environment
in the present, in the context of its past experiences and expectations of the
future.

This shaping process occurs throughout life, but is most crucial during
the years of childhood. Even short episodes of maternal deprivation have powerful neuroendocrine effects on the ability to cope with future stressful events.
Memory can be seen as the way the mind encodes elements of experience into
various forms of representation.

There is a common misconception about memory, that we are always
aware of what we have experienced and that when we remember something,
we have a feeling of recollection.

From the first day of life, infants perceive the environment around them.
This implicit memory does not require conscious processing during encoding
and retrieval. Focal attention is not required for encoding. This type of memory is independent of the medial temporal lobe and hippocampus. The mind is
capable from the very beginning of creating generalizations from experience.
Prior experiences shape our anticipatory models, and thus the term "prospec-
tive memory" has been used to describe how the mind attempts to "remember
the future," based on what has occurred in the past. Anticipating the future
may be a fundamental component of implicit memory, distinct from the capacity to plan for the future. The more complex and deliberate aspect of planning
may depend upon the explicit memory processes.

An infant who has a healthy, secure attachment has had the repeated experience of nurturing, perceptive, sensitive, and predictable caregiving respons-

es from its mother, which have been encoded implicitly in its brain. An infant with an insecure attachment may have experienced the parents as less predictable, emotionally distant, or perhaps frightening. These experiences, too, become encoded implicitly, and the infant's mind has a generalized representation of this relationship that can be filled with uncertainty, distance or fear. This state of mind, a part of the infant's emotional memory, has been implicitly learned during the first year of life. When children develop secure attachments to parents, these allow them to go out into the world to explore and develop relationships with others. The first year appears to enable implicit but not explicit encoding and retrieval.

Explicit memory requires conscious awareness and focal attention for encoding. For storage, hippocampal processing is required. Explicit memory is what most people mean when they refer to the generic idea of memory. This type of memory develops by the second birthday and reflects the maturation of the brain's medial temporal lobe (which includes the hippocampus) and orbitofrontal cortex. Explicit memory has two forms: "semantic" (factual) and "episodic" (autobiographical, or oneself in a episode of time)

The child is able to talk about his recollections of the day's events, and to remember more experiences from the past. Retrieval is a "memory modifier": the act of reactivating a representation can allow it to be stored again in a modified form.

We sense, perceive, or filter our explicit memory through the mental models of implicit memory. Forgetting is an essential aspect of explicit memory.

Interpersonal experiences appear to have a direct effect on the development of explicit memory. Elaborative parents talk with their children about what they, the children, think about the stories they read together. In contrast, "factual" parents who are found to talk only about the fact of stories, not a child's imagination or response, have children with a less developed ability for recall.

If events are filled with terror, a number of factors may inhibit the hippocampal processing of explicit memory, and therefore may block explicit encoding and subsequent retrieval. Such conditions allow implicit memory to be encoded while explicit processing is impaired. Moderate amounts of stress facilitate memory, and large amounts impair memory. The effects of high levels of stress hormones on the hippocampus may initially be reversible and involve the inhibition of neuronal growth and the atrophy of cellular receptive components called dendrites. Excessive and chronic exposure to stress hormones may lead to neuronal death in this region. Chronic stress may have direct toxic effects on the brain.

Given the important role that the hippocampus plays in learning and memory, victimized children may suffer in terms of academic achievement. During a trauma, the victim may focus his attention on a nontraumatic aspect of the environment (Rousseau focused on "mother nature" or on his imagination). By such means, at least partial escape is achieved. In this way, actual events can be forgotten, and nonexperienced "recollections" can be deeply felt to be true memories. We should remember these facts when reading *Confessions*.

Children with dysfunctional home environments have a markedly increased risk for medical illness as adults, including anxiety and mood disorders. An unresolved state of mind has important implications for the mind's functioning and for interpersonal relationships. Implicit elements of major and perhaps even minor traumatic events may continue to shape the individual's life without conscious awareness. Negative influences on development may impair mental health by blocking the normally unrestricted flow of information within the mind. Disruptive interpersonal relationships produce incoherent functioning of the individual's mind.

"Attachment" is an inborn system in the brain that motivates an infant to seek proximity to parents and to establish communication with them. The earliest attachments lead to specific organizational changes in an infant's behavior and brain function. Caregivers are the architects of the way in which experience influences the unfolding of genetically pre-programmed but experience-dependent brain development. Human connections create neuronal connections. Environmental factors play a crucial role in the establishment of synaptic connections after birth. "Developmental overpruning" refers to the toxic effect of overwhelming stress on the young brain. The release of stress hormones leads to an excessive death of neurons in areas responsible for emotional regulation.

Attachment is seen as "secure" or "insecure." When children develop secure attachments to parents, these allow them to go out into the world to explore and develop relationships with others. Implicit memory allows the mind to create generalizations and summaries of past experiences. Forming mental models is the essential manner in which the brain learns from the past and then directly influences the present and shapes future actions. If the attachment relationship is problematic, the internal working model of attachment will not give the infant a sense of a secure base, and the development of normal behaviors (such as exploration and social interactions) will be impaired. The region of the brain most central to attachment is the right orbitofrontal region, which serves by coordinating social communication, emphatic attunement, emotional regulation, stimulus appraisal, and autonoetic consciousness. Insecure attachment is not equivalent to mental disorder, but rather creates a risk of psychological and social dysfunction. Disorganized or disoriented attachments are sometimes associated with dissociative symptomatology. Such persons have deficits in attention and the regulation of emotion and behavioral impulses. For example, if an infant does not receive predictable, warm, and emotionally available communication from caregivers, he may adapt by avoiding dependence on others in the future. We will see later that our patient has tried to stay under all circumstances "independent." Interpersonal relationships in childhood shape the way the mind develops.

Avoidantly-attached children act as if the parents never left and show no outward signs of needing the parents. The internal value placed on attachment by these children has remained intact and immense. Their belief in the unimportance of relationships in development and in life are in contrast to the continued internal and non-conscious importance placed on attachment. Life stories of such people may be created by generalization of the past, as well as by nonconscious wishes for, and fantasies of, what could have been a more desirable past. This reconstructive aspect of the memory can have adaptive functions in creating a narrative sense of self that can reduce anxiety about the past as actually lived. Rousseau's *Confessions* is a good example of this.

Children with disorganized/disoriented attachment have been found to have the most difficulty later in life with emotional, social and cognitive impairments, in affect-regulating problems, social difficulties, and attentional problems.

A child uses the parent's state of mind to help organize his or her own mental processes. Nonverbal behavior is a primary mode in which emotion is communicated.

Life with the depressed parents reveals significant effects on the emotional development of the child.

Children with a history of avoidant attachment have minimal access to the nonverbal signals that reflect primary emotional states. They have a lack of awareness of others' emotions, and of their own emotions as well.

The right hemisphere is dominant in activity and development during the first three years of life. Children who experience severe emotional deprivation during this period may be at most risk of having losses in the structural components of their right hemispheres, especially in the region of the orbitofrontal cortex. The right hemisphere may require emotional stimulation from the environment in order to develop properly. The "mind-creating" module of the mind appears to be a function of the right hemisphere and develops early in life (for details see Siegel 1999).

Repeated activation of particular states—for example, a state of shame or despair—can become much more likely to be activated in the future. In this manner, states can become traits of the individual that influence both internal and interpersonal processes.

As we have seen, the inadequate parental care in the first years of life may deeply influence the brain functions of the child and create a development of the borderline personality. Masochism may be seen as a proliferation of the features of the borderline personality in a specific direction.

Theory of Masochistic Pathology

In infants, feelings of pleasure are accompanied by erections as early as the age of six to seven months. Boys will have erections any time they are excited—all day long they go through periods of penile tumescence and relaxation. Little girls go through an analogous process kept invisible by their anatomy.

From the moment of birth every human is sexual. Sexuality arrives earlier than was assumed by Freudian theory (Nathanson 1992). Later months bring increased interest in one's genitalia, which are actively discovered and stimulated. The genital sensory system matures around the age of eighteen months and at this time toddler masturbation can be observed (Haddley 1992, quoted in Shore 1994, 265). It is assumed that sexual arousal of a toddler appearing in the presence of the opposite sex plays a decisive role in the evolution of "gender identity."

In female toddlers, the brain matures earlier than in their male counterparts and early experiences can be assumed to have a different influence on the brains of women or men. Psychological gender is irreversibly determined in the first eighteen to twenty-four months of life and any later sexual change (of psychological gender) after this critical period is impossible. After that period the child states firmly: "I am a boy," or "I am a girl." Dimorphic structures and functions are set firmly and permanently by sexual steroids, which influence the maturation of the orbitofrontal cortex. At the same time, a determination of the dimorphic structure of the limbic system occurs, which is controlled by the orbitofrontal cortex.

In the second year the processes of "socialization" begins. Mother, or the person bringing up the child, makes plain that certain activities are undesirable. When the child sees the disapproving facial expressions of its educator, it reacts with a sense of shame, which is usually effective enough to inhibit the activity seen as socially "improper." The expression of disapproval in the mother's face has the effect of interrupting the emotional coupling between mother and child, which is extremely unpleasant for the latter.

Normally, the emotional coupling is rapidly reestablished. In cases where emotional uncoupling lasts too long or when its reestablishment does not occur shortly, the child tries to induce the previous emotional exchange by provocative behavior, which is inevitably followed by punishment ("Torture me, but don't abandon me," Bach 1991). The child achieves emotional contact, important even at the price of achieving it by exchange of negative emotions— punishment, which indirectly becomes a source of pleasure for the child, because it is emotionally relevant.

When erections or masturbation occur, which of course are a source of pleasure, an educator can react with further expressions of disapproval, or disgust (due to their ignorance, some mothers regard erections in toddlers as something abnormal, as a sign of hypersexuality, and can even react with consternation). If the disapproval is expressed with too much intensity or when it lasts too long, or when the toddler is punished physically, he develops intensive feelings of shame, which become connected with sexuality.

Shame is a "painful" experience. If it is additionally accompanied by the physical punishment of the toddler, a conditioned reflex can develop in which the erection becomes linked with the experience of mental or physical pain. This experience is stored during the plastic phase of orbitofrontal cortex development, which controls the lower brain centers determining sexual and affective social behavior. Pain conditions sexual arousal, which has the "advantage" that it can also be reached by imagined suffering, in one's own fantasy.

Probably only the toddler's own mother can fully understand his or her early manifestations of sexuality and even though she, in her facial expressions, does not approve of them, her love of the child is such that expressions of disapproval vanish from her face quickly. The toddler does experience feelings of shame, which teach it the lesson that erections shouldn't be displayed, but no conditioning between erection and pain develops. Masochists often miss mother (see, for example, Rancour-LaFerriere 1998. *Tolstoy on the Couch: Misogyny, Masochism, and Absent Mother*), or the relationship of mother to child is disturbed.

One can well imagine that Aunt Suzon, who looked after Jean-Jacques and was herself brought up in the puritan atmosphere of Geneva of that time, could have been terrified by the erections of the toddler, the small Jean-Jacques. She could not recognize the normality of such erections—she had no children of her own—and would react to them with exaggerated strictness, thereby unconsciously inducing the connection: pain–erection–shame–humiliation.

It may well be that moral masochism develops in families where the parents are overly strict, who wish their child to become—as soon as possible—a well-behaved and conformed child, and who try to speed up its socialization by employing hard measures. They let the child know, too early and very explicitly, that many of its joyful activities are undesirable. They communicate this message by a facial expression, which lasts a bit too long or perhaps even longer. The child is incessantly made to experience shame, which inhibits its activities. It doesn't know what it can and what it cannot do and becomes passive and insecure. In the child the impression starts to develop that the unpleasant-punishing feelings of shame and humiliation follow all activity. In this way the feeling of one's own worthlessness comes into being.

Such children can look very well-behaved, decent and obedient. They develop, however, a strict conscience, which never stops asking whether what the affected person does is correct or not. Social transgressions can never be quite eliminated. Persons brought up in this way have permanent feelings of guilt. They know, from early on, that guilt must be punished and in the end seek punishment, because they have learned to use it as a means to get rid of feelings of guilt and inferiority. Punishment purifies them and keeps up emotional relationships.

Feeling of shame and masochism are associated with feelings of humiliation, to which Rousseau tended from his youth: he was humiliated when he was accused and beaten because he broke Mlle Lambercier's comb and had never thereafter experienced "the feeling of pure happiness." He was incessantly humiliated during his apprenticeship by his master, Ducommun, and his feelings of humiliation went on for his whole life. As a true masochist he enjoyed them and never got rid of them.

Another affect, which accompanies shame and all other above-mentioned emotions, is the feeling of disgust-distaste. Gilbert (1988) emphasizes that disgust-distaste and fear can give rise to certain forms of shame. Overcoming of the feeling of disgust-distaste is a necessary condition for attaining masochistic gratification: Rousseau had to overcome himself in order to lick Mme de Warens's fingers soiled by "disgusting" ointments, he had to overcome his aversion to sexual intercourse and let Mme Larnage seduce him, etc.

Some authors regard disgust-distaste as an essential component of shame, others see disgust-distaste and shame as two different systems (Gilbert and Bernice 1998). Parents often use facial expression of disgust-distaste to show their children that they disapprove of certain behavior.

The opposite of shame is pride, which manifests intact social relationships. Pride is not to be confused with dignity. Some authors take the view that loss of dignity forms an essential part of shame. To die in dignity means to die without any greater dependence on others. For masochists, these "painful, unworthy" dependencies on others are a necessity.

Shame basically means loss of control. Narcissism constantly tries to project a positive picture for others to see and make them believe in the positive features of the narcissistic personality (beauty, talent and knowledge). Such a personality fears ordinariness and lives in fear that others might find out that he or she is not as good as pretended.

Rousseau's narcissistic features can be found especially in *Confessions* and *Dialogues*. Rousseau presents the reader with an idealized picture of his person and wants to be believed; he adjures the reader by his sincerity. Right in the beginning he states that he does not resemble any of the living. Being not better than others, he is at least different. Rousseau exhibits numerous narcissistic features. He is prophet, reformer, teacher, social critic, discoverer of new truths, he is an exceptional personality. Narcissism is a cover and apology for his inability to become an integrated member of normal human society.

Etiological Factors of Rousseau's Masochism

One can only speculate about the causes of Rousseau's masochism. The most probable explanation is a combination and synergism of several factors.

Hereditary influences

Rousseau was born into a family which was emotionally unstable, the most unstable person being his father, whom Jean-Jacques, according to testimonies of his contemporaries, resembled physically. His own emotional changes were obvious, not only to his contemporaries, but even to Jean-Jacques himself. In the first and last copy of the periodical *Persifleur* he presents his self-portrait, which, being of course a literary exaggeration, is nonetheless basically true:

> Nothing is more unlike myself than myself: That is why it would be useless to attempt to define my character by anything other than variety. Mutability is so much part of my mind that my beliefs alter from one moment to the next: sometimes I am a sombre misanthrope, at others I am intensely happy amid the charm of society and the pleasures of love. At one time I am austere and pious . . . then promptly I become a candid libertine . . . . In a word, a protean, a chameleon and a woman are all of them creatures less changeable than I.

His changing likeness forms the basis of his character. His contradictions constitute what he calls the ever-changing "weekend soul . . . Sometimes I am wisely foolish and then again foolishly wise." His sudden and groundless changes of mood are described also by his friends, Dusaulx and Mercier (cf. Grimsley 1969, 16).

Prenatal influences

Prenatal disturbance of processes of brain masculinization, of cerebral lateralization and sexual dimorphism cannot be ruled out. In this context, also, the age of his mother at the time of pregnancy has to be remembered; she was older and the incidence of pathological pregnancies increases with age.

Postnatal Influences: Deprivation, Semi-deprivation

The death of Rousseau's mother meant deprivation and the loss of feelings of security (see the previous part on neurobiology). Already as a child Jean-

Jacques must have felt that something in his life was missing—the mother who would protect and love him. This is also the reason for his incessant search, in later years, for a person who would replace her and to whom he could cling (Mme de Warens, for example).

For his whole life he was driven by a desire to find the "ideal mother," and in the end he found her in nature. Nature was the place where he wanted to be alone, together with his mother. For his whole life he tried to find "natural goodness," which would bring peace to his split character.

This inner uncertainty gave rise also to his timidity and his fear of the unknown. The latter accompanied him for his whole life and he fought it in many different ways (his fear of darkness and fear of crowds are well known).

The upbringing he received from his aunts can hardly be described as normal. The relatives (especially women) were overly sorry for the child whose mother had died, they tried to (over) protect him and carry out all his whims. In several parts of *Confessions*, Rousseau unintentionally reveals that he was pampered (even though he denies he was spoiled). He was never forced to do things and his women educators never used threats of punishment: "[The] threat of punishment was entirely unknown to me . . . No royal child could be more scrupulously cared for than I was in my early years . . . Everyone around me idolized me . . . My desires were so rarely excited and so rarely thwarted, that it never came to my head to have any."

Pampered children deem themselves worthy of being in the middle of attention and expect all their wishes to be fulfilled. They lack a sense of duty, because no duties are put on them. Too much pampering, sometimes rationalized as a necessity to "be tolerant" toward the child, results in fact in faulty socialization of the child. Pampering undermines independence, the ability to take care of oneself and self-confidence. Narcissistic character, conditioned by pampering, is associated with feelings of fear due to lack of independence. Pampered children develop into tyrannical, irresponsible adults and lack the ability to adapt to real life situations (Rueedi 1933).

Jean-Jacques was not allowed to associate with other children on the street; in this context Matějček speaks of *"peer" deprivation*, which, in Jean-Jaques, combined with *"maternal deprivation."* Mental deprivation in early childhood projects itself into a person's whole life (Matějček 1994). We know that children have a period in their development, typically around the age of eight months, in which they show signs of fear of foreign people. These signs and feelings disappear sometime later, the length of which varies from person to person.

Under normal circumstances, children overcome these feelings when they are given the freedom to meet other people. A child can then obtain its own experiences and usually finds out that other people have no intention to harm it; this experience probably plays a decisive role in the maturation of relevant brain centers. If the child cannot meet others, it does not obtain a sufficient amount of necessary experience and the relevant brain structures cannot mature; the child retains feelings of fear, shame and insecurity of this period in his or her later life. The experiments of Mr. and Mrs. Harlow show that young monkeys (Macacus rhesus), brought up without a mother and an opportunity to associate with peers, tend toward deviations in sexual appetence and defective paternal behavior as adults (Rousseau sent all his children to a foundling home).

The fundamental social task of man is to protect his woman and children. Deprived men, however, are usually neither dominant nor protective in their attitude to women; on the contrary, they attract, by their "weakness," helplessness and awkwardness, the protectiveness of women who have it to an above-average degree. They become, so to speak, their first children. But women educators can never love these children in a truly unconditional, maternal way, and, because deprived personalities are often unable to "respond emotionally," they sooner or later "repel" the protective woman (Matějček 1994).

The figure of his father was another important factor in the development of Jean-Jacques's personality. After the death of his mother, little Jean-Jacques set his heart toward his father and was emotionally dependent on him. We know that Isaac Rousseau had an unstable, explosive and irresponsible nature which was deliberately idealized in *Confessions*—Rousseau did his best to write only positive things about his father. It is known that Isaac preferred his second son to François. He probably spent long hours with Jean-Jacques, reading books.

Another known fact, however, is that he punished his children physically. Rousseau *did not mention* in *Confessions* that he was once locked in an attic room and harshly physically punished, because he had torn a Latin dictionary (Grimsley 1966, 26). Rousseau *had to* have remembered this childhood experience, but he nevertheless did not mention it in *Confessions*. Similarly he did not mention the decision of his father, after Jean Jacques's conversion to Catholicism, that "he will never again consider him his son."

This deliberate failure to mention certain facts, which did not fit into his conception, show that one has to read *Confessions* with caution. *Confessions* is, in fact, a very skillfully constructed defense of Rousseau, which is even truer of his *Dialogues*.

The irresponsibility of Isaac Rousseau can be further seen in the fact that he made no provisions for the proper schooling of Rousseau, did not take him to Nyon when he left Geneva, and kept for himself the whole income from the inheritance that came to him after his wife died. He did not support his children financially even though half of this inheritance belonged to them. Rousseau knew all of these things and the figure of his father could not have contributed to his emotional stability.

On top of that, Isaac made (seen from our perspective) a severe psychological mistake. He inoculated Rousseau with the idea that he was responsible for his mother's death: "For ten months later I was born, poor and sickly child, and cost my mother her life. So my birth was the first of my misfortunes," and further: "He seemed to see her again in me, but could never forget that I robbed him of her." In *Confessions* there is a description of the father embracing Rousseau who, however, felt that the father's caressing was mixed with suffering, which added strength to the embrace: "When he said to me 'Jean-Jacques, let us talk of your mother,' I would reply, 'Very well, father, but we are sure to cry.' 'Ah,' he would say with a groan, 'Give her back to me, console me for her, fill the void she has left in my heart! Should I love you so if you were not more to me than a son?'"

These and other emotional outpourings must have had a strong impact on the soul of a little boy. *Feelings of guilt* aroused by such remarks must have had an immense influence on the personal development of Rousseau, because he remembers them after so many years. He permanently suffered feelings of guilt, and any further wrong on his part awakened this complex deposit of guilt to new life. In this way the "shame about existing" arose (Wurmser 1997). His father blamed him for something he had not committed and which was not his fault.

It may well be that Rousseau identified with his depressive father and became attached to the traumatizing event of his mother's death in the face of which he was helpless. A feeling of guilt provokes aggression, or, in the case of a masochist, autoaggression. Aggression is connected with depressions, which are known to be accompanied by a high incidence of autoaggressions (suicides). Masochism is basically sadism turned against one's own person and that is why some authors speak of sadomasochism. The symptoms might differ, but it is quite possible that both are actually one and the same syndrome. Starobinsky (1988, 543) mentions the "sadomasochistic" structure in Rousseau.

Rousseau described how he came into this world nearly dying, with a germ of illness inside that evolved during the following years, and, of course, he was saved only through the help of his aunt (*Confessions*). But, in his *Second Discourse,* he mercilessly called for natural selection: in his description of the state of the natural world Rousseau agreed with nature, which does not allow the survival of the weak and ill and acts as ordered by the laws of Sparta in ancient Greece. Only the strong with good health should survive and others should die. He wrote in *Émile* that it is not the educator's task to attend to a weak and sickly child. In doing so, he only wastes his time caring for a useless life: "I would never take on the burden of caring for a sick and unhealthy child even if it were to live for eighty years."

It is possible that Rousseau had reached an unconscious conclusion that he was forbidden to experience pleasure in life and, in particular, that it was wrong to experience sexual pleasure. The permanent feeling of guilt over being responsible for the death of his mother could have made him believe that he must suffer. "God wants me to suffer and He knows that I am innocent" (*Rêveries*). The motif of a dead mother appears in *La Nouvelle Héloise*: Julie turns down the love of St-Preux, because she (wrongly) assumes that she bears the responsibility for the death of her mother. At the end of the novel she dies to save her son from drowning (it is possible that Rousseau resorted to this motif to deepen the literary effect).

According to psychoanalytical interpretations, Rousseau felt that sexual intercourse with a woman could kill her. He killed his mother at delivery and had no desire to kill again. He tried to overcome the feeling of fear, inoculated into him in his childhood, by submission and obedience. This attitude could have lead to his later conviction that he was chosen to be a permanent sacrifice in the world.

In *Confessions* we can find idyllic accounts of his childhood but also memories of "violence and injustice" (the accusation that he broke Mlle Lambercier's comb, the punishments of Master Ducommun). Significant numbers of his biographers saw that young Rousseau's upbringing did not teach him any discipline and that he lacked any sense of social responsibility. Any punishment, even a deserved one, could provoke in him feelings of grievance and hostility. Later on he created his own explanation for the incomprehensible punishment meted out by the world around him: he was being punished because he was better than others. His feeling of superiority drove him into social isolation. His desire to be alone probably was not as inborn as he claimed. It was a "coping mechanism" by which he sought to overcome fear and frustration.

The influence of literature on masochistic development

Another factor which influenced the development of Rousseau's character was his reading of books unsuitable for his age. When he was about five to ten years old, Rousseau consumed not only romantic, sentimental and love novels, but also books on the history of ancient Greece and Rome.

The influence of literature on a child's development is generally acknowledged and Rousseau himself was aware of the importance of this influence. For his whole life he felt himself to be exceptional, similar to the figures in Plutarch's biographies, and he tried to live according to their heroic morality. For his whole life he liked sentimental, romantic novels; for example, *Astrée* by Honoré d'Urfé, which he read several times, the last time as an old man.

This pastoral romance moistened the hankies of ladies throughout Europe, notably in England, where, after its translation, it was printed in newer and newer editions. The novels of Mlle Scudéry enjoyed the same popularity; in particular the gruesome *Artamìne, or the Big Cyrus*, ghostly stories which filled ten volumes (Cyrus was in fact Louis XIV and the heroin, Sapho, was Mlle de Scudéry herself).

Along with *Robinson Crusoe*, Rousseau also liked *Tales of the Arabian Nights* and Prévost's book, *Cleveland*. Here we see the roots of his pathos, fantasy and liking for moral heroism, and desire for life in seclusion. Already as a child he learned that all beauty and pleasure in life must be atoned for with pain.

It should be remembered that the eighteenth century has been dubbed the "women's century." Women ruled the monarchs (Mesdames de Pompadour, Dubarry, Marie Antoinette); they made men wear ladies' fashion (wigs, make-up, powder, silk, laces) and introduced a lifestyle resembling life on stage. Dreams and theatre met once again. Versailles was France in microcosm.

Promiscuity led to extreme views of love play, which culminated in the novels of Marquis de Sade.

Sexual perversions, however, invaded literature before that time. In England in 1747 and 1748, a novel by Richardson, *Clarissa, or the History of a Young Lady* was published, portraying in seven volumes (in letterform) the moral corruption of an innocent and honest girl, who fantasized masochistically that she had been killed by her cruel lover in a church and thrown into a grave in the midst of half-decomposed corpses. (One of Rousseau's favorite phrases was that he would be buried alive among the living.) Richardson's novel about persecuted virtue was also enormously successful in France, where it inspired many imitators. Among them were not only Choderlos de Laclos (*Les Liaisons dangereuses*), but also Diderot (*La Religieuse*) and Rousseau's *La Nouvelle Héloïse*. In all these novels we find exaggerated sensitivity, and the mental and physical torture of innocent girls, the virtue of whom, however, wins in the end, even when it is only in the last sentence, when the heroin leaves for heaven.

Rousseau's sexual deviation could have been influenced in particular by his reading of the history of ancient Rome and Greece. We find here descriptions of inconceivable cruelties; sadomasochistic records which, for antiquity, were quite normal. Rousseau read these histories with keen interest and lived—in his fantasy—in ancient Rome ("When I was twelve I was a Roman"); later on he wanted to translate Tacitus.

Young children are unable to separate the world of tales and legends from reality. He could not compare his experiences with the real world and contemporary society. He lived in isolation and without contacts with other children. As the sadomasochistic world of antiquity was not corrected by reality, reading of books became a reality and the cruelties of life became normal events.

Sacher-Masoch was also, in his youth, exposed to negative experiences. From prison (where his father worked) he witnessed rebellions and their violent suppression. The women masochist Marcus (1981) confirms the enormous influence literature had on her fantasies. She mentions especially the Greek myths about eternal punishment (Danaides, Sisyphus, Tantalus). The biggest influence on her was, however, the history of ancient Rome, where she found, among other things, exact descriptions of the punishment of slaves. She has acknowledged that for a masochist these books represent reality: "It was as if there were two kinds of reality—one in books and one that affected myself . . ." She felt unhappy she had to live in today's civilized times (16–17).

Rousseau, too, did not hide that, in his eyes, the cruel societies of ancient Rome and Greece were more captivating than the "decayed" Parisian society. An interesting finding in this context is the observation that in a society in which violence and criminality are on the increase, deviations from normal sexual behavior in the sadomasochistic sense occur with higher incidence. One example of this is the violent society of South Africa, where society tolerates and seeks sadomasochism more often than in other countries (see Noyes 1988). The same applies to the present-day United States.

The influence of culture on masochism.

We cannot forget also the puritan atmosphere of Geneva of that time. In the biography in Part 1, we mentioned the extent to which the government of Geneva and Puritan religion went in their efforts to regulate the life of all community members. The citizens must have developed a certain kind of habituation, because the majority of them were not aware of the oppression. Father Isaac was a good example of people who could be proud even of this regime. Regulation of every single individual in the city by strict religious decrees led to submissiveness and obedience as well as to feelings of (unconscious) fear that could not have remained without some repercussions in the psyche.

Unremitting religious pressure without the possibility of some sort of societal ventilation—often present in Catholicism—to air it out, such as the periods of carnival or the merrymaking of Shrove Tuesday, is typical of "young" religions which have not yet accumulated enough historical experience with the human psyche. Let us remember the words of Stendhal who referred to Geneva as prison. Rousseau felt good about prisons of all kinds. Isolation, too, is a solitary confinement of its kind! Paradoxically, in prison, in isolation, when he is subjected to the control of strict rules, Rousseau feels free. Gaspard Valette, (quoted in Grimsley 1969, 34) refers to a report submitted by the *préfet* of the Léman to the French Minister of the Interior, where it is stated that "Melancholy is more frequent in Geneva than anywhere else . . . It is a fact that in this city the tendency to mental disorders, and especially melancholy is hereditary."

The structure of Geneva's rigid code of ethics was such that everyone *had* to trespass against it, and this was most true in sexual matters. Sexuality aroused unconscious feelings of fear, which were further strengthened by the influence of Calvinist predestination dogmatics. Everybody was afflicted with a hereditary guilt and nobody could be sure that he would be the chosen one whose guilt would be forgiven. Rousseau modified and glorified historical Geneva according to the momentary needs of his Weltanschauung. This idealized picture of Geneva, however, was not shared by his contemporaries (see the reaction to Rousseau's *Lettre à Monsieur d'Alembert*).

In each individual, masochism is manifest with different intensity and orientation. This "borderline" deviation varies individually and the picture it presents is by no means a unified and characteristic one. The description of particular masochistic features is given in the following text. But even now it is possible to say that masochism often occurs together with other mental abnormalities and in individual combinations that can further change with time. The combination of narcissistic features, sadism, homosexuality, depression and phobias occurs quite often. Depressions are typically associated with feelings of fear, which are also characteristic for masochists. Freud describes depression as a reaction to the loss of a real or imaginary object. Rousseau lost a real person—his mother, and his losses continued. His father left Geneva; Rousseau lost his hometown, the ideals of Protestantism and his belief in the freedom of the Genevan Republic.

It is not surprising, then, that he constantly feared the loss of personal freedom.

The opposite of masochism is a paranoid personality. The masochist is frightened, he hates other people, but *punishes himself.* A paranoid personality also hates other people but punishes them, often by murdering them. Both opposite poles are consequences of disturbed interpersonal relations. Masochism can be expressed to various degrees. It is sometimes manifested only in a never-ending stream of apologies or efforts to escape others. In all its manifestations it remains a serious character and personality abnormality (Shainess 1977).

It is usually claimed that later on Rousseau fell ill with paranoid psychosis with delusions of persecution. This would suggest that Rousseau never actively fought against his persecutors. "In a certain sense, he accepts persecution as the objective guarantee of his innate goodness . . . He is good because others are wicked . . . he chooses—though not necessarily in a fully conscious and explicit manner—*to be persecuted* (Grimsley 1969, 243–244).

Part Two—The Patient Jean-Jacques Rousseau

Chapter Eight

Rousseaus Moral Masochism

Some masochistic features of Rousseau's personality have already been stressed in his biography in Part 1. This chapter supplies further information and describes some of them in more detail, particularly considering the medical ramifications.

In Rousseau's case we encounter a combination and mutual penetration of two basic forms of masochism, i.e., moral (social) and sexual masochism, which cannot be separated easily. Both of these types of masochism have some character traits in common which manifest themselves both in private and public life.

The personality of a masochist is always split in many ways. It is quite characteristic for a masochist to be split into an omnipotent self and a shamed self; grandiose self-expectations and self-images coexist with a pathetic, vulnerable, weak self and are often experienced simultaneously (Novick and Novick 1987; 1991). The fantasy of omnipotence is a particularly powerful defense against overwhelming anxiety (Morrin 1989). Masochists "avoid contact with *any* others, and maintain superiority while feeling *worthless*" (Shainess 1997).

Rousseau's personality was deeply split and the split was responsible for the paradoxes of his life as well as those of his writings. On the one hand, he regarded himself to be an exceptional person, whose goodness, naturalness and superiority made him stand high above others revealing, much like a prophet, new truths for others to follow. On the other hand, he felt like a weak person, persecuted, a "stranger without friends." The baleful looks of others made him feel he was an object of contempt and scorn; he felt like he was buried alive. Driven to solitude, he also required the idealized presence of other people. The noble savage could not "enjoy himself without the cooperation of other people." He tells us, absolute solitude is a "sad condition contrary to nature," but in another place he tells us "as soon as I am alone, I am happy."

Rousseau kept emphasizing that he wanted to exclude unpleasant things and thoughts and achieve the happiness he desired. But his fate was to remain unhappy forever because, despite all his self-assurance that he wanted to find happiness, he sought suffering—for a masochist suffering is happiness.

The main problem of his life was not his endeavor to discover a new relationship with the world, nature, or God, but to find a solution to the difficult problems of his own *interpersonal relationships*. He desperately sought to find someone who would love him, he wanted to be able to live a normal social life, to have friends and normal sexual relationships. All that, however, was denied to him, because he had missed the process of socialization and could not and was not able to become a member of society.

Rousseau's dilemma was that he wanted to live in society but knew he could not live in it (he lacked socialization). Society, and Rousseau, too, felt that he did not belong to it, that he was different: "For some years of experience had not yet radically cured me of my romantic visions, and notwithstanding all my sufferings I knew as little of the world and mankind as if I had not already paid dearly for lessons." What else could Rousseau do—he could only declare that society, which did not want to accept him, must be bad. Rousseau had not been corrupted by society and could not therefore (as he assumed) tell others how society corrupts all people. He failed to see, or did not want to see, that man is a social being and needs society in order to survive.

He considered himself "a friend of humanity." Dr. Tronchin from Geneva formulated his problem (in a letter written in March 1759) very cogently, "How is it possible that a friend of humanity stops being a friend of people?" Rousseau could save his self-esteem only as a critic of society. He could not say that he was bad and society was good. Only turning the tables and stating things the other way around enabled him to exist "outside of society."

In his life he had many opportunities to obtain a good job and turned all of them down. He could have married a girl of his own standing. He received acknowledgment for his literary work, but he could not enjoy it because of his masochistic nature. His inadequate social behavior made, probably unconsciously, even his former friends into his enemies. He desired friendship. But friendship is based on a mutual exchange of altruism, and the egocentric Rousseau was unable to offer such an exchange. His relationships with friends remained one-sided. He wanted to be able to visit them whenever he liked, but, at the same time, he controlled their visits. He wanted them to write him regularly, but took for granted that he could write them when he wanted. Mme d'Épinay gave him Hermitage as a gift, for she knew how Rousseau desired it and Rousseau himself wrote that "his life began" only there. After their rift he accused her of having made a slave of him and requiring him to live in Hermitage.

In his biography we find many such emotional reversals, which robbed him of his best friends. Every masochist is extremely egocentric. The split in his character is also partly responsible for his unsteadiness and weakness. Rousseau described himself as being as changeable as an amoeba or chameleon.

Only once in his life (in Bern) did he manage to speak in public, in front of an audience. He was never able to learn something by heart and perform it in public. It is well known that it took him a very long time to learn the speeches he intended to give in front of the Protestant representatives of Geneva in 1744 or later, in Môtiers, and which he then, at the decisive moment, totally forgot.

Those who have carefully read his biography will certainly have noticed many narcissistic moments; in his youth he imagined himself to be a Roman, Hannibal and Henry IV of France; he looked upon himself as much better educated than other people, tried to convince others in discussions, and argued against the mistaken opinions of Voltaire (the issue of theodicy) and of d'Alembert (the question of appropriateness of a theatre in Geneva).

His narcissism told him that he actually was a savior of humanity, and a discoverer of new truths (the *Discourses, Émile,* and *Social Contract).* In spite of his mental anomalies, of which he was aware, he declared, with a remarkable absence of any self-criticism, that on the whole he still regarded himself to be "the best of all people."

In a masochist, feelings of shame go hand in hand with feelings of anxiety.

Fear prevents him from acting proactively. Lack of independence and insufficient practice in social behavior in turn reinforce his feelings of fear. A masochist's fear is not real but, as is often the case with women, it has many irrational components (see the sections in this book on the right hemisphere of brain) and ultimately becomes the central problem. Fear is also the basic feature of any neurosis because fear and shame occur together.

In a masochist we usually find the fear that he could be abandoned and left alone, because he badly needs the attention of others and any kind of separation is unbearable for him. A partnership which brings him suffering is better for him; he prefers familiar unhappiness to unknown happiness. Masochists typically fear the suffering and hardness of reality, a necessary part of all people's life. The masochistic prophet, Rousseau, however, lacks the strength which would be necessary to lead suffering humanity out of its predicament. Instead of real deeds he offers illusions—his compassion is false.

Fear of criticism is another typical feature of masochists. They try to weaken it by taking preventative action and performing what might be called "self-accusation." For Rousseau this kind of self-accusation, and at the same time self-defense, takes the form of *Confessions*, which should protect him from future criticism. *Confessions* is the most outspoken evidence of his masochistic way of thinking, his fear of being accused of not behaving as he should, of breaking societal norms. Here he explains why he is "different." In *Confessions* he confronts the criticism by criticizing others.

During his stay in Paris (1770 to 1771), Rousseau read aloud from *Confessions*, but this was soon prohibited for fear of scandals. *Confessions* contained intimate knowledge of Parisian society. Still more eloquent than *Confessions* were the three dialogues written between 1772 and 1776, *Rousseau juge de Jean-Jacques. Dialogues.* Psychologically, these are much more significant than the later, poetical *Rêveries d'un promeneur solitaire.*

The masochist desires punishment and accepts it willingly, but this does not necessarily mean he does not experience fear of punishment. Masochists are fearful; they experience life situations as dangerous. They show the features of "trait-anxiety." This state is very unpleasant and masochists (but also people who are just fearful) try to transform the irrational "trait-anxiety" into concrete, more definite, so-called "state-anxiety." Taking the bull by the horns, they turn anxiety into a more concrete form of punishment, which is mentally tolerable. All of us would prefer a terrible end to terror without end. Franz Kafka, for example, suffered the irrational features of "trait-anxiety" and the masochistic features of this have been analyzed (cf. Goedde 1983).

Another fear is the masochist's apprehension that his transgressions or distortions of truth could be found out by persons in high position, to whom the masochist ascribes magical powers. Let us remember that Rousseau frequented nearly exclusively the highest walks of society. On his way to Montpellier he posed as an Englishman, though he spoke not a single English word and was horrified lest someone should discover his fraud. God-fearing people, especially, live in constant fear that they cannot fulfil the moral requirements set by their deity and are in fact sinners—disinherited sons. Children, too, regard their parents as supernatural beings, who can easily see through them.

Though already an adult man, Rousseau created his own "divine family." God was his father, nature his mother and he himself their child and prophet in one person. On his lonely walks in nature Rousseau felt happy, because he was under the protection of "his family." He had no other choice; he had to take refuge in "his family" because, owing to his deficient socialization, he was unable to live in normal society. The solitude sought in nature was his refuge, a way out of his predicament.

Fear of one's conscience is typical. The feelings of guilt, which it arouses, lead to feelings of inferiority and self-contempt. Rousseau had an unconscious, deeply rooted feeling of guilt since his childhood: his father often reproached him and "blamed" him for the death of his mother. Every new fault in his life (false accusation by the maid, Marion, his desertion of the music teacher, Le Maistre, sending his children to a foundling home and his sexual practices with Thérèse) lead to a new activation and increased his complex of guilt.

Masochists also fear that their secret ambition will be revealed. They fear that their modesty could change into pride and arrogance. Fear of arousing the envy of others makes the masochist deny and belittle himself and try to conceal the pride of his creative abilities.

The main type of fear experienced by a masochist, however, is his feeling of extreme *bashfulness* (timidity), emphasized by Rousseau himself on numerous occasions and sometimes regarded by him as a positive character trait. He affected blushes and rejected eye contact; his face expressed embarrassment, his behavior became insecure, he would sweat, experience palpitations, and his speech would lose spontaneity. Rousseau's timidity and shyness were almost insurmountable, especially in his youth and in the first years in Paris when he was still unknown. Excessive shyness made him reject the audience by the king after the successful première of his opera *The Village Soothsayer*.

If he had acted in a way that was inconsistent with his deepest conviction, it was because of the influence of his natural "shyness" and "timidity" which, in social situations, always seemed to inhibit him. Too often he had been the victim of a terrible *mauvaise honte*. Many of his alleged misdeeds, wrongly imputed by others to sinful pride, were simply "the singularities of an ardent temperament held in check by a *naturel timidé*." This shyness "bedeviled his life from the earliest years," observes Grimsley (1969, 245).

Timid people are not enterprising, they limit themselves to passive reactions and expect others to arrange things. Rousseau spoke about *paresse de penser*, which explained his tendency to allow himself to be subjugated by stronger personalities. In the more external picture of a masochist we find predominantly his fearfulness, the *"fear of fear."* This attitude inhibits aggressions and gives the impression of sheer peacefulness. When a masochist behaves aggressively, these aggressions are directed against his own personality.

In spite of this, the masochist is not free of hatred and hostility. He lives in a symbiotic partnership, which promises to bring him the fulfillment of his need of love. He puts heavy demands on his surroundings as far as care, help and understanding are concerned; such demands can be met only very seldom. In longer lasting interpersonal relationships a masochist's expectations change into demands. He asserts his claims to love, understanding, affection, friendship.

Here, of course, disappointments on both sides are necessary. But the annoyance, rage and disappointment of a masochist do not get out—they accumulate in his soul. He is dependent on his partner. This is the reason why an often ambivalently hostile attitude develops and, should this state of affairs last long, the results are aggressive outbursts. But his partner, too, who has her or his demands on the masochist as his friend, feels betrayed and responds with open rejection, which only adds to the masochist's aggressions.

Initially, the masochist relied on the leading role of his partner and restricted himself to a more subordinate position. Aggressive behavior represents his attempts to improve his position. Ambivalent acts, disagreements, mutual humiliation and fights are therefore necessary and accompany symbiotic relationships. A good example of this was Rousseau's relationship to Diderot. Rousseau became accustomed to consult with Diderot about everything, and on one occasion Diderot recommended that Rousseau write his *First Discourse* in a rather provocative way because it would increase his chances of success. He participated also on the final version of Rousseau's *Second Discourse* and Rousseau obeyed him. In the end they broke up forever, when Diderot did not meet Rousseau's expectations and did not support him in the dissension with Mme d'Épinay. The overture of their separation was a sentence from Diderot's play saying: "Only a bad man is alone," which Rousseau took personally.

As an illustration we can again use the following quotation from

Rousseau, "How many humiliations one cannot forget after a friend's hug and what wrath can still remain in one's heart!" (*Confessions*, Book Nine). He wrote this sentence after Diderot's visit in Paris in 1757. On the one hand, a masochist lets himself be abased by others when it fits and is of advantage to his conception; on the other hand, he reacts very sensitively to unexpected criticism (Goedde 1983).

No other sexual minority writes as much as masochists. The explanation offered is that there exists a close relationship between writing and the age at which a masochist learned to write—a masochist becomes fixated on this age. A more simple explanation is that masochists have to have an audience—letters and/or literary work offer the possibility to obtain it. Similar to women, who need communication, mostly in the form of verbal conversation, masochists communicate in writing and they set up correspondence circles, in which the members describe their emotional experiences.

A club in Boston where sadomasochists met to punish and obtain punishment, established for its members a very successful newspaper column "Love Whippings" to enable them to exchange descriptions of their personal experiences. A very interesting discovery was that masochists wanted the punishing person to be a woman.

Oevres complètes de Jean-Jacques Rousseau (Hachette 1865–1870) includes thirteen volumes. *Correspondence génerale* (ed. T. Dufour, P. P. Plan 1924–1934) amounts to twenty volumes. Rousseau apparently did not think much of the books which he wrote so passionately. Jakob-Heinrich Meister recorded that Rousseau said to him during his visit to Rousseau in Môtiers, "Books cause much more evil than good. They hurt those who don't understand them and are of no use for those who understand them."

When Meister's French companion, Mègre, inquired about the secret of his literary style, which he admired, Rousseau replied to him, "The only secret is that I believe firmly in what I write. No matter whether it is true or not, I believe that it is true." On the other hand, Rousseau looked upon his visitors as inferior when they knew nothing of his writings.

Rousseau always expressed views in his writings that were tinged with his masochistic deviation. Rousseau's voluminous literary work is imbued with *motifs of suffering and disaster*; the reader is presented with overwhelming emotional powers and graceful formulation. The weak nature hides in the strong formulations of his philosophy, people are bad because human society corrupts them (*First* and *Second Discourses*), and there is no escaping this suffering; no return to the original state is possible.

His *La Nouvelle Héloïse* is a drama of unhappy love, where every person taking part suffers in his or her own way. The story is embedded in an eternal triangle, which is typical of masochists. The ending is, of course, a tragic one: Julie dies and before her death she confesses to a religion which at that time must have been regarded as a heresy, and for the formulation of which, contained in "*La Profession de foi du vicaire savoyard*," Rousseau was persecuted.

Émile, too, becomes a novel with a bad ending. Already the first sentence reveals deep pessimism, "All things springing from the hands of God are good. And all things are corrupt in human hands." As everyone has to grow up in a human society, everyone's doom is predestined. In Calvinism at least the chosen ones could hope to be saved. According to Rousseau's words and ideas, all without exception are lost. Good upbringing and education do not lead to a good result and everything ends up badly; Émile becomes a slave on a galley.

In *Du Contract social* Rousseau describes an ideal social order which, however, cannot be attained—people must suffer. The whole of *Confessions* is mainly a description of Rousseau's suffering, agonies, unhappiness; these started at birth, "For ten months later I was born, a poor and sickly child, and cost my mother her life. So my birth was the first of my misfortunes." Almost every page of *Confessions* brings new references to the merciless, cruel fate, ruin, conspiracy, present and future suffering, destruction, etc. He complains that he is the victim of "inhuman persecution," and he apparently wants to believe that he is persecuted.

Masochistic aggression against others is only indirect. The character of their suffering is invariably exhibitionistic. They demonstrate their misfortune to the people about them and show it off. Moral exhibitionism should show to others how the masochist suffers; it should arouse compassion. The masochist should be comforted and loved. This also serves the purpose of showing others the wish not to be overburdened and to be spared, the need to be forgiven and punished for transgressions, to show how he is being punished by others unjustly ("Look what they have done to me"). This should arouse bad conscience in the culprits.

Others are portrayed as people trying to ridicule him, to sabotage his plans, and wanting to take their revenge on him by all possible means. Again, we find many quotations regarding this theme.

The masochist wants to be punished. He believes himself to be a good and innocent man who has been terribly wronged by evildoers. He believes that he has been "purified in the crucible of adversity" *(Rêveries)*. He will be purified, but from what? Perhaps it is a permanent feeling of guilt, which torments him. He is ashamed of his being guilty and hopes that punishment will purify him.

Rousseau punished himself by living as a hermit and refusing to accept any gifts, supposedly so that he would not "lose his independence and freedom." On the other hand, however, he needed love and admiration; he should be taken care of. The result is a totally split personality. Rousseau lived with Thérèse in his hermitage, undertook lonely walks in the country, but then, suddenly, he must go to see the château society (La Chevrette, Montlouis, Colombiere). He complained about his friends and other visitors, who disturb him, but when nobody came, he complained that he was lonely.

In his last will, signed on January 29, 1763 in which he described his illness in detail, he demanded to be dissected after his death. He offered himself as a willing corpse to the knife, for his malformation to be revealed. He wanted aggression, he wanted to be open—wrote Starobinski (1977, 557).

In all his writings and also in his behavior we can observe a more or less expressed social provocation, which is typical of masochists, "A provocation, so typical of the masochist; self-condemnation is the major problem of masochism, and it won't go away easily because hidden behind it is an even greater condemnation of all others" (Shainess 1997). Rousseau provoked with his socially unacceptable behavior, of which he was ashamed and he despised himself. At the same time he despised all others. Literary provocation was supplemented by a provocative lifestyle (rude, ill-mannered behavior, but only feigned—as Mme d'Épinay correctly observed; inappropriate clothing, wearing of Armenian caftan, etc.)

By his more or less hidden provocation the masochist makes others respond aggressively to his person, which makes it possible for him to feel the victim. Some masochists behave even in their adulthood as ill-mannered children and one simply has to punish them in the end. At first, the provocation may be initiated by simple irony, disobedience, and petty theft, verified on several occasions in Rousseau. The masochist provokes other people to punish him, physically or socially.

It should be stressed that all people seek emotional exchange with others and attempt to attain it. In the course of this, negative emotions are important (punishment, humiliation and the like)—they maintain contact with others. Rousseau's masochism, however, was not limited to the sexual sphere only. By his entire literary work he tries to provoke others and obtain social punishment, which is carefully calculated, similar to painful punishment in the sexual sphere.

It seems that his delusions of persecution, which are an established fact (he suffered them mainly in old age, till his death) and which are usually explained as resulting from his paranoid psychosis, were in fact the product of hypertrophied masochistic fantasies, occurring at a time when he could not obtain sufficient gratification from masochistic activities and when he could not produce social provocation by his writings.

The only thing remaining was his pathologically escalated imagination, which confirmed his conviction that he was surrounded by some mysterious conspiracy. He complained he was the victim of "inhuman persecution," that he was "buried alive among the living," and incessantly watched by "strange, hidden eyes," but most likely he wanted to believe that he was persecuted. Persecution brought him his badly needed suffering. For him suffering was actually happiness and he rationalized it in a religious way, "God wants me to suffer and He knows that I am innocent." He was never able to understand himself. At the end of his life he admitted in *Rêveries*, "The real, first motives of most of my actions are not as clear to myself as I had for a long time proposed."

Rousseau behaved provocatively in many different ways in Parisian salons—in socially inappropriate ways. He arrived stubble-faced and in simple clothes at the première of his opera *Le Devin du village* in Versailles, where the entire court was assembled: He provoked also by turning down the invitation to an audience with the king. As matter of fact, all his writings are provocative (unusual views on science and art, social injustice, unsuitability of French for music, etc.)

However, his provocative views were not followed by social punishment—on the contrary, they made him famous and so he had to use the most abusive provocation possible (for his century) in his works, *Émile* and *Contract*—religious heresy and the idea of a new social order. To make sure that he *would* be punished for this provocation, he insisted that both books be published under his name as author. A pseudonym could have made punishment impossible.

He put *"La Profession de foi du vicaire savoyard"* into *Émile*, though he began his work on *La Profession* as early as 1958, independently of *Émile*. Without it, *Émile* would have become a book which would not make anybody punish him. And indeed, his method produced the desired response: a warrant for his person was issued and there was a real danger of arrest—he probably waited for it and would have liked to go to prison. Only the pressure of his protectors of high standing, mainly the duchess of Luxembourg, who feared being involved in a scandal, made him leave France and thereby become an outlaw.

But even in exile, his provocative activities still went on: he criticized King Frederick II, who had offered him refuge, and did not obey his order not to write about religious and political matters. He was expelled from the Bernese territory Yverdon, but, after he left Môtiers, settled on Bernese territory again—on the Isle St-Pierre expecting to be expelled again.

In all forms of Rousseau's provocation, the martyrdom of the punished person is always stressed. By his behavior, the masochist is able to provoke in others feelings of rage, indignation and anger. Because he does not want, at the same time, to realize his provocative acts consciously, he always feels he is an innocent victim of a malevolent world. Feelings of being plotted against haunted Rousseau, especially during the last years of his life.

All Rousseau's acts are meant to *provoke "punishment."* It is possible that he was, before *Émile* and *Contract Social* were published in 1762, deeply dissatisfied with his literary work. With every single work, he wanted to provoke and arouse resistance, but to his surprise everything he wrote was accepted with enthusiasm (one of his woman admirers wrote to him, "You cannot write four lines without arousing a sensation").

He saw the *First Discourse* as his weakest work, the *Second Discourse* had, according to him (owing to Diderot's cooperation), a "coarse note" and he spoke of *Héloïse* with contempt. It was not "serious literary work," but only a romantic novel.

In the end he gained the desired punishment by his provocative religious views, unacceptable for both Catholics and Protestants, when he wrote and published *La Profession de foi du vicaire savoyard* as part of *Émile* and a chapter on religion in *Contract*, together with unacceptable political views in the same work.

Masochists want to become important martyrs (Waska 1997) and make sure they will not be able to derive pleasure from success. Rousseau, too, became what he wanted to be: an outlaw, being expelled gradually from one land after another, his books being burnt, suffering a lack of financial means, suffering from ill health, suffering from fears of being permanently spied on at the center of conspiracies.

Most of his letters dealt with himself and his various sufferings, with ill fate, which persecuted him again and again, and the betrayal and conspiracy of his former friends. All are informed right down to the last detail of his problems with urination and the necessary catheterizations. Even in places where it would be appropriate to attend to the unhappiness of others he very quickly passed over to his own suffering and hardship. In how many letters did he report he was dying or was going to die shortly! And then, even though he knew that according to the opinion of his doctors he would die soon, he made a big order of special soft wax catheters for fifty louisidors, a reserve that would have been enough for his entire life.

The masochist desires humiliation and submission to an outside power. It is a form of *infantilism*. The all-powerful influence of his temperament, which involves not merely an incapacity for action but also a veritable *paresse de penser* (for if he has sometimes "thought deeply," it has always been with a certain reluctance), which explains his tendency to allow himself to be subjugated by personalities stronger and more determined than his own; in a more general way it also accounts for his temporary corruption by "society" (Grimsley 1969, 245).

The masochist behaves as a "bad child" who deserves punishment. The punishment must be demonstrative. This necessitates an imaginary or real public, to which the humiliation could be displayed. Rousseau employed his correspondence, in which he dramatically described his entire suffering. From this point of view, *Confessions* and *Dialogues* were also accounts of his suffering and the humiliation committed against him by the entire society. He tried to convince the reader he had become the victim of a worldwide plot; he himself did nothing but stand up for (his) truth and (his) morality. He had become the victim of a corrupted society.

The ultimate aim—masochistic gratification—must be postponed till a future time, be it revenge, a feeling of superiority, or of exceptionality of one's own ego. The masochist always entertains the hope that he will be rewarded for his suffering, that he will be "redeemed" in the future.

Social masochists show signs of religious infatuation. Rousseau created his own religious system. He not only regarded himself as God's prophet, but also, as Grimsley remarks, (1969, 290), "By a curious reversal of roles, God tends to be subordinated to Jean-Jacques! He seems himself 'as impassive as God Himself.' On another occasion he imagined himself "as invisible and omnipotent as God." He would be appreciated in time to come as extraordinary and would be vindicated. He longed for immortality and this may be the reason for his intensive literary work: "He who writes will last"

The figure of a suffering but victorious young god occurs in the mythologies of many nations. The desire to be appreciated is postponed into the future: Though I'm not understood, comprehended and am seen as stupid by my contemporaries, I will be appreciated after my death. Even normal people without any special masochistic tendencies start working on big tasks with the hope that their efforts will be appreciated in the future.

The idea of success in the fantasy of pronounced masochistic characters becomes the driving force behind all behavior (Gödde, 1983). The masochist lives, in his mind, in an idealized past (for Rousseau his past included Rome, Sparta, Geneva) and his fantasy translates the glorious future into the present.

Truthfulness and the issue of truth in *Confessions*. *Confessions* is a masterfully composed work that will certainly survive and be read even when other of Rousseau's writings have fallen into oblivion. It is a hitherto unrecognized masochistic self-portrait as well. It should be remembered that Rousseau wrote *Confessions* at a time when he was already older and he knew that this work would be published only after his death. It is thus very probable that he tried to create a self-portrait for future generations that would have the quality of a photograph. The best photograph, as we know, is the one on which we look our best.

Confessions is a skillfully blended mixture of truth, facts, products of Rousseau's own fantasy and apparent sincerity and openness, which has blinded many biographers. Under the guise of unlimited sincerity there hides a deliberate manipulation of the reader. *Confessions* is about as truthful as his account of his stay in Turin that he told to Mme de Warens and about which he wrote, "Then she made me tell her my brief tale, which I did most faithfully, suppressing a few incidents, however, but otherwise neither sparing not excusing myself" (*Confessions*, 104).

Rousseau's factual mistakes caused simply by ignorance (according to him the father of his mother was pastor Bernard) are justifiable and understandable. Other mistakes were due to long time intervals, when he did not remember certain data exactly (e.g., that he lived at his uncle's home in Geneva two or three years, etc.). We can detect the inaccuracies contained in *Confessions* when we compare the data this work contains with Rousseau's letters (see for example the different accounts of the stay in Montpellier).

More serious is *that Rousseau deliberately left out and perhaps even added certain facts, making them up.* He mentioned for example that he was born with a germ of future illness inside his body resulting in urinary retention in his youth, which is impossible from a medical point of view. He also maintained that he suffered total insomnia—sleeplessness—another medically impossible fact.

He left out the following episode: his father locked him in an attic room and punished him physically following his bad behavior—he had torn a Latin dictionary. He must have known of the mysterious death of Anet and his relationship with Anet was not described truthfully. There must have arisen certain differences in his relationship with Mme de Warens; he said nothing about them, as he said nothing about differences with his father. His fantasy seduced him to manipulate his memories so long as was necessary; eventually the memories fit in with the picture he wanted to create.

We can find more such examples in *Confessions*. The composition of this book, however, is very convincing and the reader gets the impression of absolute sincerity and openness. Rousseau wrote *Confessions* not only as his confession but also as a justification and defense aimed at a future audience. He wrote in *Dialogues*, "All I want is the hope that my memory will one day be reestablished in the honor it deserves." The openness in/of *Confessions*, where he again and again adjures the truth (his life maxim was *vitam impendere vero*), is very often highly regarded by his readers, but it is merely the facade of a masochistic personality.

He felt himself to be the prophet of humanity. A prophet can err, but he can never be a deviate. Shainess (1997) remarks correctly that the essential thing is the recognition "of the extensive, defensive linguistic style of the masochist," which holds true for the whole of *Confessions*.

In *Confessions* Rousseau admitted that he had masturbated for his whole life, but did so in a very roundabout way. At the same time, however, he openly denounced masturbation. The sexual role Thérèse played in his life can be determined only by analyzing his masochistic character and the character and course of his illness. Certainly Rousseau did have "normal" sexual intercourse with her, an activity he always abhorred. We should not forget that Rousseau was also a master of literary paradox and was therefore able to employ everything and derive benefit from it, or use it for the benefit of his opinion.

Rousseau's plan has reached fulfillment. He has entered the general awareness as a reformer without reforms and a philosopher without philosophy. He has become a prophet—everyone can choose his own prophecy: of a new social order; of sociology, of a new conception of education, of openness, truthfulness and sincerity. One just chooses and then interprets appropriately.

Masochists typically live in their own fantastic worlds and try to realize what they contrive in their imagination. Rousseau, in the *First Discourse*, formed the idea that his "primitive man" was good. He tried to implement this fantastic idea by means of what he called "conversion," "reform" and transformation of society's lifestyle. He tried to become like the primitive, in his view "better," man who lives alone. But even when living alone he needed an audience to demonstrate his moral superiority. During his stay in Hermitage, Petit Montlouis, and Môtiers he continued to meet his friends and supporters. He wrote and received numerous letters, partly prepared for short-term publication.

Fantasy dominates a masochist's mental life as a source of pleasure and expectation of sainthood. In reveries, one can feel happy and look with optimism into the future without any effort whatsoever and escape the present. "Who, passing beyond the narrow prison of personal interest and petty earthly passion, rises on the wings of imagination above the mists of our atmosphere: he who, without exhausting his strength and powers in struggling against fortune and fate, knows how to leap up into ethereal regions, hover there and keep himself up by his sublime meditations, can in this way defy the onslaughts of fate and the mad judgments of men. He is beyond their attacks: he has no need for their approbation in order to be wise, or of their favor in order to be happy," wrote Rousseau in *Dialogues*.

Fantasies and dreams result in feelings of superiority over others. In fantasies one can experience satisfaction in advance, realize its anticipation. Fantasy is a masochist's instrument, by which reality is shaped to suit him or her. Reverie can be achieved in the Bastille and even in a dungeon. Marcus (1981), herself a masochist, said that with the help of imagination a masochist can achieve what would otherwise be very difficult to achieve in reality: "So in my fantasies I have deceived a lot of men, by transforming them into something they simply were not, and letting them act according to a pattern they knew nothing about, even perhaps transforming them into quite different men" (123).

Let us compare it to Rousseau's own description of how he, in his fantasies, gained the heart of every woman and made her act in compliance with his fantasies. It is a way of self-deception, but a very effective and convenient one. Rousseau used this method whenever he needed it. He would escape immediate unhappiness by taking refuge in a "land of chimeras," in "an ideal world, which his creative imagination soon filled with beings after his own heart." Ultimately he came to feel that the delights of reverie and fantasy were preferable to those of ordinary life.

His imagination, being inseparable from his emotional life, could also have more disturbing effects (Grimsley 1969, 21). "My cruel imagination always anticipates my misfortune." It had a tendency to "carry everything to extremes." He constantly complained of the misery brought upon him by his "affrighted imagination." Rousseau's greatest and at the same time unfulfilled yearning was to be loved. In his fantasies he was surrounded by imaginary friends, because he had not found, and was unable to find, real friends in his life.

The reasons a masochist willingly withdraws into his fantasies are his inability to manage his own life affairs in an independent way and his feelings of helplessness connected with impairment of purposeful behavior, as well as the inability to assert himself and achieve success. What makes Rousseau interesting is the fact that he achieved success and popularity in spite of these impairments, because he lived in the exceptional times of the eighteenth century.

His working method was not based on studying an issue, on analysis or reasoning. He repeatedly expressed his contempt for thinking. His problem-solving method relied heavily on imagination and he did not care whether his fantasies were in accordance with truth or not. The *Second Discourse* (*The Origin and Foundation of Inequality among Mankind*, 1761) was based on ideas that occurred to him during his country walks. This unscholarly approach explains why today's readers for the most part do not know any of his literary works.

On the other hand, writings of Machiavelli, Hobbes, Locke, Hume and Montesquie are outstanding for their penetrating insights into human nature and are of interest to readers even today. They are timeless because they rest on realistic psychology. The works of Rousseau are based on his fantasies; they remain compulsory reading as part of courses on political science but are without much interest for today's readers. The reader feels that the author was an autodidactic dreamer interpreting knowledge he had obtained by reading in a way that invariably supports the picture he wants to project. This was noticed by Rousseau's contemporaries.

Obviously the most successful book during his life was *La Nouvelle Héloïse*, a product of his imagination that he wrote as a romantic novel with contempt (as he claims) that turned out to be much to the taste of the ladies' similar to other ladies' novels before it *(Astré, Clarissa)*. The effeminate Rousseau knew what women's souls desire; he was a good judge of women's psychology, of which imagination is an integral part.

A masochist's ideal self is magnificent and heroic, but it exists only in his fantasies. His timidity, fearfulness and lack of healthy aggressiveness prevent him from realizing these ideals and the result is a "split personality."

The masochist has strict moral standards preventing him from taking his aggressions out on others. In certain situations, however, he can behave aggressively, especially when he believes he is on the side of right and truth and acts in the name of some authority, on its orders. Rousseau always felt himself to be a prophet and identified even with Jesus. He felt he was chosen to reveal new truths, new morals to humanity.

Imagination enables the masochist to "see" things in terms of his ideas and to manipulate reality as desired.

Pain, Hardship and Suffering

It was no secret to Rousseau's contemporaries—they knew he took pleasure in hardship, pains and suffering (see the counterfeit letter written by Horace Walpole that led to Rousseau's break with Hume). Modern biographers have not paid much attention to this interesting fact.

Hume said of him, "Surely, Rousseau is one of the most singular human beings, and one of the most unhappy. His extreme sensibility of temper is his torment: as he is much more susceptible to pain than pleasure." For his artificial and pointed poverty, Rousseau's contemporaries referred to him mockingly as the Diogenes of the eighteenth century—allegedly King Frederick II called him that. His resettlement in Hermitage in April 1756 crowned his "reform" and set the stage for still more social dependency, material hardship and the suffering he delighted in.

The social clumsiness of masochists, sometimes making the impression

of stupidity and mental retardation, was described by Reich. Many comedians and clowns are in fact masochists who have learned to make a virtue of their clumsiness and are entertaining others by it. The comedian behaves in a socially inadequate—stupid—way. The spectator can laugh because he feels himself to be superior to the stupid clown: he knows how to behave. However, the comedian knows too that he behaves in a socially inadequate way. His comic acts are calculated and derived from a good knowledge of human psychology.

The behavior of masochists, on the other hand, is not calculated and their inadequacy originates rather in their deficient socialization. The masochist usually does not know how to behave in a socially correct way, which results in various lapses. Rousseau was aware of this handicap: "Though I am not a fool, I am very often taken for one . . . Unfortunately for me, too, my face and my eyes seem to promise otherwise, and people find my stupidity all the more shocking because it disappoints their expectations . . . I should enjoy society as much as anyone, if I were not certain to display myself not only at a disadvantage but in a character entirely foreign for me. In that respect men who live in society are at a great advantage. Knowing better what not to say, they are more certain of what they say . . . but I have only to be absolutely required to speak and I infallibly say something stupid . . . In my anxiety to fulfill my obligations as quickly as possible I hastily gabble a few considered words, and am only too glad if they mean nothing at all."

This sometimes led to the accusation of "trying to be original and of acting unlike other people." He himself admitted there were "countless examples" of such inadequate behavior. He gave an example of an embarrassing remark he made in the presence of the duchess of Luxembourg, Mme de Mirepoix and Duke de Gontaut. That Rousseau behaved in society in a way that was conspicuously clumsy has been confirmed by countless evidence. Let us remember, for example, how Rousseau all of a sudden sat on the lap of a surprised Hume and tearfully began to embrace and kiss him.

The socially inadequate behavior of masochists reminds one of the right-hemispheric spontaneity of small children, who freely express what occurs to them without any rational control exerted by the left hemisphere (compare the cruelty of what is known as children's jokes).

Rousseau explained his inappropriate behavior by the fact that he had not lived in society, which was not true. As a matter of fact, Rousseau mixed in closed circles as well as in society at large for his whole life, but his socialization in early childhood had been impaired and hand in hand with it the cultural mode of thinking, together with social lies and pretension.

Added to this must be the fact that his memory functions, which require practice usually obtained in the course of normal upbringing and education, were also impaired ("I have never been able to memorize half a dozen verses in my life"). Rousseau himself found that: "In me are united two almost irreconcilable characteristics, though in a way I cannot imagine. I have a passionate temperament, and lively and headstrong emotions. Yet my thoughts arise slowly and confusedly, and are never ready till late."(See the paragraph: The Role of Memory in Future Interpersonal Relation)

His right-hemispheric "hypertrophy" affected the whole of his literary work, which is too emotional with few rational and analytical components. He was aware of it as well: "But I do not suffer from this combination of quick emotion and slow thoughts only in company. I know it too when I am alone and when I am working. Ideas take shape in my head with the most incredibly difficulty." In addition to that Rousseau was unable to force himself to perform tasks he was not enthusiastic about: "My mind is impatient of any sort of restraint, and cannot subject itself to the rules of the moment."

Masochists are usually effeminate and lacking independence and they like a reserved life. They experience difficulty in making decisions. Even minor decisions are hard for them to make but they attend to them in order to avoid the necessity of having to decide more basic issues. Indecision is accompanied by conflicts and suffering (I am in a terrible, desperate situation and I do not know what to do). The masochist finds it extremely painful when he cannot depend on a strong person, who would give him clear orders, and keeps on hesitating between different impulses.

The inability to make a decision results in severe mental conflicts. This can be exemplified by Rousseau's state of mind after he had been asked to accompany Mme d'Épinay to Geneva in the fall of 1757. He himself was reluctant to do it (probably because Mme d'Épinay had betrayed his love of Mme d'Houdetot) but all his friends advised him to accompany his supporter.

Diderot, who visited Rousseau in December 1757, shortly before Rousseau left Hermitage, bore witness to his state of mind during this conflict. Rousseau himself described this visit in *Confessions* as a pleasant encounter. Allegedly they talked about d'Alembert's article on Geneva for *Encyclopédie*. Diderot, however, described Rousseau's behavior during their encounter as that of a mentally ill person swayed between self-accusations and self-justifications, feelings of loneliness and the yearning to find love and affection. Diderot did not feel compassion for him, he felt only disgust. In his letter to Grimm he wrote that Rousseau was a madman and that he felt as if he were sitting beside the damned, "He is damned, that is for sure. I don't want to see this man anymore, he makes me believe in the devil and hell . . . His outcries can be heard across the whole garden."

The comparison of Diderot's observation (and there is no reason to doubt it) and *Confessions* shows clearly how untrustworthy *Confessions* is in some respects. Its truth was always Rousseau's subjective truth, in which he believed, "be it true or not."

In masochists, the ability to assert oneself, to achieve one's goals and actively fight for them is limited. Normal people pursue and carry through their plans and ideas with more or less intensive efforts; they try to realize their ideals. A masochist's pessimism, however, anticipates defeats and unconsciously wishes for them. So, as there is *"Zweckoptimismus"* (calculated optimism), a characteristic of a healthy man, there is also *"Zweckpessimismus"* (calculated pesimism) of a masochist, which can be observed in Rousseau's literary work. "All things springing from the hands of God are good: all things become corrupt in human hands." (*Émile*, Book One, introductory sentence).

The first chapter of *Du contract social* starts with the well-known sentence: "Man is born free but everywhere he lies in fetters." In the *First Discourse* we get to hear that man's ideal state was the state of noble savage and that science and art wrought havoc with humanity. Reversal or remedy of this state is impossible. In the *Second Discourse,* the source of all evil is seen in possession: "The first man who, having enclosed a piece of ground, bethought himself of saying, 'This is mine' and found people simple enough to believe him, was the real founder of civil society. Humanity would have been spared infinite crimes, wars, homicides, murders, if only someone had ripped up the fences or filled the ditches and said 'Do not listen to this pretender!' You are eternally lost if you do not remember that the fruits of earth are everyone's property, that the land is no one's property!"

But even this cannot be put right. His Émile received the most careful upbringing, but even the best education is no good. In his life, Émile fails. *Contract social* shows how the order of society could look. But along with it the reader gets to hear that it is impossible to realize this social system. Such a method must inevitably involve Rousseau in contradictions and paradoxes. The masochist lacks the ability to differentiate between what can be achieved and what is unattainable in this world. His fantasies carry him so high that any return becomes impossible.

Grimsley (1969, 245) observes "the all-powerful influence of his temperament, which involves not merely an incapacity for action but also a veritable *paresse de penser* . . ."

Purposeful, "agonal" behavior, aiming at the achievement of a certain goal and requiring discipline, is a function performed by the left hemisphere, particularly by its prefrontal lobe. Rousseau himself admitted that such behavior and thinking was unknown to him: "I am easily discouraged, particularly in difficult and lengthy enterprises." Thinking caused him pain and he was unable to stick to a thing for a long time.

Obedience to laws, societal moral codes and worship of authorities are not typical only for women but also for masochists. Let us remember how Rousseau refused to help the imprisoned Huguenots and referred to the fact that they had broken laws that must be respected. Faced with infringement of laws, or moral principles, the masochist behaves intransigently: "When, however, the child . . . refuses to show respect for the mother . . . then such a child should be strangled as soon as possible as a monster . . ." (*Émile*, Book One, footnote).

In *Social Contract* Rousseau enumerated positive dogmas of the bourgeois religion, which it is the duty of all to acknowledge (the existence of God, belief in life after death, happiness of the just and the sanctity of laws and social contract). Should there be someone who acknowledges them in public and then behaves as if he would not believe in them, "he should be punished by death" (*On Social Contract*, "On Bourgeois Religion").

Masochists are not passive under all circumstances. Sometimes people can be found among them who tend to perfectionism and pedantry, whose respect for the requirements and conventions of the time is exceptional and who are unable to distance themselves from them.

Wurmser (1997) speaks of absoluteness—the narcissistic stigma. It is a totalitarian superego, often with opposite demands of irreconcilable totality. They are conspicuous in that their individuality recedes into the background and they demand "for something" or "for someone."

At first glance it might seem that Rousseau was a great individualist. On closer examination, however, it becomes clear that he always acted on somebody's or something's behalf—humanity, morale, truth, divine truth— and felt himself to be the prophet of these values. He is the apostle of goodness who had sacrificed his personal comfort to the duty of proclaiming the truth to his fellow men.

It is symptomatic that Rousseau constantly looked for absolute values: absolute happiness, absolute love, ideal society. In his eyes, he probably was the best man, and surely a good one. At his birth he was endowed by a nature which released him from the necessity to seek to attain perfection of virtue. This, however, did protect him against corruption by society, so that he had been able to retain the original innocence for the first forty years of his life (*Dialogues*).

Masochists show what has been described as resignative thinking. When encountering difficulties, a masochist tends to retrospectively devise alternative behaviors which he might have, or should have, realized. Typical examples of such thoughts are: "If only I had . . ." "Why didn't I . . ." "If I were strong and good enough, all these awful things would not have happened. Whatever abuse occurs, it is all my fault." Rousseau wrote, "If I would have remained in my original state . . . to behave quietly . . . in my inadvertence I made an issue out of it . . ." (*Confessions*, Book Nine).

In addition to resignative thinking we also commonly encounter the belief in "omnipotence of thoughts," leading to the conviction that thoughts and gestures can change the world. Here magic combines with feelings of superiority and an illusory feeling of strength.

The masochist also believes in the magical helper, a strong personality, or messiah, who can bring about a decisive turn in humanity's destiny (let us remember his belief in "the law-maker" in *Contract*). The less a masochist is able to actively order his life, the greater are his expectations of a savior. Sometimes, paradoxically, he sees himself as the savior and messiah. He is not aware of his own indecisiveness. Magical thinking, in turn, is an expression of infantilism and naiveté; these do not rely on rational decisions based on reality. A masochist lacks imagination, which would depend on reality and which Goethe called *"exakte Phantasie."*

The masochist builds castles in the air unrelated to reality and which in fact represent only his *"Wunschdenken"* (wishful thinking). The masochist does not want to realize his utopias. Rousseau worked on a constitution for Corsica, but rejected visiting the island as its law-maker. Impaired social skills are related to the masochist's anxiety.

Power and love are seen as incompatible contradictions. The masochist condemns any form of power and describes his own powerlessness as an expression and ability of love. He refers to his "innocence" and does not want to see the real meaning of power. Secretly, however, he desires power, because it provides what the masochist does not have: self-confidence, zest for life, capability of normal love.

Whoever desires power necessarily wants to achieve something in life, wants to assert himself and strengthens his self-esteem. One-sided condemnation of the entitlement to power does not inhibit hostile feelings, which are the result of one's powerlessness, but has rather a strengthening effect on them. A socially powerless person has to accept his permanent feeling of anger of the powerful. Feelings of anger, envy, and revenge lead to the resentment of enmity, which is not directed against one's self but against the stronger and more powerful.

All wealth stands for moral corruption because it originates in the primary evil, i.e., inequality of people. Where there are no differences between people, the difference between poor and rich disappears as well.

Hostility can be also directed against one's best friends. Rousseau told Baron Holbach openly why he had not accepted his invitations for so long, "You are too rich." The rich and powerful person is thereby humiliated, and by his condemnation the masochist attempts to elevate his own person. In a similar way, presented with a questionnaire, citizens of the former East Germany argued: "We are not rich, but we are morally superior."

Moments of hostility flash through one's mind and are always quickly put aside, into the unconscious—into an unconscious consciousness—emotional unconscious (LeDoux 1996), from which, however, they can further influence the mind.

When a masochist lives in a power relationship, in which he accepts his submissive role, his *latent sadism* does not have to manifest itself. In closer emotional relationships of love, friendship and in the relationship to his children, however, it becomes impossible for him to hide his sadistic tendencies forever: Rousseau sent all his children to a foundling home and found all sorts of justifications, which he repeatedly changed (his own poverty, the rich take from him the bread he needs for his children, he would not be able to work, they can get a better education there, he only wants to save Thérèse's virtue, etc.).

The idea that sadism and masochism form an integrated whole was expressed by Kraftt-Ebing and Havellock Ellis. This hypothesis was held also by Freud. For the masochist it is not enough to experience suffering, he has the need to torment others, similar to the sadist, who makes other people suffer but has the need to be tormented as well.

Masochists lack positive aggressions. One of the meanings of the Latin "aggredi" is "to approach the world," which involves purposeful activity. Rousseau did not want to achieve power or wealth (even though he had opportunities to do so). His demonstrative martyr-like poverty ensures that he has a "better" character. Property corrupts the character.

The masochist hates people but he hates himself as well. He feels contempt for himself because he sees himself as a person who allows others to humiliate him. "The masochist is always willing to feel contempt for others and often torments them for features which torment him" (Salzman 1959). For this reason masochists restrict contacts with other people in order to preserve the feeling of their own superiority—by regarding others as inferior. He tries to attain a feeling of superiority over others, launching an activity which is bound to fail.

Masochism has also been called "system self-destruction" and sometimes the therapist may wish to kick a masochist: "Now and then, deeply masochistic patients evoke anger, annoyance, frustration—which even leads to a desire to kick the patient!" (Shainess 1997). He solves his personal conflicts by unconsciously taking on the role of a victim, a slave or a martyr. By "taking the bull by the horns," he gets rid of "moral" feelings of anxiety and inferiority: in his fantasy, the humiliation obtained turns into triumph. Defeat becomes victory, the masochist becomes an important person, and his ego has been rehabilitated: "Even when people did want to reach me, they could not succeed in it. Their behavior has taken away all the respect I had felt for them: any further continuation of contacts with them would be nonsensical and it would only burden me and I am a hundred times happier in my seclusion than I could ever be in coexistence with them" (*Rêveries*, Walk One).

Similarly, the masochist feels deserted and neglected by his friends, who were not able to recognize his true character. This again brings him feelings of suffering and sadness. Masochists are collectors of insults. Rousseau parted on bad terms with Grimm; criticism of Grimm and descriptions of his insults fill a disproportionately large number of pages in *Confessions*. Causes of such breaks are mostly trivial matters and remain beyond the comprehension of his friends. Let us remember Rousseau's split with Mme d'Épinay, his breaks with Diderot and Hume. Though the masochist is actually a misanthrope, hating others still more than himself, he tries to cover up this fact by saccharine-sweet communications which are full of politeness, apologies and self-humiliation.

Masochists are the creators of their own unhappiness and may even benefit from it. It would be a mistake to regard masochists merely as victims. Illness and disease can also have a positive value. Parents worry more and care more intensively for a sick child. The illness itself can serve as a means to "receive more love from parents," a fact noticed by Freud. Public demonstration of one's weakness evokes compassion. Rousseau's mysterious illnesses in Les Charmettes, where he lived absolutely carefree with Mme de Warens, fall into this category. Rousseau obviously felt that the socially-minded Mme de Warens did not find life with him to her liking and "actively" assumed the role of a "healthy patient" to encourage the weakening maternal feelings of his patron. The masochist takes pleasure in disproportionate complaining and crying, but at the same time demonstrates his extreme modesty, by which he emphasizes his importance. Both uncontrollable crying and laughing fits are "disabling" moments that eliminate self-control. Both crying and laughing fits contain obvious elements of pleasure.

Masochistic personalities, who have often been pampered in their childhood, whose wishes have been completely met and who have not been integrated into the society of other children, develop the conviction that other people have to remove all obstacles from their way. The conviction is formed that the masochist has to be free of all privations, that all his wishes must be fulfilled, because he is weak and pitiable. His modesty is only superficial. Masochists can be very demanding, especially in closer relationships. They show their weakness and helplessness in a demonstrative way, which evokes compassion in others. Behavior, like morphology, is adaptive.

How many times Rousseau portrays himself as throwing himself to the feet of one of his protectresses and wetting their hands with his tears. Practically always there is someone around who wants to help the dependent and weak human being, be it only for the reason to gain his gratitude. Masochists often live in a second-hand style in symbiotic relationships and are always at least partly dependent on others for their help. This might be the reason for their demonstrative emphasizing of independence and freedom by refusing to accept small gifts or other attentions. But they would never object to offers of more important things (see Rousseau's stay with Mme de Warens, spending one year with Baron Alcuna, acceptance of Hermitage as a refuge offered him by Mme d'Épinay, a house in Môtiers from Mme Boy, etc.)

Chapter Nine

Rousseau's Sexual Masochism: a Cause of His Disease and Death

Rousseau's lengthy reflections on his sexual masochistic deviations he described in *Confessions* are of interest from a medical point of view. They shed light on his personality and when we read these passages carefully we find out that Rousseau was well aware of the deep impact of his sexual deviation not only on his sexual life but also on his entire thinking, behavior and literary work: "Who would imagine, for instance, that I owe one of the most vigorous elements in my character to the same origin as the weakness and sensuality that flows in my veins?" (*Confession*, Book One, 1712–1728).

Rousseau dedicates much space in *Confessions* to these reflections: "Now I have made the first and most painful step in the dark and miry maze of my confessions. It is the ridiculous and the shameful, not one's criminal actions, that it is hardest to confess."

No less interesting is that no great attention has been paid to these passages from *Confessions*, probably because in recent years only very few physicians were concerned with Rousseau. According to the common view great personalities should not be subjected to inquiries into their weaknesses and deviations. Such inquiries could interfere with the established ideal picture.

This common view overlooks, however, the fact that studying these mental deviations can help to explain many aspects which would otherwise remain unclear, and to understand the works and lives of these great personalities.

Let us hear what Rousseau himself had to say when he wrote about how he first discovered his masochistic tendencies, when he was beaten by Mlle Lambercier:

> For a long time she confined herself to threats, and the threat of a punishment entirely unknown to me frightened me sufficiently. But when in the end I was beaten I found the experience less dreadful in fact than in anticipation: and the very strange thing was that this punishment

increased my affection for the inflictor. It required all the strength of my devotion and all my natural gentleness to prevent my deliberately earning another beating. I had discovered in the shame and pain of the punishment an admixture of sensuality, which had left me rather eager for a repetition by the same hand. No doubt, there being some degree of precocious sexuality in all this, the same punishment at the hand of her brother would not have seemed pleasant at all . . . Who could have supposed that this childish punishment, received at the age of eight at the hands of a woman of thirty, would determine my tastes and desires, my passions, my very self for the rest of my life and in that sense diametrically opposed to the one in which they should normally have developed.

This issue, which does not come up in the previous versions of *Confessions*, is psychologically interesting for several reasons. Rousseau wrote these lines at an advanced age, when he was reviewing his whole life. He expresses very clearly that *masochism has controlled him for his whole life* and was not, as many authors mistakenly assume, a mere excess of his youth. Medically seen, his words admit no doubts. Similar to "gender identity," the masochistic deviation develops during the first years of life and cannot be changed. Rousseau realized he had a certain kind of sexual deviation, but as he did later in other matters he seeks to minimize its importance, to trivialize it or to cast a new light on it. He was also aware that his deviation had influenced his whole life.

A second clear description of Rousseau's masochism can be found in Book One of *Confessions*. A girl of his age (eleven years or so), Mlle Goton, suggested to him that they play "a school game" where he will be the pupil and she his educator who will be allowed to punish him physically. This was exactly what Rousseau wanted and therefore never forgot.

She was indeed a strange little person, was Mlle Goton. She was not beautiful, but her face was not easy to forget. I can remember it yet rather vividly at times for an old fool . . . She had a proud, rather overbearing way with her which very well suited her schoolmistress's role, and indeed have given us the first idea for it . . . For the favors she granted me were favors to be begged for on bended knee . . . I think if I had remained longer with her it would have killed me . . . If Mlle Goton had commanded me to jump into the flames I think I should have obeyed her unhesitatingly.

During this play, which Mlle Goton herself proposed, she punished her pupil physically and he had to beg for it on his knees. "She took the greatest liberties with me, but never allowed me to take any with her. She treated me exactly as a child." Even later in Turin he ardently longed for her. "I would have given my life to have found another Mlle Goton for no more than a quarter of an hour."

His adolescent (and later adult) fantasies were not concerned with normal sexual intercourse, but with women who gave him masochistic gratification in the form of physical punishment:

> Tormented for a long while by I knew not what, I feasted feverish eyes on lovely women, recalling them carelessly to my imagination, but only to make use of them in my own fashion as so many Mlle Lamberciers . . . In my crazy fantasies, my wild fits of eroticism, and in the strange behavior which they sometimes drove me to, I always invoked, imaginatively, the aid of the opposite sex without so much as dreaming that a woman could serve any other purpose than the one I lust for.

Rousseau was thus well aware that his masochism exhibited certain streaks of madness and could lead to his destruction. Remembering Turin, he described his masochistic fantasies similarly:

> The heat in my blood incessantly filled my mind with pictures of women and girls. But not knowing the true nature of sex I imagined them acting according to my own strange fantasies, and had no idea of anything else. These thoughts, however, kept all my senses in a most troublesome state of activity.

On the other hand, however, *he saw his deviation as something positive.* He was always convinced that his masochistic tendencies had preserved his virginity (purity) longer than was the case with other youths:

> My morals might well have been impaired by these strange

tastes, which persisted with a depraved and insane intensity. But in fact they kept me pure even after the age of puberty . . . With sensuality burning in my blood almost from my birth I kept myself pure and unsullied up to an age when even the coldest and most backward natures have developed.

He considered his aversion to sexual intercourse to be the result of his upbringing by three exemplary and honest aunts. He remained "pure" because his masochistic fantasies protected him from loss of virginity. The masochistic desires protected him even as an adult man and even after the loss of "healthy morals" he did not get rid of them, he assures us. According to him, this state of affairs was not an expression of egoism but rather of his personal virtue. Shame was both the preserver of his morality and the result of his secret passions, which never failed him. He considered shame to be "the companion of an evil conscience." He asks himself the rhetorical question, "Do I have good morals because I have perverted desires?" Rousseau's logic was the logic of a typical masochist: he regarded normal sexual intercourse as something impure and bad.

He knew that his masochism was a deviation and madness, but he was prepared to justify it, e.g., by the fact that he had preserved "moral purity." According to him, masochistic practices were harmless and pure whereas real sexual intercourse was impure. He said literally, *"Always I stopped short of imagining those satisfactions, which I had been taught to loathe, and which, little though I suspected it, were in fact not so far divorced from those I envisaged."*

As a typical masochist, Rousseau *showed an aversion to normal sexual intercourse.* "Not only had I not till adolescence any clear ideas concerning sexual intercourse, but in my muddled thoughts on the subject always assumed odious and disgusting shapes." The mere thought of sexual contacts of other people aroused in Rousseau feelings of disgust: "I was always reminded of the coupling of dogs, and my stomach turned over at the very thought." He felt aversion to loose women and was not able to overcome it for his whole life: "I had a horror of prostitutes which has never left me and I could not look on a debauchee without contempt and even fear." He never spent money on them if we disregard the single occasion in Venice, where he paid one ducat to a prostitute *(padoana)* and wanted to leave her without sexual intercourse.

His second sexual intercourse experience was with the lady-friend of the parish priest Klüpffell, who asked him to have sex with her (Grimm was also asked: "We all three went in turn into the next room with the little girl, who did not know whether to laugh or to cry . . . I left the rue des Moineaux, where the little girl lived, feeling as ashamed as St-Preux . . .")

Mme de Warens probably was the only woman whom he really "loved" (in his sense). But when she decided to teach him sexual intercourse and gave him eight days to make up his mind ("which I hypocritically assured her I did not require,") he held counsel with himself for eight days trying to find an excuse and he repeated later on several occasions that he wished that the sexual intercourse had never taken place.

> It might be supposed that these eight days dragged for me like so many centuries. On the contrary, I could have wished them centuries long . . . it was made up of fright mingled with impatience. I dreaded what I desired, to the point of sometimes seriously searching my brains for some honorable excuse for evading my promised happiness . . . How, by what miracle was it that in the flower of my youth I was so little eager for my first experience?

In order to be able to have sexual intercourse with Mme de Warens, he had to deceive himself into believing he is a sinner who desecrates his maman and that his rejection might offend her. Unlike Mme Larnage, who resolutely raped him and made him have sex with her, Mme de Warens suggested sexual intercourse with her and gave him time to think about it.

What was missing in her suggestion was the order, the necessity to submit immediately to her will. With Mme de Warens, the masochistic component, necessary for him to enjoy the sexual intercourse, was entirely missing and Rousseau could not have derived much pleasure from it. On the other hand, he knew he must not turn down the offer of sexual intercourse. He was aware that when he turned down the offer he would gravely insult Mme de Warens, who took care of him, and he could lose her. Rousseau described the seduction itself as follows:

> The day came at last, more dreaded than desired. I promised all and did not break my word. My heart fulfilled my pledges with-

out any desire for the reward. I gained it nevertheless, and I found myself for the first time in the arms of a woman, and of a woman I adored. Was I happy? NO: I tasted the pleasure, but I know not what invincible sadness poisoned its charms. I felt as if I had committed incest and, two or three times, as I clasped her rapturously in my arms I wet her bosom with my tears (*Confessions*, 189–190).

Rousseau was capable of sexual intercourse (a fact doubted by some of his biographers). This is evidenced by sexual intercourse with Mme de Warens, a love affair with Mme de Larnage during the trip to Montpelier, as well as by his sexual intercourse with Thérèse, with whom he had several children. It is quite possible, however, that some of Thérèse's pregnancies were with other men and Rousseau was not the father of all five children she delivered. Rousseau was not aroused by normal sexual intercourse and experienced real orgasm only in connection with masochistic practices.

Here the reader could object that Rousseau had sexual intercourse with Mme de Larnage and was in fact proud of it: "With Mme de Larnage . . . I was proud of my manhood and good fortune, and I abandoned myself joyfully and confidently to my senses." However, more careful reading of *Confessions* reveals that the happiness he felt at this sexual intercourse was again based on masochism. Before the actual seduction, Rousseau was terribly horrified and mortally afraid lest he would offend her and he himself would be scorned: "I was restrained by the fear of offending or displeasing her, and by the still greater fear of being hissed and booed and ridiculed."

He did not seduce Mme de Larnage but she seduced him! He was her "poor victim": "So she undertook my conquest and it was good-bye to poor Jean-Jacques . . . she was determined not to accept defeat." She herself put her arms around him, kissed him and made him to have sexual intercourse with her:

She made her advances so cunningly that she would have seduced even a man off his guard . . . I was angry with myself for my stupid bashfulness, and for being unable to overcome it: but at the same time I reproached myself for it. I was in torture . . . remained silent, and looked sulky. In fact I did everything in my power to court the treatment I had feared . . . She abruptly cut the silence short by putting her arm round my neck and in a second her lips, pressed upon my own, spoke too clearly to leave me in doubt.

Rousseau did not say he had seduced Mme de Larnage. She seduced him "and though her little conquest had cost Mme de Larnage some trouble, I had reason to believe she did not regret it." Rousseau found it thrilling that he had to submit to the will of an older woman, that he, filled with anxiety, had to do something he in fact did not want to do.

Marquise de Torignan (actually Taulignan), who accompanied them, saw clearly who seduced whom and made fun of Rousseau: "He did not stop chaffing me: on the contrary, he treated me more than ever as the poor enraptured lover, *a martyr to the cruelty of his lady.*" These are Rousseau's own words, together with diction and vocabulary characteristic of a masochist.

This was what and how he really felt and what aroused him in this affair! He was forced to have sexual intercourse, which went against the grain with him and which he performed only as a masochistic order. He did not meet this duty with great enthusiasm because Mme de Larnage, though she behaved sensually, imposed a certain restraint on him, allegedly considering his health. Rousseau claimed he would never forget this neither beautiful nor young woman and said, "Were I to live for a hundred years I should never remember this charming woman without pleasure," but when he could have returned to her after his "treatment" in Montpellier, he did not do it. The masochistic component, occurring at the time of the first sexual intercourse, when he was "raped" by Mme de Larnage had evaporated over time and what remained was only the simple sexual intercourse, which did not arouse him. It is likely that it was with Mme de Larnage that Rousseau experienced orgasm of its kind, but this was only because he saw himself masochistically "tortured" in this sexual intercourse. It was therefore a special form of conjunctive masochism.

Being a sexual and moral masochist, Rousseau always had difficulties with the concept of love. For a normal person "sex without love" is identical with "love without sex." For Rousseau, however, "love without sex," which resembled the feeling connecting intensive friendship and devotion, was an affair of the "heart" but devoid of sexual intercourse. According to him, sexual intercourse degraded and destroyed feelings of love.

On the other hand, he knew and apparently practiced sex without love—in the form of urethral masturbation at Thérèse's hands. This was a purely sensual matter. The same can be said of the masochistic beatings (Mlle Lambercier and Mlle Goton) and other "symbolic" masochistic behaviors, which satisfied only his senses. These facts explain why his opinions on love are often unintelligible and unclear. Since he sometimes used the common "love" terminology and then again his own terminology, it is unavoidable that many of his ideas remain unclear and contradictory.

He said at the beginning of his affair with Mme de Larnage, "I was falling seriously in love with her." But hereafter we are informed, "If what I felt for her was not precisely love, it was at least so tender a return for her love she showed me . . ." and further again, "I have only felt true love once in my life, and that was not for her [Mme de Larnage]. I did not love her either as I had loved Mme de Warens: and it was for that reason that I was a hundred times more successful in our intercourse. With Maman, my pleasure was always troubled by a feeling of sadness, by a secret oppression at the heart, that I had difficulty in overcoming."

Rousseau wrote in Book One of *Confessions*: "I know very distinct sorts of love, both real but with practically nothing in common except that they are both extremely violent and different in every way from a mere friendly affection. The whole course of my life has been divided between these two quite separate emotions, and I have even experienced them both simultaneously." Rousseau wrote these words as an introduction of his account of the relationship to Mlle Vulson (who was ten years older), for whom he felt the love of a child, resembling the love he later felt for Mme de Warens: love as an intense relationship between friends with deep confidence, love without sexual desire.

Rousseau did not know what to do with the second, masochistic type of "love," which literally made him suffer in his boyhood, in his encounter with Mlle Goton (she was *la fouetteuse*). For him masochistic treatment was his only source of sexual gratification, but he stoped short of calling it love. In Mlle Goton's case he referred to his "love" as madness and spoke of a different kind of love and wrote finally: "My love of her, or rather my dates with her . . ."

But he never forgot the masochistic love of Mlle Goton and memories of it: "I was having very short but very passionate encounters with a little Mlle Goton, who was so kind as to play the schoolmistress to me—and that was all. But that all meant everything. It seemed the height of bliss."

If another man had been interested in Mlle Vulson, Rousseau would have felt half-hearted jealousy. "I loved her as a brother, but with a lover's jealousy. But if I had so much as supposed that Mlle Goton could lavish on anyone else the attentions I received at her hands I should have been jealous as a Turk, and savage as a tiger."

We get to know from *Confessions* that he "fell in love" easily with many different women (Mme de Malby in Lyon, Mme Dupin in Paris, etc.). Rousseau fell in love mainly with noblewomen: "Besides, seamstresses, chambermaids and shop girls hardly tempted me. I need young ladies" (*Confessions*, 132).

In Rousseau, love as emotion in fact ruled out sexual desire. It is interesting, however, that a woman Rousseau was willing to fall in love with, even though only platonically, had to have the figure of a typical woman, particularly a full and well-developed bosom, the presence of which in Mme de Warens he stressed several times. For the same reason he was unable to fall in love with Mme d'Épinay: "She was very thin, very fair, and with a chest as flat as my hand" (*Confessions*, 384).

In his life he was in love only with Mme de Warens (as he wrote in this section of *Confessions*), but he felt sadness after each sexual intercourse with her: "Instead of congratulating myself upon possessing her, I would reproach myself for degrading her." He had to find an excuse for why it was that he did not want to have sexual intercourse with a person he loved. This certainly was no problem for his overgrown imagination. He did not want to have sexual intercourse even with the beautiful courtesan Zulietta (Giulietta), "No, Nature has not made me for sensual delight," and that was why he persuaded himself that she actually was a monster, when he noticed that her bosom was slightly asymmetrical (*un téton borgne*): "I saw as clear as daylight that instead of the most charming creature I held in my arms some kind of monster, rejected by Nature, men and love" (*Confessions*, 301).

His desire for the active possession of Mme de Warens was absent. "With her I had neither transports nor desires. I was in a ravishing calm, without knowing what I was enjoying." On the other hand, when she was absent he felt an anxiety that bordered on pain.

But even in this particular relationship with Mme de Warens we can trace some masochistic elements. When he was with Mme de Warens, Rousseau was dependent upon a superior being who completed his happiness. His relation had an almost religious quality. He tells us his heart "was open before her as before God." Such a lover could not satisfy Mme de Warens's requirements. In *Rêveries* he wrote sadly: "If only I had been as sufficient for her as she was for me! What peaceful and delightful days we should have spent together!"

The insolubility of Rousseau's conflicting feelings of love can be seen in the fifth book of *Confessions*:

> When I possessed one (Rousseau used the word "possessed " as a euphemism for sexual intercourse) my senses were quiet, but my heart never. At the height of my pleasure the need for love devoured me. I had a tender mother, a dear friend: but I need a mistress. In my imagination I put one in Maman's place, endowing her with a thousand shapes in order to deceive myself. If I had thought I was holding Maman in my arms when I embraced her, my embraces would have been just as tender, but all my desire would have died. I should have sobbed with affection but I should have no physical pleasure. Physical pleasure! Is it the lot of man to enjoy it? Ah, if ever in all my life I had once tasted the delights of love to the full, I do not think that my frail existence could have endured them. I should have died on the spot.

Rousseau was unable to feel love during sexual intercourse. And where he loved (i.e., he had the feeling of intensive friendship), he was unable to have sexual intercourse, or only without any physical pleasure. As a matter of fact, Rousseau did not know love in the common sense of the word—intensive friendship coupled with a desire for sexual intercourse.

Grimsley (1969, 98) noticed correctly:

> Considerable obstacles stood in the way of all Rousseau's efforts to establish genuinely adequate relationships with women." Also correct are his observations that, "His reactions to love are not dissimilar from those involved in his search for friendship, for in each case he desires a kind of absolute emotional satisfaction which will relieve the anxieties and conflicts of his inner life, and this mood, in turn, tends to prevent him from attaining genuine personal reciprocity in his love-relationships (99).

The masochistic effort to attain absolute values and perfection is reflected also in the demands he puts on love. His dreams of love may be so "perfect" that a normal love life is thereby seriously inhibited as the individual remains imprisoned within the circle of his own unattainable desires:

> The chief psychological function of this perfectionist aspiration is that it enables a man to escape from the intolerable anxiety associated with the thought of actual physical possession. In this way he comes to interpret personal inadequacy as a mark of superiority: obsessed by his escapist dream, he refuses to treat the erotic object as a real person who may be as incomplete and fallible as himself (Grimsley 1969, 105–106).

He wrote about his relationship to Signora Basile, "I loved too sincerely, too perfectly, for me to be able to be happy."

He was concerned with love in the fourth and fifth book of *Émile* where he pathetically asks, "What is true love but chimera, illusion? We have far greater love for the image we create for ourselves than for the object to which it is appealed . . . All is merely illusion in love, I admit, but what is real are the feelings it inspires in us for the true beauty it makes us love. This beauty is not in the lover's object, it is the work of our errors . . . What is real love indeed, when not a dream, an illusion? Man loves much more the image he has created than the object to which he applies it. The full happiness of love is due to the fact that it is *not* fulfilled. Love is born from a dream and remains a mere dream illusion."

In *La Nouvelle Héloïse* he makes Julie write: "It seems to me as if love were the most virtuous bond," and before she dies, Julie says, "The world of dreams is the only thing in this world that is worthy of dwelling in." The second preface to *La Nouvelle Héloïse* has a similar sentiment: "Love is only illusion."

Rousseau cannot, however, contradict family and so family is the place where illusion is changed into reality. His educator says to the newly married couple, "I have often taken the view that if it were possible to extend the happiness of love into marriage, paradise on earth would be attained." The educator's pessimism (and Rousseaus's as well) cannot be misheard. This is why he comforts the couple by saying that passions will be replaced by "sweet habit."

More information about Rousseau's masochism also sheds new light on his often-mentioned **exhibitionism**, which in fact was not true exhibitionism.

In Turin, Rousseau showed his naked *backside* and not his penis, expecting in his unconscious as a masochist that some of the women would beat him:

> My disturbance of mind became so strong that being unable to satisfy my desires, I excited them by the most extravagant behavior. I haunted dark alleys and lonely spots where I could expose myself to women from afar off in the condition in which I should have liked to be in their company. *What they saw was nothing obscene, I was far from thinking of that: it was ridiculous.* The absurd pleasure I got from displaying myself before their eyes is quite indescribable. There was only one step for me still to make to achieve the *experience I desired* and I have no doubt that some bold girl would have afforded me the amusement, as she passed, if I had possessed the courage to wait (*Confessions, Book Three*, 1728–1732. italics added).

We know from the behavioral sciences that showing a naked backside is a gesture of submission and an invitation which provokes laughter. Rousseau's shame ("companion of the awareness of evil") joined his innate shyness and made it impossible for him to make indecent propositions to women: "Indeed, never at that time or since have I had the courage to make sexual proposals to any woman who has not more or less forced me to them by her advances, even when I have known that she was not prudish and that I was hardly likely to be rebuffed." In Book One of *Confessions* he wrote similarly: "I have never, during the whole course of my life, been able to force myself, even in a moment of extreme intimacy, to confess my peculiarities and implore her to grant the one favor which I was lacking."

Later in life he never ventured to ask women to punish him physically. His masochism was hidden behind **symbolic** behaviors. He was overjoyed if he was "at the knees of an imperious mistress, obey her orders," and to "ask her for pardon were for me very sweet joys," when he was allowed to be a passive person taking part in a love triangle.

The most outspoken of his excitement when he was allowed to lie at the feet of a woman he adored relates to the time of his stay in Turin, where he "had fallen in love" with Signora Basile. He sank on his knees behind her back and his hands were expressing an embrace. But Signora Basile saw him in a mirror and ordered him without uttering a word to lie down at her feet:

> I trembled, cried out, and threw myself down where she point-
> ed, all in a single second . . . I dared not raise my eyes, nor even,
> despite my uncomfortable position, so much as touch her on the
> knee to give myself a moment's support. I was motionless and
> dumb, but certainly not calm. Everything about me betrayed
> agitation, joy, gratitude and ardent desire, uncertain of its object
> and restrained by a fear of displeasing, which my young heart
> could not dispel.

For a masochist, such experiences possess the highest value:

> None of the feelings I have had from the possession (e.g., sexu-
> al intercourse) of a woman have been equal to those two min-
> utes spent at her feet without even the courage to touch her
> dress . . . A beckoning finger and a hand lightly pressed against
> my lips—these are all the favors I ever received from Mme
> Basile, and the memory of them, slight though they were, still
> moves me when I think of them.

The original draft of *Confessions* reveals still more clearly the nature of
Rousseau's reaction:

> On my knees before her," he says, "I was certainly in the most
> delightful but also the most constrained situation that I had ever
> experienced in my life. I dared neither to breathe nor to raise my
> eyes . . . We did not make the slightest movement: a profound
> silence reigned between us, but how many things did our hearts
> say and feel! . . . I would have passed there my whole life, nay,
> eternity itself, without desiring anything more.

A similar state of mind is revealed in another early fragment of
Confessions, where he said that "my heart was at peace in her presence and
desired nothing." Although this unnamed woman apparently treated him with
some rigor, he commented, "This severity was a hundred times more delightful to me than her favors would have been." He added significantly, "It seems
to me that she took possession of me." It was as though he obtained a certain

sensual pleasure from the thought of being possessed, adds Grimsley (1969,100).

Regarding triangular relationships, which masochists delight in, we can use Rousseau's description of the relationship between Anet, Mme de Warens and Rousseau. Claude Anet (who was Mme de Warens's lover) and of whom Rousseau wrote that he held him in high esteem, because he was "undoubtedly a rare man . . . thoughtful, circumspect in his behavior, and who was an example" to him: "as well as esteeming him, and became in some sense his pupil" must have tolerated Rousseau's presence only with great patience, unlike Rousseau who wrote: "But instead of taking a dislike for the man who had stolen her from me I actually felt the affection I had for her extending to him . . . So we lived in an alliance which brought us all happiness, and which only death was strong enough to dissolve."

At this time Rousseau had not yet had an intimate relationship with Mme de Warens. Later, after his Maman had taught him sexual intercourse, Anet died under mysterious circumstances. So Rousseau's words turned out to be right—their relationship could be dissolved only by death. It is very likely that Anet learned about the relationship between Mme de Warens and Rousseau and committed suicide, which he had already attempted once, when Rousseau came to Mme de Warens's house.

It is interesting that Rousseau turned down another triangular relationship between Mme de Warens, Wintzenried and himself, offered to him by Mme de Warens, probably because he did not think much of him and even hated him. It appears that in a love triangle the masochist must esteem the male partner and have a kind of "friendly" relationship to him. In this relationship, the masochist in fact tries to remain in a small company of people, he clings to "friendly islands" to prevent total social isolation and total abandonment, which he dreads despite all his demonstrative escapes from society.

We encounter a similar backing of his inner masochistic character in Rousseau's emotional flush for Mme d'Houdetot. As already mentioned, the masochist first dreams up in his fantasies what he then attempts to realize. From *Confessions* we learn: "I saw my Julie in Mme d'Houdetot . . ." (*Confessions*, 410); he fell in love with her only after this. Rousseau, however, was most excited by the fact that she loved another man (St-Lambert) and that she told Rousseau about her passionate love for her lover.

Rousseau delighted in being a member of a love triangle. He typically had to play a submissive role. *This* aroused the masochistic Rousseau most of all:

> She talked to me of St-Lambert like a passionate lover. How con-
> tagious is the power of love! As I listened, as I felt myself beside
> her I was seized with a delicious trembling that I had never
> experienced beside any other woman. As she spoke I felt myself
> moved . . . she inspired me with all the emotion for herself that
> she expressed for her lover. Alas, it was late in the day, and it
> was cruel indeed to be consumed by a passion as strong as it
> was unfortunate for a woman whose heart was full of love for
> another! (410).

Let us remember that Sacher-Masoch was most excited by the infidelity of a loved woman. It is most doubtful that Rousseau would have fallen in love with Mme d'Houdetot at all had she not approximately corresponded to his novel character, Julie, had she not been in love with her lover and had she not told Rousseau in vivid phrases about her relationship between herself and St-Lambert.

Rousseau's early interest in Sophie may have been stimulated by the sub-conscious thought that her steadfast devotion to St-Lambert made her unat-tainable. Rousseau admired St-Lambert and harbored no hatred for him, in spite of his relationship with Sophie. It is not impossible that Mme d'Houdetot noticed that her accounts of her love for St-Lambert excited Rousseau and that this "cruel" and "unfortunate passion" was in fact a source of pleasure for him. All triangular relationships bring a masochist still another hidden thrill of per-sonal "misdemeanor."

In this idea of triangular friendship and the *ménage à trois* we find the curi-ous mingling erotic and non-erotic elements. He is often fascinated by a type of relationship which seems to combine all the best elements in love and friendship and yet avoids the anxiety and unhappiness involved in pursuing either of them in isolation. He strove to live in peace and security and the state of emotional dependence on two "superior" people toward whom he experi-enced feelings of respect and affection without strain and anxiety.

In *Confessions* he recalled that Sophie herself spoke of "the intimate and sweet society which we might form between the three of us, when I had become reasonable." Rousseau describes it as "a charming project." He wrote to St-Lambert in 1757: "Yes, my children, be forever united: there is no other soul like yours, and you deserve to love each other until death. It is pleasure for me to be a third member in such a loving friendship." His love for Sophie could not do St-Lambert any harm: "Well! Poor Jean-Jacque, love as you will, with a safe conscience, and do not fear that your sights will do St-Lambert any harm!" (411).

Similar to his other friendships, unfortunately, this *ménage à trois* relationship was doomed to end soon. Living with a person who has not undergone the process of socialization, or has been touched by it insufficiently, borders on the impossible. Even Rousseau came to realize it and wrote in a letter to Mme de Luxembourg in 1759: "I have spent my days in a vain search for firm attachments."

Such formulations are typical of masochists to such a degree that other writers also noticed them. As Pierre Burgerline (1952, 383) put it, "Perhaps we must see in his secret masochism, a desire for humiliation which vegetates on the threshold of his consciousness and which would explain by its after-effects the extraordinary susceptibility of his pride." Grimsley (1969, 112) had a similar view: "There would thus be a link between his concern for the *ménage à trois* and his fundamental masochism . . . Whether Rousseau's obsession really did originate in these precise emotional strains and stresses may be left . . . an open question, although the idea of a connection between these reactions and the masochistic tendencies already examined is certainly plausible."

La Nouvelle Héloïse was his attempt to create a society after his own heart. He created in his imagination what could not be in life itself. His intense idealistic desire for absolute and total love impelled him to write the letters. Because Rousseau was never able to experience such completeness of feeling in real life, he dwelled with particular pleasure on this aspect of his story.

From a medical point of view, the three main characters of *Héloïse* are interesting in that Rousseau's nature and views are projected onto each of them. Taken together they again create the triangular relationship. Grimsley (1969, 129) correctly associates this relationship with Rousseau's masochism: "Here again, Rousseau's own outlook is reflected in this curious attempt to find a substitute for the complete sexual relationship, from which he had been largely excluded by his own masochism . . . he no longer feels himself alone in a hostile world since he forms part of an intimate group which seem sufficient in itself."

Rousseau's "self-portrait" is most obvious in the character of St-Preux who is just as Jean-Jacques: shy, fearful, inhibited, with moods of despair and melancholy. He has a "fiery imagination" which "carries everything to extremes." His imagination is also "disordered" and "anxious." He is extraordinarily emotionally dependent on the woman he loves. He is "weak" and "frail." St-Preux is "easy to subjugate." St-Preux reflects yet another essential trait of Rousseau's own character: his persistent tendency to see himself through other people's eyes and the constant need to feel himself the object of another's esteem.

As a true masochist, he felt bereft of his personality and became Julie's property: "I no longer belong to myself, my alienated soul is completely in you . . . Yes, my Julie, it is indeed you who form my life and being . . . Your will is enough for me . . . I shall no longer have any soul but your soul. I shall be nothing but a part of you."

Rousseau put his own views on love in Julie's mouth and made her say: "My too affectionate heart needs love, but my senses do not need a lover." Julie constantly treated their passion as a source of shame and guilt. "Their relationship was a 'criminal intercourse' which corrupted her whole being. Her sense of guilt is so strong that she sometimes gives way to an almost masochistic desire for self-abasement. Julie shows an attitude to love which is curiously reminiscent of Rousseau's own views," observed Grimsley. Though speaking constantly of shame and guilt, she seeks to minimize the extent of her misdoing by attributing it to "error" and "weakness." She is "weak and guilty," but not "depraved" and "sinful." This is Rousseau's own way of rationalizing and justifying all sorts of misdemeanors in his life.

That Julie also expresses Rousseau's views can surprise only those unacquainted with Rousseau's masochism, when she reveals that the "cold Wolmar, with his lack of passion and refusal to make absolute emotional demands was in the end more congenial to her than the intense and fiery St-Preux. He helped her to live 'happy and wise' and he was 'of all men the one who suited her best.'"

Masochistic behavior underlying seemingly irrelevant experiences is much less known. Mme de Warens made Rousseau lick her fingers smeared by ointments made of plants, the smell of which Jean-Jacques found abominable, but he was unable to resist her requests: "She made me taste the loathsome drugs. I might run away or defend myself, but despite struggles and clenched teeth, I had only to see those pretty fingers, all besmeared, approaching my face, and I was forced to open my mouth and lick them." Another episode, to be found in Book Three of *Confessions*, is also interesting from the viewpoint of sexology: "One day at table, just as she (Mme de Warens) had put some food into her mouth, I cried out that I had seen a hair in it. She spat the morsel back on her plate, whereupon I seized it greedily and swallowed it."

Such behavior is typical of masochists, as is the sexual arousal and pleasure a masochist experiences at the thought or practce of eating excrements of women. During the performance of his opera *Le Devin du village* in Versailles Rousseau was *sexually* aroused imagining that he was licking tears of sobbing women: "And yet I am sure that sexual passion counted for more at that moment than the vanity of an author: if there had only been men present I am positive that I should not have been devoured, as I continuously was, by the desire to catch with my lips the delicious tears I had evoked."

Mme Dupin in Paris asked him to look after her son for eight days until the new educator took over. Rousseau wrote: "I spent the week in an agony [!] that would have been unbearable but for my *pleasure in obliging* Mme Dupin" (*Confessions*, 273). To be looking after a child of his supporter and friend for eight days is usually an unimportant matter. Rousseau, however, retained it in his memory and recorded it in *Confessions*, because from his viewpoint as a masochist this was "martyrdom"—he had been ordered to "suffer" by a woman he loved.

This episode (totally unimportant for a normal person) is at the same time an example of the fact that the fantasies of fulfilling someone's wishes are more rewarding than real life experiences (Buss 1980). The masochist is filled with delight by the idea that he had to suffer a martyrdom imposed on him by a woman of his heart.

Rousseau's most intensive sexual pleasures had their source in such and similar events and not in sexual intercourse. He admitted that such behavior could not have filled most women with enthusiasm, but for him the flavor of masochism was necessary to stimulate his imagination and thereby also feelings of happiness.

To describe normal masturbation, which he practiced for his whole life (and which he always condemned in his writings) he used various symbolic expressions and allusions such as *"supplément."* He acquired the "technique" of masturbation in Italy: "I had returned from Italy a different person from the one who had gone there . . . I had preserved my physical but not my moral virginity . . . and learned that dangerous means of cheating Nature . . . This vice, which shame and timidity find so convenient, has a particular attraction for lively imaginations. It allows them to dispose, so to speak, of the whole female sex." During his stay in Venice, Rousseau wrote: "I had not given up my pernicious habit of satisfying my needs in another way," referring to masturbation. In Venice he probably practiced for the first time the form of urethral masturbation, because his first urinary tract infection occurred at this time.

In accounts of his life following his return from Italy, Rousseau suddenly stops talking about his masochistic tendencies with the openness which was characteristic of his descriptions of his encounters with Mlle Lambercier and Mlle Goton. It is the time of his life with Thérèse, in whom he obviously found his dreamed-up masochistic mistress and whom he had taught to provide him the suffering, which was the source of his greatest sensual gratification, i.e., urethral masturbation, which he probably had learned to perform on himself in Venice.

Urethral masturbation is the only plausible explanation of his recurrent urinary tract infections, which in the end brought ruin upon him and, at the same time is the only explanation of his life with semi-feebleminded Thérèse. It goes without saying that he could not write openly about their mutual sexual practices in *Confessions.* He confines himself merely to allusions and suggestions: "My passions have made me live, and my passions have killed me. What passions, it may be asked. Trifles, the most childish things in the world. Yet they affected me as much as if the possession of Helen or the throne of the Universe had been at stake" (*Confessions*, 209).

> Not only, therefore, did I, though ardent, lascivious, and precocious by nature, pass the age of puberty without desiring or knowing any other sensual pleasures than those which Mlle Lambercier had, in all innocence, acquainted me with; but when finally, in the course of years, I became a man I was preserved by that very perversity which might have been my undoing: *My old childish tastes did not vanish, but became so intimately associated with those of maturity* that I could never, when sensually aroused, keep the two apart. This peculiarity, together with my natural timidity, has always made me very backward with women,

since I have never had the courage to be frank or the power to get what I wanted, it being impossible for the kind of pleasure I desired—to which the other kind [sexual intercourse] is no more than a consummation—to be taken him who wants it, or *to be guessed at by the woman who could grant it.*

How much it has cost me to make such revelations can be judged when I say that though sometimes laboring under passions that have robbed me of sight, of hearing, and of my senses, though sometimes trembling convulsively in my whole body in the presence of the woman I loved, I have never, during the whole course of my life, been able to force myself, even in the moments of extreme intimacy, to confess my peculiarities and implore her to grant the one favor which I was lacking (*Confessions*, italics added).

Rousseau confesses in these quotations that his old childish pleasure (masochistic sexual arousal when punished) became associated with the second pleasure, which remains unspecified. Only a woman can grant him both pleasures and he cannot "keep the two apart" when sexually aroused. His problem here is that he did not dare to ask for both of these pleasures to be granted to him and the loved woman is not capable of guessing his wishes.

It is very likely that the second pleasure which Rousseau mentions is urethral masturbation, performed manually by a woman, which is very painful and is in fact a form of masochistic punishment. It is also very likely that the only woman to whom Rousseau could reveal his secret wishes was the primitive and semi-feebleminded Thérèse, who would obey and perform his orders. Her primitive nature had yet another masochistic attraction for Rousseau: the pain was inflicted on him by a woman who was in all respects inferior to him. He had become the slave of a primitive! His humiliation—a thing all masochists desire—was absolute: "In fact, sadomasochistic activities often involve role playing in which there is a prominent imbalance of power" (Lohr and Adams 1995, 260).

Rousseau wrote about Thérèse: "That good girl's sweet nature seemed to me so *well suited to my own* that I joined myself to her in an attachment that has defied time and injuries" (italics added). Writing about their late wedding Rousseau said:

It may be supposed that a mad passion turned my head from the first day and led me by degrees to this last extravagance: a hypothesis which will appear even more credible when the special and powerful reasons are known which would have prevented me from reaching that point. What will the reader think when I tell him, with all the sincerity that he has come to expect of me, that *from the first moment I saw her [Thérèse] till this day I have never felt the least glimmering of love for her:* that I no more desired to possess her than I had desired Mme de Warens, and that *the sensual needs I satisfied with her were for me purely sexual* and nothing to do with her as an individual? (*Confessions*, 385–386, italics added).

This paragraph is very interesting. Rousseau says explicitly that he had never loved Thérèse (in the masochistic meaning of the word), but that he also had no desire to have sexual intercourse with her (to possess her)! He only realized, with her help, his sexual masochistic fantasies. The onset and further course of his urinary tract infections shows that it could have been only urethral masturbation, in which the combination took place of his "old childish tastes . . . with those of maturity that I could never . . . keep [the two] apart."

Thérèse became his accomplice:

It was a need for intimate companionship, for a companionship as intimate as possible which was the chief reason why I needed a woman rather than a man, a woman friend rather than a man friend" (*Confessions*, 386). His desire was to find a woman accomplice for "a companionship as intimate as possible." Someone might think "that I was not made like other men, and that I was incapable of feeling love, since love did not enter into the feelings that attached me to the woman who has been dearest to me" (*Confessions*, 386). "At first I had only been out for amusement. I now saw that I had found more, that *I had won a companion* (italics added).

He wrote elsewhere:

I found in Thérèse the *substitute* that I needed. Thanks to her I have lived as happy a life as the course of events has permitted" (*Confessions*, 310–311, italics added). The word "substitute" is one of the expressions Rousseau used to refer to masturbation. "A little intimacy with this excellent girl and a little reflection on my situation made me see that while *only thinking on my pleasures,* I had contributed greatly to my happiness . . . I could find the simplicity and the *docile* heart which she had found in me (*Confessions*, 310, italics added).

At this place the reader cannot but ask what were the "pleasures" that Rousseau is referring to, when we know that these were neither the pleasures derived from sexual intercourse (possession) nor the pleasures of love which Rousseau never felt for Thérèse? These pleasures must have been masochistic pleasures. Rousseau taught his "excellent girl," who was at the same time "docile," to perform them. What Rousseau could not improve was her semi-feeblemindedness, even though he tried to do so several times: "At first I decided to improve her mind: I was wasting my time. Her mind is as Nature made it: culture and teaching have no effects on it . . . she has never been able to read properly, though she can write fairly well" (*Confessions*, 311).

Even though Rousseau did not love Thérèse and had no desire to have sexual intercourse with her, he wrote: "I lived pleasantly with my Thérèse as with the finest genius in the world . . . This sweet intimacy replaced everything for me" (*Confessions*, 311). These observations could explain one of the curious paradoxes of Rousseau's life—that this "stupid woman," as Mme de Verdelin called her, should have gained such extraordinary ascendancy over a man who was in so many ways her superior. Hume wrote in one of his letters: "She [Thérèse] governs him as absolutely as a nurse does a child," and Richard Davenport was to record that "his Gouvernante has absolute power over him and without doubt more or less influences all his actions." She became his *gouvernante.* Like many people of low intelligence and extreme ignorance, she had a highly developed animal cunning which she knew how to use with good effect (Grimsley 1969, 201).

According to available literary data, Rousseau's sexual deviation could be summed up in the following way:

Rousseau shows clear evidence of *sexual masochism* at the age of ten or eleven (Mlle Lambercier, Mlle Goton).

During his stay in Turin further evidence of his deviation can be found; this has erroneously been interpreted as exhibitionism ("exposure" of his backside in order to get punishment by women). Further, in the first phase, substituting masturbation for coitus: he started masturbation in Turin. Next was automasochistic *urethral masturbation*, which can be traced back to his stay in Venice where his first urinary tract problems occurred. Later on, the sexual masochistic urethral masturbation was performed by Thérèse, followed by coitus *(conjunctive masochism)*, and ultimately the compensatory masochistic urethral masturbation without coitus following.

Here again it should be stressed that the underlying cause of these forms of sexual deviation was the character–moral–social masochism, which served as the base for the development of Rousseau's deviations.

Starobinsky recognized the possibility that Rousseau could have infected himself during self-catheterization (551), but he assumed that Rousseau performed this catheterization on himself to relieve the urinary retention from which he suffered. He did not recognize the possibility that Thérèse catheterized Rousseau to give him sexual gratification and only later of necessity.

In one of his later (1768) letters to Thérèse, Rousseau wrote: "We both have to bewail and repent our misdemeanors." Rousseau's biographers have related this sentence to the fact that he sent all his children to a foundling home. Thérèse, however, resisted this and in this context it is hardly acceptable to refer to her as a wrongdoer.

It is more likely that this sentence relates to their mutual sexual practices. After he got to know Thérèse, Rousseau never mentioned the dangerous *supplément* or substitute of masturbation. He praises Thérèse for her being docile (a masochist always has to start by teaching his mistress what she is supposed to do) and this is followed by descriptions of incessant relapses of urethritis, prostatitis and cystitis resulting in severe multiple cicatrization of urethra and recurrent urinary retention. He never loved Thérèse. She was only an instrument to gratify his sexual masochistic needs. Gradually she gained such control over him that she could treat him as a child; she was in fact his nurse as several of his contemporaries confirm.

Masturbation of urethra in men and women is nothing unusual. Freud spoke of "urethral eroticism," in analogy to anal eroticism, which can lead to anal masturbation. As the urethra is narrower, it is often necessary to use all sorts of objects in its masturbation and these often slip into the urinary bladder. In 1862, urethral onanism in women, who used hairpins, was so widespread that it even led to the invention of a special apparatus used to remove hairpins from the urinary bladder. In men, for example, the use of knitting needles, brush handles and thermometers in urethral masturbation has been described.

This method of eroticism often results in injuries of the urethra, recurrent urethritis and prostatitis, the healing of which leads to scar formation. Free urinary flow is disturbed and infection can ascent upward, resulting in cystitis, ureteritis (inflammation of ureters) and nephritis.

This method is practiced especially by shy and effeminate men who desire femininity. Rousseau himself declared he would prefer to be a woman. He had a liking for typically feminine activities such as making bobbin lace and did not like masculine sports, e.g., fencing. Similar to a person practicing anal eroticism, the person seeking sexual gratification in urethral masturbation tends toward masochism and wants to experience cruel acts inflicted by a woman. These people experience an irresistible urgency to urinate whenever they are excited, not only sexually (see Rousseau's refusal of an audience with the king with reference to his increased urgencies; Rousseau experienced the desire to urinate also in salons, mainly when in the presence of women: "My illness was the main reason why I kept away from society, it precluded me from being with women for longer periods of time." He describes these troubles also in the letter he wanted to send to Marquis de Mirabeau.

The fact that Thérèse performed urethral masturbation on Rousseau according to his wishes (or orders) is evidenced by the fact that Rousseau did not suffer from serious symptoms of urinary tract infection before he met Thérèse in 1745, as well as by improvements of his condition when they were separated; for example, after he had gone to Switzerland in 1762. When in Yverdon and in the beginning of his stay in Môtiers, Rousseau enjoyed very good health, as he wrote in his letters to the duke and duchess of Luxembourg. After Thérèse came to Môtiers he suffered a severe relapse and in his last will (1763) he bequeathed all his possessions to Thérèse.

Other authors also have recorded the fact that Thérèse was sexually attractive to Rousseau in a special way. Starobinsky wrote that Thérèse sank down to the bottom of society and Rousseau may have identified with her at that time. He allegedly did not see in her another person, but "the help of his own flesh." Cranston (1982) wrote openly that "he no doubt also obtained from her that form of gratification to which his masturbatory habits disposed him, manual stimulation such as he was ashamed to solicit from those women of higher social status to whom he paid court." This is evidenced also by the following curious sentence in *Confessions*: "I have found in Thérèse the *supplément* I needed." Rousseau used the word *"supplément"* in *Confessions* as well as in *Émile* to refer to masturbation. We can then understand Rousseau's words that "the sensual needs, which I satisfied with her [Thérèse] were purely sexual and had nothing to do with her as an individual."

The suspicion that Thérèse manually masturbated Rousseau has thus been formulated by others. I have not, however, been able to find anywhere the assumption that this masturbation could have **been painful urethral masturbation in the sense of masochistic "torture,"** which would have been asked for by Rousseau. Every masochist must at first instruct and then educate his mistress so she knows which kind of pain he wants to suffer. In this respect every single masochist has his individual preference! The timid Rousseau cannot give such instruction to the various noblewomen with whom he met socially. The danger of indiscretion would simply be too great, as would be the discredit in society where Rousseau always played the role of a great moralist. The same applies to the impossibility of confessing these practices in *Confessions*. Future generations should see Rousseau according to his wishes.

This masochistic masturbation must necessarily have led to recurrent urinary tract infections and prostatitis, and resulted in serious cicatrization of urethra, chronic prostatitis and chronic cystitis. A vicious circle came into existence: urine, which accumulated in the urinary bladder, could not flow away and necessitated further catheterizations; these led to further deterioration and inflammatory changes and their consequences. Every patient who has had the experience of urethral catheterization or suffered urethritis, prostatitis and cystitis, will confirm how painful the procedure or the conditions are.

The urinary bladder is a hollow organ formed by a muscle (detrusor), which has at its urethral end another muscle (urethral sphincter); these two muscles form a morphological and functional unit. Functional disorders are characterized by lack of coordination of the bladder and the sphincter, which often result in incomplete emptying of the bladder and formation of residual urine. This and another consequence, thickening of the urinary bladder walls, results in frequent infections of the bladder. Functional disturbances are known to be associated with feelings of anxiety and fear. Most of the disturbances of urinary bladder emptying are caused by infravesical obstructions—obstacles in the urethra formed under the bladder. The most frequent obstacle is the enlarged prostate (in Rousseau a "scirrhous" prostate was found, which was obviously the result of chronic inflammations). Even the presence of an abscess of the prostate and strictures—narrowing of the urethra—cannot be ruled out; these strictures are also consequences of recurrent inflammations, in Rousseau's case of urethral masturbation and insertion of foreign bodies into the urethra. We know that part of one of Rousseau's catheters broke off and got stuck in the urethra.

Here the reader is led deeper into the field of medicine and it is necessary to say a few words about the prostate. The prostate is an unusual little gland, although in some respects it is not a gland at all but an organ containing about 70 percent glandular tissue and 30 percent fibromuscular tissue. The glandular portion secretes the liquid portion of semen, while the fibromuscular portion helps to open the bladder so that urine can pass. The prostate is about the shape and size of a chestnut, and it is situated just beneath the bladder. In the average adult, it weights between twenty and thirty grams, and it is encased in a thick, fibrous capsule.

Most men will experience prostate growth in their forties, fifties and sixties. Urologists refer to this as benign prostatic hypertrophy (BPH) which can be estimated by digital rectal examination (DRE). Common symptoms of BPH include decreased force of urination, trouble initiating urination, dribbling (trouble shutting off the urine stream), and a feeling of bladder fullness even after urination. There can also be painful urination and a frequent need to urinate. As BPH worsens, more urine may be retained in the bladder, the above symptoms tend to intensify, and, in addition, there may be incontinence. In a worst-case scenario, urinary blockade occurs.

The prostate causes all this botheration because of its position. The urethra, the flexible tube that transports urine from the bladder down to and through the penis, where it can be voided, passes directly through the center of the prostate. That portion is called the prostatic urethra. When a man urinates, the fibromuscular portion of the prostate contracts, dilating the prostatic urethra, thus allowing urine to flow from the bladder to the penis. Sometimes as the prostate enlarges with age or inflammations it exerts pressure on the urethra, thereby obstructing the flow of urine and causing the diversely distressing symptomatology.

In acute urinary retention, the urinary bladder is dilated by its contents and can reach up to the level of the navel. This condition can be very painful and is accompanied by the urge to urinate. Acute urinary retention can lead to chronic retention, in which an ever-increasing amount of residual urine remains in the bladder, without the patient being aware of it. A weakened stream of urine can be the first and only symptom of prostatic hypertrophy, which can also result in prolonged urination (micturition).

As the prostate enlarges and the cicatrization of the urethra becomes more pronounced, instead of acute urinary blockage—urinary retention—there can occur a slow increase of the residual urine volume at the same time the bladder capacity diminishes. The result is that the bladder voids at intervals of several minutes, or it can in the end only drip away permanently, being a sign that a condition called ischiuria paradoxa has developed (overflow incontinence). This condition is indeed characterized by urine flowing out every minute, or by urine dribbling out constantly. Ischuria paradoxa succeeds, as the next stage, acute urinary retention and is equally caused by the progressive enlargement of the prostate, i.e., subvesical obstruction.

Rousseau explained the fact that he wore the Armenian caftan because of the urge to urinate practically incessantly. If this had been the case, then he was suffering from ischuria paradoxa. This cannot be ruled out. He stopped having painful attacks of abrupt urinary retention requiring catheterization, which was usually performed by Thérèse. It remains unclear, on the other hand, how Rousseau—with urine constantly dribbling out of his urethra—could have been receiving visitors, attending theatre, or how he could have spent ten hours aboard a ship. It is certainly possible that he was using a receptacle in which he collected his urine though he never mentions this arrangement.

Urinary bladder blockage is treated by catheterization, or if this is impossible (cicatrization of urethra) a procedure called suprapubic puncture of the urinary bladder is performed (a method which was out of the question in the eighteenth century). Otherwise the urine starts to distend the ureters and accumulates in the renal pelvis of both kidneys (hydronephrosis), destroys renal parenchyma and eventually leads to inflammatory pyonephrosis. Acute pyelonephritis can turn into a chronic form and result in the development of renal abscesses, urosepsis, which cloud the brain, and death follows.

The exact cause of Rousseau's death is not known, but there is every reason to believe that the cause was renal failure and urosepsis. It is very probable that, at least after Rousseau left the Isle St-Pierre and on his journey to Strasbourg, Paris and England, he had already developed ischiuria paradoxa and his urine began to accumulate in distended ureters, renal pelves, his renal parenchyma was already disappearing and urosepsis and uremia were developing. This is supported by the fact that Rousseau did not need catheterizations after he left Switzerland. Starobinsky (1997, 551) wrote: "Ever since the delusions gain the upper hand, because the ideas of conspiracy are obsessive, we hear less of complaints about micturition and less of repeated probing."

The progressive disintegration of his personality was not so much the result of paranoia (to which it has been attributed) as it was a symptom of an organic brain syndrome due to uremia.

Rousseau died of uremia later on. The course of renal failure is usually insidious and one of its symptoms is confusion. This cause of death is also evidenced by the findings of the postmortem performed the day after Rousseau's death, on July 3, 1778: the space between brain and meninges was filled with eight ounces of a serous fluid. According to medical science of that time the cause of death was "serous apoplexy." This term has disappeared from medical terminology long ago. It survives, however, in the works of some of Rousseau's biographers, who wrote that Rousseau died of cerebral hemorrhage—apoplexy. That is why we can sometimes read, in English-speaking literature, that Rousseau died of a "stroke" (Cranston 1997), or of "apoplectic stroke" (Cohen 1953 in Introduction to *Confessions*).

The dissecting physicians did not find changes in both the urinary bladder and the urinary tract. To explain this they stated in their report that the enlargement of the prostate may have disappeared because the body was weaker and thinner as a result of advanced age. In uremia, dehydration and emaciation are common.

The cause of death leads to all sorts of speculations. Suicide and even murder (Thérèse) were mentioned as well. No one believed that "a man of Nature" could have died of natural causes. But even an exceptional man dies of banal causes (Starobinsky 1977).

Appendix 1

Chronology of Life and Work

1712	28 June	Born as son of Isaac Rousseau and mother Susanne, born Bernard, in Geneva.
	7 July	Death of mother. Rousseau is brought up by aunt, Susanne Bernard.
1719–1720		Record of reading of various genres. Semi-deprivation; he is not allowed to play with other children; father reproaches him for mother's death; spoiled by his aunts, but also physically punished by his father.
1722	October	Father Isaac leaves Geneva after a brawl with an officer, settles in Nyon. Rousseau left in the care of his uncle. With his cousin Bernard, he is sent to "school" to pastor Lambercier in Bossey. First masochistic experiences in connection with a thrashing by Mlle Lambercier.
1724		Returns to Geneva. When visiting Nyon, he falls in romantic love with Mlle Vulson and in a "masochistic" love with Mlle Goton, which he never forgets.
1725	Spring	Sent for training to the notary Masseron but is soon sacked as a "donkey." He is apprenticed to the engraver Ducommun. He is punished because of stealing and lying.

1728	17 March.	Following a walk outside Geneva the city gates are already closed. He decides to leave Geneva.
	21 March	Arrives in Annecy; meets with Mme de Warens.
	12 April	Enters the hospice Santo Spirito in Turin. Baptized on 21 April.
	Summer	Romance with Signora Basile.
	Summer	He is employed as servant of Mme de Vercelli. He shows his naked backside to women with a desire to be punished.
	Fall	Employed as secretary to Count de Gouvon. A promising career opens up before him.
1729	June	He is discharged for not meeting his duties. Returns to Mme de Warens in Annecy. Studies at the Lazarists' seminary for priests; discharged for incompetence.
	Winter	Studies in the chorus school of the local cathedral led by Le Maistre. He accompanies the latter to Lyon, where he leaves him. Returns to Annecy, but he does not find Mme de Warens there.
1730	End of June	"The idyll of a cherry orchard" (chronological inconsistency—Rousseau describes this experience in *Confessions*, Book One, 1731–1732, but according to Cranston this event took place in 1730, which is more probable).
	Summer	Journeys to Fribourg, Lausanne, Vevey, Bern, Soleure, Paris, and Lyon. Spends the winter of 1730–31 in Neuchâtel.
1731	Fall	Returns to Mme de Warens at her new residence in Chambéry. Works as clerk in the office of

King Victor Emanuel.

1732	7 June	He abandons the job in the office. He wants to earn his living by giving music lessons.
1733		Mme de Warens teaches him sexual intercourse. *Ménage à trois* with Anet and Mme de Warens.
1734	13 March	Mysterious death of Anet, who was jealous of Rousseau.
1735	Summer	Life in Les Charmettes.
1737	28 July	He comes of age (twenty-five years old) and inherits 6,000 florins from the estate of his mother.
	Fall	Mme de Warens has a new lover—Wintzenried. Rousseau leaves for Montpellier to be treated; on the way he poses as a Jacobite. Has love affair with Mme de Larnage.
1738	February - March	Returns to Chambéry. Refusal of *ménage a trois* with Wintzenried offered to him by Mme de Warens. Lonely life in Les Charmettes, where he studies but suffers from isolation.
1739	Spring	Continues lonely life in Les Charmettes. He makes up his mind he wants to earn his living with his own hands.
1740	1 May	He starts working as a tutor of the sons of M. de Mably. His contract is not renewed, probably because he stole wine from cellar.
1741	May	Returns to Chambéry. Short stay in Lyon.

Returns to Les Charmettes through the winter.

1742	First months	Works on the play *Narcisse* and develops a new system of musical notation.
1742	July–August	Departs for Paris. He tries to offer his new system of musical notation to the Academy of Sciences. Has no financial means; begins visiting salons.
1743	Spring	Introduced to Mme Dupin. Starts work on the opera *Les Muses galantes*.
	June	Accepts the offer to work as a secretary to the French ambassador in Venice (Comte de Montaigu).
	4 September	Arrives in Venice
1744	22 August	Departs from Venice after a breach with the ambassador.
1745	March	Becomes acquainted with Thérèse Levasseur.
	September	Premiere of the opera *Les Muses galantes*. Forms friendship with Condillac and Diderot.
1746	Fall	Becomes secretary to Mme Dupin and her stepson, Francueil.
1747	Fall	Meets with Mme d'Épinay. Works on the comedy *L'Engagement téméraire* while staying at Château Chenonceau. Birth of his first child (daughter) who is sent to a foundling home
1748	February	First meeting with Mlle de Bellegarde, future Mme d'Houdetot. His second child is sent to the foundling home (the time is not known)

1749	January	Writes articles on music for *Encyclopédie*.
	24 June	Diderot's imprisonment.
	August	Visits Diderot in Vincennes. Meets with Grimm.
	October	"Revelation" on the way to Vincennes. He starts working on the first *Discourse*
1750	9 June	First *Discourse* was awarded first prize in competition. Publication of the *Discourse* at the end of the year.
1751	February	Owing to success of the *Discourse* Rousseau decides to "reform" his life (he will live on note copying, wear only simple clothes, etc.).
	Spring	Birth of his third child; given to foundling home.
	Fall	Discussions about his *Discourse* in press.
1752	August	Visit of Mme d'Épinay at the Château La Chevrette.
	October 18	Successful opening of the opera *Le Devin du Village* at Fontainebleau attended by the king. He flinches from the audience with the king and forfeits a pension.
	December 18	Performance of his play *Narcisse*. Start of *"querelle des Bouffon."*
1753	November	The Academy of Dijon announces new prize competition for an essay on the origins of inequality.
1753–4	Winter	The second *Discourse* comes into existence with Diderot's aid. Even after his reform Rousseau visits the salons; meets with St-Lambert in the salon of Mlle Quinault.
1754	1 June	Journeys to Geneva with Thérèse.

		Stopover in Chambéry to visit Mme de Warens; Rousseau suggests they all live in *ménage à trois*, but Mme de Warens refuses.
	1 August	Conversion to Protestantism in Geneva; he regains Genevan civil rights.
	August	Last meeting with Mme de Warens in Geneva.
	10 October	Departs for Paris.
	Fall	Proofreading of the second *Discourse*
1755	August	Second *Discourse* appears on the bookshelves. Publication of the fifth volume of *Encyclopédie* with Rousseau's article *"Economie politique."*
	September	Mme d'Épinay invites him to move to the reconstructed Hermitage.
1756	9 April	Moves into Hermitage with Thérèse and her mother.
	August	Works on *"Lettre sur la Providence."*
	Summer	Starts writing *La Nouvelle Héloïse*.
	Winter	He reads *Héloïse* to Thérèse and Mme Levasseur.
1757	January	First visit of Mme d'Houdetot at Hermitage.
	March	Breaks with Diderot over the sentence "Only a bad man is alone."
	Spring–Summer	Love affair with Mme d'Houdetot.
	Fall	Differences with Mme d'Épinay and Grimm.
	15 December	Departs for Montmorency (Montlouis)—accompanied only by Thérèse.
1758	6 May	Mme d'Houdetot breaks off relations with him on account of Diderot's alleged indiscretion.
	Summer	Publication of *Lettre à d'Alembert sur les spectacles*.
	29 October	Dinner at the Château La Chevrette.

1759	Spring	Gets acquainted with Duke and Duchess de Luxembourg. Lives at Petit Château, works on *Héloïse, Émile, Contract Social*. Reads from *Héloïse* to the duchess.
	Summer	Completion of repair of Montlouis, moves in again.
	Fall–Winter	Completion of *Héloïse*. Gets acquainted with Marquise de Verdelin.
1760	January	Copying of *Héloïse* for Duchess de Luxembourg and Mme d'Houdetot. Correspondence with Rey about the publication of *Héloïse*.
	Summer	Meets with Comtesse de Bouffleurs, mistress of Prince de Conti.
	December	*Héloïe* is sold in London
1761	January	Sale and success of *Héloïse* in Paris.
	16 February	Publication of a second foreword to *Héloïse*, *"Préface dialoguée."* Completion of *Émile* and *Contract Social*.
	September	Sends the *"Essay sur l'origine des langues"* to Malesherbes.
	Fall	Protestants are persecution in France; he refuses to help.
	31 December	Publisher Rey asks him to write his autobiography.
1762	January	Starts writing autobiographical letters to Malesherbes (four letters).
	April–May	Publication of *Émile* and *Contract Social*.
	9 June	Condemnation by the parlement of Paris. Leaves France to escape being arrested.
	14 June	Arrives in Yverdon (in Bernese territory).
	19 June	*Émile* and *Contract* are burned in Geneva and a warrant for his arrest is issued.
	1 July	Expelled from Yverdon by Bernese authorities.

	10 July	Arrives in Môtiers (Prussian part of Neuchâtel).
	20 July	Thérèse arrives in Môtiers.
	29 July	Death of Mme de Warens.
1763	March	Publication of a defense of *Émile*: "*Lettre a Christophe de Beaumont.*"
	16 April	Naturalization on the territory of Neuchâtel.
	12 May	Renounces Genevan citizenship.
1764		Indirect involvement in political disputes in Geneva; he writes "*Lettres écrit de la Montagne.*"
	Summer	Death of Duke de Luxembourg.
	December	Decision to write *Confessions*.
1765	Spring	Dissentions with pastor Montmollin in Môtiers.
	June	First stay on the Isle St-Pierre in Lake Biel.
	1–3 Sept.	Visit of Mme de Verdelin in Môtiers, she recommends that Rousseau leave for England.
	6 September	Môtiers's citizens throw rocks at Rousseau's house.
	September	Departs for the Isle St-Pierre.
	October	Banishment from the isle by the senate of Bern.
	29 October	Departs from Biel, enthusiastic welcome in Strasbourg (2 November).
	9 December	Departs from Strasbourg, arrives in Paris on 16 December.
1766	4 January	Departs for England together with Hume.
	13 January	Arrival in London.
	January–March	Settles in Chiswick; Thérèse comes to England.
	22 March	Life in Wootton, Staffordshire.
	Summer	Controversy with Hume in public. Work on Book One of *Confessions*.
1767	March 18	King George III awards him a pension.

	1 May	Departs from Wootton.
	21 May	Departs from England.
	21 June	Life at the Château Tyre in France as Prince de Conti's guest.
		Assumes the pseudonym Renou.
	November	Publication of *Dictionaire de Musique*.
1768	11 June	Departs from Château Tyre.
	11 July	Arrives in Grenoble. Botanical studies.
	25 July	Journey to Chambéry to visit Mme de Warens's grave.
	13 August	Life in Bourgoin (Dauphiné).
	30 August	Marries Thérèse Levasseur in Bourgoin.
1769	27 April	He informs Rey he does not intend to write *Confessions*.
	November	Works on the second part of *Confessions*.
1770	10 April	Departes for Lyon.
	June	Returns to Paris where he wants to earn his living by note copying.
	November	Obsession of being plotted against.
	December	Most likely completion of *Confessions*, which he reads in the house of Marquise de Pezay.
1771	Spring	Public reading of *Confessions* in the salon of Comtesse d'Egmont.
	10 May	Mme d'Épinay asks the police to stop the readings from *Confessions*.
	April	Completion of the work "*Considérations sur le gouvernement de Pologne.*" Starts writing *Dialogues* or *Rousseau juge de Jean-Jacques*.
1773		Continuation of work on *Dialogues*. Pursuit of botany

1774		Pursuit of music. Contacts with Gluck.
1775	31 October	Successful premiere of *Pygmalion* at Comédie-Française.
		Completion of *Dialogues*.
	24 February	Fails in attempt to place the manuscript of his manifest on the high altar of Nôtre-Dame.
	April	Distribution to passers-by of the declaration "*A tout Français aimant la justice et la vérité.*"
	Summer	Works on"*Histoire du précédent écri.*"
	Fall	Starts writing first promenade of *Rêveries*.
	December	Works on the second promenade of *Rêveries*.
1777	Spring–Summer	Works on promenades number three through seven.
	August	Gives up note copying
	Winter	Completes eighth promenade.
1778	March	Completes ninth promenade.
	12 April	Starts working on the 10 promenade but never completes it.
	2 May	Confides his works to his friend Paul Moultou.
	20 May	Accepts the offer of Marquis de Giradin and settles at his Château Ermenonville.
	2 July	Death of Rousseau.
	3 July	Burial on the Ile de Peupliers in Ermenonville.
1794	9 October	Transfer of Rousseau's mortal remains to the Panthéon in Paris.

Appendix 2

Chronological Overview of Rousseau's Illnesses

1734	Chambéry	Spells of melancholy and "nervous exhaustion" following Anet's death.

1735   Chambéry   Rousseau describes his hypochondriac complaints in a letter to his father, and assumes that he will fall ill of tuberculosis.

1735   Chambéry   Melancholy, fatigue, groundless crying. Mme de Warens looks after him and cares for him "like a mother." Once again he persuaded himself that death was near.

Interpretation (assessment): A concrete illness cannot be found. The description suggests that he suffered from hypochondriac complaints, or he simulated them in order to attract attention of Mme de Warens. Sickness had become a road to happiness with her.

1735 Chambéry   Recovered from his illness "as a result of the good care of Mme de Warens," and he had also been on a journey.

1736   Les Charmettes   After a short, healthy period the hypochondriac symptoms recur: "I was sickly and my weakness increased day by day." Water treatments spoiled his stomach. He could not drink milk. He gave up all hope for cure. Once he even sustained a "blow" that hit his entire body and was followed by restlessness, palpitations, and humming in his ears. Since then he is hard of hearing, suffers from constant humming in his ears, but is not deaf. He claims to suffer from complete sleeplessness (a demonstrably incorrect claim), feeling of shortness of breath, but not complete dyspnea. This disease has destroyed his passions. "I started living when I considered myself to be a dead man." He was convinced that he would die soon. He felt half-sick after he returned from Chambéry to Les Charmettes as well. He does not have acute pains but observes that his body decomposes—a process that can be terminated only by death. He has learned "to vegetate, not to sleep and to think instead of acting."

Interpretation: The description reveals hypochondriac symptoms and aggravation, probably with the intention to tie Maman to him.

1737 Chambéry

A bottle half filled with quicklime, sulphide of arsenic and water exploded in his face. He swallowed so much of the sulphide that it almost killed him. He wrote a last will, naming the "Comtesse de Warens" as his heir.

1737   Chambéry

Hypochondriac complaints again, which he himself ascribes partially to his imagination and gloomy thoughts that are "the illness of happy people" and "the boredom of happiness," which increases susceptibility. The hypochondria was assisted by his anatomical studies. He made a self-diagnosis of "heart polyp" and decided to visit Dr. Fizes in Montpellier. His happy life with Maman à deux ended in 1737.

1738	Chambéry	Praise of Mme de Warens for leaving him in peace (in a poem). The poet's life is disturbed only by his bad health and he is very near his grave.
1739	Chambéry	He begs the King of Sardinia in a letter to award him a pension. "As a convert to Catholicism he has studied hard but the sickness has destroyed him so that he is a dying man." He lost all complaints in Lyon (May 1740–May 1741) where he was employed as tutor.
1741	Lyon	In December, when visiting Suzanne Serr, he fell ill (probably a cold) and immediately returned to Mme de Warens in Les Charmettes, who lived there in winter as well. This illness is not recorded in *Confessions*.
1742	Les Charmettes	The cold from December 1741 continues, Maman takes care of him and "brings him back from the gates of death." He dedicates to her the poem "*Fanie*" (evidenced by a letter to M. de Conzié, not recorded in *Confessions*).
1743	Paris	A bout with pneumonia, of which he allegedly nearly died. No evidence available as to whether it was genuine pneumonia, or a severe bronchitis. He states on this occasion that he used to have a similar condition as a child when he also suffered from "pleurisy" (?).
1744	Venice	First references to symptoms of urethritis and perhaps also cystitis (letter from February 1744), probably as a result of urethral masturbation ("I have not lost my unfortunate habit to cheat my passions . . ."). Arrival in Venice in September

1743, departure in August 1744.

1745	Paris	An unknown disease in the fall, perhaps ure- thritis (he met Thérèse in the spring of 1745).
1748	Paris	On 30 June in a letter to Altun, first reference to urinary retention *"une collique néphritique, la plus effrayable qu'on jamais sentie."*

In August, Rousseau writes in a letter to Mme de Warens that he got "renal colic, fever, burn- ing pain and urinary retention." He makes a self-diagnosis of a urinary stone. Besides this, he suffers from stomach pain, vomiting and diar- rhea.

1749–50	Paris	He writes in a letter to Mme de Warens (in Mach 1750) that he has a cold, suffers from fever and attacks of the old urinary complaints. Improvements of his health are allegedly only very short intervals between bouts of illness ("convalescence are simply intervals between one illness and another"). He started living in one flat with Thérèse.
1751	Paris	Rousseau suffers from an illness which remains unknown, most probably a new recurrence of urinary tract infection (Diderot informs him about the success of the first *Discourse*).
1751	Paris	He falls ill in the summer at Château La Chevrette and has to return to Paris. He has to stay in bed for five to six weeks. Mme Dupin sends for the surgeon Morand and then another surgeon, Dr. Daran, who uses special soft wax

catheters and succeeds in carrying out catheterization. Dr. Daran declares that Rousseau would not survive six months. Rousseau orders a large number of the catheters and uses them for the next eight to ten years. Other physicians consulted at that time were Helvétius, Malouin and Thierry.

1755	Paris	Summer—recurrence of urinary tract infection. It is recommended that he be seen by Dr. Tronchin but Rousseau refuses this offer.
1756	Hermitage	End of summer—recurrence of urinary tract infection accompanied by arthralgia.
1757	Hermitage	In January, common cold. In August, another (this time shorter) recurrence of urinary tract infection. In October, another recurrence of urinary tract infection—he has to use the chamber pot every five minutes.
1757	Montlouis	At the end of December recurrence of urinary tract infection with swelling in the left groin, of which Rousseau said it was a hernia. He was examined by Dr. Thierry.
1758	Montlouis	January–March. Ceaseless urinary tract infections during an extremely cold winter spent in the unheated *donjon*. He feels so sick that he bequeaths all his possessions to Thérèse. The swelling in his left groin persists, the stream of urine becomes thinner, it flows out with difficulty, and he has to press on his lower abdomen. He does not want to go to Geneva and get treated. These complaints last till May.

1758	Montlouis	Rousseau is ill practically for the entire year. A major recurrence of urinary tract infection in winter. Consultation of Dr. Thierry.
1759	Montlouis	Recurrence of urinary tract infection in winter, but this time relatively short. *Donjon* is rebuilt and heated (letter to Mme de Luxembourg).
1760	Montlouis	In the first months of the year, reference to epistaxis. In May–June "migraine" after he has been proofreading *Julie*.
	Montlouis	In December, a new recurrence of infection. He must stay in bed for six weeks (a letter to publisher Guérin, December 21, 1760).
1761	Montlouis	Petit Château in the spring—a recurrence of urinary tract infection.

Worsening in May. Rousseau refuses medical attention.

Another deterioration in June 1761 and Rousseau is convinced that he will die. He asks Mme de Luxembourg to find out about the fate of his firstborn daughter.

He is transferred to Petit Château and suffers intensive pains. The duke and duchess visit him daily and insist that Frère Côme be summoned, who succeeds in introducing a thin catheter into the urinary bladder. The operation lasts two hours. The surgeon finds a cirrhotic prostate but no urinary stone in the bladder.

Rousseau's description of this disease in *Confessions* is mistaken: he dates it to the time around Easter 1762.

He also writes that the operation was carried out in his house and not in Petit Château.

1761	Montlouis	Depression, vomiting, he cannot concentrate (letter to Mme de Luxembourg from July 20, 1761). Fall—improvement of health. In early winter an accident occurred: the soft tip of a catheter broke off ("A piece of the soft end of the catheter I have to wear, and without which I could not urinate, has stuck in the urethral canal, and makes it much more difficult for the urine to pass . . ." (letter to Moultou, 314).
1762	Montlouis	He was so ill that he was "surprised to be still alive" (letter to Mme de Verdelin from January 20, 1762). Mental strain due to controversies with publishers. He refuses to have the tip of the catheter removed, the catheterization must go on. It is not known whether or when the tip of the catheter was removed. In spring of 1762 he therefore procured the Armenian costume so as not to have to wear trousers.
1762	Môtiers	After departure from Montlouis (where he left Thérèse) he feels well. After her arrival in Môtiers (July 20, 1762) recurrences of his urinary tract infections reappear. A severe recurrence in the tough winter in December. He has a temperature and a cold. "It seems my old bladder wants to block itself up completely" (letter to Moultou). *"Je suis froid, je suis triste, je pisse mal"* (letter to Rey). In September, he once again believed he would die and wrote a testament.
1763	Môtiers	Recurrence of urinary tract infection from December lasts till the end of January 1763, an improvement does not occur before February.

		Summer—complains of bad health (probably again urinary tract infection).
		August—he is so sick that he contemplates suicide; he says goodbye to his friends.
1764	Aix les Bains	Treatment of sciatica in spa.
1764	Thonon	During a political rendezvous in bad weather, another recurrence of urinary tract infection. He remarks in the same year that he has to urinate every minute (J. Boswell – "I need a chamber pot every minute").
1765	Isle St-Pierre	When banished from the island in October, he does not feel well.
1765	Strasbourg	End of November—short unknown disease.
1765	Paris	He mentions his nearsightedness which he alleged had since his youth.
1766	London	He says to Hume in January that he wears his Armenian costume because "he needs a chamber pot every minute."
1766	England	He is more and more haunted by delusionary fantasies of persecution (uremia?).
1767	France	Ideas of being persecuted get more intense.

References

Primary sources

Rousseau, Jean-Jacques. 1865–70. *Oeuvres complètes de Rousseau.* 13 vols. Paris: Hachette

Rousseau, Jean-Jacques. 1924–34. *Correspondence générale de Jean-Jacques Rousseau.* 20 vols. Edited by T. Dufour and P. P. Plan, Paris.

Rousseau, Jean-Jacques. 1861. *Oeuvres et correspondence inédites de J.-J. Rousseau.* Edited by G. Streckeisen:Moultou, Paris.

Rousseau, Jean-Jacques. 1959. *Oeuvres complètes de Jean-Jacque Rousseau, I, "Les Confessions," autre textes autobiographiques.* Edited by B. Gagnebin and M. Raymond. Paris: Bibliothèque de la Pléiade.

Rousseau, Jean-Jacques. 1946. *Discours sur les science et les arts.* Edited by G. R. Havens, New York.

Rousseau, Jean-Jacques. 1985. *Bekenntnisse: Aus Dem Französischen von Ernst Hard. Mit einer Eiführung von Werner Krauss. Frankfurt a.M.:* Insel Verlag.

Rousseau, Jean-Jacques. 1953. *The Confessions of Jean-Jacques Rousseau.* Translated, with an introduction by J. M. Cohen. London: Penguin Books.

Rousseau, Jean-Jacques. 1964. *Les Confessions.* Paris: Garnier Frères.

Rousseau, Jean-Jacques. 1963. *Jean-Jacques Rousseau: Émile oder über die Erziehung.* Herausgegeben, eingeleitet und mit Anmerkungen versehen von Martin Rang. Stuttgart: Reclam.

Rousseau, Jean-Jacques. 1977. *Jean-Jacques Rousseau, Bürger von Genf: Vom Gesellschaftsvertrag oder Grundsätze des Staatsrechts.* Translated by H. Brockard. Stuttgart: Reclam.

Secondary Sources

Baczko, B. 1970. *Einsamkeit und Gemeinschaft.* (From Polish trans. by E. Werfel). Wien/Frankfurt/Zurich: Europa Verlag.

Begemann, C. 1987. *Furcht und Angst im Process der Aufklärung.* Frankfurt a.M.: Athäneum Verlag.

Burgelin, P. 1962. *Jean-Jacques Rousseau et la religion de Genève.* Paris: Éds. Labor et Fides.

Burgelin, P. 1952. *La Philosophie de l'existence de J.-J.Rousseau.* Paris: Presses Univ. de France.

Bensoussan, D. 1977. *L'Unité chez Jean-Jacques Rousseau.* Paris: A. G. Nizet.

Broome, J. H. 1963. *Rousseau, a Study of His Thoughts.* London: Edward Arnold.

Derathé, R. 1948. *Le rationalisme de Rousseau.* Paris: P.U.F.

Fetscher, I. 1968. *Rousseaus politische Philosophie.* Neuwied. Luchterhand.

Cranston, M. 1982. *Jean-Jacques, the Early Life and Work of Jean-Jacques Rousseau 1712–1754.* First American Edition, 1983. Suffolk: W. W. Norton.

Cranston, M. 1991. *The Noble Savage, Jean-Jacques Rousseau 1754–1762.* Chicago: The University of Chicago Press.

Cranston, M. 1997. *The Solitary Self. Jean-Jacques Rousseau in Exile and Adversity.* Foreword by Sanford Lakoff. Chicago: The University of Chicago Press.

Dale, K., Van Kley. 1996. *The Religious Origins of the French Revolution: From Calvin to the Civil Constitution 1560–1791.* New Haven/London: Yale University Press.

Grimsley, R. 1968. *Rousseau and Religious Quest.* Oxford: Clarendon Press.

Grimsley, R. 1969. *Jean-Jacques Rousseau, a Study in Self-awarness.* Cardiff: University of Wales Press.

Grimsley, R. 1973. *The Philosophy of Rousseau.* London/New York: Oxford University Press.

Hobbes, T. 1970. *Leviathan.* Stuttgart: Reclam.

Mayer-Tasch, P. C. 1976. *Hobbes und Rousseau.* Aalen: Scientia Verlag.

Nicolson, H. 1961. *The Age of Reason: The Eighteenth Century.* New York

Ogg, D. 1975. *Europe of the Ancient Regime 1715–1783.* Glasgow: Fontana Collins

Rooswelt, G. G. 1991. *Reading Rousseau in the Nuclear Age.* Philadelphia: Temple University Press.

Starobinski, J. 1977. *Rousseaus Anklage der Gesellschaft.* Konstanz: Univ. Verlag.

Starobinski, J. 1988. *Rousseau, Eine Welt von Widerständen.* München, Carl Hauser Verlag (trans. from original: Gallimard. 1971. *Jean-Jacques Rousseau: La transparence et l'obstacle.* Paris: Gallimard

Winwar, F. 1961. *Jean-Jacques Rousseau, Conscience of an Era.* New York: Random House.

Medical sources

Arborelius, L., M. J. Owens, P. M. Plotsky, and C. B. Nemeroff. 1999. The role of cortocotropin-releasing factor in depression and anxiety disorders. *J. Endocrinol.* 160 (1):1–12.

Bach, S. 1991. On sadomasochistic object relations. In *Perversions and Near-Perversions in Clinical Practice*, edited by G. I. Fogel and W. A. Myers, pp. 75–92. New Haven: Yale University Press.

Baumeister, R. F., and J. L. Butler. 1997. Sexual masochism: Deviance without pathology. In *Sexual Deviance: Theory, Assesment, and Treatment*, edited by D.R. Laws and W. T. O'Donohue et al., pp 225–239. New York: The Guilford Press.

Baumeister, R. F., K., L. Sommer. 1997. Patterns in the bizzare: Common themes in satanic ritual abuse, sexual masochism, UFO abductions, fictitious illness, and extreme love. *Journal of Social and Clinical Psychology*, vol. 16 (2): 213–233.

Baumeister, R. F. 1997. The enigmatic appeal of sexual masochism: Why people desire pain, bondage, and humilitation in sex. *Journal of Social and Clinical Psychology*, vol. 16 (2):133–150.

Bensoussan, D. 1974. *La maladie de Rousseau*. Paris: Klinsieck.

Berliner, B. 1947. On some psychodynamics of masochism. *Psychanal. Quarterly* 16: 459–471.

Biber, I. 1966. Sadism and masochism. In *American Handbook of Psychiatry*, edited by S. Arieti, vol. 3, 256–270, New York: Basic Books.

Bohus, M. L. et al. 1999. Naltrexone in the treatment of dissociative symptoms in patients with borderline personality disorder: an open-label trial. *Journal Clin. Psychiatry* 60 (9):598–603.

Bowlby, J. 1946. *Forty-four Juvenile Thieves*. London: Tyndal and Cox.

Bowlby, J. 1973. *Attachment and Loss: Separation, Anxiety and Anger*, vol. 2. London: Hogarth Press.

Brouček, F. J. 1982. Shame and its relationship to early narcissistic developments. *International Journal of Psycho-Analysis* 63:369–378.

Brouček, F. J. 1991. *Shame and the Self.* New York/London: The Guilford Press.

Buss, A. H. 1980. *Self-consciousness and Social Anxiety.* San Francisco: W. H. Freeman.

Chiron, C., L. Jambaque, R. Nabbout, R. Lounes, A. Syrota and O. Dulac, 1997. The right brain hemisphere is dominant in human infants. *Brain* 120 (6):1057–1065.

Cooper, A. M. 1988. The narcissistic-masochist character. In *Masochism,* edited by R. A. Glick and D. I. Meyers, pp. 117–139. Hillsdale, NJ: The Analytic Press.

Dawson, C. 1994. Development of emotional expression and emotional regulation in infancy. In *Human Behavior and the Developing Brain,* edited by G. Dawson and K. W. Fischer, pp. 346–379. New York: The Guilford Press.

Deutsch, H. 1944. *The Psychology of Women.* 2 vols. New York: Grune a Stratton.

Diamant, L., and R. D. McAnulty, editors. 1995. *The Psychology of Sexual Orientation, Behavior and Identity: A Handbook.* Westpoint, Connecticut/London: Greenwood Press.

Doryan, L. 1997. Masochism and the inner mother. *Psychoanalytic Review* 84 (4): 523–540.

Elosu, S. 1929. *La maladie de J.-J. Rousseau,* Paris: Fichbacher.

Erikson, E. H. 1963. *Childhood and Society.* New York: W. W. Norton.

Finell, J. S. 1992. Sadomasochism and complementarity in the interaction of the narcissistic and borderline personality type. *Psychanal. Review* 79 (3): 361–79.

Freud, S. 1924. The economic problem of masochism. In *Collected Papers,* edited by J. Strachey, vol. 2, pp. 255–268. New York: Basic Books.

Fromm, E. 1942. *The Fear of Freedom.* International Library of Sociology and Social Reconstruction. Edited by K. Mannheim and P. Kegan. London: Trench, Trubner and Co. Ltd.

Gabriel, J., and B. Stavroula. 1997. Early trauma in the development of masochism and depression. *International Forum of-Psychoanalysis,* vol. 6 (4) 231–236.

Gilbert, P. and A. Bernice, editors. 1998. *Shame, Interpersonal Behavior, Psychopathology, and Culture.* New York/Oxford: Oxford University Press.

Goleman, D. 1997. *Emoční inteligence.* Czech translation. Praha: Columbus.

Gödde, G. 1983. *Masochismus und Moral. Über das individuelle und kollektive Verlangen nach Selbstaufgabe.* Wien: Europa Verlag.

Gray, T. S., and E. W. Bingaman. 1996. The amygdala : corticotropin-releasing factor, steroids, and stress. *Crit. Rev. Neurobiol.* 10 (2):155–68.

Hanly, M. A. F., editor. 1995. *Essential Papers on Masochism.* New York/London: New York University Press.

Harder, D. W. 1995. Shame and Guilt Assessment, and Relationships of Shame-and Guilt-Proneness to Psychopathology. In *Self-Conscious Emotions. The Psychology of Shame, Guilt, Embarrasment, and Pride,* edited by J. P. Tangney, and K. W. Fischer, pp. 368–392. New York/London: The Guilford Press.

Harlow, H. F. 1958. The nature of love. *Amer. Psychol.* 13: 673–685.

Harlow, H. F. and M. K. Harlow. 1963. Social deprivation in monkeys. *Scient. Amer.* 207:137.

Harlow, H. F. and M. K. Harlow. 1966. Learning to love. *Amer Scient.,* 54: 244–272.

Heidenheim, A. 1924. *J.-J. Rousseau: Persönlichkeit, Philosophie und Psychose.* München.

Howel, E. F. 1966. Dissociation in masochism and psychopathic sadism. *Contemporary Psychoanalysis,* vol. 32 (3):427–453.

Krafft-Ebing, R., von. 1886. *Psychopathia sexualis with special reference to the antipathic sexual instinct: A medico-forensic study.* Chicago: Login Brothers.

Kreisman, J. J. and H. Straus. 1989. *I Hate You—Don't Leave Me: Understanding the Borderline Personality.* New York: Avon Books.

Koob, G. F. 1999. Corticotropin-releasing factor, norepinephrine, and stress. *Biol. Psychiatry* 46 (9):1167–80.

Lane, R.C. and W. B. Goeltz. 1998. Identity confusion, bisexuality, and flight from the mother. *Clin. Psychol. Rev.* 18 (3):259–72.

Langmeier, J. and Z. Matějček. 1974. *Psychická deprivace v dětství,* Vol 3. Praha: Avicenum.

Lansky, M. R. and A. P. Morrison, editors. 1997. *The Widening Scope of Shame.* Hillsdale, NJ: The Analytic Press.

Lebe, D. 1997. Masochism and the inner mother. *Psychoanalytic Review,* vol. 84 (4): 523–540.

Lehnert, H., C. Schulz, and K. Dietrich. 1998. Physiological and neurochemical aspects of corticotropin-releasing factor actions in the brain: The role of locus coeruleus. *Neurochem.* Res. 23 (8):1039–52.

Lewis, H. B. 1987. *Shame—the "Sleeper" in Psychopathology.* In *The Role of Shame in Symptom Formation,* edited by H. B. Lewis. Hillsdale, NJ: Erlbaum.

Links, P. S., R. Heslegrave, and R. van Reekum. 1999. Impulsivity: core aspect of borderline personality disorder. *J. Personal. Disord.* 13 (1):1–9.

Litman, R. E. 1997. Bondage and sadomasochism. In *Sexual Dynamics of Anti-social Behavior*, 2d edition, edited by L. B. Schlesinger et al. Springfield: Charles P. Thomas.

Litman, R. E. and C. Swearingen. 1966. Bondage and suicide. In *Essential papers on Suicide. Essential Papers in Psychoanalysis,* edited by J. T. Maltsberger and M. J. Goldblatt et al. New York: New York University Press.

Lohr, B. and H. E. Adams. 1995. Sexual Sadism and Masochism. In *The Psychology of Sexual Orientation, Behavior, and Identity: a Handbook,* edited by L. Diamant and R. D. McAnulty. Westpoint, CT/London: Greenwood Press.

Maccoby, E. E. 1980. *Social Development: Psychological Growth and the Parent-Child Relationship.* New York: The Analytic Press

Machizawa, S. 1994. Borderline personality disorder. *Nippon Rinsho* 52 (5): 1360–4.

Mansfield, N. 1997. *Masochism. The Art of Power.* London: Praeger.

Marcus, M. 1981. *A Taste for Pain: On Masochism and Female Sexuality.* New York: Saint Martin's Press.

Matějček, Z. 1994. *Teoretická úvaha nad pozdními následky psychické deprivace a subdeprivace.* Praha: Psychiatrické centrum.

Menzaghi, F., S. C. Heinrichs, E. M. Pich, F. Weiss, and G. F. Koob. 1993. The role of limbic and hypothalamic corticotropin-releasing factor in behavioral responses to stress. *Ann. N.Y. Acad. Sci.* Oct.29 (697):142–54.

Miller, S. B. 1996. *Shame in Context.* Hillsdale, NJ: The Analytic Press.

Millet, J. A. P. 1959. Masochism: Psychogenesis and therapeutic principles. In *Science and Psychoanalysis,* edited by J. H. Masserman, 2 44–52.

Morrison, A. F. 1989. *Shame*. Hillsdale, NJ: The Analytic Press.

Nathanson, D. L. 1992. *Shame and Pride Affect Sex, and the Birth of the Self.* New York/London: W. W. Norton.

Nemeroff, C. B. 1998. The role of corticotropin-releasing factor in the pathogenesis of major depression. *Pharmacopsychiatry* 21 (2):76–82.

Novick, K. K. and J. Novick. 1987. The essence of masochism. *The Psychoanalytic Study of the Child*. 42:353–384. New Haven: Yale University Press.

Noyes, J. K. 1998. S/M in SA: sexual violence, simulated sex and psychoanalytic theory. *American-Imago Spr.,* vol. 55 (1):135–153.

Person, E. S., editor. 1997. *On Freud's "A Child is Being Beaten."* New Haven: Yale University Press.

Pottle, F. A., editor. 1953. *Boswell on the Grand Tour: Germany and Switzerland.* New York.

Raber, J. 1998. Detrimental effects of chronic hypothalamic-pituitary-adrenal axis activation. From obesity to memory deficits. *Mol. Neurobiol.* 18 (1): 1–22.

Rancour-LaFerriere, D. 1998. *Tolstoy on the Couch: Misogyny, Masochism, and Absent Mother.* New York: New York University Press.

Reich, J. 1987. Prevalence of DSM-III-R self–defeating (masochistic) personality disorder in normal and outpatient populations. *J. Nerv. Ment. Dis.* 175 (1): 52–4.

Reich, W. 1973. *Charakteranalyse,* Frankfurt. a.M.

Reik, T. 1977. *Aus Leiden Freuden. Masochismus und Gesellschaft,* Hamburg: Hoffmann u. Campe.

Rothenhauser, H. B. and H. P. Kampfhammer. 1999. Outcome in borderline disorders. A literature review (in German). *Fortschr. Neurol. Psychiatr.* 67 (5): 200–17.

Rueedi, J. 1933. Paedagogische Ueberlegungen zum verwohnenden Erziehungsstil in Elternhaus, Kindergarten und Schule. *Zeitschrift für Individualpsychologie,* vol. 18 (4):282–293.

Sacher-Masoch, L. von. 1968. *Venus im Pelz.* Mit einer Studie über den Masochismus von Gilles Deleuze, Frankfurt: Insel Verlag.

Salzman, L. 1959. Masochism: A review and the therapy. In *Science and Psychoanalysis*, edited by J. H. Masserman, 2:1–20.

Savran, D. 1998. *Taking it Like a Man: White Masculinity, Masochism, and Contemporary American Culture.* Princeton, NJ: Princeton University Press.

Schmahl, C., C. Stinglmayr, R. Bohme, and M. Bohus. 1999. Treatment of dissociative symptoms in borderline patients with naltrexone. *Nervenarzt,* 70 (3): 262–4.

Shainess, N. 1984. *Sweet Suffering: Woman as Victim.* Indianapolis/New York: The Bobbs-Merrill Co., Inc.

Shainess, N. 1997. Masochism Revisited: Reflections on Masochism and Its Childhood Antecedents. *American Journal of Psychotherapy,* vol. 51 (4): 552–568.

Shore, A. N. 1994. *Affect Regulation and the Origin of the Self: The Neurobiology of Emotional Development.* Hillsdale, NJ: Erlbaum.

Shore, A. N. 1998. Early Shame Experiences and Infant Brain Development. In *Shame, Interpersonal Behavior, Psychopathology, and Culture,* edited by P. Gilbert and B. Andrews, pp. 55–77. New York/Oxford: Oxford University Press.

Siegel, D. J. 1999. *The Developing Mind: Toward a Neurobiology of Interpersonal Experience*. New York/London: The Guilford Press.

Sullivan, H. S. 1953. *The Interpersonal Theory of Psychiatry*. New York: W. W. Norton.

Tangney, J. P. and K. W. Fischer, editors. 1995. *Self-Conscious Emotions: The Psychology of Shame, Guilt, Embarrassment, and Pride*. New York/London: The Guilford Press.

Thomas, P. B. and M. Humpreys. 1997. Masochism: Assesment, treatment and quality of consent to injurious behavior. *Journal of Forensic Psychiatry*, vol. 8 (3): 669–667.

Thornton, D. and R. Mann. 1997. Sexual masochism: Assessment and treatment. In *Sexual Deviance and Treatment*, edited by D. R. Laws and W. T. O'Donohue et al., pp. 240–252. New York: The Guilford Press.

Tolpin, M. 1997. The development of sexuality and the self. *Annual of Psychoanalysis* 25:173–187.

Van Bockstaele, E. J., E. E. Colago, and R. J. Valentino. 1998. Amygdaloid corticotropin-releasing factor targets locus coeruleus dendrites: Substrate for the coordination of emotional and cognitive limbs of the stress response. *J. Neuroendocrinol.* 10 (10):743–757.

Waska, R. T. 1997. Precursors to masochistic and dependent character development. *American Journal of Psychoanalysis*, vol. 57 (3):253–267.

Wilhelm, S. et al. 1999. Self–injurious picking: clinical characteristics and co-morbidity. *J. Clin. Psychiatry* 60 (7):454–9.

Wurmser, L. 1993. *Das Rätsel des Masochismus*. Berlin/Heidelberg/New York: Springer Verlag.

Wurmser, L. 1997. The shame about existing: A comment about the analysis of "moral" masochism. In *The Widening Scope of Shame*, edited by M. R. Lansky and A. P. Morrison et al., pp. 367–382. Hillsdale, NJ: The Analytic Press.

Zanarini, M. C. et al. 1998. The pain of being borderline: Dysphoric states specific to borderline personality disorder. *Harv. Rev. Psychiatry* 6 (4): 201–7.

Zimmerman, M. and J. I. Mattia. 1999. Axis I diagnostic co-morbidity and borderline personality disorder. *Compr. Psychiatry* 40 (4): 245–52.

Zlotnick, C., J. I. Mattia, and M. Zimmerman. 1999. Clinical correlates of self-mutilation in a sample of general psychiatric patients. *J. Nerv. Ment. Dis.* 187 (5):296–301.

Yegdich, T. 1998. Paradox as a symptom in the borderline patient's struggle for self-differentiation. *Perspect Psychiatr. Care*, 34 (1):15–27.